D0343618

ENTRY, SEARCH AND SEIZURE:
A Guide to Civil and Criminal
Powers of Entry

AUSTRALIA AND NEW ZEALAND
The Law Book Company Ltd.
Sydney : Melbourne : Perth

CANADA AND U.S.A.
The Carswell Company Ltd.
Agincourt, Ontario

INDIA
N. M. Tripathi Private Ltd.
Bombay
and
Eastern Law House Private Ltd.
Calcutta and Delhi
M.P.P. House
Bangalore

ISRAEL
Steimatzky's Agency Ltd.
Jerusalem : Tel Aviv : Haifa

PAKISTAN
Pakistan Law House
Karachi

ENTRY, SEARCH AND SEIZURE:
A Guide to Civil and Criminal Powers of Entry

Second Edition

Richard Stone, LL.B., LL.M.
Lecturer in Law at the University of Leicester

LONDON
SWEET & MAXWELL
1989

Published in 1989 by
Sweet & Maxwell Ltd. of
South Quay Plaza, 183 Marsh Wall, London E14 9FT
Computerset by C.C.I. Technical Services Ltd.,
Hitchin, Herts.
Printed in Great Britain by
Butler & Tanner Ltd.,
Somerset.

British Library Cataloguing in Publication Data
Stone, Richard, *1951–*
    Entry, search and seizure : a guide to civil
    and criminal powers of entry. – 2nd ed.
    1. Great Britain. Powers of entry, search and
    seizure. Law
    I. Title.
    344.105′522

    ISBN 0–421–38950–8

©
Richard Stone
1989

PREFACE

The spur which set me on the road to writing this book was the case of *R*. v. *I.R.C., ex p. Rossminster* [1980] A.C. 952, which led many people to realise for the first time that it was not only the police who had the power to enter and search one's house at 7 a.m. It revived for me a concern which had lain dormant since my participation in a student production of Joe Orton's play *Loot*, which includes the following exchange between the police officer, Truscott, and one of the other characters (at p.40 of the Methuen edition):

> FAY: It's common knowledge what police procedure is. They must have a search warrant.
> TRUSCOTT: I'm sure the police must, but as I've already informed you, I am from the water board. And our procedure is different.

Could it be true that officials of certain public authorities had even greater powers than the police? (Those interested in the accuracy of Inspector Truscott's ideas as to the powers of water board officials will find the answer in Chapter Nine.)

The principal aims of this edition remain the same as that of the first, namely to provide a comprehensive and accessible guide to the wide range of powers of entry of the police and other officials, and to try to extract some general principles. Work on the first edition was affected by the enactment of the Police and Criminal Evidence Act 1984, and the growth in the use of *Anton Piller* orders. These two areas have provided a considerable amount of new material for this edition. The growing case law on the P.C.E.A. is dealt with in Chapter Three, while important *Anton Piller* decisions such as *Columbia Picture Industries* v. *Robinson*, and *Crest Homes* v. *Marks* are discussed in Chapter Five. In addition new legislation has resulted in new or amended powers of entry. For example, the Drug Trafficking Offences Act 1986, the Financial Services Act 1986, and the Consumer Protection Act 1987 are all incorporated at the appropriate points in Chapters Four, Eight and Nine. The extension of various parts of the P.C.E.A. to the Customs and Excise is dealt with in Chapter Seven.

I completed the main revision of the text in August 1988, but I have been able at proof stage to incorporate some more recent developments, such as the House of Lords decision on legal privilege (*Francis & Francis* v. *Central Criminal Court*) and the Copyright, Design and Patents Act 1988 (which is discussed as if in force).

I have tried to deal with all powers under common law or statute authorising entry on to another's property without consent. I have not attempted to cover powers under local legislation, comforting myself with the knowledge that most such powers simply re-enact existing general powers of entry (*e.g.* under section 287 of the Public Health Act 1936). Nor have I dealt with powers involving the taking of full possession of another's land, as under a compulsory purchase order. On the other hand, powers of inspection are dealt with, as well as those of search.

The book is intended to be of practical help to those who need to know about the powers exercisable by particular officials, or in particular situations. In the preface to the first edition I also expressed the hope that my attempt to extract some general principles might lead Parliament to take a more consistent approach towards entry powers. Unfortunately, however, inconsistencies are still appearing – the most notable being the apparently haphazard approach to the treatment of excluded and special procedure material in legislation passed after the P.C.E.A. This is an issue which needs to be resolved speedily, if the protection afforded to confidential documents is not to depend on the chance of whether a particular search power was enacted before or after 1984.

Finally, my thanks are due to my wife, Maggie, and my children, for putting up with my lack of availability whilst rewriting, checking proofs, preparing the index, etc.

Oadby,   RICHARD STONE
February 14, 1989

CONTENTS

Contents

Contents

TABLE OF CASES

xi

Table of Cases

TABLE OF STATUTES

Entries in **bold** *indicate paragraphs devoted to discussion of the statute or section.*

TABLE OF STATUTORY INSTRUMENTS

*Entries in **bold** indicate pragraphs devoted to discussion of the statutory instrument.*

xlix

1

BASIC ISSUES

In certain situations the law allows one person to go on to another person's property **1.01** against their will. The variety of occasions in which that will be allowed is consider-able, as will be seen in Part II. Certain issues tend to recur, however, in relation to all, or certain groups of these powers. If the entry occurs when the law does not permit it, or if a lawful entrant steps outside the scope of any permission, he or she will become a trespasser. Thus, one of the basic distinctions to be drawn is that between lawful entry and trespass. Many of the statutory powers of entry use common phraseology, *e.g.* that entry must be on the basis of "reasonable grounds" for suspicion, or can take place "at any time" during a specified period. Does the latter phrase, without more, legitimise a demand to enter at two in the morning? And in what situations may "force" be used to effect entry? Consideration of these and other basic issues is the concern of this chapter.

A. *Trespass Versus Lawful Entry*

1. Elements of trespass

The civil action for trespass has a long history, and exists as the way in which the **1.02** popular notion of the home as a castle is given practical effect. The cause of action arises as soon as there is a voluntary entry by one who has no right to enter, or where an originally lawful entry for some reason becomes unlawful. The "voluntary" nature of the entry refers only to the fact that it must be a willed act. There is no need for the entrant to be aware of the illegality of the entry—mistake of fact or law is no excuse.[1] So the policeman who enters premises on the basis of an invalid warrant, or an unreasonable suspicion, will be a trespasser. The action lies without proof of damage.[2] Full entry is not necessary for a trespass. In *Franklin* v. *Jeffries*[3] a police officer put his hand over the threshold of a motorist's property in order to arrest him. This was a trespass which rendered the arrest invalid.

Once the basic elements of trespass have been shown to exist, then it is up to the defendant to show that there was a lawful excuse for his presence on the plaintiff's property. Much of the rest of this book is concerned with specific statutory powers which can provide such a defence. But often the defendant will claim that he was invited in by the person in control of the premises—in effect that he had a "licence" to be where he was, and therefore not a trespasser. Two questions arise

---

[1] *Basely* v. *Clarkson* (1682) 3 Lev. 37.
[2] See below, Chap. Two, para. 2.25.
[3] *The Times*, March 11, 1985; *cf. R.* v. *Collins* [1973] 1 Q.B. 100.

1

from this. First, in what situations will a person be regarded as having a licence to be on another's property? And secondly, who has the power to grant or withdraw a licence, and what form should any withdrawal take?

(a) *Creation of licence*

1.03   **(i) Express.** A licence may be created by words or conduct, or both. Few problems arise as regards an express licence created verbally, except on the evidential level of what exactly was said. It seems, however, that an express licence may also arise from conduct alone. In *Faulkner* v. *Willetts*[4] the appellant's wife, having opened the door to a police officer, and being told the reason for his visit, thereupon opened the door fully and walked back into the house. The Divisional Court held that this could be construed as an invitation for the officer to follow. On the other hand, if the police wish to *search* premises, as opposed to, for example, entering to talk to the occupants, written consent should be obtained.[5]

1.04   **(ii) Implied.** In some situations a licence will be implied in the absence of any indications to the contrary. For example, it is well established that there is an implied licence to pass through an unlocked garden gate, and walk up to the front door of a house if a person has or reasonably thinks he has legitimate business with the occupier.[6] Presumably this would extend to business with a member of the occupier's household. Would it cover entry to the common parts of a block of flats, or of a house divided into flats? In *Knox* v. *Anderton*[7] the Divisional Court found that the staircases and landings of a block of flats in a council housing estate were, in the absence of any restriction of access, places to which the public have or are permitted to have access.[8] Here the staircase and landings were "open to the atmosphere"; the position where there is a "main door" to a block of flats, or a house divided into flats, might well be different. In *Heads* v. *Chief Constable of Humberside Police*,[9] the view was taken that where the block had a door which was habitually open during the day but locked at night, the common parts were a "public place" for the purposes of the Public Order Act 1936[10] at any time when the door happened to be open (including times when it was usually locked). In any case, it is suggested that there should only be a licence implied where it is necessary to go to the front door of a particular flat in order to attract the individual occupier's attention, *i.e.* where there are no bell pushes or other devices for this purpose at the main entrance.[11]

---

[4] [1982] Crim.L.R. 453; [1982] R.T.R. 159, D.C.

[5] Code of Practice B (under the Police and Criminal Evidence Act 1984, s.66), para. 4.1. See below, para. 3.05

[6] *Robson* v. *Hallett* [1967] 2 Q.B. 939; *Lambert* v. *Roberts* [1981] 2 All E.R. 15; [1981] R.T.R. 113; *Bailey* v. *Wilson* [1968] Crim.L.R. 617. A rather wider implied licence is supported by some authorities on the powers of bailiffs. But such an extension is undesirable, and it is suggested that these authorities should not be applied beyond their own facts—see further, Chap. Five, paras. 5.40–5.44.

[7] (1983) 76 Cr.App.R. 156; [1983] Crim.L.R. 114, D.C.

[8] And therefore a "public place" for the purposes of the Prevention of Crime Act 1953.

[9] May 12, 1986, Divisional Court (unreported).

[10] Section 9 of the 1936 Act defined a public place as including "any highway and any other premises or place to which at the material time the public have or are permitted to have access, whether on payment or otherwise."

[11] The question of who would have the power to revoke such a licence is considered below, para. 1.08.

2

(iii) Implied by necessity. Certain old cases establish the necessity of preserving **1.05** life or property as a defence to trespass,[12] but there do not seem to be any modern examples of its successful use. It was accepted in *Handcock* v. *Baker*,[13] that where a woman feared that her husband was about to murder her and she called out for assistance, her potential rescuers were justified in making a forcible entry in order to save her. But it was not clear how far such a power would be taken to go. In particular, would fear of a lesser offence than murder justify entry? As far as the police are concerned their power in these circumstances exists now under section 17(1)(e) of the Police and Criminal Evidence Act 1984, and is thus limited to "saving life or limb or preventing serious damage to property."[14] The position of private individuals is uncertain, but it would be surprising if they had greater powers than the police.

As far as preventing crime is concerned the question is only likely to arise where it is the occupier of property who is committing the offence. It is unlikely that the occupier is going to bring an action for trespass against a person who has entered the property with the sole purpose of preventing a crime being committed against the occupier, his family, or his property.

(b) *Withdrawal of licence*

A licence, whether express or implied, may be withdrawn at any stage, and if the **1.06** erstwhile licensee does not remove himself with reasonable speed he will become a trespasser.[15] The withdrawal may take several forms. If the hostility to the other's entry is made clear at a sufficiently early stage, of course, it may operate to prevent a licence arising at all: for example, if the front gate is kept locked, or a notice is displayed saying "Police Keep Out."[16] More difficulty arises where the occupier wishes to terminate an express or implied licence. The question of whether the licence has been withdrawn is a question of fact alone.[17] The occupier will be well advised to make his wishes perfectly clear, because although in some cases magistrates have appeared to take a fairly lenient approach, as for example in *Lambert* v. *Roberts*,[18] where the statement of fact "this is private property: you are trespassing," was enough to withdraw the licence, without there being a specific request to leave, in others they have decided that uttering a common expletive, such as "fuck off," was to be regarded as mere vulgar abuse. As such it would not lead to the withdrawal of a licence. The Divisional Court supported the magistrates in this view.[19] *A fortiori* it will be difficult to establish a withdrawal of licence from conduct unsupported by words. Indeed Ormrod L.J. has expressed the view that only an express withdrawal

---

[12] *Dewey* v. *White, Maleverer* v. *Spink* (1538) Dyer 35b, 36b.
[13] (1800) 2 Bos. & P. 260.
[14] See further, para. 3.25.
[15] *Robson* v. *Hallett* [1967] 2 Q.B. 939.
[16] *Lambert* v. *Roberts* [1981] 2 All E.R. 15, 19.
[17] *Ibid*; and *Snook* v. *Mannion* [1982] Crim.L.R. 601; [1982] R.T.R. 321, D.C.
[18] [1981] 2 All E.R. 15.
[19] *Snook* v. *Mannion* above.

of the licence would be workable, because of the practical problem of "where to draw the line."[20]

(c) *Who may grant or withdraw a licence?*

1.07   In some situations the question will arise as to who has the power to grant or revoke a licence. In particular this will be the case where several parties have an interest in the property, *e.g.* where it is held under a lease or the occupier himself is merely a licensee. Of course, the owner in possession will always have the power to grant licences, but in other situations difficulties may arise.

1.08   **(i) Owner absent—property empty.** In this case the party wishing to enter will have to rely on implied licence of some kind, or else actually seek out the owner, or other person controlling the means of entry.[21]

(ii) Owner absent—property lawfully occupied by third party. The question here will be whether the third party has a right of *exclusive* occupation. If he does, *e.g.* as a tenant under a lease, then he will have the right to admit or exclude people from the property which is the subject of the tenancy, and the landlord will have no right to interfere.[22] It was noted above (para. 1.04) that the extent of any implied licence to enter a building leased to a number of tenants was unclear. The same difficulty arises in relation to the granting or revoking of a licence. For example, the police are making inquiries. They enter a block of flats and knock at one of the doors. The tenant of the flat, on answering the door tells the police to leave the property. He can clearly prevent them entering his own flat (unless they have a warrant or other lawful authority), but can he demand that they leave the block entirely? If he tries to expel them, will he be obstructing or assaulting a police officer in the execution of his duty? It is possible that such questions could be determined by looking at the precise terms of the lease in each case. But in the absence of authority, and in the interests of certainty, a more robust approach would be preferable. This might be that the tenant should be regarded as having authority over the common parts, if not as a result of his tenancy agreement, then under an implied authority from the landlord. This would provide a workable solution for all cases except the unusual one where there was a conflict between two tenants as to whether the police should stay or go. In that situation it is suggested that the most workable solution would be for the objection of one tenant to be sufficient to terminate the licence.[23] If the other tenant wishes the police to remain he should invite them into his own flat, where he has exclusive rights.

1.09   This solution is satisfactory as regards the common parts of leased premises. But it

---

[20] *Ibid.* 326.

[21] *Jewish Maternity Society's Trustees* v. *Garfinkle* (1926) 97 L.J.K.B. 766.

[22] Unless there is damage to the reversion.

[23] Though the decision of the Court of Appeal in *Slade* v. *Guscott* (1981) (unrep.), in relation to co-owners, might suggest a different view—see S. H. Bailey and D. J. Birch [1982] Crim.L.R. 475, 478, n. 13.

does not resolve all difficulties which may arise with single premises in multiple occupation. It is clear that the law recognises that the owner of premises may expressly or impliedly delegate authority to allow others on to the premises to others who are in lawful occupation, *e.g.* members of his family.[24] It is also clear that the owner will in some circumstances be able to override an invitation given by a person with a lesser interest in the property.[25] It might be thought that the qualification in the last sentence is unnecessary, and that the owner of property should always have the last word on the termination of licences. In *R.* v. *Thornley*,[26] however, the Court of Appeal ruled otherwise. Here the invitation to enter the property had been issued by the wife of the owner following a domestic dispute between herself and her husband. The husband told the police to leave, and tried to eject them forcibly, which led to his being charged with assault occasioning actual bodily harm. The Court of Appeal ruled that there was no need to consider whether the husband had used excessive force, since he had no power to revoke the licence issued by his wife until the police had completed the investigation which she had requested them to make. The problems raised by this decision are obvious.[27] In what situations can the owner's wishes be overridden? Is it only wives (or husbands) who have such a power, or does it extend to other members of the owner's family, or to anyone with authority to issue an initial invitation? And does the rule apply only to the police, or to any invitee? Because of these difficulties it will be as well if *Thornley* is applied very restrictively. The rationale of the decision, which was presumably the desire to protect the wife in such a situation, could often be more satisfactorily fulfilled by using a different basis for legitimising the police presence, such as the statutory right to enter to save life or limb,[28] to effect an arrest,[29] or the common law power to prevent a breach of the peace.[30]

One other problem may arise out of the grant of a licence on the basis of implied **1.10** authority. How does the person seeking entry know whether the person letting him in has such authority? The door may be opened by a child, or by an employee who has been expressly forbidden to allow anyone on to the premises. The only practical answer is to apply an objective test; was it reasonable in all the circumstances for the entrant to assume that the person granting the licence had authority to do so?

A sub-tenant will be in the same position as a tenant, provided he has exclusive possession.[31] But the requirement of exclusive possession will place people such as lodgers, guests at hotels and boarding houses, and servants, in a much weaker position. It is clearly established that this type of possession, *i.e.* that of a bare or

---

[24] *Robson* v. *Hallett* [1967] 2 Q.B. 939; *Lambert* v. *Roberts* [1981] 2 All E.R. 15; *Jones & Jones* v. *Lloyd* [1981] Crim.L.R. 340.
[25] *Ibid.* and *cf. R.* v. *Jones and Smith* [1976] 3 All E.R. 54.
[26] (1981) 72 Cr.App.R. 302; [1981] Crim.L.R. 637.
[27] See, *e.g.* the comments of D. J. Birch [1981] Crim.L.R. 638.
[28] Police and Criminal Evidence Act 1984, s.17(1)(*e*).
[29] *Ibid.* s.17(1)(*b*).
[30] See below, Chap. Three, para. 3.02, and *cf. McGowan* v. *Chief Constable for Kingston upon Hull* [1968] Crim.L.R. 34.
[31] *Lane* v. *Dixon* (1847) 3 C.B. 776.

contractual licensee, does not carry with it the right to sue for trespass.[32] Equally it cannot therefore by itself give the right to grant or revoke a licence. Of course, as in the domestic field, the licensee may be given such power by the express or tacit approval of the owner. It is not suggested that if a hotel guest invites a friend back to his room, that friend will automatically be a trespasser. Unless the owner or his manager has let it be known that such behaviour is unacceptable, the guest will be taken to have an implied authority to bring in the friend.

1.11   If the occupier exercises *his* power to admit others to the premises there is little the licensee can do about it. For example, if the owner of a boarding house gives the police permission to enter a room the police will be lawful entrants under the licence granted by the occupier, despite any objections from the person paying for the room. Equally, if the entry takes place in the licensee's absence he will have no grounds for complaint against the entrants, though he may have against the owner.[33] This will depend on the terms of his licence.

1.12   **(iii) Owner absent—property unlawfully occupied by third party.** The principal category here is that of squatters. There is authority for saying that *de facto* possession is sufficient to entitle the possessor to undisturbed possession of the property as against all but the true owner.[34]

If this is so it would seem to give the squatter the right to prevent anyone from entering the property, other than the owner, those acting on his instructions, or those relying on some other authority (*e.g.* statutory power or warrant). The Criminal Law Act 1977 even gives the right to exclude the lawful owner in some circumstances.[35] In effect the squatter seems to be in much the same position as a licensee.

B. The Use of Force

1.13   Where a power of entry exists it does not automatically follow that there is a right to use force to effect an entry. Some statutory powers specifically allow for the use of force "if necessary"; others are silent on the matter. The circumstances in which force may be used in support of a power is considered below at paragraph 1.15. First we must consider what constitutes "force."

1. Meaning of "force"

1.14   It is clear that "forcible entry" could mean any entry where no permission has

---

[32] *Allan* v. *Liverpool* (1874) 9 L.R.Q.B. 180, dicta of Blackburn J., approved by the Court of Appeal in *Appah* v. *Parncliffe* [1964] 1 W.L.R. 1064; *Smith* v. *Overseers of St. Michael's Cambridge* (1860) 3 E. & E. 383.

[33] The Code of Practice under the Police and Criminal Evidence Act 1984 states that a search should not be made solely on the basis of the landlord's consent unless the tenant is unavailable, and the matter is urgent—para. 4A.

[34] See *Graham* v. *Peat* (1801) 1 East 244; *Nicholls* v. *Ely Beet Sugar Factory* [1931] 2 Ch. 84. Note also the decision in *Scarborough Borough Council* v. *Adams* (1983) 47 P. & C.R. 133; (1983) 147 J.P. 449; [1983] J.P.L. 673, D.C., where it was held that squatters could be "occupiers" for the purposes of the Town and Country Planning Act 1971.

[35] s.6(2). But note the powers given to the police under s.17(1)(c)(ii) of the Police and Criminal Evidence Act 1984, and under the Public Order Act 1986, s.39.

been obtained from the occupier. Does "force" imply anything more than that? There is surprisingly little authority on the issue. The most recent reported consideration of it was in the case of *Swales* v. *Cox*[36] in relation to the police power to enter to effect an arrest, by virtue of section 2(6) of the Criminal Law Act 1967 (now replaced by section 17(1) and (2) of the Police and Criminal Evidence Act 1984). Without referring to any authority, Donaldson L.J. suggested the following approach (from which Hodgson J. did not dissent) to the meaning of force[37]:

> "In the context of outside premises of course there is no problem about force unless there is a gate or something of that sort. The constable simply enters the place and is authorised to do so by section 2(6). But if he meets an obstacle then he uses *force if he applies any energy to the obstacle with a view to removing it.* It would follow that, if my view is correct, where there is a door which is ajar but is insufficiently ajar for someone to go through the opening without moving the door and energy is applied to that door to make it open further, force is being used. A fortiori force is used when the door is latched and you turn the handle from the outside and then ease the door open. Similarly if someone opens any window or increases the opening in any window, or indeed dislodges the window by the application of any energy, he is using force to enter. ... "
> [emphasis added.]

This approach has much sense, but it could give rise to one or two surprising results. For example, the references to whether or not the door is sufficiently ajar to allow entry might require consideration of the girth of the proposed entrant. And is it intended that the same approach should apply to windows? The concluding words of the above quotation would seem to indicate that it is. But it seems odd, if not positively wrong, to remove climbing through a window, albeit an open window, from the category of forcible entries. There are, however, dicta to the same effect by the Court of Appeal in *Grove* v. *Eastern Gas Board*,[38] and so the definition given above must be taken to represent the law. It is submitted, however, that it would be preferable to use the approach taken by the Crown Court in *Swales* v. *Cox, i.e.* that "entry by force meant entry upon premises without an invitation to do so."[39] This would result in anything other than an entry "with permission" being a "forcible entry." A particular difficulty with such an approach, though it exists to some extent whatever definition of force is adopted, is that where an entry power is given without a power to use force, the power would seem to have little effect. If permission must be obtained, and there is no power to use force, why bother to give the entry power at all? In some circumstances the answer will be that the occupier refusing admission will be liable to prosecution for obstruction. An alternative answer is suggested below, in the light of authorities which hold that *any* power of entry carries with it the right to use force in certain circumstances.[40]

---

[36] [1981] Q.B. 849.
[37] *Ibid.* 854.
[38] [1952] 1 K.B. 77, 87, *per* Jenkins L.J.
[39] [1981] 1 Q.B. 849, 852.
[40] See para. 1.16.

2. When may force be used?

1.15   It seems to be generally accepted that at common law the exercise of entry powers
could only be effected by force where permission to enter had been sought and
refused.[41] The case which is usually cited as authority for this proposition is *Burdett* v.
Abbott,[42] which concerned the execution of a warrant for arrest for contempt of
Parliament. Lord Ellenborough C.J., considered that since contempt was a matter
of public as opposed to private interest, "breaking the house, after due notification
and demand of admittance without effect, is justifiable."[43]

A similar approach towards statutory powers was shown in *Launock* v. *Brown*,[44]
which concerned the execution of a search warrant issued under a statute which
made no mention of force.[45] Again it was held by the King's Bench that forcible entry
following a previous demand and refusal was justifiable.[46]

A different view was taken in *Grove* v. *Eastern Gas Board*[47] where the Court of
Appeal was considering a statutory power of entry in a form similar to many modern
statutes which give such powers to local and central government inspectors. The
statutory provision itself,[48] made no mention of force, simply providing for entry "at
all reasonable times" and " on production of some duly authenticated document"
showing the officer's authority. The Court of Appeal nevertheless held that the
production of authority was not required if there was no one to whom it could be
produced, and that a power of entry conferred by a statute must prima facie
authorise forcible entry if necessary. As Somervell L.J. commented[49]:

> "There would be no need for statutory authorisation if all that the representa-
> tives of the gas board were allowed to do was enter and read the meter if the
> consumer was willing to admit them."

In deciding that this power did justify the use of force, the court looked at the
power in the context of the rest of the statute. Some weight was given to the fact that
there was an obligation to leave unoccupied premises secure against trespassers, and
to pay compensation for any damage resulting from the entry. Both these factors, in
the court's opinion, suggested that force must be available under this power.

1.16   In *Swales* v. *Cox* the court was concerned with a power under a statute which
specifically permitted the use of force "if necessary." It was of the opinion that there
was no need for a prior request in order to justify forcible entry. But the feasibility of
making such a prior request was a relevant factor in the decision as to whether the
use of force was necessary. For example, it might be that

---

[41] *Swales* v. *Cox* [1981] 1 Q.B. 849, 853. And see the comments of Bailey and Birch [1982] Crim.L.R.
479, 480.
[42] (1811) 14 East 1; 104 E.R. 501.
[43] *Ibid.* 158, 561.
[44] (1819) 2 B. & Ald. 592; 106 E.R. 482.
[45] 22 & 33 Car. 2 (c. 25), s.2.
[46] Although Abbott C.J. who gave the main judgment limited his comments to misdemeanours rather
than felonies.
[47] [1952] 1 K.B. 77 (C.A.).
[48] Gas Act 1948, Sched. III, para. 34.
[49] [1952] 1 K.B. 77, 82.

"a criminal is at large and the public ... are warned not to approach him because he is known to be a very dangerous man. If a constable is following such a man into premises, it may be essential for his own protection that he shall give no warning of his approach by asking the leave of the criminal to enter the premises."[50]

The law in this area is not entirely coherent or consistent. It is suggested, however, that the following represents the current situation as to when force may be used to effect an entry on to the premises. In each of the following categories force will only be available "if necessary." This is purely a question of fact, and the burden is on the entrant to justify the use of force in particular circumstances.[51]

(a) Where the entrant is relying on common law powers of entry there must be a request and refusal before force may be used—except perhaps in an emergency, such as in *Handcock* v. *Baker*.[52]

(b) Where a statutory power, under warrant or otherwise, does not refer to force, force may nevertheless sometimes be used as a last resort. If there is someone present on the property, his permission to enter must be sought. Only if he refuses may force be used. Even then, if there is an alternative procedure available, such as obtaining a warrant, that should be followed. If there is no one on the premises whose permission can be sought, then force may be used, unless, again, there is an alternative procedure.[53]

(c) Where a statutory power allows the use of force, no prior request and refusal is needed, even if there is someone on the property.

Where force is permitted, only "reasonable" force is allowed. This again is a question of fact to be judged in the light of all the circumstances, including the reason for seeking entry. A higher level of force, for example, would be reasonable for a police constable entering premises to arrest an escaped murderer armed with a gun, than for a trading standards officer, investigating weights and measures offences.

C. Reasonable Grounds

There are three situations related to entry powers where the question of whether someone involved in the exercise of his power had reasonable grounds for his action may arise: **1.17**

(a) where a warrant is issued the justice or judge issuing the warrant will generally have to be satisfied that the person seeking the warrant has reasonable grounds for doing so;

(b) a person executing a warrant, having gained entry to premises under it, may be required to have reasonable grounds for suspicion before taking further action, such as arresting a person, or seizing property, found on the premises;

---

[50] [1981] 1 Q.B. 849, 855.
[51] *Ibid.*
[52] (1800) 2 Bos. & P. 260.
[53] *Launock* v. *Brown* (1819) 2 B. & Ald. 592; *Grove* v. *Eastern Gas Board* [1952] 1 K.B. 77 (C.A.).

(c) where a police officer or other official takes action under a power which does not require a warrant, again there will generally be a requirement that reasonable grounds for suspicion exist, before the action is taken.

In all three situations it now seems to be settled law that the question of whether or not there were reasonable grounds at the time is an objective one.[54]

"The test whether there was a reasonable and probable cause for the arrest or prosecution is an objective one, namely, whether a reasonable man, assumed to know the law and possessed of the information possessed by the defendant, would believe that there was a reasonable and probable cause."[55]

Successful challenges to the existence of such reasonable grounds have depended on the point in time at which the challenge is made. This problem is considered further in Chapter Two.[56] For the moment the discussion is confined to the content of alleged "reasonable grounds." This has been accepted to be a question of law, albeit reluctantly at times,[57] though, of course, whether such grounds did exist is a question of fact. It should therefore be possible to decide, within fairly broad limits, what amounts to "reasonable grounds," and what factors the person making the decision on the spot is entitled to take into account in reaching a decision.[58] The Code of Practice on Stop and Search,[59] Annex B, also contains some useful guidance as to the kind of factors which are relevant to establishing reasonable grounds.

It must be remembered that what we are considering here is simply "reasonable grounds for *suspicion*" of a person's guilt or of the existence of certain circumstances. The amount of information required before such a suspicion may be said to be based on reasonable grounds is obviously at a fairly low level. Certainly there is clear authority for saying that nothing in the nature of a prima facie case is required.[60] Moreover factors which would not be admissible in evidence in establishing a prima facie case, such as the suspect's known character and previous convictions, may be taken into account in establishing the existence of reasonable grounds for suspicion.[61]

1.18   But it is also clear that it is not enough simply to allege that the suspect's behaviour was "suspicious"; some basis for the suspicion must be shown, of a kind capable of evaluation by an objective third person.[62] This may be no more than

---

[54] *Nakkuda Ali* v. *Jayaratne* [1951] A.C. 66—approved by the House of Lords in *R.* v. *I.R.C., ex p. Rossminster* [1980] A.C. 952.

[55] *Dallison* v. *Caffery* [1965] 1 Q.B. 348, 371, *per* Diplock L.J.

[56] Para. 2.33.

[57] *e.g.* Lord Chelmsford in *Lister* v. *Perryman* (1870) L.R. 4 H.L. 521.

[58] See also L. H. Leigh, *Police Powers in England and Wales* 2nd ed., (1985), pp. 160–163; P. Polyviou, *Search and Seizure*, pp. 279–281.

[59] Under s.66 of the Police and Criminal Evidence Act 1984.

[60] *e.g. Dumbell* v. *Roberts* [1944] 1 All E.R. 326, C.A.

[61] *McArdle* v. *Egan* (1933) 150 L.T. 413, (*per* Lord Wright), *obiter*; *Shaabin Bin Hussien* v. *Chong Fook Kam* [1970] A.C. 942. *cf.* Code of Practice on Stop and Search, Annex B, para. 2.

[62] *Mure* v. *Kaye* (1811) 4 Taunt. 33; 128 E.R. 239. Code of Practice on Stop and Search, Annex B, para. 1.

information received from a reliable informant.[63] In this case all that will be required is for it to be shown that the person against whom the power is exercised did match the information.[64] There are no hard and fast rules as to what is reasonable; each case must depend on its own circumstances,[65] and it has been suggested that different, and presumably lower, standards of reasonableness apply to policemen as opposed to the ordinary private citizen.[66] Some recent decisions, however, have shown the courts being unwilling, even as regards the police, to accept "hunches" as reasonable grounds for suspicion.[67] This trend is strongly reinforced by the guidance in the Code of Practice on Stop and Search.

Most of the authorities in this area have arisen in relation to the exercise of arrest powers. The most recent House of Lords decision, however, concerned powers of entry and search as exercised by officials of the Inland Revenue in connection with tax fraud.[68] The existence of reasonable grounds was in question here in relation to both the issue of the warrant under section 20C of the Taxes Management Act 1970, and the seizure of property as a result of the ensuing search. As regards the warrant the House of Lords considered, though it was not a point argued by the respondents, whether the warrant was invalid because it did not state that the circuit judge who issued it was satisfied that there were reasonable grounds for suspicion, as he was required to be by the statute. The majority (Lord Salmon dissenting) thought that if the circuit judge issued the warrant it was to be assumed that he had fulfilled the statutory requirements, satisfying himself that there were reasonable grounds for suspicion, and not simply relying on the statement on oath of the Inland Revenue officer that there were reasonable grounds. They were not prepared, in other words, to look behind the warrant. The result of this decision would seem to be that once a warrant has been issued the question of whether there were reasonable grounds is dead, except in the unlikely event that some evidence is available that the person issuing the warrant had not satisfied himself of the existence of the reasonable grounds.[69]

In relation to seizure, the respondents argued that the quantity of material taken **1.19** and the speed at which the search was carried out meant that the officers carrying out the search could not have had "reasonable cause to believe" that each item they were taking might be required as evidence of tax fraud, as was required under section 20C(3). The Court of Appeal had been prepared to accept this argument,[70]

---

[63] *McArdle* v. *Egan* (1933) 150 L.T. 412, C.A.; *Haynes* v. *Mervis* (1826) 5 L.J. (o.s.) K.B. 47; *Lister* v. *Perryman* (1870) L.R. 4 H.L. 521.

[64] *King* v. *Gardner* (1979) 71 Cr.App.R. 13.

[65] *Lister* v. *Perryman* (1870) L.R. 4 H.L. 521.

[66] *Dallison* v. *Caffery* [1965] 1 Q.B. 348, C.A.

[67] See S. H. Bailey and D. J. Birch [1982] Crim.L.R. 475.

[68] *R.* v. *I.R.C., ex p. Rossminster Ltd.* [1980] A.C. 952.

[69] The new requirements as to warrants in the Police and Criminal Evidence Act 1984, see below, para. 3.07, may well provide slightly more protection, in that they require certain additional information to be included on the warrant over and above the minimal amount required by their Lordships in *Rossminster*—but these generally only apply to police search warrants, and so would not affect the Inland Revenue, or any other authority with the power to obtain warrants. See further, below, paras. 3.05–3.11.

[70] *R.* v. *I.R.C., ex p. Rossminster Ltd.* [1980] A.C. 952, 967.

and made a final declaration that the seizures were unlawful. The House of Lords however unanimously held that because there was a conflict of evidence a final declaration should not have been granted,[71] and also took the view that the fact that a document was not looked at before it was seized did not necessarily mean that there were no reasonable grounds for seizing it[72]:

> "If the fraud suspected involved inter-company transactions between a large number of companies, it would not take up much time to decide that a file relating to one of the companies might reasonably be believed as likely to contain material which might be required as evidence; and such a conclusion might properly be reached without looking at every document in the file."

In *Reynolds* v. *Commissioner of Police for the Metropolis*[73] the Court of Appeal had to consider another case where large quantities of documents had been removed, this time by the police. The view was taken that the police had to have reasonable cause for suspicion as regards each "file, book, bundle or separate document,"[74] but need not go through each file or bundle examining individual sheets.

The cases on this point thus indicate a fairly lenient approach to what will amount to "reasonable grounds for suspicion." It is submitted that it is not going too far to suggest that it is only where the searcher fails to produce any reason at all for the suspicion that the court is likely to say that there were no reasonable grounds.

D. Warrants

1. Form

1.20   "There is no mystery about the word "warrant": it simply means a document issued by a person in authority under power conferred in that behalf authorising the doing of an act which would otherwise be illegal."[75]

Thus a warrant does not at common law need to take any particular form, and need only contain a minimum of information to be valid. Search warrants issued to the police and some other officials,[76] now have to comply with the slightly more detailed requirements under section 15 of the Police and Criminal Evidence Act 1984,[77] but all other warrants are subject to the common law. All that a warrant is required to contain, according to the House of Lords in *Rossminster*, is:

(a) the authority under which it is issued (*i.e.* generally the relevant statutory provision);

(b) the name of the person to whom it is addressed (*i.e.* the official who is to carry out the entry);

---

[71] See further Chap. Two, para. 2.36.

[72] *R.* v. *I.R.C., ex p. Rossminster Ltd.* [1980] A.C. 952, 1006, *per* Viscount Dilhorne. See also, *Reynolds* v. *Commissioner of Police for the Metropolis* [1984] 3 All E.R. 649.

[73] [1984] 3 All E.R. 649.

[74] *Ibid.* at 655.

[75] *R.* v. *I.R.C., ex p. Rossminster Ltd.* [1980] A.C. 952, 1000, *per* Lord Wilberforce. See also Polyviou, *Search and Seizure* pp. 277–287.

[76] See below, para. 3.05.

[77] *Ibid.*

(c) the address of the premises to be entered.

There is no need for the warrant to be specific as to any suspected offences which lead to the issue of the warrant, nor to state the grounds for suspicion, nor even to say that the person issuing the warrant was satisfied that reasonable grounds existed. Whilst it may be desirable in some case to specify these things, their absence does not invalidate the warrant.

It should be noted that because of the limited nature of a warrant it will often amount to no more than the "key to the door," in that it makes what would otherwise be a trespass a lawful entry, but does not in itself prescribe what can be done in the way of search, seizure or arrest once entry has been gained. These matters will often be dealt with by other statutory provisions, or by the common law, or a mixture of the two. If the entrant exceeds in any way the powers given, he will thereupon become a trespasser, despite the fact that the original entry was under the authority of a warrant.

2. Issue

The warrant is obtained by presenting a justice of the peace (or whoever is empowered to issue the warrant) with an information on oath in the form of a deposition setting out the facts on which the warrant is sought,[78] together with the warrant itself. The issuing authority must be satisfied that sufficient grounds exist for the issue of the warrant, and may question the applicant to this end. The applicant is not expected to identify informants, but the issuer may wish to know whether the informant is known to the applicant, and whether it has been possible to make further inquiries to verify the information.[79] If satisfied, the issuer will see that the applicant has signed the information, and will then himself sign both the information and the warrant.[80] It must be remembered that the above, in particular whether or not the issuer is satisfied, will be subject to only the most minimal judicial review.[81]

1.21

3. Execution

A warrant issued by a magistrate in England and Wales may be executed by any person to whom it is directed, or by any police constable acting within his police area.[82] If issued by any other authority, then it may generally only be exercised by the person to whom it is directed (unless the statute itself provides for wider exercise). It seems that the warrant itself may grant a power of entry to persons not specifically mentioned in the statute. In *Rossminster* the warrant referred to the officers entering "with such constables as they may require," whereas the statute referred only to "an officer of the Board" being allowed to enter. There seems little

1.22

---

[78] *Herniman* v. *Smith* [1938] A.C. 305.
[79] Lord Chancellor's advice to those training magistrates—Royal Commission on Criminal Procedure, *Law and Procedure*, Cmnd. 8092–1, para. 31. See also Code of Practice B, para. 2A.
[80] *Stone's Justices Manual*, Vol. 1, p. 34.
[81] *R.* v. *I.R.C., ex p. Rossminster Ltd.* [1980] A.C. 952.
[82] Magistrates' Courts Act 1980, s.125(2).

reason for giving the police a power of *entry* here; the justification is presumably that they will be there to prevent breaches of the peace, but their common law powers would probably be sufficient to cover this.[83] However, no objection on these grounds was raised in *Rossminster*, and it therefore seems that the courts have given tacit approval to the inclusion of police constables in the warrant, even where it is directed to some other official.[84]

With the exception of warrants for the arrest of a person charged with an offence,[85] all warrants must be in the possession of the person purporting to exercise rights under them at the time of execution.[86] "Possession" does not necessarily mean physical possession. As Roskill L.J. commented in *R. v. Purdy*[87] "having something in one's possession does not mean of necessity that one must actually have it on one's person." In *Purdy* the warrant was in a police car some 60 yards away. But provided it was near enough for it to be produced as "part and parcel of the operation,"[88] an arrest could be validly made under the authority of the warrant. With respect to a search warrant it seems reasonable to expect the searcher to produce his authority if challenged (and some statutes will require this), and there seems no practical reason for having a rule such as that in the Magistrates' Courts Act 1980, s.125(3) in relation to search warrants.[89]

4. Expiry of warrant

1.23   Warrants of arrest issued by a justice of the peace under a statute remain in force until executed or withdrawn.[90] There is no similar provision relating to search warrants, but it is submitted that unless a time limit is imposed by statute,[91] a warrant for entry would likewise remain in force until executed or withdrawn. Statutes allowing entry "at any time or times" always impose a time limit, so there is no possibility of an entry power existing indefinitely and allowing repeated entries.[92]

E. Time

1.24   The form of words used in the statutes which provide for entry powers varies in a number of ways in relation to the time at which, or within which, the power may be exercised. Where the power is under warrant, the commonest form is to state that entry may be "at any time," or "at any time or times" within a given time limit. For powers of entry without warrant, entry at "a reasonable time" is usually stipulated. The particular form used will have its own effect in limiting the scope of the power.

---

[83] See para. 3.02.

[84] Note that this was a warrant issued not by a magistrate but by a circuit judge, and so the provisions of the Magistrates' Courts Act 1980, s.125(2) could not be used to justify the inclusion of the police.

[85] See the Magistrates' Courts Act 1980, s.125(3).

[86] *Codd* v. *Cabe* (1876) 1 Ex. D. 352; *Galliard* v. *Laxton* (1862) 2 B. & S. 363; *R.* v. *Purdy* [1975] Q.B. 288.

[87] [1975] Q.B. 288, 298.

[88] *Ibid.*

[89] But see to the contrary, L. H. Leigh, *Police Powers in England and Wales* 2nd ed., (1985), p. 99.

[90] Magistrates' Courts Act 1980, s.125.

[91] As it is for police search warrants under the Police and Criminal Evidence Act 1984—see para. 3.10.

[92] See also the next section.

Dealing first with the widest form, *i.e.* "at any time," in *I.R.C.* v. *Rossminster*, Viscount Dilhorne, while commenting with disfavour on the fact that the Inland Revenue had chosen to carry out their search at 7 a.m., continued[93]:

> "It cannot, however, be said that they acted illegally by demanding entry at that time for a warrant issued under section 20C authorises entry 'at any time,' even in the middle of the night."

And in *R.* v. *Adams*,[94] which concerned the exercise of a power under a statute which was silent on the issue,[95] the Court of Appeal was clearly of the view that the search could be conducted by night or day.[96] Thus, unless the statute specifically limits the hours within which the power may be exercised, there is no restriction.

Some statutes refer to a search, particularly under warrant, being exercisable at any time within a specified period; others to it being exercisable at any time or times within that period. The former formulation was considered in *R.* v. *Adams*,[97] where the police had made two searches under a warrant, and the accused challenged the legality of the second. The Court of Appeal accepted that the form of words used in the Obscene Publications Act 1959 only permitted one entry per warrant, and that the police had acted illegally in returning for a further search. This ruling has now been given statutory force as regards all police search warrants by the Police and Criminal Evidence Act 1984, s.15.[98] While the Court of Appeal was reluctant to set a precedent for the interpretation of other powers,[99] it seems likely that its approach would be followed, and that only where the statute specifically uses the phrase "time or times" will more than one entry be permitted.

The vast majority of powers exercisable without warrant restrict entry to "reasonable time" or a "reasonable hour." This phrase has received little judicial attention in the context of entry powers. In *Small* v. *Bickley*,[1] the issue was raised as to whether three o'clock on a Sunday afternoon was a reasonable time to seek entry to a butcher's shop in the course of an inquiry into the sale of unfit meat. The magistrates thought that it was, and the Divisional Court said that there was no need for them to add anything on the point, presumably because the issue was one of fact alone, on which they were not prepared to interfere with the magistrates' decision. If this is so, then the nature of the power, the type of premises to be entered, and the seriousness of the investigation, should all be relevant. The way in which the phrase is used in the Police and Criminal Evidence Act 1984, however, suggests a slightly more limited approach. This is discussed further in Chapter Three.[2]

[93] *R.* v. *I.R.C., ex p. Rossminster Ltd.* [1980] A.C. 952, 1001.
[94] [1980] 1 All E.R. 473.
[95] *i.e.* the Obscene Publications Act 1959. The position under this Act is now changed by the Police and Criminal Evidence Act 1984—see para. 3.10.
[96] [1980] 1 All E.R. 473, 478.
[97] *Ibid.*
[98] Below, para. 3.10.
[99] [1980] 1 All E.R. 473, 479.
[1] (1875) 40 J.P. 119.
[2] Para. 3.10.

F. Notice

1.25 Entry powers are frequently exercisable only after a specific period of notice has been given, generally "not less than" a certain period of days. It seems to be well established that such a period, *e.g.* "not less than seven days," means seven clear days, not including the day the notice is received, nor the day on which the power is exercised. This was the view of the Court of Criminal Appeal in *R.* v. *Turner,*[3] in relation to section 10(4)(*b*) of the Prevention of Crime Act 1908, following *Chambers* v. *Smith,*[4] which concerned the time for return of a writ. It was followed in *Re Hector Whaling Ltd.*[5] in connection with notice of meetings under the Companies Act 1929. The approach thus seems to be accepted as a general rule in a number of areas of law, and has not been challenged in recent times.

That any notice given must be specific was made clear in *Stroud* v. *Bradbury.*[6] In this case a local authority wrote to the defendant in February stating that they intended to "proceed under section 290(6) of the Public Health Act 1936," which authorised them to carry out work on premises where the occupier had failed to do so. In the following June, a sanitary inspector arrived to carry out the work, but was refused entry by the defendant. Lord Goddard, and the rest of the Divisional Court, had no doubt that the occupier was within his rights. The entry power relied on was given not by section 290 itself, but by section 287(1) of the same Act, which requires 24 hours' notice of an intention to enter.[7] The February letter could not possibly fulfil this requirement. Unfortunately, the precise reason for the court's decision is not clear. Was it simply that the notice did not refer to the right section, or was the lapse of time also relevant? It is submitted that *both* points are important. A notice of intention to enter a person's private property (and particularly their home) should spell out precisely the authority which is being relied on, and explain what is to happen as plainly as possible. But it is also desirable that it should be as specific as possible as to time. In most cases it should be possible to state a particular day, if not the exact time on that day, when entry will be sought. As yet there is no authority making this mandatory, but it is surely desirable practice.

G. Authority

1.26 It is common for an inspector, particularly in relation to central and local government powers, to be required to produce documentary evidence of his authority before entering premises. It is possible, of course, for a person to be specifically authorised for each occasion. The more common practice, however, is for a person likely to need to use entry powers to be provided with a document on appointment, setting out his authorisation to seek entry under a variety of statutes. An example of

---

[3] [1910] 1 K.B. 346.
[4] (1843) 12 M. & W. 2.
[5] [1936] Ch. 208.
[6] [1952] 2 All E.R. 76.
[7] See para. 9.03.

such a document set out in Clay's *Handbook of Environmental Health*,[8] lists nearly 30 statutes. The requirement that a person should be authorised to enter for a particular purpose thus becomes something of a formality. Perhaps a wider use of the more restrictive requirement contained in the Health and Safety at Work, etc. Act 1974 would make this type of provision more useful to the occupier, and discourage unnecessary "authorisations."[9]

H. Land, etc.

An entry power may state that it applies to any "place," or it may use some more **1.27** specific word, such as "land," or "premises." The effect of the use of particular words is difficult to determine. Sometimes the statute itself provides a definition, but in the absence of this, do these words have a settled meaning? The three words discussed here, because they are the most frequently used, are "land," "premises," and "dwelling-house."

"Land" is the only one of the three which is defined in the Interpretation Act 1978. This states that the word "includes buildings and other structures, land covered with water, and any estate, interest, easement, servitude or right in or over land." This is a fairly comprehensive definition. But it is clear that in some statutes the word is used to exclude buildings, *e.g.* the Gas Act 1965, Schedule 6.[10] "Premises" on the other hand, may be said to require there to be buildings. The word was considered by the House of Lords in *Maunsell* v. *Olins*,[11] in relation to the Rent Act 1968. Viscount Dilhorne stated that:

> " 'Premises' is an ordinary word of the English language which takes colour and content from the context in which it is used. A reference to Stroud's Judicial Dictionary shows this to be the case. It has, in my opinion, no recognised and established primary meaning. Frequently it is used in relation to structures of one kind or another. No one would, I think, in the ordinary use of the English language refer to farm land as 'premises' though farm buildings may often be referred to as 'farm premises.' "

The House was unanimous in accepting Viscount Dilhorne's suggestion that the word must be looked at in context, but this approach led only a majority to the view that the word was limited to premises of a residential character and so could not apply to a "farm" as a whole. On this view a cottage on a farm did not form part of larger "premises." In a case on the Rent Act 1965, however, a Divisional Court had been prepared to accept a caravan together with the land on which it was sited as being "premises."[12] And in a case on the Petroleum (Consolidation) Act 1928, it was accepted that the forecourt of a petrol station was part of "premises," though a

---

[8] 15th ed., p. 23.
[9] See below Chap. Eight, para. 8.31.
[10] See below, Chap. Nine, para. 9.95.
[11] [1975] 1 All E.R. 16.
[12] *Norton* v. *Knowles* [1969] 1 Q.B. 572, apparently not cited in *Maunsell* v. *Olins* [1975] 1 All E.R. 16.

tanker standing on it was not.[13] As these cases show, the meaning of the word does need to be considered afresh in each provision in which it is used, but it is suggested that in the absence of indications to the contrary, "premises" must have some buildings on them, but that the land surrounding the buildings will form part of the premises.[14]

1.28   The word "dwelling-place" is generally used as part of a limitation on a power of entry, *i.e* the power is expressed to be unavailable as regards premises used "only as a dwelling-place."[15] Plainly the word must apply only to residential property, but, as with premises, land surrounding or "belonging to" the residence should probably be included.[16] In *G. E. Stevens (High Wycombe) Ltd.* v. *High Wycombe Corporation*,[17] on the Housing Act 1957, Diplock J. said that premises occupied by a company could not be a private dwelling, even if they were used for residential purposes. Otherwise, the only difficulty seems to be with the qualification often applied, that the premises must be used "only" as a dwelling. Premises used partly for business and partly as a dwelling will fall outside this. But it is unclear what the position is as regards living accommodation which is, for example, directly attached to a shop. Presumably it will be a question of fact in each case whether the living accommodation formed part of business premises, or could be regarded as a separate entity. It should not be the case, however, that a shopkeeper who keeps his account books in the living room thereby turns his house into business premises. The statute will often provide for entry under warrant which is not limited to business premises, and this would be the appropriate power to use if entry was required in such circumstances.

Finally, one building can comprise more than one set of premises, *e.g.* a block of flats, or offices, is itself "premises," but so is each individual unit.

I. Obstruction

1.29   It is not uncommon where a statutory power of entry is given to find that it is specifically made an offence to "obstruct" the person who is given the power. And, of course, wilful obstruction of a police officer in the execution of his duty is an offence under the Police Act 1964, s.51(3). Most of the cases on the meaning of "obstruction" have, in fact, arisen under the Police Act provision, but there is no reason to suppose that the courts would interpret the word differently in any other context.

Unarguable cases of obstruction will arise where the entry is physically resisted by the occupier, or some other person. This will include "passive resistance" of the type adopted by the demonstrators in *R.* v. *Chief Constable of Devon and Cornwall, ex p. Central Electricity Generating Board*,[18] which involved lying down in front of moving

---

[13] *Grandi* v. *Milburn* [1966] 2 Q.B. 263.

[14] See also *Customs and Excise Commissioners* v. *Cope* [1981] S.T.C. 532; *Crownlion* v. *The Commissioners of Customs and Excise* [1985] V.A.T.T.R. 188.

[15] Or "dwelling-house," or "dwelling." See, *e.g.* the Trade Descriptions Act 1968, s.28; Chap. Nine, para. 9.72.

[16] But *cf.* Public Order Act 1986, s.8, which refers specifically to "structures."

[17] [1962] 2 Q.B. 547.

[18] [1982] Q.B. 458.

18

vehicles, chaining themselves to equipment, and sitting down where work was to be done. In Scotland, at least in relation to police powers, nothing less than physical obstruction will do,[19] the word having been construed *eiusdem generis* with "assault" and "resist." In England and Wales the courts have not been so limited in their interpretation. So it has been held that giving a warning of police presence can amount to obstruction, including a warning by non-verbal communication, if the warning is given to a person who is committing, or is suspected of committing or being about to commit, an offence.[20] Indeed, almost any positive act which makes it more difficult for someone to carry out their duties can amount to obstruction. But what of the householder who simply sits behind an already locked door, or the owner who refuses to hand over the keys of his warehouse? Mere passive unhelpfulness, even if undertaken with the intention of frustrating the police, has been held not to be obstruction.[21] In *Dibble* v. *Ingleton*,[22] where a motorist's drinking of whisky after he had ceased to drive, in order to avoid a breath test, was held to be wilful obstruction, Bridge J. commented[23]:

> "I would draw a clear distinction between a refusal to act, on the one hand, and the doing of some positive act on the other. In a case, as in *Rice* v. *Connolly*, where the obstruction alleged consists of a refusal by the defendant to do the act which the police constable asked him to do—to give information, it might be, or to give assistance to the police constable—one can see readily the soundness of the principle, if I may say so with respect, applied in *Rice* v. *Connolly*, that such a refusal to act cannot amount to a wilful obstruction under section 51 *unless the law imposes on the person concerned some obligation in the circumstances to act in the manner requested by the police officer.*" [emphasis added.]

The precise implications of the passage in emphasis have not been worked out by the courts, but it has been argued that, if someone is given the right to enter premises, there will be a corresponding duty on the occupier to let him in.[24] If there is such a duty to co-operate, a refusal to do something requested by the entrant in order to further the entry, will amount to obstruction.[25] If this is right, and it seems a correct inference from Bridge J.'s statement, then the person sitting behind the locked door, or refusing to hand over, or reveal the whereabouts of, the keys to his property, will be "obstructing" the person trying to enter, and will be committing an offence if the required mental element is proved.   **1.30**

The mental element in obstruction offences related to powers of entry is most commonly expressed in terms of "wilfulness." It is now clear that this requires the   **1.31**

---

[19] *Curlett* v. *M'Kechnie* 1938 S.C.J. 176.

[20] *Betts* v. *Stevens* [1910] 1 K.B. 1; *Hinchcliffe* v. *Sheldon* [1955] 3 All E.R. 406; *Green* v. *Moore* [1982] Q.B. 1044.

[21] *Rice* v. *Connolly* [1966] 2 Q.B. 414—refusal to answer questions.

[22] [1972] 1 Q.B. 480.

[23] *Ibid.* 488.

[24] J. C. Smith and B. Hogan, *Criminal Law* (5th ed.), p. 370. And see also T. Gibbons [1983] Crim.L.R. 21, and K. W. Lidstone [1983] Crim.L.R. 29.

[25] *cf. Stunt* v. *Bolton* [1972] R.T.R. 435—refusal to hand over car keys. Also *Liepins* v. *Spearman* [1986] R.T.R. 24.

prosecution to prove that the defendant intended or realised that what he was doing would have the effect of obstructing the exercise of the power. The case of *Willmott* v. *Atack*,[26] appeared to suggest that an element of "hostility" towards, in this case, the police, had to be proved as well. In *Moore* v. *Green*,[27] and *Hills* v. *Ellis*,[28] this was explained as simply meaning that the defendant's conduct had to be "aimed at" the police. Even this has now been doubted, however, in *Lewis* v. *Cox*[29] where Webster J. said that the only facts that it was necessary for a court to find were:

> "whether the defendant's conduct in fact prevented the police from carrying out their duty or made it more difficult for them to do so; and whether the defendant intended that conduct to prevent the police from carrying out their duties, or to make it more difficult for them."

Thus "wilful" is now treated as being synonymous with "intentional." This corresponds to a recent change in the drafting of obstruction offences, where it has become the practice to use "intentional" rather than "wilful."

In some statutes no *mens rea* word is attached to the offence.[30] In prosecutions for these offences the court need only concern itself with the first of Webster J.'s questions (above).

1.32   The penalty for obstruction (and other offences) is often expressed in terms of a fine not exceeding a certain level on the "standard scale." The current amounts of the various levels of the standard scale are set out in Appendix Two.

---

[26] [1977] Q.B. 498.
[27] [1983] 1 All E.R. 663.
[28] [1983] 1 All E.R. 667.
[29] [1984] 3 W.L.R. 875.
[30] I have been careful in the descriptions of the offences only to leave out the *mens rea* word where the statute itself does so.

Chapter Two

REMEDIES

If an unlawful entry is attempted or takes place the occupier will want to seek some **2.01**
remedy. If he is sure of his ground self-help, in the form of refusal of entry, or ejection
of the trespasser may be the most effective approach, but it is surrounded by
dangers, as will be seen below. Injunctions or court orders might also be tried, but
the delay in obtaining them may often render them ineffective. And finally there may
be an action in tort for damages. These issues are discussed in Part I of this chapter.

In Part II the focus is on the position when property has been seized as the result
of a search. To what extent can evidence resulting from an unlawful search be
challenged? And how can a person recover property, or compensation for its loss or
damage?

I. CHALLENGING THE INITIAL ENTRY

A. Self-help

In Chapter One various situations were considered where a licence might be given **2.02**
for an entry. If an entrant has no such licence, or the licence has been withdrawn,
and there is no other authority for the entry, under a warrant or statutory power, he
will be a trespasser. The person having authority to grant a licence to enter will now
also have the authority to refuse entry, or to require the trespasser to leave.

The right to require a trespasser to leave will include the right to use reasonable
force to achieve this end.[1] If the trespass or attempted trespass is carried out by force
then the occupier may use reasonable force to remove or repel the trespasser
forthwith, without the need for any request for the trespasser to depart.[2] If, however,
the entry took place peaceably then force may not be used until there has been a
request to depart, and an opportunity given for the trespasser to comply.[3]

In *Robson* v. *Hallett*,[4] a police officer, who had originally been given permission to **2.03**
enter the premises, had his licence revoked. He started to leave at once, but was
attacked while on his way. The court had no doubt that he had been assaulted while

---

[1] *Davis* v. *Lisle* [1936] 2 K.B. 434; *Thomas* v. *Marsh* (1833) 5 Car. & P. 596; *Dean* v. *Hogg* (1834) 10 Bing.
345; *Roberts* v. *Tayler* (1845) 1 C.B. 117; *Brett* v. *Mullarkey* (1873) Ir.Rep. 7 C.L. 120.
[2] *Weaver* v. *Bush* (1798) T.R. 78; *Polkinhorn* v. *Wright* (1845) 8 Q.B. 197.
[3] *Green* v. *Goddard* (1704) 2 Salk. 641; *Polkinhorn* v. *Wright* (1845) 8 Q.B. 197; *Robson* v. *Hallett* [1967] 2
Q.B. 939; *Kay* v. *Hibbert* [1977] Crim.L.R. 226.
[4] [1967] 2 Q.B. 939.

in the execution of his duty. In *Davis* v. *Lisle*,[5] on the other hand, where the request to leave was met by an attempt to produce a warrant card, this action was taken as an assertion of a right to remain on the premises, taking the police officer outside the scope of his duty. The immediate use of reasonable force by the occupier was therefore justified.

Just as an occupier may use reasonable force to remove a trespasser, so he may use force on the threshold to resist an attempted forcible trespass. Once again there is no requirement on the occupier to precede his use of force by a request to desist from attempting to enter.[6]

2.04   It is at this point that the rights of an occupier tend to merge with the basic criminal law defences of self-defence or prevention of crime. Since the way in which these issues generally arise before a court is where the occupier is charged with some form of assault against the alleged trespasser, these defences may be pleaded in addition to the basic self-help rights of the occupier. Their availability will of course depend on the accused showing that the trespasser, potential or actual, was committing, or was about to commit a criminal offence. In the situations with which we are chiefly concerned, *i.e.* purported entries under some lawful authority, where that authority does not in fact exist, this might be an assault, criminal damage, or an offence under the Criminal Law Act 1977, s.6, whereby

> "any person who, without lawful authority, uses or threatens violence for the purpose of securing entry into any premises for himself or for any other person is guilty of an offence."

2.05   There are several limitations on this offence.

(1) There must be violence threatened or used (though it can be directed against the person or property).[7] "Violence" is undefined, but presumably it means something more than simply "force."[8] Thus slipping a Yale lock would presumably not amount to "violence," though breaking it off the frame would.[9] But it will probably also cover *any* use of force against a person, *e.g.* by pushing a door when there is someone on the property pushing from the other side.[10]

(2) A threat is sufficient for the offence to be committed, *e.g.* "Are you going to open the door, or are we going to have to do it for you?"

(3) If "lawful authority" exists then there will be no offence, but it must be an authority to use violence, not simply to enter.[11] A defective warrant would not be "lawful authority."

---

[5] [1936] 2 K.B. 434.
[6] *Polkinhorn* v. *Wright* (1845) 8 Q.B. 197.
[7] s.6(4).
[8] For which, see Chap. 1, para. 1.14.
[9] Law Commission Report No. 76, para. 2.61. See also Glanville Williams, *Textbook of Criminal Law* (2nd ed., 1983), p. 920; Griew, *The Criminal Law Act 1977*, note to s.6; Smith and Hogan, *Criminal Law* (6th ed., 1988), p. 803.
[10] Law Commission Report No. 76, para. 2.61.
[11] Law Commission Report No. 76, para. 2.66.

(4) There must be someone on the premises at the time who opposes the entry, and the prospective entrant must be aware of that fact.[12]

1. Reasonable force

In all situations involving self-help, in tort as well as under the criminal law, the occupier is expected only to use such force as is reasonable in the circumstances. It is true that in *R. v. Hussey*,[13] the Court of Criminal Appeal approved a passage in Archbold which stated that a person may kill a trespasser who would forcibly dispossess him of his house.[14] In that case the occupier, a tenant, had shot and wounded two people, who, under the direction of the landlady, were unlawfully trying to evict him. But the dictum was not necessary for the decision, and the better view seems to be that a test of reasonableness must be applied.[15] Shooting to kill could only possibly be reasonable if all other methods of defending one's property had failed (and perhaps not even then). What the decision in *Hussey* does emphasise is the fact that a person's *home* is a very special place in need of greater protection than other property that he may own, such as a shop or a factory. For if he is turned out of his home, where else can he go?

However, the situations discussed in this book do not involve attempts to dispossess the occupier, but merely to gain entry for some other purpose, such as a search. In such cases there seems no doubt that it is simply a question of fact as to what force is reasonable in the circumstances. In this context it is useful to look further at *Davis v. Lisle*.[16] In that case the accused was charged with assaulting a police officer in the execution of his duty, and with "wilfully and maliciously tearing" the policeman's tunic. The court had no doubt that the police officer, having had his licence terminated by a request to leave the premises, and having no other authority for remaining, was no longer acting in the execution of his duty when he stayed put. So the assault conviction could not stand. But the Divisional Court was more than happy to allow the conviction for tearing the tunic to stand. The damage had been caused by blows to the chest and stomach following closely on the request to depart, and it seems clear from the tone of the judgments that the court would have been of the opinion, if the issue had been before them, that the degree of force used was not justifiable in the circumstances.

The variables which may exist, and the fact that the issue is primarily one of fact, make it difficult to give guidelines as to what is acceptable, but it is tentatively suggested that the following are likely to be relevant considerations:

(1) Pushing or manhandling is more likely to be judged reasonable than a direct assault (as in *Davis v. Lisle*).

(2) If the trespasser resists, or ignores the initial application of force, an increase

2.06

2.07

2.08

---

[12] s.6(1)(*a*) and (*b*).
[13] (1924) 18 Cr.App.R. 160.
[14] But *cf.* 2 Inst. 316; *Moriarty v. Brooks* (1834) 6 C. & P. 684.
[15] As in *Collins v. Renison* (1754) 1 Sayer 138.
[16] [1936] 2 K.B. 434.

will be permissible—though whether to the level approved of in *Hussey* must be doubtful.[17]

(3) An imbalance in physical prowess between the trespasser and the occupier may be relevant. If the trespasser is burly and the occupier weak, it may be reasonable for the occupier to use a weapon. If the balance of power is the other way a much lesser degree of force may be reasonable.

(4) The urgency of the situation, or any other circumstances which might affect the judgment of the reasonable man as to the amount of force to be used, should be taken into account.[18]

2. Mistake of fact

2.09   The above discussion has been conducted on the basis that the facts are as they are perceived to be by the occupier, *i.e.* that the entry or continued presence of the other party does constitute a trespass. What is the position if the occupier, as the result of a genuine mistake, has wrongly categorised the status of the entrant?

(a) *Criminal law*

2.10   If the occupier is facing a criminal charge as a result of action taken on the basis of a mistake, the question of his liability will depend on the nature of the mistake and the definition of the offence with which he has been charged. If the mistake is one of law, *e.g.* as to whether a certain official has any power of entry, then it will be no defence. If it is one of fact, then the consequences will depend on the actual offence charged, since, following *D.P.P.* v. *Morgan*[19] a mistake as to an essential element of an offence need only be honestly made in order to entitle a defendant to an acquittal.

The most common charge in the situations under consideration will be "obstruction," or some form of "assault." For obstruction, if the offence is defined as having to be committed "wilfully," then any mistake need only be honest; otherwise it will have to be reasonable.[20]

2.11   If the charge is one of "assault," the defendant's mistake may lead him to think that he is acting lawfully in self-defence. In *R.* v. *Gladstone Williams*[21] the Court of Appeal held that such a defence was available, even if the mistake was unreasonable, because "unlawfulness" was an essential element of assault. Subject to the proviso that the mistake must not be the result of voluntary intoxication, this line has been followed in subsequent cases.[22]

2.12   One decision of the Court of Appeal, however, *R.* v. *Fennell*[23] (which was not cited in *Gladstone Williams*) suggests that even a reasonable mistake will not provide a

---

[17] *R.* v. *Hinchcliffe* (1823) 1 Lew. C.C. 161.
[18] *Att.-Gen. for Northern Ireland's Reference (No. 1 of 1975)* [1977] A.C. 105.
[19] [1976] A.C. 182.
[20] See also Chap. One, paras. 1.29–1.31.
[21] (1984) Cr.App.R. 276.
[22] *Beckford* v. *The Queen* [1988] A.C. 130 (P.C.); *R.* v. *O'Grady* [1987] 1 Q.B. 995; *R.* v. *Jackson* [1985] R.T.R. 257.
[23] [1971] 1 Q.B. 428.

defence in some circumstances. In that case the defendant's son had been arrested. The defendant thought that the arrest was unlawful because there were no reasonable grounds for the police officer's suspicion (a question of fact), and having unsuccessfully demanded his son's release, struck one of the police officers. He was charged with assaulting a police officer in the execution of his duty. He pleaded that he had made a reasonable mistake as to the lawfulness of the arrest, and was therefore entitled to use reasonable force to secure his son's release. In delivering the judgment of the court that the father's plea must fail, Lord Widgery said[24]:

> "Where a person honestly and reasonably believes that he or his child is in imminent danger of injury it would be unjust if he were deprived of the right to use reasonable force by way of defence merely because he had made some genuine mistake of fact. On the other hand, if the child is in police custody and not in imminent danger of injury there is no urgency of the kind which requires an immediate decision and a father who forcibly releases the child does so at his peril. If in fact the arrest proves to be lawful the father's use of force cannot be justified."

The implications of this decision for the use of self-help remedies are serious if the case means that no defence of mistake will be allowed unless there is an "imminent danger of injury." It would mean that, as Lord Widgery says, the occupier would act at his peril, unless he was absolutely sure that the trespass was unlawful. It is suggested that this is out of line with the other cases cited above, and should be limited in its application to the situation of releasing third parties from arrest by the police. Certainly, as regards its reference to "reasonable" mistakes it is incompatible with *Gladstone Williams*.[25]

(b) *Tort*

In tort it seems that a mistake, reasonable or not, will not provide a defence to an **2.13** action for an intentional tort, such as assault and battery.[26]

B. Challenging Evidence

1. Criminal law

The importance of the remedies outlined above becomes even greater when the **2.14** approach of the courts to the exclusion of evidence is considered. One curb on the unlawful use of entry powers would be the use of an exclusionary evidence rule such as that which operates in the United States. In England and Wales the position is governed by the House of Lords decision in *R. v. Sang*,[27] and by section 78 of the

[24] [1971] 1 Q.B. 428, 431.
[25] *R. v. Asbury* [1986] Crim.L.R. 258, C.A.
[26] *Consolidated Co.* v. *Curtis* [1892] 1 Q.B. 495; *Hollins* v. *Fowler* (1875) L.R. 7 H.L. 757; *Basely* v. *Clarkson* (1682) 3 Lev. 37.
[27] [1980] A.C. 402, taking the same approach as the Privy Council in *Kuruma* v. *R.* [1955] A.C. 197. See also *R.* v. *Heston-Francois* [1984] Q.B. 278.

Police and Criminal Evidence Act 1984. The relationship between section 78 and the common law is unclear. Some courts have taken the view that the section simply restates the common law; others suggest that it should be regarded as stating a new principle. As will be seen,[28] at the moment there are conflicting views at Court of Appeal level. Pending resolution of this by the House of Lords, the pre-1984 position still needs to be considered. *Sang* itself concerned an agent provocateur, but their Lordships took the opportunity to give their considered views on the whole area of the court's power to exclude evidence. The opinion of the House is summarised in Viscount Dilhorne's formulation of their reply to the question put to them by the Court of Appeal. This question was[29]:

> "Does a trial judge [including magistrates] have a discretion to refuse to allow evidence—being evidence other than evidence of admission—to be given in any circumstances in which such evidence is relevant and of more than minimal probative value?"

The answer given was in two parts:

(1) A trial judge in a criminal trial has always a discretion to refuse to admit evidence if in his opinion its prejudicial effect outweighs its probative value.

(2) Save with regard to admissions and confessions and generally with regard to evidence obtained from the accused after the commission of the offence, he has no discretion to refuse to admit relevant admissible evidence on the ground that it was obtained by improper or unfair means.[30]

2.15   In the context of the rest of the opinions delivered by their Lordships the following points seem to be clearly established:

(1) The court is concerned primarily with the fair conduct of the trial, and not with the manner in which evidence was obtained. Thus the mere fact that the evidence was acquired as the result of an illegal entry and search is irrelevant to the question of whether that evidence should be excluded.[31] It is unfairness in the context of the trial, rather than the manner of obtaining evidence, that is the crucial consideration.

(2) The main example of unfairness in the use of evidence is where its prejudicial effect outweighs its probative value, *e.g.* as in "similar facts" cases.

(3) Admissions or confessions which have been unfairly obtained may be excluded.

2.16   The difficulty lies with the question as to whether the judge's discretion extends any further. The speeches of their lordships do not appear unanimous on this, despite their agreement with the formulation given above. The ambiguity arises from the phrase "and generally with regard to evidence obtained from the accused after the commission of the offence" in paragraph (2) above. Some of the speeches, in particular those of Lord Diplock and Viscount Dilhorne, apparently leave little

---

[28] See below, para. 2.19.
[29] *R.* v. *Sang* [1980] A.C. 402 at p. 424.
[30] *Ibid.* 437.
[31] *e.g. Jeffrey* v. *Black* [1978] Q.B. 490.

room for giving any content to this phrase. They seem to be saying that unless the evidence is such that it in effect amounts to a confession and is equivalent to the accused incriminating himself as a result of a trick or other improper pressure on him, then there is no scope for the exercise of any discretion.[32] Lord Salmon, Lord Fraser, and Lord Scarman were prepared to go a little further. In Lord Salmon's view the judge always has a discretion to reject evidence on the ground that it would make the trial unfair, and this is not confined to the specific cases outlined above: "In my opinion the category of such cases is not, and never can be closed, except by statute."[33] Lord Fraser felt that subject to a limitation that the discretion should only apply to evidence obtained from the accused himself or from his premises, judges should be left to exercise their discretion "in accordance with their individual views of what is unfair or oppressive or morally reprehensible."[34] And Lord Scarman, with a similar reluctance to tie the hands of the judge at the trial stated that

> "the principle of fairness, though concerned exclusively with the use of evidence at trial, is not susceptible to categorisation or classification, and is wide enough in some circumstances to embrace the way in which after the crime, evidence has been obtained from the accused."[35]

The majority of their Lordships were therefore not prepared to give a detailed **2.17** description of the precise limits on the judge's discretion, nor were they prepared to go very far in providing examples of situations in which they considered the discretion should be exercised in favour of the accused, other than those clear cases listed above. Undoubtedly previous and subsequent decisions of the courts on specific situations of alleged unfairness will continue to be of considerable importance. For our purpose, the most directly relevant is the case of *Jeffrey* v. *Black*.[36] The accused was arrested by members of the police drug squad, for the theft of a sandwich. After he had been charged, but before he was bailed, he was told by the police officer that they intended to search the place where he lived. The accused went with police officers to his home, and showed them the room which he occupied. The police found drugs on the premises, and the accused was charged with the unlawful possession of these drugs. At his trial the defence objected to the evidence of the search being presented, because it was the fruit of an unlawful search. The justices accepted that the accused had not in fact consented to the search, and refused to allow the evidence of what had been found. On a case stated, the Divisional Court agreed that the police officers in this situation had no power to search the accused's premises without his consent.[37] But they held that this was not sufficient to allow the magistrates to exclude relevant admissible evidence.

> "[T]he simple unvarnished fact that evidence was obtained by police officers

[32] *e.g. R.* v. *Payne* [1963] 1 W.L.R. 637.
[33] [1980] A.C. 402, 445.
[34] *Ibid.* 450.
[35] *Ibid.* 456.
[36] [1978] Q.B. 490.
[37] See further below, para. 3.24.

who had gone in without bothering to get a search warrant, is not enough to justify the magistrates in exercising their discretion to keep the evidence out."[38]

2.18   Something additional must be shown in the way of trickery, deception, or oppression. This additional factor must presumably now be considered in the light of *Sang*, and relate to unfairness in the context of the trial, and not simply in the acquisition of the information (unless it is the equivalent of a confession). At any rate it is clear that it is only in a very exceptional case that exclusion will be considered: unlawful entry in itself not being sufficiently exceptional.

The same view was taken by the Divisional Court in an unreported case in 1980 involving an alleged unlawful entry by a local authority official. In *Cameron* v. *Charles Simpson Motors*[39] the accused was charged with offences under the Caravan Sites and Control of Development Act 1960. The magistrates dismissed the information because they held that the evidence had been obtained in the course of an unlawful entry, and they decided to exercise their discretion to exclude it. The Divisional Court held that in fact the entry had been legal, but went on to say that even if it had been illegal the evidence should not have been excluded under the principles in *Kuruma*[40] and *Sang*.[41] They seem to have taken a very restrictive interpretation of *Sang*, construing the general words in paragraph (2) of Viscount Dilhorne's formulation, referring to evidence obtained from the accused after the commission of the offence, as applicable only to such things as involuntary confessions. A similar line was taken in *Tunbridge Wells* v. *Quietlynn*[41a] in connection with the inspection of a sex shop under the Local Government (Miscellaneous) Provisions Act 1982.[41b]

2.19   How is the common law affected by section 78 of the Police and Criminal Evidence Act 1984? Section 78(1) states:

> "In any proceedings the court may refuse to allow evidence on which the prosecution proposes to rely to be given if it appears to the court that, having regard to all the circumstances, including the circumstances in which the evidence was obtained, the admission of the evidence would have such an adverse effect on the fairness of the proceedings that the court ought not to admit it."

It is clear that this is no narrower than the common law,[42] but is it any wider? In *R.* v. *Mason* the Court of Appeal took the view that "section 78 does no more than to restate the power which judges had at common law before the 1984 Act was passed."[43] If that is so then the phraseology used, and in particular the meaning of "fairness of the proceedings" will have to be interpreted in the light of *Sang*.[44] But in

[38] [1978] Q.B. 490, 498.
[39] [1980] C.L.Y. 2630.
[40] [1955] A.C. 197.
[41] [1980] A.C. 402.
[41a] [1985] Crim. L.R. 594.
[41b] See below, para. 4.11.
[42] The common law power to exclude evidence is effectively preserved by s.82(3).
[43] [1988] 3 All E.R. 481.
[44] [1980] A.C. 402.

two cases decided after Mason, *R.* v. *Samuel*[45] and *R.* v. *O'Leary*,[46] differently constituted Courts of Appeal have ruled that otherwise admissible evidence may be excluded under section 78 even in the absence of any impropriety in the way it was obtained. This clearly goes further than *Sang*. In *O'Leary* the test was put in this way:

> "It is the duty of the court to take into account all the circumstances of the case and then answer the question: 'Will the admission of the relevant evidence have such an effect on the fairness of proceedings that I, the court, ought not to admit it?' "

Most of the cases on section 78 have been concerned with the admission of evidence obtained during interviews with the defendant, and the operation of the Codes of Practice.[47] In some cases a breach of the relevant Code has been regarded as giving rise to the possibility of excluding evidence,[48] but other decisions have been more restrictive.[49] **2.20**

A case on entry powers which was decided by the Divisional Court on the day before *Mason*, while claiming to simply apply *Sang*, does seem to take a slightly broader approach. In *Matto* v. *Wolverhampton Crown Court*[50] police officers had knowingly trespassed in order to administer a breath test. Woolf J. ruled that the Crown Court had been wrong to refuse to consider exercising its discretion under section 78, in relation to evidence obtained subsequently at the police station. The bad faith, and oppressive conduct, of the trespassing police officers could have affected the fairness of proceedings *at the police station*. This extends the scope of section 78 beyond the fairness of *the trial*, which seemed to be the limit of the scope of *Sang*. On the other hand, it is clearly in line with *Sang* in that it is concerned with the exclusion of incriminating evidence obtained as a result of improper pressure.[51] Similarly in *Mason* the Court of Appeal ruled that a confession obtained by a trick should be excluded. It seems that section 78, while producing a considerably body of case law,[52] is likely to produce only minor changes in the general trend of the law in this area. *Cameron* v. *Charles Simpson Motors*,[53] for example, would almost certainly be decided the same way under section 78. Even in a case like *Jeffrey* v. *Black*[54] exclusion would be unlikely, assuming that the police officers were found to have acted in good faith, and without knowledge of their lack of authority.

2. Civil proceedings

In civil proceedings the problems of unlawfully obtained evidence arise less **2.21**

---

[45] [1988] 2 All E.R. 135.
[46] *The Times*, May 18, 1988, C.A.
[47] *i.e.* under s.66 of the Police and Criminal Evidence Act 1984.
[48] *R.* v. *Samuel* [1988] 2 All E.R. 135.
[49] *R.* v. *Alladice, The Times*, May 11, 1988.
[50] [1987] Crim.L.R. 641.
[51] In contrast to the situation in *Fox* v. *Chief Constable of Gwent* [1985] 3 All E.R. 392, see below, para. 4.26.
[52] See in addition to the cases dealt with here, *R.* v. *Vernon* [1988] Crim.L.R. 445; *R.* v. *Sat-Bhambra* [1988] Crim.L.R. 453; *R.* v. *Lunnon* [1988] Crim.L.R. 457; *R.* v. *Hughes* [1988] Crim.L.R. 519.
[53] See above, para. 2.18.
[54] See above, para. 2.17.

frequently than under the criminal law. But the area has recently come to be considered as a result of the growth of the use of *Anton Piller* orders.[55] If, in the course of exercising an *Anton Piller* order information is acquired which is irrelevant to the action in hand, but may be relevant to some other action, what use may be made of it? The general approach in the civil law was stated by the Court of Appeal in *Helliwell* v. *Piggott-Sims*,[56] to be that a judge has no discretion to refuse evidence which is relevant, whether or not it has been obtained unlawfully. This would seem to follow logically from the *Sang* view that the only justification for the exercise of the discretion in a criminal trial is to avoid prejudice to the accused. The same considerations of a "fair trial" do not apply in quite the same way in civil proceedings, where the parties are in more balanced opposition. Nor does the rule against self-incrimination have any relevance, except in the area of discovery.[57] This is the one area where the courts have been prepared to be strict in their control of the use to which information may be put. In *Riddick* v. *Thames Board Mills*[58] the Court of Appeal ruled that a document obtained on discovery in an action could not be used as the basis of a subsequent action. The application of this ruling has fallen to be considered in two later cases. In *I.T.C. Film Distributors* v. *Video Exchange*,[59] as a result of a rather bizarre chain of events, one side obtained possession of some of the other side's papers. Some of these documents were exhibited to an affidavit sworn by the defendant, and the defendant, while accepting that he might not make use of, and must return the other documents, sought to retain the use of those that were attached to the affidavit for the purpose of his present action. Warner J. held that since the documents had been obtained by stealth or a trick, the case was *a fortiori Riddick's* case, where the document had been obtained lawfully. On the other hand, his Lordship had already looked at some of the documents in question, because, although they had not formally been put in evidence, they had in fact been used as evidence in the cross-examination of one of the plaintiff's witnesses, which had been taken early for the witness's convenience, and at the plaintiff's request. These documents, his Lordship felt, could not now be excluded, and he allowed their continued use by the defendant.[60]

2.22   It seems unlikely that the particular facts of this case would recur, but it does raise some points of interest as to the general principles to be applied in this area. The plaintiff forestalled the defendant's use of most of the documents by seeking an injunction and delivery up; those that had been used in evidence were allowed to remain in use. To that extent the case is in line with the general principle of relevance being the crucial factor, not how the evidence was obtained. However, Warner J. was prepared to treat this case as analogous to discovery. With respect there seems no pressing reason why this analogy should hold. The documents were not obtained

[55] See below, paras. 5.02–5.35.
[56] [1980] F.S.R. 582.
[57] See *Rank Film Distributors* v. *Video Information Centre* [1982] A.C. 380, below, Chap. 5, para. 5.17.
[58] [1977] 1 Q.B. 881.
[59] [1982] Ch. 431.
[60] In *Guess? Inc.* v. *Lee* [1987] F.S.R. 125, the Hong Kong C.A. refused to follow Warner J. on this issue, taking the view that even this evidence should have been excluded.

by discovery or any similar process, but either by chance or, more probably, by a trick. A party obtaining information on discovery undertakes to use that information only for the present proceedings. Contempt of court will lie for breach of this undertaking.[61] No such undertaking is possible where the information is obtained without the other side's knowledge or consent. It is difficult to see why the general rule as stated by the Court of Appeal in *Helliwell* v. *Piggott-Sims* should not apply to the use of this information in any subsequent action, and the other party be left to his civil remedies (as is the accused in criminal proceedings) if the information has been obtained tortiously. If the suggested conclusion seems unsatisfactory it suggests, perhaps, that there is something unsatisfactory about the normal exclusionary rule.

The second case where these issues were considered was *Sony Corporation* v. *Time Electronics*.[62] Here, while executing an *Anton Piller* order relating to headphones the plaintiff's solicitor observed on the defendant's premises cassettes which he suspected were counterfeit. Accordingly he set up a test purchase of the cassettes, and when his suspicions were confirmed, made a new application for an *Anton Piller* order in relation to the cassettes. The defendant objected that this amounted to a breach of the undertaking always attached to an *Anton Piller* order, not to use information acquired through its exercise for any purpose other than the current or imminent proceedings. Goulding J. rejected this argument on two grounds. **2.23**

(1) The real foundation of the new action was the information obtained from the test purchase, not from the exercise of the *Anton Piller* order.

(2) In any case, the facts fell outside the scope of *Riddick* v. *Thames Board Mills*, because the information which the solicitor obtained by his observation was not something that the court had ordered to be disclosed.

Both these arguments seem rather strained. First, the test purchase would not have been set up if the solicitor had not made his observation while executing the original order. Secondly, the observation, while not something specifically within the scope of the original order could not have been obtained if that order had not been made. The information was obtained as a direct result of the exercise of the *Anton Piller* order, and it is submitted that it should have been regarded as falling within the undertaking imposed by that order.[63]

In *Piver S.A.R.L.* v. *S. & J. Perfume Ltd.*,[64] however, Walton J. came to a similar conclusion, though without referring to the *Sony* case. A private investigator participating in the execution of an *Anton Piller* order pocketed a carton which suggested the infringement of rights of another of his clients. As a result, this client successfully obtained an *Anton Piller* order. Walton J. ruled that, although it was important that *Anton Piller* orders should not become oppressive, provided that full disclosure was made to the court of how evidence was obtained, and it did not concern trade secrets or other confidential material, it could be admitted.

Apart from the problems raised by the above cases, related to discovery and *Anton* **2.24**

---

[61] *Home Office* v. *Harman* [1983] A.C. 280.
[62] [1981] F.S.R. 333.
[63] For further discussion of the scope of this undertaking, see Chap. 5, paras. 5.32–5.33.
[64] [1987] F.S.R. 159.

Piller orders, the law relating to the use of evidence in civil proceedings is clear, in that there is a total non-exclusion rule, without any of the nebulous areas of discretion which exist in criminal proceedings.

C. Actions in Tort

Trespass to land

(a) *Availability of the remedy*

2.25   Trespass to land is actionable *per se*. Moreover, if the trespass is the result of "oppressive, arbitrary, or unconstitutional action by servants of the Government,"[65] exemplary damages may be awarded. So the action in tort is a very real remedy for the occupier. But it should be noted that whereas self-help may be employed by a person acting under the authority, express or implied, of a person in possession of the property, it is only the possessor himself who can maintain an action for trespass. Thus a lodger may, unless his landlord says otherwise, repel trespassers from his room. But if he is unsuccessful, or happens to be out when the trespass occurs, he will not be entitled to seek compensation through an action for damages.[66] For further discussion of the question as to who has sufficient possession to maintain an action, see Chapter One, paras. 1.02–1.12.

(b) *Measure of damages*

2.26   The basic principle will be *restitutio in integrum*. Where there has been damage to the fabric of the premises in the course of the trespass the basis of any award will generally be the reduction in value of the property, but in some circumstances the cost of repair may be used.[67] In addition, damages will be awarded for the fact of the trespass, though in the absence of any damage, or of oppressive conduct these will only be nominal.[68]

(c) *Exemplary damages*

2.27   As has been seen "oppressive, arbitrary or unconstitutional action," by servants of the Government will lead to the possibility of exemplary damages. In *Holden* v. *Chief Constable of Lancashire*[69] the Court of Appeal held that unconstitutional conduct, such as an unlawful arrest, did not need to be "oppressive" in order to justify an award of exemplary damages. "Servants of the Government" may be taken to include local government officials and the police, in addition to those directly

---

[65] *Rookes* v. *Barnard* [1964] A.C. 1129.

[66] Unless perhaps other property of his which was in the room has been damaged.

[67] See *Clerk and Linsell, on Torts* (15th ed.), paras. 22–43, and Lawson, *Remedies of English Law* (2nd ed., 1980), pp. 120–121. Also *Heath* v. *Keys* (1984) 134 New L.J. 888.

[68] The courts may also be prepared to award something to take account of the invasion of privacy involved in the unlawful entry.

[69] [1986] 3 All E.R. 836.

employed by central government.[70] It is not clear whether it would also cover officials of statutory bodies such as the Gas, Electricity, or Water Boards, but there seems no strong reason why these (even when "privatised") should not also fall within the scope of Lord Devlin's principles.

If exemplary damages are awarded they should be used "with restraint" to avoid **2.28** overpunishment of the defendant.[71] But recent cases have shown that courts are prepared to make very substantial awards where they think it is appropriate. In particular, the case of *White* v. *Metropolitan Police Commissioner*,[72] which involved an unlawful police raid, at 12.30 a.m., on the home of the plaintiffs, in the course of which police officers used "excessive, unreasonable, and unnecessary force." The householder and his wife sued for false imprisonment, assault, and malicious prosecution. On top of aggravated damages of £4,500, and £6,500, Mars-Jones J. awarded a further £20,000 to each of the plaintiffs by way of exemplary damages, because of the "shameful" nature of the police conduct.[73]

By way of contrast, in *Simper* v. *Metropolitan Police Commissioner*[74] a county court **2.29** judge awarded damages of only £300 for distress, injury, and property damage (to an attaché case), in an action for trespass resulting from an unlawful police search, refusing to award exemplary damages because the police had acted in the honest but mistaken belief that they had lawful authority to search.

It is interesting to note that in *White* there was no action for trespass to the house. It is likely that any unlawful entry, particularly if resisted by the occupier, is going to involve the commission of other torts, particularly assault or false imprisonment. So that if an action is brought for the trespass, the plaintiff may well want to sue for other torts, which will compensate specifically for the unlawful behaviour surrounding the trespass. In this context the damages awarded for the trespass itself may play a relatively small part in any eventual award.

(d) *Injunctions*

In theory an injunction would be a possible remedy against an unlawful entry. In **2.30** practice, however, the speed of events, and the fact that the occupier will be unlikely to know until he hears the knock on the door that the unlawful entry is going to take place, make it an unrealistic remedy. The only exception might be in relation to those powers, generally given to officials of central or local government, which require notice of an intended entry to be given.[75] But these powers will generally contain their own right of "appeal" against the proposed entry.

In addition, injunctions will normally only be granted in respect of repeated or

---

[70] *Cassell* v. *Broome* [1972] A.C. 1027.
[71] Lord Devlin in *Rookes* v. *Barnard* [1964] A.C. 1129.
[72] *The Times*, April 24, 1982.
[73] See also *Reynolds* v. *Commissioner of Police for the Metropolis* [1982] Crim.L.R. 600, where a £12,000 jury award against the police was approved by the Court of Appeal in an action for wrongful arrest and false imprisonment.
[74] [1982] C.L.Y. 3124.
[75] See below, Chaps. Eight and Nine.

continuing torts, not one-off unlawful acts, for which the remedy in damages is considered sufficient. If however, the tort is a continuing one an injunction may be granted even though no actual damage is caused.[76]

Another limitation on the usefulness of injunctions is that by virtue of the Crown Proceedings Acts, no injunction will issue against the Crown, or an officer of the Crown.

(e) *Quia timet injunctions*

2.31   If the occupier should get to know beforehand that an unlawful entry on to his property is proposed, then he might seek a *quia timet* injunction. However the court will require very strong evidence that the trespass is going to occur.

(f) *Interlocutory relief*

2.32   Because of the need for speed it is almost inevitable that the plaintiff in this type of situation will first seek an interlocutory injunction prior to trial of the action, in order to call an instant halt to the defendant's activities. If there is sufficient urgency the request may be made *ex parte*. The court will decide whether or not to issue such an injunction by considering the principles laid down by the House of Lords in *American Cyanamid Co.* v. *Ethicon Ltd.*[77] These require the court to be satisfied initially that there is a "serious question to be tried"—which is a lesser standard than the requirement of a prima facie case. Indeed in *Patel* v. *W. H. Smith (Eziot)*[78] the Court of Appeal held that in relation to trespass against an undisputed owner, the burden is on the defendant to raise sufficient evidence to establish a "serious question." Otherwise the injunction must issue. If there is a "serious question" then the court should consider which way the "balance of convenience" tilts as to whether the injunction should in fact be granted. All the circumstances should be considered, and in particular the adequacy of damages as a remedy and the importance of maintaining the status quo between the parties.[79] One hazard for the impecunious plaintiff seeking interlocutory relief is that he will be expected to give an undertaking in damages to cover any losses suffered by the defendant should a perpetual injunction be refused. If the court is not satisfied as to the plaintiff's undertaking on that score, this will be a ground for refusing the interlocutory injunction. The strength or otherwise of the plaintiff's case is only to be considered where the balance is level after all other factors have been weighed. But, of course, it is quite possible, if the facts are not in dispute, for the application to be treated as the trial of the full action. The merits of the case will be considered, and a perpetual injunction issued, if appropriate.

Damages may be awarded where an injunction has been applied for (including a *quia timet* injunction), in addition to or in substitution for the injunction. If the

[76] See *Goodson* v. *Richardson* (1874) 9 Ch.App. 221, quoted by Sir George Jessel in *Cooper* v. *Crabtree* (1882) 20 Ch.D. 774.
[77] [1975] A.C. 396. See also *Patel* v. *W. H. Smith (Eziot) Ltd.* [1987] 2 All E.R. 569.
[78] [1987] 2 All E.R. 569.
[79] *Hubbard* v. *Pitt* [1976] Q.B. 142.

injunction is not granted the award will take account of future damage as well as actual damage. Whether or not the court exercises its discretion in this area will largely depend on the seriousness and extent of the defendant's conduct. It is submitted that a court is likely to regard the deliberate entry on to another's property without any lawful excuse as a matter of some seriousness, and therefore appropriate for the issue of an injunction if the plaintiff has made out his case.

D. Judicial Review

The most direct method of challenging an alleged unlawful entry may be by an **2.33** application for judicial review under R.S.C., Ord. 53 (particularly since under this order the court has the power to grant an injunction, if, in its opinion, it would be "just and convenient" to do so). In *R. v. Inland Revenue Commissioners, ex p. Rossminster Ltd.*,[80] for example, the plaintiffs sought:

(i) an *order of mandamus*, commanding the Inland Revenue Officers, *inter alia*, to act in accordance with law in deciding which property might be seized, and to allow reasonable access to all documents which were seized; and

(ii) *declarations* that the officers were bound to act in the way set out in (i) above; and

(iii) an *order of certiorari* to quash the warrants under which the entry was effected.

Although the House of Lords eventually rejected all the applications, it was assumed throughout that the Order 53 procedure was an appropriate one for determining the issues in this sort of situation.

The orders of certiorari, prohibition, and mandamus will now be looked at in turn, followed by the remedy of a declaration.

1. Certiorari

Where the entry takes place as a result of the issue of a warrant, certiorari would **2.34** seem the most apropriate remedy. It is accepted that magistrates or judges should act judicially in deciding whether or not to issue a warrant, and their decision should therefore be subject to review. However, *Rossminster* showed the formidable obstacles that exist if, as is usual, the statutory power only requires the issuing authority to be satisfied that reasonable grounds exist for the suspicion which resulted in the request for the warrant. The burden of proof is on the applicant to show that the issuer did not act judicially, and it will obviously be very difficult in most cases to find the evidence on which to base such a claim. Nor is an application based on error on the face of the warrant, which was the form the application took in *Rossminster* itself, very likely to be successful, given the very limited formal requirements for a valid warrant,[81] even under the Police and Criminal Evidence Act 1984.[82]

If, however, the entry power is exercised without warrant, then there will perhaps

---

[80] [1980] A.C. 952.
[81] See above, para. 1.20.
[82] s.15. See below, para. 3.07.

be slightly more possibility of a challenge. For the test now will be the objective one of whether there was a proper basis for the exercise of the power. But again, as long as the power is based on the existence of "reasonable grounds," the applicant's task will be the difficult one of proving a negative, *i.e.* that there were no reasonable grounds on which the official could have acted. In the absence of evidence of something akin to malice on the part of the official, it is difficult to imagine many situations where the court would be prepared to reach such a conclusion.

2. Prohibition and mandamus

2.35   Neither of these orders appears to have any practical use in the situations we are considering. Mandamus may, however, be used to deal with an abuse of power in relation to the seizure of property as a result of a legal, or illegal entry, or search, and will therefore be discussed in that context below.[83]

3. Declaration

2.36   A declaration may well be the most useful remedy against Crown Servants, against whom an injunction will not be granted. Moreover its scope is wider than an injunction, in that there does not have to be something to prohibit. It covers virtually all the ground covered by certiorari, mandamus, and prohibition, and provided the applicant has locus standi (which will not be a problem where the alleged unlawful acts affect his property rights), it appears the most useful of the remedies so far considered. It does however have the considerable disadvantage, particularly in comparison to the injunction, that the court will not issue an "interim declaration." This well-established rule was confirmed in *Rossminster*, where the Court of Appeal tried to circumvent it by issuing a final declaration on the basis of the affidavits. The House of Lords refused to sanction this, and indeed it is difficult not to have sympathy with Lord Scarman's comment that it would be "absurd" to have a court "declaring one day in interlocutory proceedings that an applicant has certain rights and on a later day that he has not."[84]

II. RECOVERING PROPERTY OR COMPENSATION

2.37   Where property has been seized in connection with legal proceedings, and at the end of the proceedings it is not ordered by the court to be returned to the person from whose possession it was taken, that person may wish to take proceedings to recover it. In addition, if the property was taken in the course of an unlawful entry, or as a result of an unlawful exercise of power in the course of a lawful entry, he may wish to seek compensation for that illegality.[85] The courses of action which are available to the owner include self-help; tortious actions for trespass, conversion, replevin, and possibly negligence; motion for judicial review under R.S.C., Ord. 53; and action under the Police (Property) Act 1897.

[83] Para. 2.53.
[84] [1980] A.C. 952, 1027.
[85] See also above, action for trespass to land, para. 2.25.

A. Self-help

The owner of goods which have been wrongfully seized, or which, after a lawful **2.38**
seizure, are retained without authority, is entitled to recover the goods without
resort to the courts. As with all forms of self-help, however, such action is surrounded by pitfalls. This is particularly so in the situations covered by this work,
where the property is likely to be in the possession of some public authority with
ample funds, rather than an impecunious defendant who might dispose of the
property, and then be unable to meet any claim for damages. The need to rely on
self-help becomes less pressing in this type of situation, and therefore its use less
reasonable.

Extent of the right

There seems no doubt that the owner may enter the land of the person who is **2.39**
guilty of the initial wrongful appropriation of the property.[86] He will be expected to
explain to the occupier the basis for his claim to the property, if challenged.[87] If his
attempt to retake his property is resisted, the owner may use reasonable force to
pursue his claim. If however, the property is on the land of an innocent third party
who has committed no tort in respect of it, it is unclear whether the owner has any
right to exercise self-help. The better view would seem to be that he probably does
not, unless the property was originally taken by a criminal act, or arrived on the
third party's land as a result of an inevitable accident. A mere refusal of the third
party to return the property will not justify the owner in entering to retake.[88] In the
light of these uncertainties, and of the fact that the repossessor might well find
himself facing not only a tortious action but also a charge of theft,[89] it is suggested
that self-help should be viewed with great circumspection.

B. Actions in Tort

1. Trespass to goods

Any physical interference with goods, *e.g.* damaging or removing them, will **2.40**
amount to trespass. The trespass may be intentional or negligent,[90] though of course,
in the latter case there will be an overlap with the tort of negligence. Thus a person
will be liable if, in the course of a search he damages the plaintiff's goods, or if he
unlawfully takes possession of those goods, or if having lawfully taken possession of
them he damages them. Mere unlawful retention after a lawful seizure would not
amount to trespass, though it might amount to conversion.[91]

Right to sue

The right to sue for trespass is based on possession. Only a person who was in **2.41**

[86] *Patrick* v. *Colerick* (1838) 3 M. & W. 483.
[87] *Anthony* v. *Haney* (1832) 8 Bing. 186, 191–192.
[88] *cf. Anthony* v. *Haney* (1832) 8 Bing. 186, with *British Economical Lamp Co. Ltd.* v. *Empire Mile End Ltd.*
(1913) 29 T.L.R. 386.
[89] See *R.* v. *Turner (No. 2)* [1971] 1 W.L.R. 901; [1971] 2 All E.R. 441.
[90] As to the burden of proof in unintentional trespass see *Fowler* v. *Lanning* [1959] 1 Q.B. 426.
[91] For which see below, paras. 2.42–2.43.

possession of the goods at the time of the unlawful interference may bring an action.[92] Unfortunately, possession in law is not confined to actual physical control, and this leads to some difficulties, particularly with such things as bailments. If, for example, a person has delivered a watch to a jeweller for repair, and the jeweller's shop is searched by the police, who are looking for stolen goods, and the watch is seized, unlawfully, by the police, can the owner of the watch sue the police in trespass? According to the case of *Wilson* v. *Lombank*,[93] the answer would seem to depend on the contract between the owner of the watch and the jeweller. In that case it was held that an immediate right to possession was sufficient to maintain an action for trespass. So that, if, as would often be the case, the jeweller had a lien over the goods because of repairs he had carried out, the owner would have no right of possession sufficient to maintain his action. But if, as in *Wilson* v. *Lombank*, the owner had a monthly credit account with the repairer, or for some other reason there was no lien, then trespass would lie against the police.

2. Conversion

2.42   The tort of conversion now covers the areas previously covered by the two separate torts of conversion and detinue.[94]

The tort may be committed by any unlawful dealing with the goods, including taking possession of them, damaging or destroying them, or refusing to return them.[95] The mere receipt of goods which are unlawfully transferred may also amount to a conversion, even though the receiver is innocent,[96] unless he can rely on one of the exceptions to *nemo dat* or some similar defence.

2.43   As with trespass, possession is an important element in deciding who has the right to sue for conversion. Ownership is neither necessary nor sufficient. Once again the court will look for an "immediate right to possession." This causes few problems where the goods are seized from the owner's possession. If the seizure is unlawful, or if the goods, having been seized lawfully, are retained beyond a legitimate period,[97] the owner will be able to sue in conversion. On the other hand, if the goods are seized from a bailee, to whom the bailor has surrendered his right of possession, he will have more problems in establishing his right to sue. Suppose, for example, A Ltd., a legitimate hirer of videocassettes, hires one or more cassettes to B, who unknown to A Ltd., intends to make copies, and distribute them in breach of copyright. If C Ltd., who has got to know of previous similar activities by B, obtains an *Anton Piller* order to search B's premises, and in the course of that search unlawfully seizes A Ltd.'s cassettes, can A Ltd. recover those cassettes from C Ltd. by an action in conversion? At first sight it would seem not: A Ltd. does not have sufficient possessory interest to

---

[92] N.B. *Winfield and Jolowicz on Torts* (12th ed., 1984), p. 478, for some alleged exceptions.
[93] [1963] 1 W.L.R. 1294.
[94] See Torts (Interference with Goods) Act 1977, s.2.
[95] There is thus obviously some overlap with trespass.
[96] *Souhrada* v. *Bank of New South Wales* [1976] 2 LL.Rep. 44; *Wilkinson* v. *King* (1809) 2 Camp. 335; *Farrant* v. *Thompson* (1822) 3 Stark 130; *Dyer* v. *Pearson* (1824) 3 B. & C. 38; *Hilbery* v. *Hatton* (1864) 2 H. & C. 822; *Ingram* v. *Little* [1961] 1 Q.B. 31 (C.A.).
[97] *cf. Roandale* v. *Metropolitan Police Commissioner* [1979] Crim.L.R. 254 (C.A.).

maintain the action, which could therefore, somewhat incongruously, only be brought by the wrongdoer, B. The only possibility for A Ltd. would seem to lie in the argument that B was in breach of an express or implied term of the hiring (because of his intended illicit use of the cassettes), and that the bailment was therefore at an end at the time C Ltd. took possession of the cassettes. This result would seem to go a little further than previous authority, as laid down by the Court of Appeal in *Moorgate Mercantile Co.* v. *Finch*[98] but it would at least provide a reasonable solution to an unsatisfactory situation, and would probably result in A Ltd. having actions in conversion against either B or C Ltd. It would not of course provide any remedy for the true owner where the bailee has acted with total propriety in relation to the goods. In this case it seems that the owner must rely on the bailee to take action to recover the goods.

If the owner of goods is in a position where he can take action against a person who has seized the goods unlawfully, he should first request their return. A refusal to comply with this request will be evidence of a wrongful detention of the goods, and found the basis for a subsequent conversion action.

An owner of goods who is temporarily out of possession may also have a right of action if the goods are permanently lost or damaged, on the basis of injury to his reversionary interest in them.[99]

3. Replevin

This ancient form of action, based on an unlawful *taking* of goods is now only of **2.44** practical importance in relation to distress. If the court's officers in exercising a distress warrant[1] have wrongfully taken the plaintiff's property, the plaintiff may apply to the registrar of the county court. The goods will be restored to the plaintiff subject to his giving security to prosecute an action of replevin in the county court or High Court.[2]

4. Negligence

If, of course, goods are damaged or lost through negligence, this in itself will **2.45** provide a cause of action for the owner, or other person having an interest in them.

5. Forms of relief

The types of relief available to the successful plaintiff in any action for the **2.46** wrongful interference with goods are set out in the Torts (Interference with Goods) Act 1977, s.3(2), and comprise:

(i) an order for delivery of the goods, and for payment of any consequential damage; or

---

[98] [1962] 1 Q.B. 701 (use of car for carrying uncustomed watches, which led to its forfeiture under the Customs and Excise Act 1952, see below, para. 7.20).

[99] *Mears* v. *London & South Western Ry.* (1862) 11 C.B.(N.S.) 850; *Lancashire Waggon Co.* v. *Fitzhugh* (1861) 6 H. & N. 502; *Tancred* v. *Allgood* (1859) 4 H. & N. 438.

[1] See below, para. 5.35.

[2] *cf.* the interlocutory relief provided generally for actions dealing with the wrongful interference with goods by virtue of the Torts (Interference with Goods) Act 1977, s.4, below, para. 2.46.

(ii) an order for the delivery of the goods, but giving the defendant the alternative of paying damages by reference to the value of the goods together in either alternative with payment of any consequential damages; or

(iii) damages.

Remedy (i) is available only at the court's discretion, but the plaintiff may choose between the other two.[3] As part of its general discretion to impose conditions on an order for delivery, the court may require the plaintiff to pay something to the defendant, *e.g.* where if damages had been awarded instead of delivery, they would not have been for the full value of the goods.[4]

The Act also contains provisions protecting the wrongdoer from double liability,[5] and enabling the court to make allowance for any improvements made to the goods by a mistaken but honest "improver."[6]

6. Measure of damages

2.47   Where damages are awarded in relation to the wrongful detention of property there are three heads under which compensation may be sought: the loss of the property itself, be it temporarily or permanently; damage to the property, if it is returned; and consequential losses resulting from the unavailability of the property to the plaintiff. For the purposes of exposition it will be easiest to divide the discussion on the basis of whether or not the property is returned to the plaintiff.

(a) *Permanent loss of the property*

2.48   Where a court refuses to order the return of the goods, or return is impossible because the defendant has disposed of the goods, or they have been destroyed, the basis of the award of damages will be the "value" of the goods. The value will be taken to be the "market value," or, if there is no market, the cost of replacement, assessed at the time of the tortious act.[7]

The approach to be taken where the market value has changed significantly between commission of the tort and the time of judgment is considered below under "consequential losses."

(b) *Temporary loss of the property*

2.49   Where the plaintiff recovers goods, as a result of a court order or otherwise, then, subject to the goods not being damaged, or the plaintiff not having suffered any other consequential loss, it would seem that the principle of *restitutio in integrum* has been satisfied, and any difference in market value would be irrelevant. In one case,

---

[3] s.3(3)(*b*).
[4] s.3(6).
[5] s.7.
[6] s.6.
[7] See Winfield and Jolowicz, p. 500, n. 92: the only doubt as to whether this was the correct time arose in connection with detinue cases, *e.g. Sachs* v. *Miklos* [1948] 2 K.B. 23—but with the abolition of detinue by the 1977 Act, it is to be assumed that the assessment of damages in all actions based on wrongful interference will take place on the same basis.

however, *Solloway* v. *McLaughlin*,[8] which involved shares, the Privy Council held that the defendants were liable for the difference in value of the shares between their conversion and redelivery. But, as is pointed out by Ogus,[9] unless it could be shown that the plaintiff had lost a definite sale at the highest value, the most that he should be entitled to recover should be compensation for the loss of a *chance* to sell at that price.

The power of the court to order payment from the plaintiff to the defendant in appropriate circumstances, when an order for redelivery is made, should also be noted.[10]

Apart from these two situations, the main consideration in assessing damages as a result of temporary deprivation will be the amount to be awarded for any consequential losses.

(c) *Consequential loss*

As we have seen above, consequential losses may fall to be compensated where the plaintiff has been deprived of his property either permanently or temporarily. This will cover losses arising from the unavailability of the property to the plaintiff, and (as regards a temporary deprivation), damage to the property.   **2.50**

An example of a case where damages were awarded for the loss of the use of goods is *Bodley* v. *Reynolds*,[11] where a carpenter was awarded £10 special damages in respect of the loss of his tools, over and above their actual value. There is no reason why the plaintiff should not claim for any profitable use that he might have made of the property during its removal from his possession, subject to the normal rules of remoteness. It may well be that lost profits on a sale are best treated as a type of consequential loss, and thus subject to the remoteness rules, rather than as relating to the establishment of the value of the property.[12]

(d) *Damage*

Damage to property for which the plaintiff will be entitled to recover compensation may occur: **2.51**

(i)   in the course of an unlawful search, any damage being tortious;
(ii) in the course of a lawful search as a result of unnecessary or excessive force;
(iii) while the property is being lawfully detained, through (a) misuse or negligence, or (b) dismantling as part of the investigation;
(iv) while being unlawfully retained.

Category (iii) (b) raises problems of liability, and will be considered separately. In all the other cases the person responsible for the damage will be clearly liable in

---

[8] [1938] A.C. 247.
[9] *Law of Damages*, p. 159.
[10] Tort (Interference with Goods) Act 1977, s.3(6).
[11] (1846) 8 Q.B. 779.
[12] *The Arpad* [1934] P. 189; *France* v. *Gaudet* (1871) L.R. 6 Q.B. 199; *cf. Solloway* v. *McLaughlin* [1938] A.C. 247, para. 2.49, above.

trespass, conversion (if the goods are destroyed), or negligence. The measure of damages in all these cases will be the reduction in the value of the goods over the cost of restoring the goods to their previous condition, whichever is the less, except where the goods are destroyed, where it must be the value of the goods.[13] Consequential losses will be recoverable in the same way as for deprivation of the goods.[14]

2.52   Where the damage occurs as part of the investigation into the nature of the property, *e.g.* a car, or furniture, which is dismantled as part of a search for drugs, it would seem that as long as the search itself is lawful, there will be a defence provided that what was done was reasonable in the circumstances. There does not seem to be any obligation on the searchers to "make good" any damage caused by an unlawful search; they may legitimately leave the car or furniture in pieces, even if nothing was found. This seems to be a loophole in the law which it would be desirable to fill, though probably not through making the searcher liable in tort, but through some statutory scheme for compensation. If, of course, the search goes beyond what is reasonable, and is adjudged unlawful, it will amount to a trespass, and be compensable on that basis.

C. Judicial Review

2.53   In *Ghani* v. *Jones*[15] the plaintiffs, who were trying to recover their passports from the police, obtained an order of mandamus for their return. This order is the one which most obviously provides a remedy for the plaintiff who seeks the return of his property because it has been unlawfully seized or is being unlawfully retained. Certiorari might also be applicable if what is complained of is some specific decision to seize or retain the goods. But mandamus is more likely, as in *R.* v. *I.R.C., ex p. Rossminster.*[16]

There is a requirement before the court will issue the order that there has been a prior demand for the property to be returned, and a refusal to do so. There must be a duty to return the property, but the order itself merely calls upon the person to whom it is addressed to do his or her duty, so the prior demand is necessary to indicate what exactly is expected.

D. Police (Property) Act 1897

2.54   When, as a result of a search, or some other aspect of the criminal process, the police are in possession of goods, problems may arise as to its disposal on the conclusion of any criminal proceedings. Of course, where statutes provide for forfeiture or other means of disposing of goods the police will simply carry out the orders of the court. But there will arise cases where, either the court has no power to make, or omits to make, any order, or where not all of the property seized by the police is made the

---

[13] See discussion above concerning market value, etc.
[14] See above, para. 2.50.
[15] [1970] 1 Q.B. 693.
[16] [1980] A.C. 952.

subject of criminal proceedings (*e.g.* on a handling charge it may not be established by the court proceedings that all the goods seized are in fact stolen goods). As far as England, Wales and Northern Ireland are concerned, this situation is largely, though not comprehensively covered by the Police (Property) Act 1897. This provides that where property is in the possession of the police in connection with their investigation of a suspected offence, or under certain enactments, a court of summary jurisdiction may, on application, either by an officer of police, or by a claimant of the property, make an order for the delivery of the property to the person appearing to the court to be the owner, or if the owner cannot be ascertained, make such order as may seem appropriate to the court.

The application for an order may be made by the police, or by someone claiming ownership of the property. It will be most appropriate for the police to use the statute where there is no claimant, and in this situation the application may well be made orally.[17] Where one or more people do lay claim to the property the police can leave it to them to initiate action under the statute.

The question of the correct procedure to be adopted came before the courts in *R.* v. **2.55**
Uxbridge JJ.,[18] where the question was raised as to whether it was permissible to use the "complaint" procedure to initiate proceedings, despite the fact that section 1 refers to an "application." The Court of Appeal held that it was (Lord Denning dissenting), though the practice in metropolitan magistrates' courts of using a special "application" form was also approved (Sir Stanley Rees dissenting). If the complaint procedure is used then the magistrates have power to award costs by virtue of the Magistrates' Courts Act 1980, s.64, but they should use this power sparingly, particularly where the application has not been opposed.

Once an order has been made under section 1(1) anyone claiming an interest in **2.56**
the property has six months in which to bring proceedings for the recovery of the property.[19] Once again the burden is on the claimant to establish that he is the "true owner" of the property.[20] Possessory rights are insufficient. Once the six months has expired no proceedings may be brought. The arguments of Professor Smith to the contrary, although attractive, seem to go against the clear wording of section 1(2).[21]

Where property to which the Act applies is in police possession, but no one has claimed it, and no court order has been made, the Police (Disposal of Property) Regulations apply.[22] These provide that, with three exceptions (see below), once the property (other than money) has been in police possession for a year it shall be sold and the proceeds of sale paid to the Police Authority and kept in a separate account, to be called the Police Property Act Fund. Any money to which the Act applies

---

[17] See Sir Stanley Rees, *R.* v. *Uxbridge Justices* [1981] 1 Q.B. 829, 847.
[18] [1981] 1 Q.B. 829.
[19] s.1(2).
[20] *Irving* v. *National Provincial Bank* [1962] 2 Q.B. 73.
[21] Smith, *Law of Theft* (5th ed.), para. 445.
[22] S.I. 1975 No. 1474.

should also be paid into the Fund on the expiration of a similar period. There are three exceptions to these procedures:

(1) the Chief Officer of Police has the power, if he is satisfied that the nature of the property is such that it is not in the public interest that it should be sold, to direct that it should be destroyed or otherwise disposed of.[23]

(2) If the property is perishable, or its custody involves unreasonable expense or inconvenience, it may be sold at any time, but the proceeds must be retained for a year from the date of sale before being paid into the Fund.

(3) Where the property is in police possession by virtue of an order under section 43 of the Powers of the Criminal Courts Act 1973, it shall not be disposed of until six months from the date of the order, or if someone claims the property within that period, or an appeal is made against the conviction which preceded the order, until the claim or the appeal has been determined.

Administration of the fund

2.57   The administration of the Fund is in the hands of the Police Authority, though they may delegate their powers to the Chief Officer of Police.[24] As well as being used to defray the expenses of dealing with property in connection with the execution of the Regulations, the Fund may also be used to pay reasonable compensation to persons by whom property has been delivered to the police (*e.g.* the unwitting recipient of stolen goods), and to make payments to charity.[25] This list of uses appears to be exclusive.

E. Which Remedy?

2.58   As has been shown there is a wide range of remedies available to the person whose property has been seized or damaged unlawfully. Which remedy is sought will depend on the circumstances, and there may well be occasions where self-help, despite its dangers, or an application for judicial review, will be the most appropriate course of action. In the majority of cases, however, the choice will fall upon one of two approaches. If the property is in the hands of the police, and the main concern is for its speedy return, the easiest and quickest remedy will be an application under the Police (Property) Act 1897.[26] If the property is in the hands of officials other than the police, or of private individuals, or in any case where there is consequential loss, or aggravated or exemplary damages are sought because of the illegality of the seizure, then one of the tort remedies will be most appropriate. Their versatility and usefulness has been greatly increased by the provisions of the Torts (Interference with Goods) Act 1977 relating to the availability of orders for the return of the goods in place of, or in addition to damages,[27] and by the provisions of

---

[23] Reg. 4(3).
[24] Reg. 4(8).
[25] Reg. 4(7).
[26] Above, para. 2.54.
[27] s.3, above, para. 2.46.

section 4 which allow for interlocutory relief pending proceedings for wrongful intereference. The procedure is governed by R.S.C., Ord. 29, r. 2A, and C.C.R., Ord. 13, r. 7, and may well mean that the remedies of replevin and mandamus arerendered unnecessary, since a plaintiff can obtain equivalent relief in connection with an action for trespass, conversion, or negligence.

CHAPTER THREE

POLICE: GENERAL POWERS

3.01 General powers of entry have not played a notable part in the range of powers available to the police, probably as a result of the decision in *Entick* v. *Carrington*,[1] which clearly established the hostility of the English courts to any power of entry not based on specific and clear authority. Chapter Four is concerned with the specific narrowly defined statutory powers of entry available to the police. This chapter is concerned with the more general powers under the Common Law, and under the Police and Criminal Evidence Act 1984 (the "P.C.E.A."). That Act also sets out some general rules applying to all police entries. These are also dealt with below.

I. COMMON LAW

3.02 Section 17(5) of the P.C.E.A. states that, with the exception of those powers relating to breaches of the peace, "all the rules of common law under which a constable has power to enter premises without a warrant are hereby abolished." In fact, probably for the reasons outlined in the preceding paragraph, there were very few such powers under the common law. Professor Leigh, in 1975,[2] could identify only two, illustrated by the cases of *Handcock* v. *Baker*,[3] and *Thomas* v. *Sawkins*,[4] both of which could be said to have been concerned with breaches of the peace, of a more or less serious nature. The *Handcock* v. *Baker* power has been given statutory form as far as the police are concerned by section 17(1)(*e*) of the P.C.E.A.,[5] so we need only consider *Thomas* v. *Sawkins*.

This case arose out of a meeting on private premises to which the public were invited.[6] Two police officers were present at the meeting, despite the fact that it had been made clear by the organisers, both beforehand and at the time of entry, that their presence was unwelcome. A steward attempted to eject one of the officers, and was prevented from doing so by the other, Sergeant Sawkins. A private prosecution for assault was brought against the Sergeant. The magistrates acquitted, and the Divisional Court was called on to decide whether the police officers' presence at the meeting was lawful, or a trespass. In unanimously deciding that it was lawful, the

---

[1] (1765) 19 State Tr. 1065. See, *e.g.* L. H. Leigh, *Police Powers in England and Wales* (2nd ed.), (1985), pp. 199–201.

[2] *Op. cit.* (1st ed.) p. 172.

[3] [1800] 2 Bos. & P. 260, and see above, para. 1.05.

[4] [1935] 2 K.B. 249.

[5] See below, para. 3.25.

[6] See D. G. T. Williams, *Keeping the Peace*, pp. 142–149, for the background to this case, and a discussion of its implications.

court made several statements which have been the subject of criticism.[7] The first related to the power of the police to act to prevent breaches of the peace which are anticipated, as well as to stop those which are already taking place. Prior to the case it had been widely accepted (though not confirmed by any authority) that the police could only enter premises once a breach of the peace was taking place.[8] The court in *Thomas* v. *Sawkins* considered that the police were entitled to enter if they reasonably anticipated a breach of the peace. This view has not been seriously challenged since, and the general power of the police to act on reasonable apprehension of a breach of the peace (though not specifically in the context of entering premises) was recently confirmed by the Court of Appeal in *R.* v. *Howell*.[9]

The second criticism of *Thomas* v. *Sawkins* arose from the fact that the lawfulness of **3.03** the police's presence was said to flow from their anticipation not only of a breach of the peace, but also of the commission of various offences (*e.g.* sedition).[10] This problem no longer exists since section 17(5) and (6) of the P.C.E.A. make it clear that the *Thomas* v. *Sawkins* power only survives to the extent that it is concerned with actual or anticipated breaches of the peace.

The final problem comes from the fact that the meeting took place on private premises. Does the power of entry recognised in the case only apply to meetings to which the public are invited, or are the police entitled to enter any premises on which a breach of the peace is occurring, or is likely to occur? The judges in *Thomas* v. *Sawkins* appeared to attach importance to the fact that they were dealing with a public meeting, but the difficulties of using this as a distinguishing factor have been well pointed out by Goodhart.[11] The general law of trespass makes no distinction between public and private meetings.[12] If those attending a meeting on private premises do so on the basis of a licence from the occupier, then that licence may be withdrawn, from the police as much as anyone else. If the police have the power to override the withdrawal of a licence, then there seems no reason why that power should not exist on all occasions. The result is that the case gives the police a power to enter any premises to prevent or deal with a breach of the peace. Although this is a wide power, it does not appear to have caused problems in practice, presumably because the police have been reluctant to use it in relation to private occasions on private premises, at least until it is clear that a breach of the peace is actually occurring. It is significant that *Thomas* v. *Sawkins* has only been cited in three reported cases since the war,[13] and in none of them was the principle important to the decision.

The final issue to consider in relation to this power, is what is meant by a "breach **3.04** of the peace." This has been the subject of some judicial consideration in recent

---

[7] See A. L. Goodhart (1936–38) 6 C.L.J. 22; D. G. T. Williams, *loc. cit.* above, n. 6.
[8] See Goodhart, *op. cit.*
[9] [1982] Q.B. 416. See also *Moss* v. *McLachlan* [1985] I.R.L.R. 76.
[10] [1935] 2 K.B. 249, 255 (Lord Hewart), and 256 (Avory J.).
[11] *Op. cit.* above, n. 7, p. 25.
[12] See above, para. 1.02.
[13] *R.* v. *Waterfield*; *R.* v. *Lynn* [1964] 1 Q.B. 164; *Robson* v. *Hallett* [1967] 2 Q.B. 939; *R.* v. *Chief Constable for Devon and Cornwall, ex p. C.E.G.B.* [1982] Q.B. 458.

years. The currently favoured definition seems to be the one proposed by the Court of Appeal in *R.* v. *Howell.*[14] The case arose from a disturbance in a street, following complaints about the noise from a party. The appellant was convicted of assaulting a police officer who was trying to arrest him to prevent an imminent breach of the peace. In upholding the conviction, the Court of Appeal nevertheless made it clear that mere noise and rowdiness did not of itself constitute a breach of the peace[15]:

" ... we cannot accept that there can be a breach of the peace unless there has been an act done or threatened to be done which either actually harms a person, or in his presence his property, or is likely to cause such harm, or which puts someone in fear of such harm being done."

In other words, violent behaviour, or the reasonable apprehension of it, is a necessary element of a breach of the peace. A wider definition was proposed by Lord Denning in the later case of *R.* v. *Chief Constable of Devon and Cornwall, ex p. Central Electricity Generating Board.*[16] This case involved the duties of the police in assisting the Board to remove demonstrators from land which the Board wished to survey.[17] Lord Denning took the view that the obstruction of the Board's work was itself a breach of the peace, entitling the police to intervene[18]:

"There is a breach of the peace whenever a person who is lawfully carrying out his work is unlawfully and physically prevented by another from doing it."

This line was not followed by the other members of the court, who preferred to argue that if the demonstrators resisted removal by the Board's employees, this would be likely to lead to violence, and thus justify police intervention. The view of the majority is consistent with *R.* v. *Howell* (which was cited by counsel, but not referred to in any of the judgments), and is therefore to be preferred. In *Parkin* v. *Norman,*[19] a Divisional Court, faced with the differing views outlined above, followed the *Howell* definition in the context of a breach of the peace for the purposes of section 5 of the Public Order Act 1936.[20] If, as seems likely, *Howell* remains the governing authority, it will mean that the police will not be justified in entering a meeting simply because a noisy and acrimonious debate is taking place, but only if this leads to a reasonable anticipation of a fight, or some other violent behaviour.[21]

II. POLICE AND CRIMINAL EVIDENCE ACT 1984

3.05 This statute went a long way (though not the whole way) to consolidating police powers in England and Wales. Some of the provisions of the Act are of general

---

[14] [1982] Q.B. 416.
[15] *Ibid.* 426.
[16] [1982] Q.B. 458.
[17] See below, para. 9.89.
[18] [1982] Q.B. 458, 471.
[19] [1983] Q.B. 92.
[20] This section was repealed by the Public Order Act 1986. The replacement offences do not use the concept of "breach of the peace."
[21] See also *Marsh* v. *Arscott* [1982] Crim.L.R. 827, and *Read* v. *Jones* (1983) 77 Cr.App.R. 246.

application; *i.e.* they apply to police powers under whatever statute they arise. Other parts of the Act specifically create new entry powers. Both are dealt with in this chapter. The Act also provides for the issue of Codes of Practice for the search of premises and the seizure of property.[22] Contravention of a Code will not give rise to any criminal or civil liability, but will render the police officer in question liable to disciplinary proceedings.[23] In addition, a civil or criminal court may take account of the breach of the Code in determining any proceedings to which the breach appears to it to be relevant.

A. Basic Provisions

The general provisions of the P.C.E.A. which are of relevance to entry powers are those relating to the formalities of warrants, privileged material, and powers of seizure. Any provision of the Act which confers a power on a police officer to act without requiring the consent of some other person, carries with it the power to use reasonable force.[24]   **3.06**

1. Warrants

Sections 15 and 16 of the P.C.E.A. contain provisions which apply to all warrants to enter and search premises issued to a constable, under any enactment. The limitations on the scope of these provisions are important. They only apply to warrants issued to constables, not any other official, such as an Inland Revenue officer. They have, however, been extended to Customs and Excise officers,[25] and officers enforcing the Food and Environment Protection Act 1985.[26] As far as the police are concerned the sections only apply to warrants to both enter and search. A warrant simply to enter and inspect, or an arrest warrant which is used to legitimise entry,[27] is not covered by these provisions.   **3.07**

In situations where sections 15 and 16 do apply, an entry or search which fails to comply with them is unlawful.[28] This simply means that the occupier of the premises will have his usual remedies in trespass, etc.: it does not render any fruits of the search inadmissible, unless it would affect the fairness of the trial.[29]

In *R. v. Longman*[29a] the Court of Appeal had some difficulty interpreting section 15(1), insofar as it says that "an entry on or search of premises under a warrant is unlawful unless *it* complies with this section and section 16 below."[29b] The problem lay with the word "it." Was it intended to refer to the "entry or search" or to the

---

[22] s.66.
[23] s.67(7) and (8).
[24] s.116.
[25] By S.I. 1985 No. 1800 (as amended by S.I. 1987 No. 439), made under s.114 of the P.C.E.A. See further below, Chap. 7, para. 7.02.
[26] See further below, Chap. 8, para. 8.26.
[27] s.17(1)(a).
[28] s.15(1).
[29] See s.78, and the discussion in Chap. Two, paras, 2.14–2.20.
[29a] [1988] 1 W.L.R. 619.
[29b] Emphasis added

warrant? With some hesitation, and without finally deciding the issue, the Court was inclined to think that it was the warrant that was being referred to.[29c] With respect, however, this cannot have been the draftsman's intention, since section 16 is not concerned with the validity of the warrant. It is suggested that what is meant is that the entry or search must comply with the sections. Section 15, despite being labelled "Search warrants—safeguards," *is* concerned with entries, in that an entry will not comply with the sections if it is made on the authority of a warrant obtained in breach of the provisions of section 15.

The sections impose requirements at each stage, of application for, issue, execution, and return of a warrant.

(a) *Application*

3.08   The application is to be made *ex parte* to a justice of the peace or judge, as required by the provision under which the warrant is being sought.[30] It must be supported by an information in writing. The constable must answer on oath any question which the justice or judge asks.[31] In particular the constable has a duty to make clear:

   (i)   the grounds on which he is making the application;
   (ii) the enactment under which the warrant would be issued;
   (iii) the premises to be entered and searched; and
   (iv) so far is practicable, the articles or persons sought.[32]

The Code of Practice gives further guidance as to the procedure which should be adopted. An officer receiving information which appears to justify an application for a warrant, should check its accuracy, etc., as far as possible. In particular he should not act on information from an anonymous source without seeking corroboration.[33] He should also try to establish the nature and location of the article to be searched for, the nature of the premises, whether anything is known about the occupier, and whether the premises have previously been searched, and if so how recently.[34] No application should be made without the authorisation of an officer of at least the rank of inspector, except in a case of urgency, when the senior officer on duty may give approval.[35] Similarly, if there is reason to believe that a search might adversely affect relations between the police and the community, the local police community liaison officer should be consulted.[36]

When making the application, the officer must be prepared to answer questions

---

[29c] [1988] 1 W.L.R. 619, 623.
[30] s.15(3).
[31] s.15(4).
[32] s.15(2).
[33] Code of Practice, para. 2.1.
[34] *Ibid.* paras. 2.1–2.4.
[35] *Ibid.* para. 2.4.
[36] *Ibid.* para. 2.5.

about the accuracy of the information, and the reliability of the source from which it came, though he should not have to disclose the identity of an informant.[37]

(b) *Issue*

Section 15(6) requires a search warrant to contain a certain minimum of information. It must specify the name of the person applying for it, the date of issue, the enactment under which it is issued, and the premises to be searched. In addition it must, as far as is practicable, identify the articles or persons to be sought.[38] Here, as with the provisions under section 15(2), it will presumably be up to the individual issuing justice or judge to decide what degree of generality is acceptable, *e.g.* whether a phrase such as "stolen goods" would in itself be sufficient. **3.09**

Two copies must be made of the warrant, which should be clearly certified as such.[39]

(c) *Execution*

A search warrant will authorise entry on one occasion only.[40] It must be executed within one month of the date of issue.[41] Statutory provisions setting a different time limit are amended by Schedules 6 and 7. **3.10**

The warrant may be executed by any constable.[42] It may authorise other people to accompany the constable,[43] and these should presumably be identified as precisely as possible. It is to be hoped that phrases such as "together with such other persons as he may deem necessary" will be avoided. Section 16(1) does *not* authorise a constable to execute a warrant which has been issued to some other official.

Timing of entry. Normally a search warrant should be executed "at a reasonable hour."[44] It is not clear what this phrase means. The Code of Practice, paragraph 5A states that the officer in charge should, among other things, have regard to the times of the day at which the occupier is likely to be present, and should not search at a time when the occupier, or any other person on the premises, is likely to be asleep, unless this is unavoidable. "A reasonable time" cannot here mean "a time that is reasonable in all the circumstances," since the second half of section 16(4) recognises that a search may take place at an "unreasonable hour" if the purpose of the search might otherwise be frustrated. It seems that "reasonableness" is to be determined by the nature of the premises (*i.e.* business, domestic, etc.), and the identity of the occupants (if any). The reasons for, and objects of the search, are irrelevant, unless the police wish to search other than at a reasonable hour.[45]

---

[37] *Ibid.* para. 2A.
[38] s.15(6).
[39] s.15(7) and (8).
[40] s.15(4). This puts into statutory form the ruling in *R.* v. *Adams* [1980] Q.B. 575—see above, para. 1.24.
[41] s.16(3).
[42] s.16(1). Provisions requiring the officer to be named have generally been repealed (Scheds. 6 and 7) but see also para. 4.18.
[43] s.16(2).
[44] s.16(4).
[45] See also above, para. 1.24.

Occupied premises. If at the time the warrant is to be executed the occupier is present, the constable must identify himself to him. If the constable is not in uniform he must produce documentary evidence that he is a constable.[46] The Code of Practice makes it clear that these steps should be taken *before* entry, unless there is reasonable ground to believe that to alert the occupier, or other person entitled to grant access, would frustrate the object of the search, or endanger the officer concerned or any other person.[47] This was confirmed by the Court of Appeal in *R. v. Longman*.[48] The police had entered premises by subterfuge in order to execute a search warrant under the Misuse of Drugs Act 1971. In the circumstances, the court held that the police were justified in not revealing their identity or purpose prior to entry, on the basis of paragraph 5.4(iii) of the Code of Practice. But where entry was effected in this way the requirement was that at the very earliest the constable should, after entry and *before search*, announce his identity, produce his authority, and, at the first reasonable opportunity, give the occupier a copy of the search warrant.[49] If the occupier is not present, but some other person who appears to the constable to be in charge of the premises is, the constable has the same obligation to identify himself, etc., as regards that person as he would to the occupier.[50] In the absence of any person appearing to the constable to be in charge of the premises, he must leave a copy of the warrant in a prominent place on the premises.[51] This will apply not only where the premises are totally unoccupied: it might also be the appropriate procedure where, for example, the only persons present were the occupier's young children.

Limitations on search. The final general provision relating to search warrants is contained in section 16(8), which states that:

> "A search under a warrant may only be a search to the extent required for the purpose for which the warrant was issued."

This enacts one of the recommendations of the Royal Commission on Criminal Procedure, to the effect that a search, for example, for stolen video recorders, should not entitle the police to search filing cabinets.[52] The further recommendation of the R.C.C.P. that the fruits of an inappropriate search should be inadmissible evidence has not, however, been followed. Once again the aggrieved occupier is left to his civil remedies.

(d) *Return*

3.11   The constable executing a search warrant is required to make an indorsement on it stating whether the articles or persons sought were found, and whether any

---

[46] s.16(5).
[47] Code, paras. 5.3 and 5.4.
[48] [1988] 1 W.L.R. 619.
[49] *Ibid.* at 626 (emphasis added); and s.16(5).
[50] s.16(6).
[51] s.16(7).
[52] Royal Commission on Criminal Procedure, *Report*, Cmnd. 8092, para. 3.49.

articles other than those sought were seized.[53] Should the constable chance to find a wanted criminal on the premises, and arrest him, it seems that there is no need to make mention of this. The purpose of the indorsement is presumably to allow the issuing judge or justice to see that the police have acted properly, and also to provide evidence where an occupier, or owner of goods, wishes to complain.

An executed warrant, or a warrant which has not been executed before expiry, must be returned to the clerk to the justices, or the appropriate court officer, depending on whether it was issued by a justice or a judge.[54] It must be retained for 12 months from its return,[55] and if during that period the occupier of the premises to which it relates asks to inspect it, he shall be allowed to do so.[56] No one other than the occupier has a right to inspect the warrant, but presumably there is nothing to stop the clerk or court official allowing others to see it, if it was thought appropriate. This might be, for example, where goods seized belonged to someone other than the occupier, and the owner wishes to inspect the warrant.

2. Privileged material

The Act creates three categories of privileged material, in respect of which the police cannot obtain an ordinary search warrant.[57] Access to items subject to "legal privilege" cannot be obtained at all. For "excluded" and "special procedure" material, the police normally have to follow the procedures set out in Schedule 1 to the Act, and outlined below (para. 3.28).[58] Within both these latter categories there is a sub-category of "journalistic material."   **3.12**

(a) *Legal privilege*

This category is defined in section 10. Legal privilege attaches to the following items when held by a person entitled to possession of them.   **3.13**

First, communications between a professional legal adviser and his client, or any person representing his client, made in connection with the giving of legal advice to the client, are privileged. The "legal advice" need not relate to any legal proceedings, actual or intended. Secondly, if legal proceedings are taking place, or being contemplated, then privilege attaches not only to communications between the adviser, his client, and the client's representative, but also any communication made for the purposes of the proceedings between any of these three and any other person. Thirdly, privilege attaches to items (presumably generally documents) enclosed with or referred to in communications falling within one of the first two categories, and made in connection with the giving of legal advice or in connection

---

[53] s.16(9).
[54] s.16(10).
[55] s.16(11).
[56] s.16(12).
[57] s.9(2). Other officials having power to obtain search warrants are not limited by this provision—it applies only to the police.
[58] s.9(1). Note the limitations in respect of this protection as regards entry powers given under legislation passed subsequent to the P.C.E.A.: see para. 3.28 below.

with or contemplation of legal proceedings, and for the purposes of such proceedings. It will not, however, cover straightforward records of transactions, such as conveyancing documents.[59]

The Act does not define "communications." There seems no reason why the word should not include, in addition to letters, or other typed, printed or handwritten communications, recordings of conversation or telephone calls. Similarly, copies or transcripts of any of the above should be covered, if the scope of the privilege is not to be unduly narrow.

Section 10(2) provides that "items held with the intention of furthering a criminal purpose are not items subject to legal privilege." Two cases have considered the scope of this limitation on privilege. In *R. v. Crown Court at Snaresbrook, ex p. D.P.P.*[60] the item in question was a legal aid application. It was thought that it might provide support for a prosecution for attempting to pervert the course of public justice. The relevant form was in the hands of the local Law Society. The judge to whom application for access to the form was made held that it was subject to legal privilege. On the D.P.P.'s application for judicial review of this decision the Divisional Court had no doubt that a legal aid application came within the scope of section 10(1), even though it might include untrue statements.[61] It was argued on behalf of the D.P.P., however, that if the person submitting the form had the intention of furthering a criminal purpose, section 10(2) would operate to remove the privilege. The Divisional Court refused to read the section in this way, ruling that the "intention" in section 10(2) must be the intention of the person "holding" the material. In this case the Law Society was holding the material. The judge had therefore been right to refuse access.

A different view was taken, however, in *Francis & Francis v. Central Criminal Court,*[62] which concerned an application for an order under section 27 of the Drug Trafficking Offences Act 1986.[62a] The definition of legal privilege in section 10(1) of the P.C.E.A. is specifically incorporated into this Act. The items sought here were correspondence and attendance notes held by a firm of solicitors relating to property transactions undertaken by one of their clients. The police suspected that the funds for these transactions were provided by one of the client's relatives out of the proceeds of drug trafficking. In this case the House of Lords (by a majority of three to two) upheld the Divisional Court's view that although the solicitors holding the documents had no criminal intention, the purposes of the client's relative were sufficient to bring section 10(2) into operation. They reached this somewhat surprising conclusion by reference to the common law approach exemplified by *R. v. Cox and Railton.*[63] Stephen J. had held that communications "criminal in themselves, or

---

[59] *R. v. Crown Court at Inner London Sessions, ex p. Baines & Baines* [1987] 3 All E.R. 1025; *R. v. Central Criminal Court, ex p. Francis & Francis* [1988] 1 All E.R. 677, 679.

[60] [1988] 1 All E.R. 315.

[61] *Ibid.* 319.

[62] [1988] 3 All E.R. 775.

[62a] See below, para. 4.04.

[63] (1884) 14 Q.B.D. 153.

intended to further any criminal purpose" were not privileged.[64] This clearly covered the intention of the client. The majority of their Lordships thought that section 10(2) should be interpreted in the same way, and even extended to cover the intention of a third party, in this case the client's relative.

This decision obviously has a serious limiting effect on legal privilege. Indeed, in any case where the police are searching for items which constitute evidence of an offence they will normally be able to show that *someone* has a criminal purpose in relation to those items.[65] There is thus a danger that the decision in *Francis & Francis* will render section 10 redundant. Lord Goff, however, who gave the main speech for the majority, did not recognise one situation where section 10 would still apply. Referring to the *Snaresbrook* case (above), he accepted that the reasons for the decision could not stand. But he did not feel that that necessarily meant that the decision itself was wrong. This was because he thought that legal privilege could not be excluded by the *Cox & Railton* exception

> "in cases where a communication is made by a client to his legal adviser regarding the conduct of his case in criminal or civil proceedings, merely because the communication is untrue and would, if acted on, lead to the commission of the crime of perjury in such proceedings."[66]

The precise scope that this leaves to section 10 remains to be worked out. But is does seem to give protection to a client who, between the commission of an offence and trial, tells lies to his solicitor, for example by claiming to be innocent when in fact guilty. Such a narrow area of protection is surely not what was intended by Parliament. It should be remembered, however, that even if legal privilege is lost, material held by a solicitor on behalf of a client will almost certainly constitute either "excluded" or "special procedure" material (below 3.14–3.15) and thus have some protection from seizure.

(b) *Excluded material*

This is defined by section 11. There are three types of excluded material. **3.14**

(i) Personal records. These must be held in confidence by a person who acquired or created them in the course of a trade, business, profession or other occupation, or for the purposes of a paid or unpaid office.[67] Records are held in confidence for the purposes of the Act if they are held subject to an express or implied undertaking to that effect, or to a statutory restriction or obligation of secrecy (*e.g.* under the Official Secrets Act 1911).[68] Section 12 explains that "personal records" means records (documentary or otherwise) concerning an individual (living or dead), from which he may be identified, and which relate to:

---

[64] *Ibid.* 167.
[65] Note that under the Drug Trafficking Offences Act the material does *not* have to be evidence of an offence.
[66] [1988] 3 All E.R. 775, 800.
[67] s.11(1)(*a*).
[68] s.11(2).

(a) his physical or mental health;
(b) spiritual counselling or assistance given or to be given to him; or
(c) counselling or assistance given or to be given to him, for the purposes of his personal welfare, by a voluntary organisation, or an individual who because of his office or occupation has responsibilities for the person's welfare, or who is responsible for supervising him under a court order.

Records held by doctors, clergymen, probation officers, or voluntary organisations such as the Samaritans, for example, would be covered by this. Some educational records might also be covered, but not general personnel files held by an employer, except in so far as they relate to the above matters. Many such records would in any case not be "relevant evidence"[69] because of the hearsay rule.[70] One possible exception would be a situation such as that reported in *The Times* for June 15, 1984, concerning an investigation into alleged fraud against the National Health Service by consultants. Personal records were checked to see whether people had actually received treatment which was recorded. In any case the evidence does not necessarily have to be admissible if, apart from the P.C.E.A., it could have been obtained by a search warrant under some other legislation.[71]

(ii) Human tissue or tissue fluid. The material must have been taken for the purposes of diagnosis or medical treatment, and be held in confidence.[72] The requirement of confidentiality (which is defined in the same way as for personal records, above) should be a fairly easy one to satisfy in such circumstances.

(iii) Journalistic material. The material must consist of documents, or records, and satisfy the definition of "journalistic material" in section 13. The definition is in fact rather circular, in that it states that journalistic material means "material acquired or created for the purposes of journalism"—this word not being further defined. The definition is further limited by section 13(2) which requires the material to be in the possession of a person who acquired or created it for the purposes of journalism if it is to attract the protection of the Act. The reporter who deposits such material with a friend for "safekeeping" may thus achieve the opposite of his aim.

As with the other two categories, journalistic material must be held in confidence to be excluded material. But here there is an additional requirement that it must have been held in confidence continuously, by one or more persons, ever since it was first acquired or created for the purposes of journalism.[73]

One type of document which would be covered by this category and which the police might wish to have produced, or to search for, would be a document covered

---

[69] *i.e.* admissible evidence—s.8(4). And see below, para. 3.16.
[70] See s.68.
[71] See Sched. 1, para. 3.
[72] s.11(1)(*b*).
[73] s.11(3).

by the Official Secrets Acts which had been "leaked" by a civil servant to a journalist.

(c) *Special procedure material*

This is defined in section 14. The category covers, first, all journalistic material **3.15** which is not excluded material.[74] This does not need to be held in confidence. Secondly, it covers certain other material (not being excluded material) which is held in confidence as a result of an express or implied undertaking by the person holding it, or by virtue of a statutory obligation (as defined in s.11(2)(*b*), above, para. 3.14).[75] Within these limits the phrase includes any material in the possession of a person who acquired or created it in the course of a trade, business, profession, or other occupation, or for the purpose of a paid or unpaid office.[76] It does not have to consist of documents or records. But special procedure material not in this form may be obtained by a search warrant under another Act without using the Schedule 1 procedure. Section 8 of the P.C.E.A., however, cannot be used in relation to *any* special procedure material.[77]

There are certain limitations on the scope of special procedure material held by employees or a company. As regards material acquired by an employee from his employer in the course of his employment, or by a company from an "associated company,"[78] it will only be special procedure material if it was such immediately before its acquisition.[79] Thus the status cannot be gained for otherwise unprotected material simply by extracting an undertaking of confidentiality from an employee to whom it is transferred. Similarly, if material is created by an employee in the course of his employment, or by a company for an associated company, it will only be special procedure material if it would have been such had the employer or associated company created it.[80]

Examples of items which have been dealt with as special procedure material include the accounts of a Youth Association,[81] photographs held by newspapers,[82] conveyancing documents in the possession of a solicitor,[83] and details of bank accounts.[84]

3. Seizure

Section 19 of the P.C.E.A., contains general provisions relating to the seizure of **3.16** items by a constable who is lawfully on premises, whether by virtue of a warrant,

---

[74] See the previous paragraph.
[75] s.14(1) and (2).
[76] s.14(2)(*a*).
[77] s.9(2).
[78] A company will fall into this category if it would be so treated for the purposes of the Income and Corporation Taxes Act 1970—s.14(6).
[79] s.14(3).
[80] s.14(4) and (5).
[81] *R.* v. *Central Criminal Court, ex p. Adegbesan* [1986] 3 All E.R. 113.
[82] *R.* v. *Bristol Crown Court, ex p. Bristol Press and Picture Agency* (1986) 85 Cr.App.R. 190.
[83] *R.* v. *Crown Court at Inner London Session, ex p. Baines & Baines* [1987] 3 All E.R. 1025.
[84] *R.* v. *Crown Court at Leicester, ex p. D.P.P.* [1987] 3 All E.R. 654.

statutory power, or the consent of the occupier.[85] On the basis of the decision in *Foster* v. *Attard*[86] the constable does not need to be aware of the lawful basis for his presence in order to take advantage of it. The provisions of section 19 replace the common law rules set out in *Ghani* v. *Jones.*[87] Generally the P.C.E.A. power is slightly wider than that under the common law, but in one respect it is more restricted. Items which the constable has reasonable grounds for suspecting to be subject to legal privilege,[88] may never be seized, whatever the basis of the constable's presence.[89] This seems more restrictive than the approach to this issue adopted by Swanwick J. in *Frank Truman Export Ltd.* v. *Metropolitan Police Commissioner,*[90] since items which are evidence of an offence may still be protected by the privilege. Presumably "reasonable grounds" will require more than a mere statement by the owner that they are subject to legal privilege. The constable may well be entitled to inspect the documents to a limited extent in order to ascertain their character.[91] Apart from this restriction, however, the constable may seize anything (including excluded or special procedure material) which he has reasonable grounds for believing has been obtained in consequence of the commission of an offence (*e.g.* stolen goods), or is evidence in relation to an offence he is investigating, or any other offence.[92] The offence need not be a serious one, nor need the article be in possession of someone suspected of being implicated in the offence,[93] but the constable must have reasonable grounds for believing that the seizure is necessary to prevent the concealment, loss, alteration, or destruction of the item. In addition, items obtained from the commission of an offence may be seized to prevent damage to them.[94] The likelihood of evidence being damaged (rather than destroyed) is an insufficient ground for seizure.[95]

It is unfortunate that section 19 uses the word "evidence" rather than the phrase "relevant evidence." In section 8(4) "relevant evidence" in relation to an offence is defined for the purposes of the Act as anything which would be *admissible in evidence* at a trial for the offence. It is to be hoped that the simple word "evidence" will be interpreted in the same way, but there is clearly a danger that a court might be persuaded that the omission of the qualifying adjective was deliberate, and that the

---

[85] s.19(1). Note that the Code of Practice states that a search by consent should normally only take place on the basis of written permission, and after giving the occupier full information as to the purpose of the search—paras. 4.1 and 4.2.

[86] *The Times,* January 4, 1986.

[87] [1970] 1 Q.B. 693, 708. See also *Chic Fashions Ltd.* v. *Jones* [1968] 2 Q.B. 299; *Garfinkel* v. *Metropolitan Police Commissioner* [1972] Crim.L.R. 44; *Reynolds* v. *Commissioner of Police of the Metropolis* [1984] 3 All E.R. 649.

[88] As defined in s.10, above.

[89] s.19(6).

[90] [1977] Q.B. 952.

[91] *cf. A.M. & S. Europe Ltd.* v. *Commission of the European Communities,* [1983] Q.B. 878—see below, paras. 8.81–8.82.

[92] s.19(2) and (3).

[93] *cf.* the first and third of Lord Denning's requirements in *Ghani* v. *Jones* [1970] 1 Q.B. 693, 708 and see also *Wershof* v. *Metropolitan Police Commissioner* [1978] 3 All E.R. 540.

[94] s.19(2)(*b*).

[95] s.19(3)(*b*).

word should be given a wider meaning, perhaps closer to its popular use, rather than the technical concept of "admissible evidence."

(a) *Computers*

If a constable has reasonable grounds for believing that information which is **3.17** evidence in relation to an offence he is investigating, or any other offence, or which has been obtained in consequence of the commission of an offence, is contained in a computer, and that it might otherwise be concealed, lost, tampered with, or destroyed, he may require it to be produced in a visible, legible, and removable form.[96] Printout would satisfy these requirements, but discs or tapes would not. The computer need not be situated in the premises entered, but simply accessible from them. With the growth in electronic communications systems, this might mean a computer situated on the other side of the world.

Section 20 extends a similar power to require the production of information held in a computer to any situation where a constable, having entered premises in the exercise of a statutory power, has a power of seizure under section 8 or 18 of, or paragraph 13 of Schedule 1 to, the P.C.E.A., or under any other Act. The power is on one reading very wide, in that it is not necessary for the seizure power itself to cover documents, nor does the power depend on reasonable suspicion on the part of the constable. Since, however, the power under section 20 only arises where there is a power of seizure, it should be taken as being limited by the terms in which that power of seizure is granted. Thus, if a constable is exercising a power of seizure under section 3 of the Obscene Publications Act 1959,[97] he should be limited to requiring the production of information which he has reasonable cause to believe constitutes an obscene article, or, more plausibly, relates to the trade or business carried on at the premises.

Neither the power under section 19(4) nor that under section 20 gives a power to seize as such. Once the information has been produced in the required form, it may only be taken away if this is justified by some other power (*e.g.* s.19(3)).

(b) *Receipts*

Contrary to the recommendation of the Royal Commission on Criminal Proce- **3.18** dure,[98] there is no obligation on an officer to supply a receipt for what has been seized, unless he receives a request from a person showing himself to be the occupier of the premises where the seizure occurred, or to have had possession or custody of the thing seized immediately before it was seized.[99] The request may be made at the

---

[96] s.19(4).
[97] See below, para. 4.06.
[98] *Report*, Cmnd. 8092, para. 3.47.
[99] s.21(1).

time of the search or later: no time limit is specified. The officer must provide a record of what was seized within a "reasonable time" of the request being made.[1]

(c) *Access, copies, and photographs*

3.19   Section 21 imposes certain duties on an officer in charge of an investigation to allow access to, or to provide copies or photographs of, things which have been seized by a constable. All these are subject to the restriction in section 21(8) that there will be no such duty where the officer has reasonable grounds for believing that to allow access, or supply a photograph or copy, would prejudice the investigation for which the thing was seized, or the investigation of any other offence, or criminal proceedings brought as a result of such investigations.[2]

If there are no such grounds, however, the investigating officer, on receipt of a request for access from a person having custody or control of the seized item immediately before it was seized, or from someone acting on their behalf, must allow access, under the supervision of a constable.[3] Similarly, if such a person requests a photograph or copy of a seized item, the officer must either allow access to it for the purpose of photographing or copying it, again under the supervision of a constable, or must himself supply, within a reasonable time, a photograph or copy.[4] In *Allen v. Chief Constable of Cheshire*,[4a] the Divisional Court held that the proper way to challenge a refusal by the police to allow access, etc., was by an application for judicial review, rather than by seeking an injunction and damages for wrongful interference with goods.

In addition to these duties the police have a general power to photograph or copy anything which they have the power to seize.[5]

(d) *Retention*

3.20   The general principle is that seized items may be retained for as long as is necessary in all the circumstances.[6] In particular an article may be retained for use as evidence in a trial, or for "forensic" (presumably meaning "scientific") examination, or other investigation in connection with an offence.[7] But nothing may be retained for these purposes if a photograph or copy would be sufficient.[8] An article may also be retained in order to establish its lawful owner, where there are reasonable grounds for believing that it has been obtained in consequence of the commission of an offence.[9]

If an item has been seized on the ground that it might be used to cause physical

---

[1] s.21(2).
[2] s.21(8).
[3] s.21(3).
[4] s.21(4), (5) and (6).
[4a] *The Times*, July 16, 1988.
[5] s.21(7).
[6] s.22(1).
[7] s.22(2)(a).
[8] s.22(4).
[9] s.22(2)(b).

injury, to damage property, to interfere with evidence, or to assist in escape from police detention, it may only be retained while the person from whom it was seized is in police custody, or the custody of a court, and has not been released on bail.[10]

None of the above provisions affects the power of a court to make an order under the Police (Property) Act 1897.[11]

(e) *Recording information*

The P.C.E.A. does not require the police to record information following a search **3.21** other than on the warrant itself,[12] or for the purpose of fulfilling the obligation under section 21 to supply a record of what has been seized.[13] Paragraph 8.1 of the Code of Practice, however, requires each sub-divisional police station to keep a search register. The officer in charge of a search should, on arrival at a police station, make, or have made, a record of the search, and this should be entered in the search register. The record should include the address of the premises searched, the names of the officers conducting it and of any persons on the premises (if known), whether force was used, and if so, why, and a list of any damage caused, and the circumstances.[14] The record should also include the authority under which the search took place. If this was a warrant, or written consent, a copy should be attached to the record, or kept in a place identified in the record. If the authority was a statutory power of entry without warrant, the record should include the power. Finally, the record should include a list of articles seized, or a note of where such a list is kept. If any of the articles was not covered by a warrant, the reason for the seizure should be stated.[15]

B. *Specific Provisions*

The P.C.E.A. itself creates or re-enacts a number of entry powers, both with and **3.22** without warrant. Powers exercisable without a warrant are dealt with first, then those requiring a warrant, and finally, those requiring the special procedure in Schedule 1 to the Act. In relation to all these powers section 117 of the Act will apply, so that, unless the exercise of the power depends on consent, reasonable force may be used, if necessary.

1. Search after an arrest

The powers to search premises after an arrest are to be found in sections 18 and 32. **3.23**

(a) *Section 32*

This power arises where a person has been arrested, other than at a police station.

[10] s.22(3).
[11] s.22(5). See above, para. 2.54.
[12] See above, para. 3.11.
[13] See above, para. 3.18.
[14] Code of Practice, para. 7.1.
[15] *Ibid.*

The arrest does not have to be for an "arrestable offence."[16] The section empowers a constable to enter and search the premises where the arrest occurred, or which the arrested person had left immediately before the arrest.[17] The purpose of the power is to allow the constable to search for evidence relating to the offence for which the person has been arrested, and the constable must have reasonable grounds for believing that such evidence is on the premises.[18] As with the other powers of search under the Act, the power only extends as far as reasonably required for the purpose of discovering such evidence.[19] Once on the premises, of course, the constable will be able to use the powers under section 19 (above, para. 3.16) to seize evidence of other offences which he may come across in the course of his search.

There is special provision in section 32 for the situation where the premises on which the arrest occurred consists of two or more separate dwellings. Section 32(7) limits the power to search to the dwelling in which the arrest took place or which the arrested person left immediately prior to his arrest, and any parts of the premises which occupiers of that dwelling use in common with the occupiers of other dwellings.

There is no time limit on the exercise of the power under section 32(2)(*b*), though it is clearly designed principally to allow a search immediately following an arrest. It is clearly within the scope of the power, however, for the police to return at a later stage to the scene of an arrest and search it in the light of information obtained as a result of questioning the arrested person. This may be an attractive power to the police, given that a warrant is unnecessary, the power refers to "evidence" rather than "relevant evidence,"[20] and it allows a search for excluded or special procedure material without the need to use the Schedule 1 procedure.[21] In *R. v. Badham*,[22] however, a Crown Court refused to regard an attempted entry some four hours after an arrest as lawful under section 32. Although no time limit was given, this was an immediate power, and it would be wrong to have an open-ended right to go back to premises where an arrest had occurred. It is surely right that, in view of the width of the power it should be used sparingly, and not as a means of circumventing the protective provisions attaching to searches under warrant.

(b) *Section 18*

3.24   Whereas section 32 is concerned with searches of the premises where an arrest occurred, section 18 applies to any premises occupied or controlled by a person who has been arrested for an "arrestable offence." The definition of an "arrestable offence" (*i.e.* an offence for which an arrest may be made without a warrant) is contained in section 24. It covers,

(i) offences for which the sentence is fixed by law (*e.g.* murder);

[16] See below, para. 3.24.
[17] s.32(2)(*b*). The section also gives powers to search the arrested person—s.32(1) and (2)(*a*).
[18] s.32(6).
[19] s.32(2). See above, para. 3.10.
[20] See above, para. 3.16.
[21] See below, para. 3.28.
[22] [1987] Crim.L.R. 202.

(ii) offences for which a person over 21 may be sentenced on first conviction to five years' imprisonment[23];

(iii) offences for which a person may be arrested under the Customs and Excise Acts[24]

(iv) offences under the Official Secrets Acts 1911 and 1920, not falling within (ii) above;

(v) offences under sections 22 or 23 of the Sexual Offences Act 1956;

(vi) offences under section 12(1) or 25(1) of the Theft Act 1968.

In addition, in relation to any of the above offences, conspiracy, attempt, incitement, aiding, abetting, counselling, or procuring, is also an arrestable offence.[25]

Supervision of the exercise of the power of search under section 18 is given to officers of the rank of inspector or above.[26] Such an officer must authorise the search in writing. In *R. v. Badham*[27] the Crown Court judge ruled that the authorisation should be in the form of an independent document which the constable could take with him to the premises to be searched. The mere recording of the fact of authorisation in the inspector's notebook was insufficient. No written authorisation is required, however, if the search takes place before the arrested person has been taken to a police station, because his presence at a place other than a police station is necessary for the effective investigation of the offence.[28] In that case the constable conducting the search must, as soon as is practicable, inform an officer of the rank of the inspector or above that he has made it.[29] The officer authorising or being informed of the search is required to make a record in writing of the grounds for the search, and the nature of the evidence which was sought.[30] Where at the time the record is made a person who was in occupation or control of the premises at the time of the search is in police detention, the record should be made on that person's custody record.[31]

The power given by section 18 is to enter and search premises, if the constable has reasonable grounds for believing that there is on the premises evidence,[32] other than items subject to legal privilege, that relates to the offence for which the person has been arrested, or any other arrestable offence connected with or similar to that offence.[33] This would cover the situation where the police are searching for evidence relating to the theft of a car used in a robbery for which someone has been arrested,

---

[23] Or might be so sentenced but for the restrictions imposed by section 33 of the Magistrates' Courts Act 1980. N.B. that this covers common law offences as well as those created by statute—*cf.* Criminal Law Act 1967, s.2(1).

[24] See Customs and Excise Act 1979, s.1(1).

[25] s.24(3).

[26] s.18(5). But N.B. the provision in s.106, allowing a sergeant to act as an inspector in certain circumstances.

[27] [1987] Crim.L.R. 202.

[28] s.18(4) and (5).

[29] s.18(6).

[30] s.18(7).

[31] s.18(8).

[32] Not necessarily "relevant evidence"—see above, para. 3.16.

[33] s.18(1).

since the offences would be "connected," and also where someone has been arrested for a burglary, and the police wish to search for evidence of earlier burglaries which he may also have committed, since here the offences would be "similar." It would not cover a case such as *Jeffrey* v. *Black*,[34] where the flat of a person arrested for stealing a sandwich was searched for drugs. The precise scope of these words will, however, have to await judicial interpretation.

Section 18 does not specifically require the authorising officer to be satisfied of the reasonable grounds for the constable's belief. And, as with section 32, the power may be used to search for excluded or special procedure material without using the Schedule 1 procedure.

The power to search is limited to a power to search to the extent reasonably required to discover the evidence which the constable believes to be there.[35]

2. Entry for the purpose of arrest, etc.

3.25   Section 17 gives a number of powers of entry without warrant. All but one of them are concerned with a power of arrest. Provided that the constable has reasonable grounds for believing that the person he is seeking is on the premises,[36] he may enter in order to:

(i)   execute a warrant of arrest issued in connection with or arising out of criminal proceedings;

(ii) execute a warrant of commitment issued under section 76 of the Magistrates' Courts Act 1980;

(iii) arrest a person for an arrestable offence;

(iv) arrest a person for an offence under section 1 of the Public Order Act 1936, or section 4 of the Public Order Act 1986;

(v)   arrest a person for an offence under section 6, 7, 8, or 10 of the Criminal Law Act 1977—in this case the constable must be in uniform[37];

(vi) recapture a person "unlawfully at large" and whom he is pursuing.

As regards the last power, it is presumed that a person cannot be "unlawfully at large" at least until he has been arrested.[38] Thus the constable who witnesses a non-arrestable offence, and pursues the offender in order to exercise the power of arrest under section 25 of the P.C.E.A., would not be able to rely on this section in order to follow the person on to private property.[39] This analysis is supported by the fact that a specific power to enter is given in relation to arrestable offences.[40] There would be no need for this if "unlawfully at large" covered the suspected offender who has not yet been detained.

In all the above cases the powers to search are limited in relation to premises consisting of two or more separate dwellings, to a power to enter and search:

[34] [1978] Q.B. 490.
[35] s.18(3). See above, para. 3.10.
[36] s.17(2)(a).
[37] s.17(3).
[38] cf. *Hart* v. *Chief Constable of Kent* [1983] Crim.L.R. 117, D.C.
[39] cf. also *Clowser* v. *Chaplin, Finnigan* v. *Sandiford* [1981] 1 W.L.R. 837.
[40] s.17(1)(b).

(i) any parts of the premises which are used in common by the occupiers of two or more dwellings;

(ii) any dwelling in which the constable has reasonable grounds for believing that the person who he is seeking may be.

There is a further power to enter under section 17 which is not subject to this limitation. This is the power to enter to search premises for the purpose of saving life or limb, or preventing serious damage to property. There is no requirement of "reasonable belief" here, either, so presumably all that is required is for the constable's "purpose" genuinely to fall within the scope of the section.[41]

3. Search under warrant

Prior to the passing of the 1984 Act the police had no general power to obtain a **3.26** warrant to search for evidence, only the specific powers outlined in the next chapter, under a variety of statutory provisions. This gave rise to particular problems with common law offences. It had long been an absurd gap in police powers, for example, that they were unable to obtain a warrant to search for a murder weapon or a corpse. Similar difficulties were highlighted by the case of *McLorie* v. *Oxford*,[42] where, following the arrest of a driver of a car who was then charged with attempted murder, the police had no power to enter private premises to seize or examine a car suspected of having been used in the offence.

The Royal Commission on Criminal Procedure recommended that this gap should be filled. But they considered that a power to search for evidence without consent should be available only as a last resort.[43] They suggested a two-stage procedure, under which the police would usually seek an order of court for the production of evidence. Only if this failed, or seemed likely to fail, and certain other conditions were satisfied, would a warrant be issued. In the event the 1984 Act only adopts the two-stage procedure in respect of excluded and special procedure material.[44] In other circumstances a warrant may be issued to a constable who applies to a justice of the peace,[45] following the procedure set out in section 15,[46] provided a number of conditions are satisfied. The first four of these are cumulative, *i.e.* they must *all* be satisfied before a warrant may be issued.

The justice must first be satisfied (1) that there are reasonable grounds for believing that a serious arrestable offence has been committed. A serious arrestable offence is defined in section 116 and Schedule 5. The offences which are always serious arrestable offences are treason, murder, manslaughter, rape, kidnapping, incest with a girl under the age of 13, buggery with a boy under 16 or a person who has not consented, indecent assault constituting an act of gross indecency, or an

---

[41] *cf.* the common law version of this power, as recognised in *Handcock* v. *Baker* (1800) 2 Bos. & P. 260, above, para. 1.05.
[42] [1982] Q.B. 1290.
[43] *Report*, Cmnd. 8092, para. 3.42.
[44] See paras. 3.14, above, and 3.28 below.
[45] The R.C.C.P. suggested a circuit judge, *Report*, para. 3.45.
[46] See above, para. 3.08.

offence under the Explosive Substances Act 1883, s.2,[47] the Sexual Offences Act 1956, s.5,[48] the Firearms Act 1968, ss.16, 17, or 18,[49] the Road Traffic Act 1988, s.1,[50] the Taking of Hostages Act 1982, s.1, the Aviation Security Act 1982, s.1,[51] or various "drug trafficking offences."[52] In addition any arrestable offence (as defined in s.24, above, para. 3.24) becomes serious if its commission has led, or is intended or likely to lead to certain consequences.[53]

3.27   These consequences are[54]:

(i) *Serious harm to the security of the State or to public order.* The question of what amounts to "serious" harm, etc., in this and the following provisions is an objective one, on which a court would have the power to rule. It is not determined by the reasonable belief of a person exercising the power, though it is likely that a court would be reluctant to go against the decision of a justice issuing a warrant. In the case of the security of the State a court might well rely on a Ministerial ruling.[55]

(ii) *Serious interference with the administration of justice or with the investigation of offences or of a particular offence.*

(iii) *The death of any person.*

(iv) *Serious injury to any person.* "Injury" includes any disease and any impairment of a person's physical or mental condition.[56] "Serious" here will presumably mean much the same as "grievous bodily harm" under the Offences Against the Person Act 1861.

(v) *Substantial financial gain to any person.*

(vi) *Substantial financial loss to any person.* The seriousness of a loss here (though not of a gain under the previous provision) has to be judged by its effect on the person who suffers it.[57] Thus the theft of a van, essential for a one-man business, might be a serious arrestable offence, whereas the theft of an identical van from a firm owning a fleet of them would not. And the status of an offence involved in, for example, snatching a handbag, will depend on the state of the victim's bank balance.

In addition to being satisfied as regards suspicion of a serious arrestable offence, the justice must also be satisfied (2) that there are reasonable grounds for believing that there is material on the specified premises which is likely to be of substantial value (by itself or with other material) to the investigation of the offence, (3) that the

---

[47] Causing an explosion likely to endanger life or property.
[48] Intercourse with a girl under the age of 13.
[49] Possession with intent to injure; use to resist arrest; carrying with criminal intent.
[50] Causing death by reckless driving.
[51] Hi-jacking.
[52] As defined in s.38(1)(a)–(d) of the Drug Trafficking Offences Act 1986.
[53] s.115(3).
[54] ss.115(6).
[55] *cf. Chandler* v. *D.P.P.* [1964] A.C. 763.
[56] s.115(8).
[57] s.115(7).

material is likely to be relevant evidence,[58] and (4) that it does not consist of items subject to legal privilege, or excluded or special procedure material.[59]

If all the above four conditions are satisfied, then the justice must consider whether there are reasonable grounds for believing that one or more of the following further conditions applies[60]:

(i) that it is not practicable to communicate with any person entitled to grant entry to the premises;

(ii) that it is practicable to communicate with such a person, but not practicable as regards the person entitled to grant access to the evidence;

(iii) that entry to the premises will not be granted unless a warrant is produced;

(iv) that the purpose of a search may be frustrated or seriously prejudiced unless a constable arriving at the premises can secure immediate entry to them.

A warrant may then be issued and executed in accordance with sections 15 and 16 (above, para. 3.07). The constable will be entitled to seize and retain anything for which a search has been authorised under these provisions.[61]

In *R. v. Guildhall Magistrates, ex p. Primlaks Holding Company*[61a] the police had obtained a warrant under the above powers in relation to the premises of "two well-known firms of solicitors of high reputation". The Divisional Court refused to accept that the justice could have been satisfied that the material sought did not prima facie consist of either legally privileged or special procedure material, or that any of the conditions (i) to (iv) above had been satisfied. In such circumstances, the police should not have applied for a warrant *ex parte* under section 8, but should have used the *inter partes* procedure under Schedule 1, described below.

4. Access to excluded or special procedure material

If the police wish to gain access to excluded or special procedure material, they will normally have to do so by means of an application under Schedule 1 to the Act.[62] This applies even where the material could previously have been obtained by a search warrant issued under some other statute.[63]   **3.28**

As regards search warrant powers included in legislation passed after the P.C.E.A., the Act is silent.[64] The position therefore seems to be that if the later Act itself contains no limitation, the police will be able to search for excluded, special procedure, and even legally privileged, material with an ordinary search warrant.

---

[58] *i.e.* admissible in evidence at a trial for the offence—s.8(4).

[59] See above, para. 3.12.

[60] s.8(1)(*e*), and s.8(3).

[61] s.8(2).

[61a] *The Times*, December 30, 1988.

[62] s.9(1).

[63] s.9(2).

[64] *cf.* s.15(1) which specifically applies the provisions relating to the issue of warrants to legislation passed after the P.C.E.A.

They will have the option,[65] however, where a serious arrestable offence is being investigated, of using Schedule 1 of the P.C.E.A. to obtain access to special procedure material.[66] They will not be able to use the Schedule in relation to excluded material, because this would involve satisfying the second set of access conditions. The condition in paragraph 3(b) of these refers to the issue of a warrant affected by section 9(2). Section 9(2) has no effect on Acts passed after the P.C.E.A., and so this condition could never be satisfied.

Because of the serious implications of this for the policy behind the introduction of the Schedule 1 procedure, it is to be hoped that Parliament will in the future make specific reference to privileged material when enacting, or re-enacting, search warrant powers.[67]

There are two methods which may be used to give access under the Schedule. First, a circuit judge may make an order for production or access. Secondly, he may issue a search warrant.

(a) *Order*

3.29   The process is initiated by an application from a constable to a circuit judge. Since the hearing of the application will be *inter partes*,[68] notice of the application must be given, following the procedures in paragraphs 8, 9 and 10. It is not necessary for notice of the application to be given to anyone other than the person from whom access is sought.[69] A person on whom such notice is served will be forbidden to conceal, destroy, alter or dispose of the material to which the application relates without the leave of a judge, or the written permission of a constable.[70] The sanction for breaking this obligation is unclear, but it would presumably be dealt with as a contempt.[71] The obligation continues until the application is dismissed or abandoned, or there has been compliance with an order made as a result of the application. In *R.* v. *Adegbesan*[72] the Divisional Court ruled that the police should set out in the notice a description of all that is sought to be produced or discovered, sufficient to enable the person on whom the notice is served to comply with the obligation not to interfere with material subject to it.[73] In addition, in *R.* v. *Central Criminal Court, ex p. Carr*,[74] Glidewell L.J. thought that the notice ought to indicate the general nature

---

[65] The police normally have no choice—they *must* use Schedule 1 in relation to excluded or special procedure material; they *cannot* use it in relation to other material. See Stone, "PACE: Special Procedures and Legal Privilege" [1988] Crim.L.R. 498, 499.

[66] By virtue of s.9(1).

[67] This was done, *e.g.* in the Cinemas Act 1985, s.13, (see below, para. 9.58) but not in the Public Order Act 1986, s.24 (see below, para. 4.53).

[68] Sched. 1, para. 7.

[69] *R.* v. *Crown Court at Leicester, ex p. D.P.P.* [1987] 3 All E.R. 654. In this case the person under investigation by the police had claimed the right to notice of the hearing.

[70] Sched. 1, para. 11.

[71] *R.* v. *Adegbesan* [1986] 3 All E.R. 113, 117.

[72] [1986] 3 All E.R. 113.

[73] If the police fear that giving notice may lead to the disappearance of such items, they should seek a warrant *ex parte*, under paras. 12–14 of the Schedule: *ibid.* 118. See also Stone, "PACE: Special Procedures and Legal Privilege" [1988] Crim.L.R. 498.

[74] Divisional Court, February 27, 1987 (unreported).

of the offence or offences under investigation (*e.g.* "fraud," "riot," "wounding") and the address of the premises where the material is alleged to be. Further information, such as the facts relied on by the police as showing that the material was in the person's possession, or the details of the offences suspected, and who was suspected of committing them, was not necessary.[75] In some circumstances it may be acceptable for the required information to be given orally, but the written notice should then identify the person to whom the information has been given.[76]

At the *inter partes* hearing the judge must be satisfied that one of the two sets of "access conditions" contained in paragraphs 2 and 3 of the Schedule has been satisfied. Paragraph 3 ("the second set of access conditions") applies where, but for section 9(2) of the Act, the constable would have been able to obtain a search warrant under some other Act. The judge must be satisfied that there are reasonable grounds for believing that excluded or special procedure material is on the premises specified, and that the issue of such a warrant would have been appropriate. This presumably means simply that all the other conditions for the issue of a warrant under the other Act have been fulfilled. It is only under this set of access conditions that an order relating to *excluded* material may be made.

The alternative set of access conditions, under paragraph 2 ("the first set of access conditions"), is more complex, but to some extent follows the provisions of section 8(1) which apply to ordinary search warrants under the P.C.E.A.[77] Thus there must be reasonable grounds for believing that a serious arrestable offence has been committed, and that there is on specified premises, special procedure material which is likely to be of substantial value to the police's investigations,[78] and to be relevant evidence.[79] In addition, however, the judge must be satisfied that other methods of obtaining the material have been tried without success, or have not been tried because it appeared that they were bound to fail.[80] And finally, the judge must be satisfied that it is in the public interest that the material should be produced or access to it given.[81] In deciding what is in the public interest, regard should be had to the benefit likely to accrue to the investigation if the material is obtained, and to the circumstances under which the person in possession of the material holds it. The first of these factors is relatively easy to comprehend, in that, presumably, the more likely it is that access to the material will provide a successful conclusion to the police investigation the greater the public interest in that access. The second factor, related to the circumstances in which it is held, is more difficult to give concrete form. Presumably material which, for example, has been obtained in contravention of the Official Secrets Acts, will be more likely to be made the subject of an order than information which is simply held in confidence by an employer.

The issue of the "public interest" was considered in *R. v. Bristol Crown Court, ex p.*

---

[75] *Ibid.*
[76] *R. v. Manchester Crown Court, ex p. Taylor* [1988] Crim.L.R. 386 (D.C.).
[77] See above, para. 3.26.
[78] Whether by itself, or together with other material.
[79] Sched. 1, para. 2(*a*). And see above, para. 3.16, for the meaning of "relevant evidence."
[80] *Ibid.* para. 2(*b*).
[81] *Ibid.* para. 2(*c*).

Bristol Press and Picture Agency.[82] The police were seeking access to photographs of rioting taken by press photographers. The agency in possession of the photographs argued that to hand them over would be contrary to the public interest in that it would prejudice the impartiality of the press, and increase the risk of photographers being attacked. The judge rejected the first of these arguments because the photographs would only have been handed over under the compulsion of a court order, and the second because he could not see that photographers ran greater risks by taking pictures that might be ordered to be handed over to the police, than pictures which would be published in newspapers or used in television broadcasts.[83] The Divisional Court thought that he had approached the issues before him entirely correctly, and refused judicial review.[84] Indeed it is difficult to imagine many circumstances where a judge will be willing to hold that it is contrary to the public interest to allow the police access to relevant evidence which may be of substantial value to the investigation of a serious arrestable offence.[85]

If at the *inter partes* hearing of the application, the judge is satisfied that one of the sets of access conditions is satisfied, he may order the person having possession of the material to produce it to a constable, or give a constable access to it, within seven days.[86] If the material consists of information held in a computer, it must be produced in a form in which it can be taken away, and in which it is visible and legible.[87]Anything produced in response to an order must be dealt with in accordance with the provisions of sections 21 and 22 of the Act as to access, copying, and retention, as if it had been seized by a constable.[88]

Failure to comply with an order is to be dealt with by the judge as if it were a contempt of the Crown Court.[89]

(b) Warrant

3.30   The issue of a warrant to search for excluded or special procedure material should clearly be a last resort. This is confirmed by the additional non-statutory safeguards set out in the Code of Practice, paras. 5.12 and 5.13, below.

It is a prerequisite for the issue of a warrant that the circuit judge to whom the (*ex parte*) application is made, should be satisfied that one of the sets of "access conditions" outlined above in relation to orders has been fulfilled.[90] He must also be satisfied of the existence of one of the following further conditions. The first two of these are that it is not practicable to communicate with the person having power to grant entry to the premises, or access to the material, as under section 8(3) (above,

---

[82] (1986) 85 Cr.App.R. 190. I am grateful to Mr. David Newell of the Newspaper Society for providing me with a transcript of Stuart-Smith J.'s judgment in this case.
[83] The same approach was taken by Lord Denning in *Senior* v. *Holdsworth, ex p. Independent Television News Ltd.* [1976] 1 Q.B. 23, 33.
[84] (1986) 85 Cr.App.Rep. 190.
[85] See also Stone, "PACE: Special Procedures and Legal Privilege" [1988] Crim.L.R. 498.
[86] Sched. 1, para. 4. The order may itself specify a longer period.
[87] *Ibid.* para. 5. *cf.* s.19(4), above, para. 3.17.
[88] *Ibid.* para. 6. See above para. 3.19.
[89] *Ibid.* para. 15.
[90] *Ibid.* para. 12.

para. 3.27).[91] The third relates to the nature of the information. The condition will be fulfilled if the material is subject to a statutory restriction on disclosure,[92] and is likely to be disclosed in breach of this if the warrant is not issued.[93] This would apply, for example, to information covered by the Official Secrets Acts. The fourth possible condition is that service of notice to apply for an order under paragraph 4 of the Schedule may seriously prejudice the investigation.[94] This is obviously the widest of the conditions, and will need close supervision by the issuing judge if it is not to lead to abuse. This was emphasised by Macpherson J. in *R.* v. *Maidstone Crown Court, ex p. Waitt,* [94a] where he commented that the Schedule constitutes

> "a serious inroad upon the liberty of the subject. The responsibility for ensuring that the procedure is not abused lies with circuit judges. It is of cardinal importance that circuit judges should be scrupulous in discharging that responsibility".

The police had sought warrants to enter a number of premises, including those of the applicant, who was a solicitor. The court refused to accept that in relation to a solicitor's office, any of the grounds for the issue of a warrant could have been satisfied. The police should have used the *inter partes* procedure to obtain an order for production.[94b]

If the applicant is relying on the second set of access conditions, *i.e.* that a search warrant would have been obtainable in relation to the material but for the P.C.E.A.,[95] there is an additional ground on which a warrant may be issued. This is where an order under paragraph 4 has not been complied with.[96] Non-compliance with an order does not justify the issue of a warrant where it is the first set of access conditions which is being relied on. This will simply fall to be treated as a contempt.[97]

The warrant will authorise a constable to enter the premises and search them.[98] He may seize anything for which the warrant authorises him to search. A warrant issued under Schedule 1 also falls within the scope of the general provisions in sections 15 and 16 of the Act.[99]

The Code of Practice contains a number of additional provisions relating to the **3.31** execution of warrants issued under Schedule 1. An officer of at least the rank of

---

[91] *Ibid.* para. 14(*a*) and (*b*).
[92] As under s.11(2)(*b*)—see above, para. 3.14.
[93] *Ibid.* para. 14(*c*).
[94] *Ibid.* para. 14(*d*).
[94a] *The Times,* January 4, 1988.
[94b] *cf* the decision in *R.* v. *Guildhall Magistrates, ex p. Primlaks Holding Company, The Times,* December 30, 1988, above, para. 3.27.
[95] See above, para. 3.29.
[96] Sched. 1, para. 12(*b*).
[97] *Ibid.* para. 15—see above, para. 3.29.
[98] *Ibid.* para. 12.
[99] See above, para. 3.07.

inspector should take charge of the execution of the warrant.[1] He is enjoined to ensure that the search is conducted with discretion, and with the least possible disruption of the business or other activities on the premises.

Before searching the premises the inspector should ask for the material in question to be produced. He might also ask for indices to files on the premises to be produced, and seek to inspect any files which an index seems to show might contain any of the material sought. Only if these procedures are refused, or ineffective, or for some other reason the inspector thinks that a physical search of the premises is necessary, should one be carried out.[2]

[1] Code of Practice, para. 5.11.
[2] *Ibid.* para. 5.12.

CHAPTER FOUR

POLICE: SPECIFIC POWERS

This chapter deals with the specific powers of entry which the police have under a **4.01** number of statutes. Search warrants issued in respect of these have to comply with the Police and Criminal Evidence Act 1984 (P.C.E.A.), as described in Chapter Three.[1] It may be that these more specific powers will be used less now that the police have the general power to obtain a search warrant under the P.C.E.A., s.8. But this only applies to "serious arrestable offences," and in some cases (perhaps where it is proposed to use other procedures under an Act, *e.g.* the forfeiture procedures under the Obscene Publications Act 1959[2]) the specific powers may anyway be thought more appropriate. It may also be necessary to use them to seize items (*e.g.* stolen goods, or drugs) covered by the power, but not intended to be used as evidence.

All powers of entry exercisable under a search warrant will be subject to the provisions of sections 15, 16 and 19 of the P.C.E.A., and the effect of these sections is not repeated in this chapter in respect of the individual powers. Reference should be made to Chapter Three for detailed discussion of these sections, but *inter alia* they provide that all search warrants must be executed within one month of their issue, that only one entry may be made under each warrant, and that reasonable force may be used to gain entry.[3] Those powers of entry which do not depend on a warrant, or depend on a warrant permitting, *e.g.* inspection, rather than search, will be subject only to section 19.

A. Stolen Goods

The Royal Commission on Criminal Procedure found that the most frequently used **4.02** police search powers were those in relation to theft offences.[4]

1. Theft Act 1968

A warrant to enter premises to search for stolen goods (as defined in s.24) may be obtained under section 26. A justice of the peace must be satisfied by information on oath that there is reasonable cause to believe that a person (who might be innocent of any offence) has stolen goods in his custody or possession or on his premises. The

---

[1] See above, para. 3.07.
[2] See below, para. 4.06.
[3] See Chap. Three, paras. 3.06–3.21.
[4] Royal Commission on Criminal Procedure, *The Law and Procedure* Cmnd. 8092–1 (1981) App. 7. See also M. McConville, "Search of Persons and Premises: New Data from London" [1983] Crim.L.R. 605; and K. W. Lidstone, "Magistrates, the Police and Search Warrants" [1984] Crim.L.R. 449.

warrant must be addressed to a constable.[5] The constable will be authorised to enter and search the premises, and seize any goods which he believes to be stolen goods.[6] The belief does not have to be reasonable. The wide definition of "stolen goods" in section 24 means that property believed to be the proceeds of the disposal of goods stolen or obtained by deception or blackmail, may also be seized.

The power of a superintendent to authorise a search has been repealed by the P.C.E.A.

Seized goods must be dealt with in accordance with the provisions of section 19 of the P.C.E.A. The court, however, has power on conviction to make certain orders for restitution or compensation under section 28 of the 1968 Act, or for forfeiture under section 43 of the Powers of Criminal Courts Act 1973. It was held in *Malone* v. *Metropolitan Police Commissioner*,[7] that the police were not entitled to retain property not required as evidence, simply on the grounds that it was likely that an order under section 28 or section 43 would be made in respect of it. Section 28(3) refers to compensation payments being made from money taken out of the convicted person's possession on his apprehension. The section does not, however, legitimise seizure for this purpose. At the time the money is taken the constable seizing it must believe it to be stolen property, or the proceeds of stolen property.[8]

2. Public Stores Act 1875

It is an offence under section 5 of this Act to obliterate marks denoting Her Majesty's property. Under section 12,[9] a justice of the peace may issue a search warrant if it is made to appear by information on oath that a person has in his custody or possession, or on his premises, stores in respect of which an offence under section 5 has been committed. The warrant will authorise a constable to search for and seize the stores, in the same way as for stolen goods under the Theft Act 1968.[10]

The Police (Property) Act 1897 applies to goods seized under this section.[11]

3. Fugitive Offenders Act 1967

Where a warrant is issued under section 6 of this Act for the arrest of someone accused of theft, or receiving, or any other property offence, a justice of the peace may also issue a warrant to search for the property.[12]

B. Drugs

1. Misuse of Drugs Act 1971

4.03   Two powers of entry are given by section 23 of the Misuse of Drugs Act 1971. The

---

[5] Except under the authority of an enactment expressly so providing.
[6] s.26(3).
[7] [1980] Q.B. 49.
[8] s.26(3).
[9] As substituted by the Theft Act 1968, Sched. II.
[10] Above.
[11] See above, para. 2.54.
[12] s.6(5).

first, under section 23(1), applies only to premises of a person carrying on business as a producer or supplier of controlled drugs. It is exercisable, without warrant, by a constable, or a person authorised by the Secretary of State, for the purposes of the execution of the Act. It does not have to be exercised at a reasonable time, nor is the entrant required to give any notice of the intended entry, or to produce evidence of his authority. On entry he may demand the production of, and inspect, books and documents relating to dealings in controlled drugs, and inspect any stocks of such drugs. This subsection does not give a power of seizure, but under section 23(2), if a constable has reasonable grounds to suspect that a person is in possession of a controlled drug in contravention of the Act, he may, for the purposes of proceedings under the Act, seize and detain anything which appears to him to be evidence of an offence under Act. Intentional obstruction of person exercising powers under section 23(1) is an offence, as is concealing from such a person any books, documents, stocks or drugs mentioned in that section, or failing without reasonable excuse to produce books or documents demanded by a person exercising the power. In each case the offence is punishable on summary conviction with a fine not exceeding £1,000, or up to six months' imprisonment, or both, and on indictment with a fine, or up to two years' imprisonment, or both.

The more general power of entry is given by section 23(3). A justice of the peace must be satisfied by information on oath that there are reasonable grounds for suspecting that either;

(a) controlled drugs are, in contravention of the Act in the possession of a person on any premises, or
(b) a document directly or indirectly relating to a transaction which was or would be an offence under the Act,[13] is in the possession of a person on any premises.

He may then issue a warrant authorising a police constable to enter the premises named in the warrant and search them and any person found there. Force may be used if necessary, and the entry must take place within one month of the date of the warrant. The section refers to entry "at any time or times," but this is limited to one entry only, by the P.C.E.A., s.15(5).

If in the course of the search the constable finds controlled drugs, in relation to which he has reasonable grounds for suspecting that an offence under the Act *has been* committed, or a document which he has reasonable grounds to believe to fall within (b), above, he may seize and detain the drugs or document.[14] Under section 27, where a person is convicted of an offence under the Act, the court may order anything shown to its satisfaction to relate to the offence, to be forfeited and either destroyed, or dealt with as the court may order. The power is not available in respect of convictions for conspiracy.[15] A person claiming to be the owner, or otherwise having an interest in the property, must have an opportunity to be heard, before

---

[13] Or under the law in force in the place where the transaction was, or is to be, carried out.
[14] See P.C.E.A., s.19, for provisions relating to seized items—see above, para. 3.16.
[15] *R.* v. *Cuthbertson* [1981] A.C. 470 (H.L.).

such an order is made. An order under section 27 is in the nature of a "sentence," and is therefore subject to section 11(2) of the Courts Act 1971.[16]

2. Drug Trafficking Offences Act 1986

4.04   This Act gives the police powers to obtain access orders and search warrants in relation to material which is likely to be of substantial value to investigations into drug trafficking.[17] The powers are modelled on those contained in Schedule 1 to the Police and Criminal Evidence Act 1984.[18]

(a) *Access orders*

Under section 27 a constable can apply to a circuit judge for an order directing a person in possession of material either to produce it to a constable, or to give a constable access to it. Unlike the procedure under the P.C.E.A. Schedule 1, the application will be made *ex parte*. There is no provision for notice to be given. Where the order is that the constable is to be given access to the material, it may be coupled with an order requiring the person appearing to the judge to be entitled to grant entry to the premises to allow the constable to enter.[19] No power of search attaches to this power of entry. It simply allows the constable to take possession of the material specified in the order. The period for compliance with an order of either kind is seven days, subject to the discretion of the judge to substitute a shorter or longer period if appropriate.[20]

The conditions for the grant of an application are, first, that there are reasonable grounds for suspecting that a specified person (not necessarily the person in possession of the material) has carried on or has benefited from drug trafficking. The judge must also be satisfied that there are reasonable grounds for suspecting that the material is likely to be of substantial value to the police's investigation, but that it does not consist items subject to legal privilege, or "excluded material."[21] The scope of "legal privilege" in this context was considered by the House of Lords in *Francis & Francis* v. *Central Criminal Court* which is discussed above (para. 3.13). Finally, the judge must be satisfied that there are reasonable grounds for believing that the public interest is in favour of access being given.[22] Surprisingly, the judge does not need to be satisfied that there are reasonable grounds for believing that the material is on specified premises.

"Special procedure" material under the P.C.E.A.[23] is not given any special status under these provisions, and the section is specifically stated to apply to material

[16] *R.* v. *Menocal* [1980] A.C. 598 (C.A.). *cf. R.* v. *Saville* [1981] Q.B. 12 (C.A.).
[17] As defined in s.38.
[18] See above, Chap. 3, paras. 3.28–3.31.
[19] s.27(5).
[20] s.27(3).
[21] s.27(4)(*b*)(ii). By s.29(2), "legal privilege" and "excluded material" have the same meaning as in the P.C.E.A.: see above, para. 3.13. Note that "special procedure" material is not protected.
[22] s.27(4)(*c*).
[23] See above, Chap. 3, para. 3.15.

subject to obligations of secrecy or restrictions on disclosure, statutory or otherwise. It also covers material in the possession of an authorised government department.[24]

(b) *Search warrants*

The power to obtain a search warrant is contained in section 28. Once again the **4.05** application must be made to a circuit judge. He may issue a search warrant in relation to specified premises in one of three sets of circumstances.

The first is that an order made under section 27 has not been complied with.[25]

The second is that the conditions for the issue of an order under section 27 exist, but it is impracticable to communicate with any person entitled to produce or give access to the material or premises, or the investigation might be seriously prejudiced unless a constable could secure immediate access.[26]

The third set of circumstances arises where there are reasonable grounds for suspecting that a specified person has carried on or benefited from drug trafficking, and that there is on the specified premises material relating to that person or the trafficking which would be of substantial value to the investigation, but it is not possible at the time to particularise the material so as to enable an order under section 27 to be made.[27] The judge must also be satisfied that it is not practicable to communicate with the person entitled to give entry to the premises, or that any request to enter without a warrant will be refused, or that the investigation might be seriously prejudiced unless a constable arriving at the premises can gain immediate access.[28]

There seems to be a gap in the powers here. If the police are unable sufficiently to identify the material they are seeking in order to be entitled to an order under section 27, but the person in charge of the premises where the material is thought to be is happy to allow the police to enter (but not to search) the premises, no warrant can be issued, and the police have no means of obtaining the material.

Once on premises by virtue of a section 28 warrant, the police may seize and retain any material, other than items subject to legal privilege or excluded material,[29] which is likely to be of substantial value to the investigation for which the warrant was issued.[30] The police will of course also have their general powers under section 19 of the P.C.E.A.[31]

C. Obscenity and Indecency

1. Obscene Publications Act 1959

The main provision in this area is section 3 of the Obscene Publications Act 1959. **4.06**

---

[24] s.27(9).
[25] s.28(2)(a).
[26] s.28(3).
[27] s.28(4).
[28] s.28(4)(c).
[29] See n. 5, above.
[30] s.28(5).
[31] See above, Chap. 3, para. 3.16.

This provides for the issue of a warrant by a justice of the peace, on his being satisfied by information on oath that there are reasonable grounds for suspecting that obscene articles are, or are from time to time, kept for publication for gain in premises specified in the information.[32] The warrant will empower a constable to enter and search the premises, and seize and remove any articles which the constable has reason to believe to be obscene articles kept for publication for gain.[33] If any such articles are seized the constable may also seize and remove any documents which relate to a trade or business carried on at the premises.

The test of obscenity which the constable has to apply is the tendency of an article to deprave and corrupt those likely to read, see or hear, the matter contained or embodied in it.[34] Articles intended solely for export may come within this.[35] "Article" means any description of article containing matter to be read or looked at or both, any sound record, and any film or other record of a picture or pictures (including video-cassettes).[36] It does not therefore cover such "sex-aids" as inflatable rubber sex-dolls.[37]

Any articles seized under section 3(1) must either be brought before magistrates with a view to forfeiture, or returned.[38] In practice, where large quantities of material have been seized, the police may take some time to sort through it, and to decide whether a prosecution under section 2 of the Act is to be brought, or simply forfeiture proceedings. It seems that the police will be allowed a reasonable time to do this.[39] The proper remedy for undue delay is to apply for an order of mandamus.[40]

Forfeiture proceedings under section 3 allow the person from whom articles were seized, or the owner, author, or maker of the articles, or any other person through whose hands the articles have passed before being seized, to appear to show cause why they should not be forfeited.[41] They may argue that the articles are not obscene, or that, despite their obscenity, publication would be for the public good.[42] If the court does not order forfeiture, costs may be ordered to be paid by the person laying the information to any person appearing to argue against forfeiture.[43]

---

[32] The power also applies to "stalls" and "vehicles."

[33] s.3(1).

[34] Obscene Publications Act 1959, s.1(1). See also *R.* v. *Penguin Books* [1961] Crim.L.R. 176; *Calder* v. *Powell* [1965] 1 Q.B. 509; *Shaw* v. *D.P.P.* [1962] A.C. 220; *R.* v. *Calder and Boyars* [1969] 1 Q.B. 151; *D.P.P.* v. *Whyte* [1972] A.C. 849; *R.* v. *Anderson* [1972] 1 Q.B. 304; *cf. R.* v. *Skirving* [1985] 2 All E.R. 705, and Stone, "Obscene Publications: the Problems Persist," [1986] Crim.L.R. 139.

[35] *Gold Star Publications* v. *D.P.P.* [1981] 2 All E.R. 257.

[36] s.1(2); *Att.-Gen's. Reference (No. 5 of 1980)* [1980] 3 All E.R. 816.

[37] *Conegate Ltd.* v. *Customs and Excise Commissioners* [1986] 2 All E.R. 688.

[38] s.3(3). No provision is made for business documents seized—these should be dealt with in accordance with P.C.E.A. s.19.

[39] *Roandale* v. *Metropolitan Police Commissioner* [1979] Crim.L.R. 255, (C.A.). Here the Court of Appeal clearly felt that the police had not been unreasonable in taking two months to sort 179,118 articles, and to schedule and list them under 452 titles. See also *R.* v. *Snaresbrook Crown Court, ex p. Commissioner of the Metropolis* (1984) 79 Cr.App.R. 184 (D.C.).

[40] *Ibid.*

[41] s.3(5).

[42] Obscene Publications Act 1959, s.4. See also *D.P.P.* v. *Jordan* [1976] 3 All E.R. 775.

[43] s.3(6).

2. Children and Young Persons (Harmful Publications) Act 1955

In contrast to the Obscene Publications Act 1959, this Act has hardly been used.   **4.07**
It was aimed against "horror comics." Thus, it applies to books, magazines, or other
similar works which are of a kind likely to fall into the hands of children or young
persons and consist wholly or mainly of stories told in pictures (with or without
writing) portraying:

  (a) the commission of crimes; or
  (b) acts of violence or cruelty; or
  (c) incidents of a repulsive or horrible nature

in such a way that the work as a whole would tend to deprave and corrupt a child or
young person into whose hands it might fall.[44] The power to issue a search warrant
arises where a justice of the peace has issued a summons, or warrant for the arrest of
a person, for a publication offence under section 2 of the Act, and he or another
justice is satisfied by information on oath that that person has in his possession or
under his control a copy or copies of a work to which the Act applies, or a plate or
photographic film for printing such works. The section empowers the constable to
enter the premises named in the warrant, and search them, as well as any vehicle or
stall used by the person for his trade or business. Any works which the constable has
reasonable cause to believe fall within the Act may be seized, as may any photographic plates or films reasonably believed to have been prepared for producing
such works.

On conviction the court may order forfeiture of any copies of a work to which the
conviction relates, found in the possession or control of the person convicted. A
plate, or photographic film, prepared for printing the work may similarly be
forfeited.[45]

3. Protection of Children Act 1978

This Act is concerned with indecent photographs (including films) of children   **4.08**
under 16.[46] Where a justice of the peace is satisfied by information on oath that there
are reasonable grounds for suspecting that, in any premises within his area, there are
indecent photographs of children, he may issue a warrant authorising a constable to
search the premises, and seize and remove any articles which he reasonably believes
to be or to include such indecent photographs.[47] Articles seized should be dealt with
in the same way as articles seized under the Obscene Publications Act 1959, s.3,[48]
and section 5 contains almost identical forfeiture provisions.[49]

---

[44] s.1.
[45] s.3(2).
[46] See s.1, s.2(3), and s.7. "Indecency" is not defined, and is thus a question of fact—*cf. R.* v. *Stanley*
[1965] 2 Q.B. 327; *R.* v. *Anderson* [1972] 1 Q.B. 304. See also, s.160 of the Criminal Justice Act 1988.
[47] s.4(2).
[48] s.4(3).
[49] See above, para. 4.04.

4. Indecent Displays (Control) Act 1981

4.09   The public display of indecent matter constitutes an offence under this Act.[50] A constable has the power to seize any article which he has reasonable grounds to believe to be or to contain indecent matter and to have been used in the commission of an offence under the Act.[51] In addition, if a justice of the peace is satisfied on information on oath that there are reasonable grounds for suspecting that an offence under the Act has been or is being committed on any premises, he may issue a warrant authorising a constable to enter those premises, and to seize any articles which the constable has reasonable grounds to believe to be or to contain indecent matter, and to have been used in the commission of an offence under the Act.[52] There is no specific power of *search* under this Act, so it is not clear whether it is covered by sections 15 and 16 of the P.C.E.A. The fact that the provision as to time of execution of the warrant has been repealed by the P.C.E.A. suggests that Parliament thought that it was.

There is no power of forfeiture under this Act. The powers of seizure are designed primarily to enable the police to obtain possession of the evidence on which to base a prosecution.

5. Criminal Libel Act 1819

4.10   Where a person has been convicted of blasphemous or seditious libel, section 1 of this Act gives the court a power to order the seizure of all copies of the libel in the possession of the person convicted, or held by any other person named in the order for the use of the person convicted. Evidence on oath to this effect must have been given to the court. The order will empower a constable to search the premises of any person alleged to be in possession of the copies. Force may be used only if admission is initially refused. Copies found may be seized, and held or disposed of at the court's direction.[53]

6. Local Government (Miscellaneous Provisions) Act 1982

4.11   Under section 2 of this Act a local authority may resolve that "sex establishments" (*i.e.* sex cinemas and sex shops)[54] in its area should be governed by the controls contained in Schedule 3 to the Act. This provides for a licensing system for sex establishments.

A licensed sex establishment may be entered and inspected by a constable at any reasonable time, with a view to seeing:

(i)   whether the licence is being complied with;
(ii) whether any person disqualified from holding a licence is employed in the business;

---

[50] s.1(1) "Indecent" is not defined—see note 30, above.
[51] s.2(2).
[52] s.2(3).
[53] N.B. also s.2, as regards appeals.
[54] As defined in paras. 3 and 4 of Sched. 3 to the Act. See also *Lambeth London Borough Council* v. *Grewal* (1985) 82 Cr.App.R. 301.

(iii) whether any person under the age of 18 is in the establishment;
(iv) whether any person under 18 is employed in the business.

In addition, there is a power of entry under warrant obtainable from a justice of the peace by a constable or authorised local authority officer.[55] This will authorise the entry and inspection of a sex establishment if the constable or authorised officer has reason to suspect an offence under paragraph 20, 21, or 23 of the Schedule. These paragraphs make it an offence, *inter alia*, to operate a sex establishment without a licence, to employ people disqualified from holding a licence, to allow contraventions of the terms of a licence,[56] to make false statements to obtain a licence,[57] or to employ, or to allow on the premises, a person under 18.[58]

Refusal without reasonable excuse to allow a constable or authorised officer to enter under a warrant is a summary offence punishable with a fine not exceeding level 5 on the standard scale.[59]

Neither of the entry powers under the schedule gives a power to search, or seize, and so neither is covered by the provisions of the P.C.E.A. An authorised officer must, however, produce his authority, if required to do so, before exercising his powers under paragraph 25.[60]

7. Video Recordings Act 1984

A system of censorship and classification for video recordings was established by this Act. A power of entry is given by section 17. A constable may obtain a warrant to enter and search premises by satisfying a justice of the peace by information on oath that there are reasonable grounds for suspecting that an offence under the Act has been or is being committed on the premises, and that evidence of this is on the premises.[61] On entry, the constable may seize anything which he has reasonable grounds to believe may be required as evidence in proceedings for an offence under the Act.[62]

4.12

Following a conviction for an offence under the Act, video recordings produced to the court, and shown to the satisfaction of the court to relate to the offence, may be forfeited.[63] Anyone claiming to be the owner, or otherwise interested in, the recordings, must be given an opportunity to show cause why an order for forfeiture should not be made.[64]

[55] Para. 25(2) and (4). In *Tunbridge Wells B.C.* v. *Quietlynn* [1985] Crim.L.R. 594, the fact that the local authority officers had entered premises without a warrant did not in itself render their evidence inadmissible.
[56] Para. 20.
[57] Para. 21.
[58] Para. 23.
[59] Para. 25(6).
[60] Para. 25(5).
[61] s.17(1).
[62] s.17(2). Note also the powers of trading standards officers to enforce the provisions of this Act: Criminal Justice Act 1988, s. 162 below, para. 9.76.
[63] s.21(1).
[64] s.21(2).

D. Forgery and Fraud

1. Forgery and Counterfeiting Act 1981

4.13   This is the principal Act in this area. There are powers of entry under warrant under sections 7 (forgery) and 24 (counterfeiting).

(a) *Forgery*

A justice of the peace may issue a warrant under section 7 if it appears to him from information on oath that there is reasonable cause to believe that a person has in his custody, or under his control:

  (i) anything which he, or someone else, has used, or intends to use, in contravention of section 1 or 2 of the Act (making or copying a "false instrument")[65];
  (ii) any false instrument, or copy of a false instrument which he or someone else has used or intends to use in contravention of section 3 or 4 (using a false instrument, or copy of a false instrument);
  (iii) anything (*e.g.* money orders, share certificates, passports) the custody or control of which, without lawful authority or excuse, is an offence under section 5.

The warrant will authorise a constable to enter the specified premises to search for and seize the object in question.[66] Once the object has been seized a constable may at any time apply to a magistrates' court for an order for forfeiture and destruction or disposal.[67] The court must be satisfied that the object falls within (i), (ii), or (iii), above, and that it would be conducive to the public interest to make the order. A similar order may be made by a court on a conviction for an offence under Part I of the Act in relation to an object shown to the satisfaction of the court to relate to the offence.[68] In either case, an order for forfeiture must not be made where a person claiming to be the owner, or otherwise interested in the object, applies to the court, unless he has been given an opportunity to show cause why the order should not be made.[69]

(b) *Counterfeiting*

The power of entry under warrant in respect of counterfeiting is in very similar terms to the power just discussed. It is given by section 24 of the Act. The main difference from section 7 is that, in place of the categories of objects under section 7(1) (*i.e.* (i), (ii), and (iii), above), the justice of the peace must be satisfied that a person has under his custody or control:

---

[65] As defined in ss.8 and 9.
[66] s.7(1). See also *Reynolds* v. *Commissioner of Police for the Metropolis* [1984] 3 All E.R. 649, as regards the extent of the police's powers of seizure under the Forgery Act 1913.
[67] s.7(2).
[68] s.7(3).
[69] s.7(4).

(i) a counterfeit of a currency note or a protected coin, or a reproduction made in contravention of section 18 or 19 of the Act;

(ii) anything which the person or someone else has used or intends to use to make such a counterfeit or reproduction.

Otherwise, the powers of entry, search and seizure; and the powers to order forfeiture, are given in exactly the same terms as in section 7.[70] An additional provision appears in section 24(5), which makes it clear that the power to order forfeiture includes the power to direct that the object in question be passed to an authority with power to issue notes or coins, or to a person authorised by such an authority to receive the object.

2. Criminal Justice Act 1987

This Act created the Serious Fraud Office. Under section 2, the Director of the **4.14** Office has the power to demand the production of documents[71] relevant to an investigation. In support of this power, section 2(4) enables the Serious Fraud Office to obtain a warrant. A justice of the peace must be satisfied by information on oath from a member of the office that a person has failed to comply with an obligation to produce documents, or that it is not practicable to serve a notice demanding production, or service of a notice might seriously prejudice the investigation. The justice must also be satisfied that the relevant documents are on premises specified in the information.

The warrant will authorise a constable (who should, if practicable be accompanied by a member of the Serious Fraud Office, or someone authorised by the Director) to enter the premises, by force if necessary, and search them. Documents appearing to be those specified in the information may be seized, or steps taken to preserve, or prevent interference with them.

Section 2(9) gives protection to documents covered by legal professional privilege. In addition, section 2(10) protects confidential information held in the course of a banking business, unless the person to whom the confidence is owed consents, or the Director, or a specially designated member of the Serious Fraud Office, has authorised the requirement of disclosure. "Special procedure" and "excluded" material are not protected.[72]

E. Sexual Offences

Rape and certain other sexual offences are serious arrestable offences under the **4.15** P.C.E.A.,[73] but the Sexual Offences Act also contains provision for two powers of entry under warrant.

1. Sexual Offences Act 1956, s.42

Where it appears by information on oath that there is reasonable cause to suspect

---

[70] s.24(1)–(4).

[71] "Documents" include information recorded in any form. If not recorded in legible form, the obligation to produce means produce in a legible form: s.2(18).

[72] See above, Chap. 3, paras. 3.14–3.15.

[73] See above, para. 3.26.

that any house or part of a house is being used by a woman for the purposes of prostitution, and that a man residing in or frequenting the house is living wholly or in part on her earnings, a justice of the peace may issue a warrant empowering a constable to enter and search the house, and arrest the man.

2. Sexual Offences Act 1956, s.43

The power to issue a warrant under this section arises where a justice of the peace is satisfied by information on oath that a woman is being detained in any place for the purposes of unlawful sexual intercourse (with one or more men). The information may be laid by the woman's parent, relative, guardian, or any other person who in the opinion of the justice is acting in her interests. The justice must also be satisfied that the woman is:

(a) detained against her will; or
(b) under 16; or
(c) a mental defective[74]; or
(d) under 18, and detained against the will of her parent or guardian.

The warrant will authorise a constable to enter premises specified in the warrant, search for the woman and detain her in a place of safety until she can be brought before a justice of the peace. The constable must allow the person laying the information to accompany him, unless the justice issuing the warrant directs otherwise.[75]

F. Criminal Damage

4.16 Some criminal damage will fall within the definition of "serious arrestable offence" in the P.C.E.A.,[75a] but in addition, there is a power of entry under warrant in section 6 of the Criminal Damage Act 1971. It must be made to appear to a justice of the peace by information on oath that there is reasonable cause to believe that a person has in his custody, under his control, or on his premises, something which there is reasonable cause to believe has been used or is intended for use without lawful excuse, to destroy or damage property belonging to another,[76] or to destroy or damage any property (including his own) in a way likely to endanger the life of another. The warrant will authorise a constable to search for and seize the item in question, and for that purpose to enter and search the premises specified, and seize anything which he has reasonable cause to believe to have been used or to be intended for use as above.

Disposal of property seized is governed by the Police (Property) Act 1897.[77]

---

[74] As defined in s.45.
[75] s.43(4).
[75a] See above, para. 3.26.
[76] As defined in s.10(2).
[77] s.6(3). See above, para. 2.54.

G. *National Security and Terrorism*

1. Official Secrets Act 1911

The main offences under this Act concern spying and sabotage,[78] and unauthori- **4.17**
sed communication of information.[79] These may be "serious arrestable offences."[80]
In addition, material subject to the Act will be held "in confidence" and thus may be
excluded or special procedure material for the purposes of the P.C.E.A.[81] Subject to
this, section 9 of the Act contains two powers of entry. First, if a justice of the peace is
satisfied by information on oath that there is reasonable ground for suspecting that
an offence under the Act has been or is about to be committed, he may issue a
warrant authorising entry by a constable to any premises or place named in the
warrant. The justice does not apparently have to be satisfied as regards the presence
on the premises of what is to be searched for, but simply as to the commission of the
offence. On entering, the constable may search the premises, and anybody on them,
and seize any sketch, plan, model, article, note or document, and anything of a like
nature, in connection with which he has reasonable ground for suspecting that an
offence under the Act has been, or is about to be committed. He may also seize
anything else which is evidence of an offence, and about which he has similar
grounds for suspicion.

The second power arises where it appears to a police superintendent that the case
is one of "great emergency," and that immediate action is necessary in the interests
of the State.[82] The phrase "great emergency" is not defined, and the superintendent's belief does not, apparently, have to be reasonable. The section gives him
power to issue a written order to a constable, giving him the same powers as are
given by a warrant issued under section 9(1). Most other powers of this kind were
repealed by the P.C.E.A.

2. Incitement to Disaffection Act 1934

It is an offence under this Act to try to seduce a member of Her Majesty's Forces **4.18**
from his duty or allegiance.[83] In recent years the Act has been most used in respect of
attempts to discourage troops from serving in Northern Ireland.[84] There is a power
of entry under warrant under section 2. Unusually the power to issue the warrant is
given to a High Court judge, rather than a justice of the peace. The judge must be
satisfied by information on oath that there are reasonable grounds for suspecting
that an offence under the Act has been committed, and that evidence of this is to be
found at a place or premises specified in the information. The application must be
made by an officer of at least the rank of inspector, and must relate to an offence

---

[78] s.1, and see *Chandler* v. *D.P.P.* [1964] A.C. 763.
[79] s.2, and see *R.* v. *Simington* [1921] 1 K.B. 451; *R.* v. *Crisp and Homewood* (1919) 82 J.P. 121; *R.* v. *Galvin*
[1987] 2 All E.R. 851.
[80] See above, para. 3.26.
[81] See above, paras. 3.14–3.15.
[82] s.9(2).
[83] s.1.
[84] See, *e.g. R.* v. *Arrowsmith* [1975] Q.B. 678.

suspected to have been committed in the previous three months. The section states that the warrant will authorise entry by a named officer of at least the rank of inspector, together with any other persons named, and any other police officers. It is not clear whether this formulation brings the section within the scope of sections 15 and 16 of the P.C.E.A. which applies to warrants issued to "constables." A police officer of the rank of inspector or above will have the powers of a "constable," and so the sections may apply. If so, then the warrant may be executed by any police officer, the rank being irrelevant.[85] On the other hand, it seems to have been Parliament's intention to limit the number of police officers having powers of search, and it may be significant the words "named in the warrant" are not specifically repealed by the P.C.E.A., as are similar phrases in other statutes. The following description of the powers under the section is written on the basis that the P.C.E.A. does *not* apply; if it does then, where there is a conflict, the standard provisions in sections 15 and 16 of the P.C.E.A. will prevail.

Entry must take place at any time within one month of the issue of the warrant, and force may be used if necessary. The premises or place may be searched, together with any person found on them. Anything which the officer searching has reasonable grounds to suspect to be evidence of an offence under the Act may be seized. Following a search of premises, the officer in charge must notify the occupier, and supply him with a list of items removed. In addition, any person from whom documents are seized should be supplied with a list of these. Anything seized may be held for one month, or until the conclusion of proceedings.[86] The Police (Property) Act 1897 applies to such things.[87]

Following a conviction under the Act, a court may order the destruction, or other disposal, of any documents connected with the offence.[88]

3. Public Order Act 1936

4.19   Section 2 of this Act is concerned with preventing the organisation, training, etc., of quasi-military groups. If a High Court Judge is satisfied by information on oath from an officer of at least the rank of inspector that evidence of an offence under the section is to be found on any premises or place specified in the information, he may issue a search warrant to an officer of at least the rank of inspector and others named in the warrant. The same problems as to the applicability of the P.C.E.A. to this section arise as with the Incitement to Disaffection Act 1934.[89] The warrant will authorise those named in it, and any other police officers, to enter the premises or place, to search them and any person found on them, and to seize anything which the officer has reasonable ground for suspecting to be evidence of the commission of an offence under the section.

[85] P.C.E.A., s.16(1).
[86] s.2(4).
[87] *Ibid.* See above, para. 2.54.
[88] s.3(4).
[89] See above, para. 4.18.

4. Emergency Laws (Re-Enactments and Repeals) Act 1964

4.20 This Act gives power to the relevant Minister to make orders concerning hire-purchase controls, the provision of welfare foods, and the prices of medical supplies and milk. There is a power of entry under warrant in paragraph 2 of Schedule 1 to the Act. A justice of the peace must be satisfied by information on oath laid on behalf of a "competent authority,"[90] that there is reasonable ground for suspecting that there are on any premises documents which have not been produced as required by paragraph 1 of the Schedule.

The warrant will authorise constables, together with other persons named in it, to enter and search the premises specified in the information. Documents appearing to be documents required to be produced may be seized, or other steps taken in relation to them as appears necessary to preserve them or prevent interference with them. Documents seized may be retained for three months, or until the conclusion of proceedings started within that period.[91]

There is a specific obstruction offence under paragraph 2(4), punishable on summary conviction with a fine not exceeding level 3 on the standard scale, or three months imprisonment, or both.

5. Biological Weapons Act 1974

4.21 Section 4 of this Act gives a power of entry under warrant. A justice of the peace must be satisfied by information on oath that there is reasonable ground for suspecting that an offence under section 1 of the Act (development, etc., of biological agents, toxins, or weapons) has been, or is about to be committed. The warrant will authorise a constable, and any person named in the warrant, to enter and search the premises or place named in it. On entry, various other powers arise. Any person found on the premises may be searched; any documents may be seized or detained; any equipment inspected, seized and detained; and any substance inspected, sampled, seized and detained. There is apparently no need for a constable to have reasonable grounds for suspicion of an offence before taking any of these actions.

6. Aviation Security Act 1982

4.22 This Act is concerned with the protection of aerodromes and aircraft against acts of violence.[92] The Secretary of State may give a direction in writing to the manager of an aerodrome requiring him to use his best endeavours to secure that searches under section 13 are carried out by constables or other persons specified in the direction.[93] Searches under section 13 may be carried out without warrant. If a constable (or other specified person) has reasonable grounds to suspect that any firearms, explosives, or other dangerous articles, are in, or may be brought into, any part of the aerodrome, he may search the aerodrome, and any things or people found on it. To

---

[90] *i.e.* the Minister, or other person given powers by virtue of the Act.
[91] Para. 2(3).
[92] As defined in s.10(1). See also below, para. 8.54, for other powers under this Act.
[93] s.13(1).

this end he may enter any building, works, or land in the aerodrome, by force if necessary, and stop and detain any aircraft, vehicle, goods, or people.[94]

Failing to comply with a direction under the section, or wilfully obstructing a search, is an offence punishable on summary conviction with a fine not exceeding £1,000, and on indictment with a fine, or up to two years' imprisonment.[95]

7. Prevention of Terrorism (Temporary Provisions) Act 1984

4.23   The provision as to search warrants under this Act are reproduced almost without change from the Prevention of Terrorism (Temporary Provisions) Act 1976, except that there is now no power to obtain a warrant to search for evidence of the offence of withholding information about acts of terrorism.[96] A justice of the peace must be satisfied by information on oath from a police officer of at least the rank of inspector that there are reasonable grounds for suspecting that there is to be found in any premises or place[97]:

(a) evidence of the commission of an offence under section 1 (membership or organisation of "proscribed organisations"), section 9 (breach of an "exclusion order"), or section 10 (contribution towards acts of terrorism); or

(b) evidence sufficient to justify an order proscribing an organisation under section 1, or an exclusion order under section 3.

The warrant will authorise the applicant, together with any other police officer to enter the premises or place and search them and any person found on them.[98] Anything suspected, on reasonable grounds, of being evidence falling with (a) or (b) above, may be seized.[99]

In addition, if an officer of the rank of not less than superintendent has reasonable grounds for believing that the case is one of great emergency, and that in the interests of the State immediate action is necessary, he may, by written order, authorise any police officer to exercise the same powers as are available under a warrant issued under paragraph 4,[1] or which would have been available but for section 9(2) of the P.C.E.A.[2] The order may not authorise a search for items subject to legal privilege.[3]

H. Explosives

4.24   The offence under section 2 of the Explosive Substances Act 1883 (causing explosion likely to endanger life or property) is a serious arrestable offence under the P.C.E.A.[4]

---

[94] s.13(3).
[95] s.13(4).
[96] s.11.
[97] Sched. 3, Pt. II, para. 4(1).
[98] There is a similar problem as to the rank of police officer entitled to execute a warrant under this Act, as there is under the Incitement to Disaffection Act 1934—see above, para. 4.18.
[99] Para. 4(3).
[1] Para. 4(4).
[2] P.C.E.A., Sched. 6, para. 27.
[3] As defined in the P.C.E.A., s.10.
[4] See above, para. 3.26.

In addition, entry powers in connection with explosives are to be found in the Offences Against the Person Act 1861, and the Explosives Act 1875.

1. Offences Against the Person Act 1861

Under section 65 a justice of the peace may issue a search warrant upon reasonable cause assigned by oath that there is in any place gunpowder, or some other explosive, dangerous or noxious substance or thing, or any machine, engine, instrument or thing suspected to be made, kept, or carried for the purpose of being used in committing one of the offences under the Act for which a person (not previously convicted) may be tried on indictment otherwise than at his own instance. The warrant will authorise a search of the suspected place, and the seizure and removal of any gunpowder etc. (together with its containers) which the searcher has good cause to suspect to be intended to be used in committing an offence as above.

2. Explosives Act 1875

A general power of search is given by section 73. It is exercisable by a constable either on the basis of a warrant issued by a justice of the peace on reasonable grounds assigned by oath, or on the basis of a written order from a police officer of at least the rank of superintendent, where it appears to that officer that the case is one of emergency and that the delay in obtaining a warrant would be likely to endanger life. The constable must have reasonable cause to believe that an offence with respect to an explosive has been or is about to be committed in the place to be searched, or that any explosive is in that place in contravention of the Act, or that the provisions of the Act are not being observed there. He may enter and examine the place, search for explosives, and take samples of anything being, or reasonably supposed to be, an explosive or an ingredient of an explosive. Where the entry took place on the basis of a written order rather than a warrant, a written report must be sent to the Secretary of State.

A person who fails to admit a constable demanding entry under section 73, or obstructs him, commits an offence punishable on summary conviction with a fine not exceeding the prescribed sum, and on indictment with an unlimited fine. In addition he will be liable to forfeit all explosives, and ingredients, which are at the time in his possession or under his control at the place where the search power is being exercised.

The procedure to be adopted as regards items seized, or liable to forfeiture is set out in section 74.

I. Offensive Weapons

1. Offences Against the Person Act 1861

4.25 The power under section 5 of this Act, discussed above, paragraph 4.24 in relation to explosives, seems wide enough to cover "offensive weapons" of most types, provided the suspicion of the relevant purpose can be established.

2. Crossbows Act 1987

This Act places restrictions on the purchase, hire and possession of crossbows with a draw weight of 1.4 kilogrammes or more, by persons under the age of 17. Under section 4 a constable has a power of search and seizure where he suspects with reasonable cause that a person under 17 has possession of a crossbow, not being under the supervision of a person aged at least 21.[5] In order to exercise this power, the constable may enter any land other than a dwelling-house.[6]

3. Criminal Justice Act 1988

Section 142 of the Criminal Justice Act 1988 introduced a power to obtain a search warrant in relation to flick knives or gravity knives (as defined in section 1(1) of the Restriction of Offensive Weapons Act 1959), and weapons specified in orders made under section 141 of the Criminal Justice Act.[7]

A justice of the peace must be satisfied, on application from a constable, that there are reasonable grounds for believing that such weapons are on the specified premises, and that one of the following conditions applies. These are, that it is not practicable to communicate with any person entitled to grant entry to the premises or access to the weapons, or that entry will not be granted unless a warrant is produced, or that the purpose of the search may be frustrated or seriously prejudiced unless a constable arriving at the premises can secure immediate entry to them.

J. Road Traffic

4.26 The breathalyser has caused some problems to the police in the past as regards entry powers, in that section 7 of the Road Traffic Act 1972, as originally drafted, gave no power to enter property to conduct a breath test. As a result the police, if pursuing a motorist whom they suspected of drunken driving, could not follow him on to his own property, unless they could rely on the usual implied licence.[8] If the motorist entered a third party's property as a trespasser, the position was not clear, but the House of Lords in *Morris* v. *Beardmore*,[9] seemed to be of the opinion that in this situation the police would be entitled to follow him in order to seek a specimen of breath. Section 7 was substituted by the Transport Act 1981,[10] and has since been repealed and replaced by the Road Traffic Act 1988, s.6, which gives a limited power of entry. The first requirement for the power to arise is that an accident has occurred owing to the presence of a motor vehicle on a road or other public place.[11] If, in addition, a constable has reasonable cause to suspect that the accident involved injury to another, he may, for the purpose of administering a breath test to a person

[5] See s.3.
[6] s.4(3).
[7] At the time of writing, no such orders had been made.
[8] As in *Pamplin* v. *Fraser* [1981] R.T.R. 494, and see above, para. 1.04. See also *Morris* v. *Beardmore* [1981] A.C. 446; and *R.* v. *Allen* [1981] R.T.R. 410 (licence withdrawn).
[9] [1981] A.C. 446.
[10] Sched. 8.
[11] Road Traffic Act 1988, s.6(2).

whom he has reasonable cause to believe was driving or attempting to drive or in charge of the vehicle at the time of the accident, enter any place where that person is, or where the constable reasonably suspects him to be.[12] Force may be used if necessary. In *Fox* v. *Gwent*,[13] the House of Lords reaffirmed that the constable must have some basis for believing that someone has been injured. The discovery of a crashed vehicle, which had been abandoned, did not provide such a basis, and the subsequent entry in pursuit of the driver, and demand for a specimen of breath, was unlawful, following *Morris* v. *Beardmore*.[14] However, the motorist was then arrested (unlawfully) and taken to a police station, where a specimen of breath was obtained. The House of Lords refused to hold that the specimen was unfairly obtained, and therefore inadmissible.[15]

A different conclusion was reached by the Divisional Court in a subsequent similar case, *Jit Sing Matto* v. *D.P.P.*[16] in applying section 78 of the P.C.E.A. The difference was that on this occasion the police officers were clearly aware that they had no right to remain on the suspect's property after being told to leave. There was thus an element of *mala fides* about their actions which tainted the arrest and the breath test subsequently taken at the police station. This evidence should not have been admitted.[17]

The same power of entry may be used to arrest a person who, as a result of a breath test the constable has reasonable cause to believe has more than the prescribed proportion of alcohol in his breath or blood, or a person who the constable has reasonable cause to suspect has alcohol in his body, and who has failed to provide a specimen of breath for a breath test as required.[18] The arrest power does not apply where the person is at hospital as a patient.

K. Immigration

The Immigration Act 1971 gives a police officer a power of entry under warrant.[19] A **4.27** justice of the peace must be satisfied by information on oath that there is reasonable ground for suspecting that a person liable to be detained on the authority of an Immigration Officer under paragraph 16 of Schedule 2 to the Act (and therefore liable to arrest under paragraph 17) is to be found on specified premises. The constable may enter the premises named in the warrant for the purpose of searching for and arresting the person.

L. Mental Health

Two powers of entry under warrant are given to the police by the Mental Health Act **4.28**

---

[12] *Ibid.*, s.6 (5)(6)

[13] [1985] 3 All E.R. 392.

[14] [1981] A.C. 446—the accused committed no offence by refusing to supply a specimen of breath in these circumstances.

[15] *cf.* above, paras. 2.14–2.19.

[16] [1987] Crim.L.R. 641.

[17] See also the discussion of s.78, above, paras. 2.14–2.20.

[18] Road Traffic Act 1988, s.6 (5).

[19] Sched. 2, para. 17.

1983, s.135. Under section 135(1) the initiative must be taken by an approved social worker, who must satisfy a justice of the peace by information on oath that there is reasonable ground to suspect that a person believed to be suffering from mental disorder has been, or is being, ill-treated, neglected, or not kept under proper control, or is living alone and unable to care for himself. The patient need not be named in the warrant.[20] The warrant will empower the constable, who must be accompanied by an approved social worker and a registered medical practitioner,[21] to enter the premises in which the person is believed to be, by force if necessary. On entry, the constable may, if thought fit, remove the person to a place of safety,[22] with a view to making an application under Part II of the Act,[23] or other arrangements for his treatment or care. Detention at a place of safety as a result of the execution of a warrant under section 135 should not exceed 72 hours.[24]

The second power of entry under warrant, under s.135(2), requires a constable, or other person authorised under the Act to take a patient to any place, or to take or retake a patient into custody, to apply to a justice of the peace. The justice must be satisfied that there is reasonable ground to believe that the patient is to be found on specified premises, and that admission to the premises has been refused, or such refusal is apprehended. The warrant will authorise a constable to enter the premises, and remove the patient. The heading to the section refers to a "search" but the text of the section itself does not. It seems likely that a power to search would be implied here.

M. Children

4.29   The powers of police officers to enter premises to search for children are generally given in support of powers given to court officers, or local authorities.[25] They cover a number of areas.

1. Ill-treatment

4.30   Under section 40 of the Children and Young Persons Act 1933 an information must be laid before a justice of the peace by a person who is, in the opinion of the justice, acting in the best interests of a child or young person. It must appear to the justice that there is reasonable cause to suspect that the child or young person has been or is being assaulted, ill-treated, or neglected, in a manner likely to cause unnecessary suffering, or injury to health, or that an offence under Schedule 1 to the

---

[20] s.135(1).
[21] s.135(4).
[22] Defined in s.135(6) as "residential accommodation provided by a local social services authority under Pt. III of the National Assistance Act 1948 or under paragraph 2 of Schedule 8 to the National Health Service Act 1977, a hospital as defined by [s.145(1)] of this Act, police station, mental nursing home, or residential home for mentally disordered persons, or any other suitable place the occupier of which is willing temporarily to receive the patient."
[23] "Compulsory Admission to Hospital and Guardianship."
[24] s.135(3).
[25] For which, see below, para. 9.63.

Act has been or is being committed in respect of the child or young person.[26] The justice may issue a warrant authorising a constable, who may be accompanied by the person laying the information, unless the justice directs otherwise, and a doctor, if the justice so directs, to enter a specified house, building or place, and search for the child. The child need not be named in the information or warrant.[27] If the suspicions outlined above are found to be fulfilled, the victim may be taken to a place of safety,[28] until he can be brought before a juvenile court.

2. Unlawful absence or taking

(a) *Children and Young Persons Act 1969*

Under section 32(2A) of this Act,[29] a magistrates' court may issue a search **4.31** warrant if satisfied by information on oath that there is reasonable ground to believe that a child or young person who is absent from local authority care, a remand home, a special reception centre, a training school, or a place of safety, is in premises specified in the information.[30] The warrant will authorise a constable to search the specified premises for the person.

(b) *Adoption Act 1976, s.29*

Sections 27 and 28 of the Adoption Act 1976 impose restrictions on the removal of a child from his current home while an adoption order is pending. If a child has been taken away in breach of section 27 or 28, and an order has been made under section 29(1) of the 1976 Act, a power of entry arises. If a justice of the peace is satisfied by information on oath that there are reasonable grounds for believing that such a child is in premises specified in the information he may issue a search warrant.[31] This will empower any constable to search for the child, and return him to the person on whose application the order under section 29(1) was made.

This power backs up the power given to an officer of the court under section 29(3) to search premises under the authority of a court order.

(c) *Children Act 1975, s.42*

Here a justice of the peace must be satisfied by information on oath that there are reasonable grounds for believing that a child to whom an order under section 42(1) (return of child taken away in breach of an order under s.41) relates, is in premises specified in the information. He may then issue a warrant empowering a constable to search for the child, and return him to the person upon whose application the order under section 42(1) was made.[32]

---

[26] s.40(1).
[27] s.40(5).
[28] As defined in s.107(1).
[29] As added by the Children Act 1975, s.68.
[30] N.B. the restrictions on who may lay the information in s.32(2B).
[31] s.29(4).
[32] The form of the warrant is governed by S.I. 1985 No. 1695, r. 17(3).

Again, this supports a power given to an officer of the court, under section 42(3).

3. Employment

4.32   In connection with the controls over the employment of children, two powers of entry are given by section 28 of the Children and Young Persons Act 1933. The first arises where it appears to a justice of the peace that there is reasonable cause to believe that the provisions of Part II of the Act (other than those relating to employment abroad) are being contravened. He may then issue an order (not a warrant) to a local authority officer or a constable, empowering him to enter any place in which the person is, or is believed to be, employed, taking part in a performance, or being trained. The order may be sought by the local authority, or a constable. The entry must take place at a reasonable time within 48 hours of the making of the order, and simply empowers the officer or constable to make inquiries about the person.

The second power of entry, again given to a local authority officer or a constable, arises without the need for an order or warrant. It enables the constable or officer to enter any place used as a broadcasting, cable programme or film studio or for recording a performance for broadcast, or use in a cable programme or in a film for public exhibition, and make inquiries as to any children to which section 37 of the Children and Young Persons Act 1963 applies.[33] The officer or constable may similarly enter any place in which a person is authorised by a licence under that section, or a licence for training for dangerous performances, to perform or to be trained. Again the power is simply to make inquiries with respect to the child.[34]

Obstruction, or refusing to answer inquiries, or giving false answers, is an offence punishable on summary conviction with a fine not exceeding level 2 on the standard scale.

N. Animals

1. Protection of Animals Act 1911

4.33   A constable has the right to enter a knackers' yard at any hour of the day, or whenever business is apparently, or usually, carried on, to check compliance with the Act.[35] Refusal of admission, or obstructing or impeding a constable, is a summary offence, punishable with a fine not exceeding level 1 on the standard scale.

2. Performing Animals (Regulation) Act 1925

4.34   Section 1 of this Act requires a trainer or exhibitor of performing animals to obtain a certificate from a local authority. A constable, or duly authorised local authority officer, may at any reasonable time, enter any premises in which performing animals

---

[33] s.28(2)(*a*). s.37 of the 1963 Act contains restrictions on children under 16 taking part in public performances, etc.
[34] s.28(2)(*b*).
[35] s.5.

are being trained or exhibited, or kept for training or exhibition. He may inspect the premises, and any animals found there, and require anyone whom he has reason to believe is a trainer or exhibitor of performing animals, to produce his certificate.[36] This power does not entitle a constable or officer to go on or behind the stage during a public performance of performing animals.[37] Obstruction, wilful delay, concealing an animal from inspection, or failing without reasonable excuse to produce a certificate, is an offence punishable on summary conviction with a fine not exceeding level 3 on the standard scale.[38]

3. Animals (Scientific Procedures) Act 1986

Controls are imposed under this Act on the performing of experiments on ani- **4.35** mals, and the breeding of animals for experiments. Under section 25 a justice of the peace, on information on oath that there are reasonable grounds for believing that an offence under the Act has been or is being committed at any place, may issue a warrant authorising a constable to enter, by force if necessary. On entry the constable, who may be accompanied by an inspector appointed under the Act,[39] may search the place and require any person found there to give his name and address. Refusing to give a name or address, or giving a false one, or intentionally obstructing the constable or inspector, is a summary offence, punishable with up to three months imprisonment, or a fine not exceeding level 4 on the standard scale, or both.

O. Poaching

Under section 2 of the Game Laws (Amendment) Act 1960, a constable who has **4.36** reasonable grounds for suspecting that a person is committing an offence under section 1 or section 9 of the Night Poaching Act 1828, or section 30 or section 33 of the Game Act 1831 (which relates to daytime poaching) may enter land where he suspects that the offence is being committed, in order to exercise his powers under section 31 of the Game Act 1831, or to carry out an arrest under section 25 of the Police and Criminal Evidence Act 1984.[40]

P. Gaming

1. Betting, Gaming and Lotteries Act 1963

Despite its title this Act is now solely concerned with betting, the other two topics **4.37** having been taken over by the Gaming Act 1968, and the Lotteries and Amusements Act 1976, which are dealt with below. Two powers of entry without warrant are

---

[36] s.3(1).
[37] s.3(2).
[38] s.4(1).
[39] If this is authorised by the warrant, which it must be if the place is a "designated establishment" under the Act.
[40] The power is not exercisable in relation to land occupied by certain Government departments, and other bodies—s.2(3).

given. First, under section 10(4), a constable may enter a licensed betting office to check whether it is being managed in accordance with Schedule 4 to the Act. Secondly, under section 23, a constable may at all reasonable times enter on a "track,"[41] to check whether the provisions of Part I of the Act are being complied with. This power may also be exercised by a person authorised in writing by the licensing authority, on production, if demanded, of his authority. In respect of the power under both section 10 and 23, obstruction is a summary offence punishable with a fine not exceeding level 1 on the standard scale.

The Act also gives a power of entry under warrant.[42] A justice of the peace must be satisfied by information on oath that there are reasonable grounds to suppose that an offence under the Act is being, has been, or is about to be committed in any premises or place.[43] The warrant will authorise a constable to enter the premises, search them, and seize and remove any document, money or valuable thing, instrument, or other item found on the premises, which the constable has reasonable cause to believe may be required as evidence in proceedings for an offence under the Act. He may also search any person found on the premises whom he has reasonable cause to believe to be committing or to have committed such an offence. Where a person is convicted, and the court is satisfied that items produced to it relate to the offence, it may order the forfeiture and destruction, or other disposal, of the items.[44]

2. Gaming Act 1968

4.38   The entry powers under this Act are contained in section 43. They apply also to the Gaming (Bingo) Act 1985.[44a] There is a basic power of entry in respect of premises licensed under the Act, which may be exercised by a constable (or Gaming Board inspector) at any reasonable time. He may inspect the premises, any machines or other equipment on them, and also any books or documents, in order to discover whether there is, or has been, a contravention of the Act.[45]

There is also a power of entry under warrant.[46] A justice of the peace must be satisfied by information on oath that there are reasonable grounds for suspecting that an offence under the Act is being, has been, or is about to be committed on the premises or place specified in the information. The warrant will authorise a constable, with or without one or more inspectors, to enter and search the premises or place. The powers to seize items, and search persons found on the premises, are in exactly the same terms as those under section 51 of the Betting, Gaming and Lotteries Act 1963 (above).[47] Where a person is convicted of an offence, section 46 similarly gives the court power to order the forfeiture, etc., of items produced to it,

---

[41] *i.e.* premises on which races of any description, athletic sports, or other sporting events take place.
[42] s.51.
[43] s.55(1).
[44] s.52(4). See *R. v. Edmonton Justices, ex p. Stannite Automatics* [1965] 2 All E.R. 750 on the meaning of "produced to the court"—see below, para. 4.38.
[44a] s.4(3).
[45] s.43(2).
[46] s.43(4).
[47] Para. 4.37.

and shown to relate to the offence. In *R.* v. *Edmonton Justices, ex p. Stannite Automatics*,[48] the Divisional Court had to decide what was meant by "produced to the court." The items in question were heavy gaming machines, which were difficult to move. They had apparently been in the courthouse, but had not been brought into court. The Divisional Court ruled that physical production was not necessary, but that[49]:

> "the objects to which the order is going to be related must be properly identified as being objects which were concerned in the offence, and they must be available for the court to look at, if it wishes to do so."

A person claiming to be the owner, or otherwise interested in what is to be forfeited, has a right to be heard before any order is made.[50]

4. Lotteries and Amusements Act 1976

This Act covers lotteries, prize competitions, and amusements with prizes. It **4.39** contains a power of entry under warrant in section 19 in virtually identical terms to the Betting, Gaming and Lotteries Act 1963, s.51.[51] The only difference is that there is a power to arrest a person found on premises being searched whom the constable has reasonable cause to believe to be committing or to have committed an offence under the Act.[52]

There is the same power to order forfeiture, etc, as under the 1963 Act.[53]

Q. Liquor Licensing

The main provisions giving entry powers in relation to the sale or supply of **4.40** "intoxicating liquor" are to be found in the Licensing Act 1964 ("the 1964 Act").

There is a general power of entry without warrant under section 186.[54] It applies to any licensed premises, a licensed canteen, or premises for which a special hours certificate under section 78 of the Act is in force. It may be exercised by a constable for the purpose of preventing or detecting the commission of offences under the Act. The times at which the power may be exercised vary, according to the nature of the premises. Licensed premises, or a licensed canteen may be entered during the "permitted hours" under the licence, and the first half hour after the end of any period forming part of those hours.[55] He may also enter at any other time when he reasonably suspects that an offence is being, or is about to be committed.[56] Premises subject to an occasional licence may be entered during the hours specified in the

---

[48] [1965] 2 All E.R. 750—the case was actually concerned with s.52(4) of the Betting, Gaming and Lotteries Act 1963.

[49] *Ibid.* 752.

[50] s.46(2). Note also the provisions of s.43(9) concerning fire regulations—see below, para. 9.28.

[51] See above, para. 4.37.

[52] The equivalent provision in the 1963 Act was repealed by the P.C.E.A.

[53] s.20(2).

[54] As substituted by the Licensing (Amendment) Act 1977, s.1. See also the Licensing (Occasional Permissions) Act 1983, below, para. 4.44.

[55] s.186(1A)(*a*).

[56] s.186(1)(*b*).

licence.[57]Premises subject to a special hours certificate, may be entered between 11 p.m. and 30 minutes after the end of the permitted hours (under s.76).[58]

A person who fails, by himself, or by any person acting in his employment or with his consent, to admit a constable demanding entry under this section, commits an offence punishable on summary conviction with a fine not exceeding level 1 on the standard scale.[59]

The 1964 Act also contains three powers of entry under warrant.

1. Retail

4.41   Under section 187 a justice of the peace may issue a search warrant if satisfied by information on oath that there is reasonable ground for believing that intoxicating liquor is being sold by retail,[60] at any place where it may not lawfully be sold by retail. The warrant will authorise a constable to search the place for intoxicating liquor. He may seize and remove any that he finds (together with its containers) which he has reasonable grounds to suppose to be in the place for the purpose of unlawful sale (there or elsewhere).[61] Any person found on premises on which a constable seizes intoxicating liquor under this power is liable, unless he proves that he was there for a lawful purpose, on summary conviction, to a fine not exceeding level 1 on the standard scale.[62]

Where the owner or occupier of the premises is convicted of an offence connected with the sale, exposing for sale, or possession of intoxicating liquor, the liquor and its containers are to be forfeited.[63] While this forfeiture is automatic, and not dependent on any court order, it was held in *R. v. Lewes Justices, ex p. Trustees of the Plumpton and District Club*,[64] interpreting the equivalent provision in the Licensing Act 1953, that it only occurred when *all* "owners and occupiers" had been convicted. Subject to this, forfeited liquor or containers must be sold, or otherwise disposed of at the direction of the court. If sold, the proceeds are to be applied as if they were a fine.[65]

2. Clubs

4.42   In order for a search warrant to be issued under section 54 of the 1964 Act in respect of club premises,[66] a justice of the peace must be satisfied that there are reasonable grounds for believing that one of two sets of circumstances exists. The first is that grounds exist for cancelling, in whole or in part, the club's registration certificate,[67] and that evidence of this is to be obtained at the club premises. The second set of circumstances is that intoxicating liquor is sold or supplied by or on

---

[57] s.186(1A)(*b*).
[58] s.186(1A)(*c*).
[59] s.186(2).
[60] Or exposed or kept for sale by retail.
[61] s.187(1).
[62] s.187(3). There is also an obligation to provide a name and address—s.187(4).
[63] s.187(2).
[64] [1960] 2 All E.R. 476 (D.C.).
[65] s.194(3).
[66] As defined in s.39(6).
[67] The grounds for such cancellation are set out in s.44(2).

behalf of a club in club premises for which the club does not hold a registration certificate or justices' licence, or is kept in club premises for sale or supply in contravention of Part II of the 1964 Act.

The warrant will authorise a constable to enter the club premises, search them, and seize any documents relating to the business of the club.

3. Parties

Section 84(1) of the 1964 Act provides that it is unlawful, outside general licensing **4.43** hours, to supply or consume intoxicating liquor at a party organised for gain, and taking place in premises kept or habitually used for such parties at which intoxicating liquor is consumed. A power to issue a search warrant is given to a justice of the peace who is satisfied by information on oath that there are reasonable grounds for believing that specified premises are kept or habitually used for parties at which the provisions of section 84 are contravened.[68] The warrant will authorise a constable to enter and search the premises, and seize and remove any intoxicating liquor found there which he has reasonable grounds for supposing to be there for the purpose of being supplied or consumed in contravention of section 84(1).

Where a person is convicted of an offence under section 84, any liquor, and its containers, are to be forfeited.[69] Forfeited items should be dealt with in accordance with section 194(3) of the 1964 Act.[70]

4. Occasional permissions

Under the Licensing (Occasional Permissions) Act 1983 justices may authorise **4.44** representatives of organisations not carried on for private gain to sell intoxicating liquor at functions connnected with the activities of their organisations. The Act contains a power of entry without warrant under paragraph 9 of the Schedule to the Act. It is exercisable by a constable in respect of authorised premises, at any time during the hours specified in the occasional permission, for the purpose of preventing or detecting the commission of an offence under the Schedule.[71] This is backed up by the fact that a person who, by himself or through someone acting with his consent, fails to admit a constable who demands entry under this power, commits an offence, punishable on summary conviction with a fine not exceeding level 1 on the standard scale.[72]

5. Sporting events

As part of the attempt to control the consumption of alcohol at sporting events, the **4.45** Secretary of State has power under section 9 of the Sporting Events (Control of Alcohol, etc.) Act 1985 to "designate" grounds or events. Section 7 provides that a constable may at any time during the period of a designated sporting event at any

---

[68] s.85.
[69] s.85(3).
[70] See above, para. 4.41.
[71] Para. 9(1).
[72] Para. 9(2) and 10. *cf.* 1964 Act, ss.186 and 187, above, para. 4.40.

designated sports ground, enter any part of the ground for the purpose of enforcing the provisions of the Act.

R. Entertainments

1. Theatre

4.46　The powers of entry without warrant in relation to premises licensed under the Theatres Act 1968 are dealt with in Chapter Nine.[73] There is also a power, under section 15(1) of the Act to obtain a warrant to enter. A justice of the peace must be satisfied by information on oath that there is reasonable ground for suspecting that a performance of a play involving the commission of an offence under section 2 (obscenity), section 6 (provocation of a breach of the peace), or section 20 of the Public Order Act 1986 (incitement to racial hatred), is to be given at specified premises. The warrant will simply empower a constable to attend any performance given on those premises.

A similar power to obtain a warrant exists where an offence under section 13(1) (unlicensed performance) is suspected. In this case the warrant may be executed by a constable, or an officer of the licensing authority, who will be entitled to inspect the premises.

Neither of the warrants available under section 15(1) involves a power of search, so sections 15 and 16 of the P.C.E.A. will not apply.

2. Cinema

4.47　For the powers of entry under the Cinemas Act 1985, see Chapter Nine.[74]

3. Children

4.48　Where an entertainment for children is provided in a building, or the majority of people attending an entertainment are children, and in either case the number of children attending exceeds 100, section 12 of the Children and Young Persons Act 1933 requires the attendance of an adequate number of adults to control safety.[75] A constable may enter any building in which he has reason to believe that such an entertainment is being, or is about to be, provided, to see whether the provisions of the section are being adhered to.[76] The power does not extend to a private dwelling-house.

4. Hypnotism

4.49　Exhibitions of hypnotism to which the public are admitted are controlled by the Hypnotism Act 1952. A constable may enter any premises where any entertainment

[73] See below, para. 9.61.
[74] See below, para. 9.58.
[75] s.12(1).
[76] s.12(4). A authorised officer of the licensing authority has a similar power as regards a building licensed as a cinema, theatre, or for music and dancing.

is held if he has reasonable cause to believe that anything contrary to the Act is being, or may be, done there.[77]

5. Late Night Refreshment Houses Act 1969

A constable may, at any time when he thinks fit, enter a "late night refreshment house"[78] licensed under the Act. If the licensee, or one of his employees, or any person acting on his direction, refuses admission, he will commit an offence punishable on summary conviction with a fine not exceeding level 4 on the standard scale, or up to three months imprisonment, or both.[79] The constable, in his turn, has a duty to assist in expelling drunken, riotous, quarrelsome, and disorderly persons.[80] **4.50**

S. Copyright

Powers of search in relation to copyright were first given to the police in the Copyright (Amendment) Act 1983. They are now contained in sections 109 (infringing copies) and 200 (illicit recordings) of the Copyright, Designs and Patents Act 1988. A justice of the peace may issue a warrant if satisfied by information on oath that there are reasonable grounds for believing that an offence under section 107 or 198 connected with the making, importation, or distribution of infringing articles or illicit recordings has been or is about to be committed on any premises, or that evidence of such an offence is on the premises. The power does not extend to items subject to legal privilege, or excluded or special procedure material, as defined in the Police and Criminal Evidence Act 1984.[81] Nor, it seems, could the procedures under Schedule 1 of the P.C.E.A. be used in relation to such material. A warrant may authorise persons to accompany the constable to whom the warrant is issued, and will remain in force for 28 days.[82] In reflection to infringing copies, though not illicit recordings, the constable may on entry seize any article if he reasonably believes that it is evidence that *any* offence (not necessarily one for which a search warrant may be issued) under section 107(1) has been or is about to be committed.[83] **4.51**

T. Scrap Metal

Controls over scrap metal dealers are largely in the hands of local authorities, under the Scrap Metal Dealers Act 1964.[84] Section 6(1), however, gives a constable a power of entry without warrant as regards a place registered under the Act as a scrap metal store, or as occupied by a scrap metal dealer for the purposes of his business. On entry the constable may require the production of, and inspect, any scrap metal, **4.52**

[77] s.4.
[78] As defined in s.1.
[79] s.10(1).
[80] s.10(2).
[81] ss.109(2), 200(2).
[82] ss.109(3), 200(3).
[83] s.109(4).
[84] See below, para. 9.21.

and any books or receipts required to be kept under the Act. He may take copies of or extracts from such books and receipts.

No force may be used to obtain entry under this power.[85] But obstructing a right of entry or inspection, or failing to produce books or documents, is a summary offence, punishable with a fine not exceeding level 1 on the standard scale.

U. Incitement to Racial Hatred

4.53   The Public Order Act 1986 created a new offence of possession of racially inflammatory material.[86] Under section 24 a search warrant may be obtained from a justice who is satisfied by information on oath laid by a constable that there are reasonable grounds for suspecting that a person is in possession of such material in contravention of section 23. Reasonable force may be used, if necessary, to enter and search the premises where it is suspected the material is situated.[87]

"Excluded" or "special procedure" material, or items subject to legal privilege have no special status under this Act.[88] This could be significant where allegedly racially inflammatory is being held with a view to publication in a "newssheet", and is therefore arguably journalistic material.[89]

---

[85] If force is needed the constable would have to seek a warrant under s.6(3)—see below, para. 9.21.
[86] s.23.
[87] s.24(3) "Premises" includes vehicles, vessels, aircraft or hovercraft; offshore installations; and any tent or movable structure; s.24(4).
[88] See above, paras. 3.12, 3.28.
[89] See above, paras. 3.14-3.15.

CHAPTER FIVE

CIVIL PROCEDURES

At two points in the civil process power may be given to one of the parties to an **5.01** action to enter on to the premises of another. At an early stage, before trial, and in some cases even before the issue of a writ, a plaintiff may be allowed to obtain an order requiring the defendant (or potential defendant) to give access to his property for the purpose of obtaining evidence.

At the other end of the process, a debt may in some circumstances be enforced by seizing the debtor's property. The two circumstances where this may arise are in the execution of a judgment of a court, and through distress for rent, rates, or taxes. Only enforcement of judgments and distress for rent are dealt with in this chapter, distress for taxes and rates being dealt with in Chapters Six, Seven and Nine.

I. OBTAINING EVIDENCE—THE "ANTON PILLER" ORDER

Under Order 29, r. 2 of the Rules of the Supreme Court, the High Court has a **5.02** general power to authorise entry on to the property of any party to an action in order that property which is the subject-matter of the action, or about which questions may arise in the course of the action, may be detained, preserved or inspected. Technological developments in the area of communications, and in particular the increasing availability of ever cheaper means of recording sound and pictures by means of cassettes and tapes, have fed the amazing growth since the mid-seventies of a related order, sometimes called a "civil search warrant." These "warrants" are in fact orders issued by the High Court (most often the Chancery Division), *ex parte*, under the authority of the above order, combined with the inherent jurisdiction of the court to make orders of this type in order to preserve evidence.[1] They are generally known as *Anton Piller* orders, after the plaintiffs in the first case of this type to receive the seal of approval of the Court of Appeal.[2]

In that case the plaintiffs were concerned that their agents in England were **5.03** revealing trade secrets to the plaintiffs' rivals. In particular it was thought that the secrets surrounding a valuable new product were in danger. So they applied to the

---

[1] *cf.* the almost parallel development of the "Mareva Injunction," from *Nippon Yusen Kaisha* v. *Karageorgis* [1975] 2 Ll.Rep. 137 and *Mareva Compania Naviera SA* v. *International Bulkcarriers SA* [1975] 2 Ll.Rep. 509. The parallel lines have now met in such cases as *Johnson* v. *L & A. Philatelics Ltd.* [1981] F.S.R. 286.

[2] *Piller K.G.* v. *Manufacturing Processes* [1976] 1 Ch. 55. As the Court of Appeal pointed out, judges at first instance in several previous cases had been prepared to grant the order, the only reported example being *E.M.I. Ltd.* v. *Pandit* [1975] 1 W.L.R. 302.

Chancery Division, *ex parte* because of the need not to alert the agents to their suspicions, for interim injunctions against the defendants, restraining them from further breach of copyright or disclosure of confidential information. These were granted, but the plaintiffs also sought a further order that they should be allowed into the defendant's premises to inspect all documents and articles relating to the plaintiffs' products, and to remove certain articles into the custody of the plaintiffs' solicitors. Brightman J. refused to grant this further order, and the plaintiffs appealed.

The Court of Appeal unanimously reversed Brightman J.'s ruling, and allowed the order to be made in the form suggested. In the course of so doing the Court of Appeal laid down a number of guidelines and safeguards, which have, for the most part, been adhered to in later cases.[3]

It was the fact that the application was *ex parte*, preventing the defendant from challenging the issue of the order, which most concerned the Court of Appeal. Indeed, apart from this aspect, the order for inspection and delivery up was governed by previous authority,[4] and by R.S.C., Ord. 29, r. 2(1) and (2).[5]

5.04   The Court of Appeal, however, thought that it was necessary to accept the realities of the situation, which were that there was a real danger of evidence being suppressed. This evidence was vital to the plaintiffs' action in protecting their rights, and it was therefore proper to issue the order. Nevertheless, Lord Denning was careful to point out the limits to what was being ordered.[6]

> "[T]he order sought in this case is not a search warrant. It does not authorise the plaintiffs' solicitors or anyone else to enter the defendant's premises against his will. It does not authorise the breaking down of any doors, nor the slipping in by a back door, nor getting in by an open door or window. It only authorises entry and inspection by permission of the defendant. The plaintiffs must get the defendants' permission. But it does do this: it brings pressure on the defendants to give permission—with, I suppose, the result that if they do not give permission, they are guilty of contempt of court."

Once the enforcement of the order is backed up by the threat of contempt proceedings, the differences between this and a search warrant exercised by a police officer, backed up by the threat of criminal proceedings for obstruction, perhaps appear a little subtle.[7] But there are other safeguards for the defendant, dealt with below, which mean that the division between the two types of procedure is distinct, though by no means broad.

The whole practice and procedure surrounding *Anton Piller* orders was compre-

---

[3] See below, para. 5.07 for the guidelines, But N.B. the comments of Whitford J. in *Systematica Ltd.* v. *London Computer Centre* [1983] F.S.R. 313, criticising the too free use of *Anton Piller* orders.
[4] *i.e. United Company of Merchants of England, Trading to the East Indies* v. *Kynaston* (1821) 3 Bl.(o.s.) 153.
[5] *Piller K.G.* v. *Manufacturing Processes* [1976] 1 Ch. 55, 56, *per* Lord Denning.
[6] *Ibid.* p. 60.
[7] As Lord Denning acknowledged in the next sentence of his judgment. *cf.* the comments of Scott J. in *Columbia Picture Industries Inc.* v. *Robinson* [1986] 3 All E.R. 338, 367.

hensively reviewed by Scott J. in *Columbia Picture Industries Inc.* v. *Robinson.*[8] He was very critical of the recent use of the orders, feeling that they had been granted too readily, and with insufficient safeguards for respondents.[9] His specific criticisms are considered at the appropriate points below.

Having considered the general nature of the order, its various aspects are now **5.05** examined in more detail, in the following order:

1. The timing of the application.
2. The circumstances in which the order will be made.
3. The form of the order.
4. The exercise of the order.
5. Challenging the order.
6. Use of the information acquired.
7. Failure to comply, and contempt.

1. Timing of the application

An application for an *Anton Piller* order will often be made before a writ has been **5.06** issued. Normally the application will be supported by affidavits sworn by the plaintiff. It was, however, accepted by the Court of Appeal in *WEA Records Ltd.* v. *Visions Channel 4 Ltd*[10] that in cases of sufficient urgency an order might be granted where the plaintiff's counsel was "armed only with a draft writ and instructions as to the nature and results of the plaintiffs' inquiries."[11] But the court disapproved of the fact that the judge in that case had received information from the plaintiffs' counsel which the plaintiffs were not prepared to give to the defendants' solicitors.

If the application is granted before a writ has been issued, the plaintiff should be expected to undertake to issue one forthwith. And the Court of Appeal has made it clear, in *Hytrac Conveyors* v. *Conveyors International*[12] that the order must not be used simply as a "fishing expedition" to discover evidence on which to found a later action[13]:

> "Those who make the charges must state right at the beginning what they are, and what facts they are based on. They must not use the Anton Piller orders as a means of finding out what charges they can make."

The element of secrecy which is of such importance in *Anton Piller* proceedings, and justifies the application being heard *ex parte*, means that it should also be heard *in camera*. It is the responsibility of the applicant's counsel to make it clear at the outset that the nature of the application requires this.[14] An appeal against the refusal

---

[8] [1986] 3 All E.R. 338.
[9] *Ibid.* 371.
[10] [1983] 2 All E.R. 589.
[11] *Ibid.* 591.
[12] [1982] 3 All E.R. 415.
[13] *Ibid.* 418.
[14] *Vapormatic Co. Ltd.* v. *Sparex Ltd.* [1978] F.S.R. 451, 454.

of an *ex parte* order[15] should generally be heard in open court, relying on the discretion of the law reporters and the press. If counsel for the applicant feels for some special reason that the appeal should be heard *in camera*, he should give his reasons in writing to the registrar. This would not be a submission on behalf of his client, but a statement of his personal professional view. The court should then decide whether proceedings are to be *in camera* or not.[16]

2. In what circumstances will the order be made?

5.07   Many of the subsequent cases on *Anton Piller* orders have referred back to the three essential preconditions for the making of the order set down by Ormrod L.J.[17] These were that

    (a) there must be an extremely strong prima facie case.
    (b) the damage to the plaintiff, potential or actual, must be very serious.
    (c) there must be clear evidence that the defendants have in their possession incriminating documents or things, and that there is a real possibility that they may destroy such material before any application *inter partes* can be made.

5.08   These requirements are to be read in conjunction with Ormrod L.J.'s view that, since the order is at the extremity of the courts' powers, it should only be used where there is no alternative way of ensuring that justice is done to the applicant.[18] Or as Shaw L.J. put it "where the normal processes of law would be rendered nugatory if some immediate and effective measure was not available."[19]

Ormrod L.J. thought that *Anton Piller* orders would be made only "very rarely." In fact, largely owing to the technological developments noted earlier, the orders have been sought and granted on a regular basis since 1976. In *Columbia Picture Industries Inc.* v. *Robinson*[20] it was stated that one firm of solicitors alone obtained some 300 orders in a 10-year period: *i.e.* an average of two to three each month. In practice, Ormrod L.J.'s three conditions have not been considered quite as strictly as he might have intended.[21]

Of the conditions, the ones which the courts have been most inclined to play down have been the second, to the extent that it calls for *very serious* damage, and the second part of the third, referring to the likelihood of evidence being destroyed.[22] So that at times it has seemed almost enough for the plaintiff to show simply a very strong prima facie case combined with evidence that relevant documents or articles are in

---

[15] See below, paras. 5.26–5.31, re appeals against an order.
[16] *Practice Note* [1982] 3 All E.R. 924 (C.A.).
[17] *Piller K.G.* v. *Manufacturing Processes* [1976] 1 Ch. 55, 62.
[18] *Ibid.* 61.
[19] *Ibid.* 63.
[20] [1986] 3 All E.R. 338, 369.
[21] See the remarks to this effect by Wilkinson J. in *Thermax Ltd.* v. *Schott Industrial Glass* [1981] F.S.R. 289, 298, and Whitford J. in *Systematica* v. *London Computer Centre* [1983] F.S.R. 313 and *Jeffrey Rogers Knitwear Productions Ltd.* v. *Vinola (Knitwear) Manufacturing Co.* [1985] F.S.R. 184, 189, in addition to Scott J.'s comprehensive criticism in *Columbia Picture Industries Inc.* v. *Robinson* [1986] 3 All E.R. 338, 372.
[22] See the dissenting judgment of Donaldson L.J. in *Yousif* v. *Salama* [1980] 1 W.L.R. 1540, 1543.

the defendant's possession. Later cases have, however, reasserted the importance of the defendant's "character."[23]

It is because of this that it becomes vital that the court should act in full knowledge **5.09** of all relevant circumstances. Affidavits in support of an application "ought to err on the side of excessive disclosure."[24] For example, the fact that the defendant is not simply a one-man business, but is a subsidiary of a large and well-respected corporation may well be crucial in deciding whether the defendant is likely to abscond or destroy the evidence.[25] If the plaintiff fails to reveal the true nature of the company to the court, then the order may well be set aside on the defendant's application.[26] In *Randolph M. Fields* v. *Watts*,[27] the Court of Appeal held that it was not appropriate to issue an order against practising barristers and their clerks, since there was no possibility of documents being concealed or destroyed.

The main use of the order has been in copyright and passing-off cases, but there is **5.10** no reason why it should be limited to these areas provided the other conditions for its issue are satisfied. In *Emanuel* v. *Emanuel*[28] the court made an order in relation to an application for ancillary relief in divorce. The previous attitude of the husband had showed that he was ready to "flout the authority of [the] court and to mislead it if he thinks it is to his advantage to do so."[29] As a consequence the judge felt that the normal process of law was liable to be rendered nugatory.

> "I am quite satisfied that the wife has a strong prima facie case to the effect that relevant documentation has not been produced in the past and is most unlikely to be produced in the future without the present order. Such essential documents are at risk."

In these circumstances Wood J. thought that it was appropriate, and within the limits set by the Court of Appeal to make an *Anton Piller* order, enabling the wife to inspect and copy those documents in the husband's possession which were relevant to her claim.[30]

In reaching this decision, Wood J. placed considerable reliance on the Court of Appeal's decision in *Yousif* v. *Salama*.[31] This case was also concerned with access to documents and information, rather than the seizing of infringing copies (which is the main object in the copyright area). In *Yousif* v. *Salama* the applicant was a commission agent who was trying to recover his commission from the defendant, and was

---

[23] See *Thermax Ltd.* v. *Schott Industrial Glass* [1981] F.S.R. 289; *Dunlop Holdings* v. *Staravia* [1982] Com.L.R. 3; and *Randolph M. Fields* v. *Watts, The Times*, November 22, 1984.

[24] Scott J. in *Columbia Picture Industries Inc.* v. *Robinson* [1986] 3 All E.R. 338, 372.

[25] See *Thermax Ltd.* v. *Schott Industrial Glass* [1981] F.S.R. 289, and *cf. Gallery Cosmetics Ltd.* v. *Number One* [1981] F.S.R. 556 (Ch.D.).

[26] See also below, para. 5.30. But the lack of disclosure must be important: *Gallery Cosmetics* v. *Number One* [1981] F.S.R. 556.

[27] *The Times*, November 11, 1984.

[28] [1982] 2 All E.R. 342; [1982] 1 W.L.R. 669 (Fam.D.).

[29] *Ibid.* 348.

[30] An order was granted in a similar situation in *K.* v. *K.* (1983) 13 Fam.Law. 46. For a discussion of the use of *Anton Piller* orders in the Family Division see Meisel (1982) 12 Fam.Law 123. See also *Collins* v. *Collins* [1987] 1 F.L.R. 226.

[31] [1980] 1 W.L.R. 1540.

concerned about the safety of certain accounts which he had seen in the defendant's possession. The Court of Appeal (Donaldson J. dissenting) considered that the documents were vital to the applicant's action, that there was prima facie evidence that they were at risk, and that the order should therefore be made.[32]

5.11   In two cases the courts have allowed the order to be used to protect the applicant's rights *vis-à-vis* a third party. In *Ex p. Island Records*[33] the defendant's "bootlegging" activities—*i.e.* making unauthorised recordings from live performances—involved criminal offences under the Dramatic and Musical Performers' Protection Act 1958, but no breach of copyright. However, a record company had exclusive agreements with the performers, and the Court of Appeal (Shaw L.J. dissenting) held that these agreements constituted sufficient private rights over property that the applicant was entitled to use the remedies sought to prevent the defendant's unlawful interference with them. In *Lonhro* v. *Shell Petroleum*,[34] however, doubts were cast on the correctness of this decision, and the Court of Appeal in *R.C.A.* v. *Pollard*[35] considered that it must be taken as being overruled. There was no interference with the performance of a contract, only a reduction in its value. This was not enough on which to base a cause of action. The position is further complicated by the decision in *Rickless* v. *United Artists*[36] where the Court of Appeal held that the 1958 Act does give a civil right of action to *performers*: the decision in *Pollard* was limited to the position of recording companies. The Copyright, Designs and Patents Act 1988, however, makes it a breach of statutory duty to infringe the rights of performers, or those owning recording rights.[36a] This would seem to restore the position to that following the Court of Appeal's decision in *Ex p. Island Records*.

The second case in which a third party's rights were taken into account was *Carlin Music Corporation* v. *Collins*.[37] Here, the Mechanical Copyright Protection Society Ltd. (the M.C.P.S.), which was the collecting agent for certain copyright holders, sought an *Anton Piller* order as a result of the defendant's alleged illegal import of records. Such illegal imports would result in lost fees and a drop in commission for the M.C.P.S. Megarry V.-C. refused the order because he felt that the Society had not made out a prima facie case that the defendant had committed the tort of interference with the plaintiff's business by unlawful means. He felt that this case lacked the necessary interference between a third party and the plaintiff, and that the tort did not extend to cases which simply involved the non-payment of debts. The Court of Appeal allowed the appeal by the M.C.P.S., holding that the potential loss of commission constituted a sufficient interference with the Society's business. Moreover they were not seeking to enforce a debt, but suing in tort for damages (which would be measured by the amount of lost fees).

---

[32] See below, n. 39 for the particular form of the order in this case.
[33] [1978] 1 Ch. 122.
[34] [1981] 2 All E.R. 456 (H.L.).
[35] [1983] Ch. 135.
[36] [1987] 1 All E.R. 679.
[36a] s.194.
[37] [1979] F.S.R. 548.

This case, together with *Emanuel* v. *Emanuel* shows that the potential scope for the **5.12** use of the order is very wide.[38] It is available for use not only in respect of the protection of copyright holders themselves, but also their agents, and, it seems, in any cases where evidence relevant to some legal action by the applicant against the defendant is in danger.[39]

3. The form of the order

In a number of cases the full text of the order has been published.[40] This, together **5.13** with the comments of judges in other cases as to what the order should contain, makes it possible to give some account of the elements which must be, or which typically are, included in an *Anton Piller* order.

If the order is sought before a writ has been issued, it will normally be on the basis of affidavits provided by the applicants.[41] The order should have attached to it these affidavits, or copies of other evidence on the strength of which the order was obtained.[42] This is to enable the defendant to see what is being alleged against him, and so make it more practicable for him to exercise his right to challenge the order.[43]

There will follow a number of undertakings by the applicant. These will normally **5.14** include an undertaking that service will be by a solicitor (as an officer of the court); that anything removed will be retained by the applicant's solicitor in safe custody; that the applicant will abide by any order of the court as to damages to be paid to the defendant as a result of the *Anton Piller* order. It will probably include an undertaking not to use any documents, articles, or information obtained under the order save for the purpose of civil proceedings connected with the current dispute between the parties.[44] Breach of these undertakings may involve the plaintiff in the payment of substantial damages,[45] as well as providing the basis for a challenge to the order itself.[46] The consequences of a breach of these undertakings is considered further below in relation to the defendant's right to challenge the order.[47]

---

[38] Note also *Loose* v. *Williamson* [1978] 1 W.L.R. 639, where a similar *ex parte* order was granted in relation to an action alleging infringement of fishing rights. The decision in this case would now fall foul of the ruling of the House of Lords in the *Rank* case, below, paras. 5.17–5.20 and would not be rescued by the Supreme Court Act 1981, s.72.

[39] See also *Yousif* v. *Salama* [1980] 1 W.L.R. 1540; and *Johnson* v. *L. & A. Philatelics Ltd.* [1981] F.S.R. 286, where an *Anton Piller* order was used in conjunction with a *Mareva* injunction to take into custody certain of the defendant's property which it was feared would otherwise be removed from the country, leaving insufficient assets to meet a debt allegedly owed to the applicant. But *cf.* now *C.B.S.* v. *Lambert* [1982] 3 All E.R. 237.

[40] *e.g. Vapormatic Co. Ltd.* v. *Sparex Ltd.* [1976] F.S.R. 451, 455; *Gates* v. *Swift* [1981] F.S.R. 57; *Johnson* v. *L & A. Philatelics* [1981] F.S.R. 286; *Emanuel* v. *Emanuel* [1982] 2 All E.R. 342, 349; [1982] 1 W.L.R. 669, 678; *Columbia Picture Industries* v. *Robinson* [1986] 3 All E.R. 338.

[41] But see *WEA Records Ltd.* v. *Visions Channel 4 Ltd.* [1983] 2 All E.R. 589, above, para. 5.06.

[42] See the comments of Graham J. in *International Electronics Ltd.* v. *WeighData Ltd., The Times*, March 13, 1980.

[43] As to which see below, paras. 5.27–5.31.

[44] Though the orders in *Johnson* v. *L. & A. Philatelics Ltd.* [1981] F.S.R. 286, and *Emanuel* v. *Emanuel* [1982] 2 All E.R. 342, [1982] 1 W.L.R. 669 contained no such undertaking. Would one be implied anyway? *cf. Home Office* v. *Harman* [1983] 1 A.C. 280, and see *Sony* v. *Anand* [1981] F.S.R. 398.

[45] In *Columbia Picture Industries* v. *Robinson* [1986] 3 All E.R. 338, the sum of £10,000.

[46] See below, para. 5.29.

[47] *Ibid.*

In appropriate cases, *e.g.* where the defendant is unlikely to have legal advice readily available, there may also be an undertaking that the solicitor serving the order should offer to explain its meaning and effect in everyday language.[48]

Following the undertakings come the mandatory orders addressed to the defendant. These will usually require him first to refrain from dealing with the articles, documents, etc., which are relevant to the action until after a specified date. Then will come the order peculiar to this type of procedure, *viz.*, that the defendant shall allow certain specified people to enter the premises. The number ordered to be allowed to enter will be small—perhaps four or five—made up of two representatives of the applicant, and two or three from the applicant's solicitors. The premises themselves must be identified clearly. General words, such as "premises under the control of" the defendant will not be allowed in the absence of some special reason.[49]

It is unclear whether the courts have the power to make an order exercisable in premises outside the jurisdiction. In *Protector Alarms* v. *Maxim Alarms*[50] the applicant sought an order in relation to premises in Scotland. Without deciding that he had no power to do so, Goulding J. exercised his discretion to refuse the order. It was preferable that the applicant should seek relief from the Court of Session, if possible. In *Altertext* v. *Advanced Data*,[51] however, Scott J. took the view that since an *Anton Piller* order acts *in personam*, it would be permissible to serve it on a defendant within the jurisdiction in respect of premises outside it. But here the applicant was seeking service out of the jurisdiction, which Scott J. refused to allow without giving the defendant a chance to challenge leave under R.S.C., Order 11. This, of course, would have defeated the purpose of the *Anton Piller* order.

5.15 A specific period during which the order may be exercised will be set out in the order, *e.g.* "on any weekday at any time between 9 o'clock in the morning and 7 o'clock in the evening."[52] The outer limits of the times appearing in orders which have been published have been 8 a.m. and 10 p.m. There does not seem to be any particular reason for the choice of times, other than that it is clear that the courts expect the order to be served during the day or early evening. This emphasises the fact that there should be a great difference between the civilised entry and search under an order of the court, and a police "raid."[53]

5.16 Assuming that the applicant gains entry to the defendant's premises, the order may then empower him to do a number of things:

    (a) search for and inspect various items or classes of items, which should be clearly specified by the order. If they are in the custody of a third party the court should follow the guidelines set out in *Z Ltd.* v. *A-Z and AA-LL*[54];

---

[48] See, *e.g. Emanuel* v. *Emanuel* [1982] 2 All E.R. 342; [1982] 1 W.L.R. 669; *Gates* v. *Swift* [1981]F.S.R. 57.

[49] *Protector Alarms* v. *Maxim Alarms* [1978] F.S.R. 442 (Ch.D.).

[50] [1978] F.S.R. 442 (Ch.D.).

[51] [1985] 1 All E.R. 395.

[52] *Gates* v. *Swift* [1981] F.S.R. 57, 58.

[53] But *cf. I.T.C. Film Distributors Ltd.* v. *Video Exchange Ltd.*, *The Times*, November 18, 1981, below, para. 5.23.

[54] [1982] Q.B. 558 (C.A.). See *C.B.S. United Kingdom Ltd.* v. *Lambert* [1983] Ch. 37 (C.A.).

(b) remove items into the custody of the applicant's solicitor. If the court is not satisfied that the applicant's solicitor has suitable safe custody for what is to be removed it should appoint a receiver[55]

(c) take photographs or make copies;

(d) test machinery.[56]

The above is not intended to be a comprehensive list of what may be ordered; that is limited only by what the applicant is seeking and what the court thinks it appropriate to allow. In *Bayer AG* v. *Winter*[57] the Court of Appeal granted an injunction restraining the defendant from leaving the jurisdiction, and ordering the surrender of his passport to the person serving the *Anton Piller* order. Because, however, this involved a serious interference with the liberty of the subject, the extent of the order was limited to the time thought necessary to execute the *Anton Piller* order—in this case two days.[58]

In addition to these orders involving the discovery, examination, and delivery of **5.17** articles or documents, the defendant may well be ordered to disclose the names and addresses of those with whom he has had relevant business dealings. This type of addition to the *Anton Piller* order received the approval of the Court of Appeal in *E.M.I. Ltd.* v. *Sarwar Haidar.*[59] It has proved very useful in the copyright area in enabling the copyright holder to catch all the participants in what may be a fairly complex chain of activity, by obtaining an *Anton Piller* order against one link in the chain. In *Rank Film Distributors Ltd.* v. *Video Information Centre,*[60] this type of order was challenged in that it might involve the defendant in self-incrimination. The House of Lords accepted that where the information sought might show involvement in a serious crime such as conspiracy to defraud, the defendant should not be compelled to reveal it.[61] The very limiting effect which this decision might have had on the usefulness of the *Anton Piller* order was swiftly removed by Parliament in the Supreme Court Act 1981. Section 72 of this Act provides that, in certain circumstances, incriminating evidence, provided as a result of compliance with an order, will not be admissible against the person, or the spouse of the person, from whom the evidence was obtained, in subsequent proceedings for certain criminal offences.[62] Given this protection from having the evidence used against him, the defendant's right to refuse to answer is removed.[63]

---

[55] *Ibid.*

[56] *e.g. E.M.I. Ltd.* v. *Pandit* [1975] 1 All E.R. 418 (Ch.D.)—testing typewriters to see if they had been used in connection with an alleged forgery.

[57] [1986] 1 All E.R. 733.

[58] See also *Bayer* v. *Winter (No. 2)* [1986] 2 All E.R. 43, where Scott J. refused to extend this order to allow time for the defendant to be cross-examined.

[59] [1977] F.S.R. 146.

[60] [1982] A.C. 380.

[61] This does not apply, it seems, where it would show liability for a petty offence, *e.g.* under s.21 of the Copyright Act 1956—see Lord Wilberforce [1982] A.C. 380, 441.

[62] s.72(3). For the relevant criminal offences, see below, para. 5.19.

[63] s.72(1).

5.18   The section does not, however, apply to all orders, but only to those issued in connection with civil proceedings in the High Court[64]:

(a) for infringement of rights pertaining to any intellectual property or passing-off;
(b) brought to obtain disclosure of information relating to any infringement of such rights or to any passing-off; or
(c) brought to prevent any apprehended infringement of such rights, or any apprehended passing-off.[65]

5.19   "Intellectual property" is defined as "any patent, trade mark, copyright, registered design, technical or commercial information or other intellectual property." The most common situations in which the *Anton Piller* order has been used will clearly fall within the scope of the section. It must be doubtful, however, whether cases such as *Carlin Music Corporation* v. *Collins*[66] which involved a kind of indirect copyright protection, would fall within the section. However, it may be that the situation would be regarded as being sufficiently analogous to the protection of intellectual property to receive benefit of the section. In other cases it will depend on how far the court is prepared to stretch the phrase "rights pertaining to some intellectual property" in section 72(2).

It is clear, of course, that cases involving the wider use of the *Anton Piller* order (*e.g. Emanuel* v. *Emanuel*) fall outside the scope of section 72, and the *Rank* decision will still apply to them. This is discussed further below.[67]

In situations where section 72 does apply, the proceedings in which evidence will be inadmissible are, where infringement is alleged to have taken place already, proceedings for any offence committed by or in the course of the copyright infringement or passing-off, or any offence involving fraud or dishonesty committed in connection with that infringement or passing-off.[68] Where, however, the infringement is merely apprehended, the evidence will be inadmissible in proceedings for *any offence* revealed by the facts on which the applicant relies in his action to prevent the infringement.[69] In *Universal City Studios* v. *Hubbard*[70] the Court of Appeal had no doubt that the wider wording of section 72(5)(*b*) should be given its full effect. The fact that the evidence obtained by the exercise of the order might have shown that the defendant was involved in copying pornographic films on to tape did not take the case outside the scope of section 72. The privilege was lost, though of course the evidence could not be used in any subsequent proceedings.

In any case evidence will always be admissible in proceedings for perjury or contempt.[71]

---

[64] Or on appeal from the High Court, s.72(6).
[65] s.72(2).
[66] [1979] F.S.R. 548.
[67] See para. 5.20.
[68] s.72(5)(*a*).
[69] s.72(5)(*b*). N.B. proceedings for a "related penalty" are also covered.
[70] [1984] 1 All E.R. 661.
[71] s.72(4). It is doubtful whether the privilege extends to these offences anyway: see para. 5.20, below.

Residual applicability of the Rank decision

Because of the limited scope of section 72 there is still life left in the House of Lords **5.20**
decision in *Rank Film Distributors* v. *Video Information Centre*[72] and it is necessary to
consider the precise effect of the case.

It was given some consideration by Wood J. in *Emanuel* v. *Emanuel*.[73] There was
prima facie evidence that the husband might have committed perjury, and Wood J.
felt obliged to consider whether any provision should be made in order to protect
him from self-incrimination. Referring to the case of *Rice* v. *Gordon*[74] he found that
there was no reason to make such provision. In *Rice* v. *Gordon*, which had also
concerned the danger of the defendant incriminating himself as regards perjury, the
Vice-Chancellor, Sir L. Shadwell, had drawn the distinction between offences
committed prior to the institution of proceedings between the parties, and those
committed during the proceedings themselves, such as perjury. In the latter case, to
allow the defendant to plead self-incrimination would be "holding out an induce-
ment to a defendant to commit perjury in an early stage of the cause, in order to
prevent the Court from administering justice in the suit." *Rice* v. *Gordon* had been
cited (without disapproval) in the Court of Appeal in the *Rank* case[75] and since in the
present case the possible perjury had been committed in an earlier stage in the
proceedings between husband and wife, Wood J. felt able to follow it and not require
any special clause to be inserted in the order to encourage the husband to invoke the
principle of privilege against self-incrimination. Presumably the same reasoning
would apply to any criminal prosecution arising out of the conduct of the suit itself,
e.g. for contempt.[76]

If the criminal offence is committed before the start of proceedings, then the
privilege will undoubtedly apply in most cases, the only doubts arising in connection
with "petty offences," particularly those which are committed in the course of the
very acts concerning which the civil proceedings have been instituted. It was not
necessary for the House of Lords to decide this in *Rank*, since far more serious
offences were also involved, but there was a clear reluctance among their Lordships
to allow possible liability for some minor, and possibly regulatory, offence, to give
rise to the privilege.[77] This distinction does not appear in any other of the authorities
or statutes related to privilege, *e.g.* the Civil Evidence Act 1968, s.4, which refers
simply to "criminal offences under the law of any part of the United Kingdom and
penalties provided for by such law."

4. The exercise of the order

(a) *Service*

On arrival at the defendant's premises the order must be served and accepted **5.21**

[72] [1982] A.C. 380.
[73] [1982] 2 All E.R. 342; [1982] 1 W.L.R. 669 (Fam.D.).
[74] (1843) 13 Sim. 580.
[75] [1982] A.C. 380, 422.
[76] *cf.* Supreme Court Act 1981, s.72(4).
[77] See, *e.g.* [1982] A.C. 380, 441, *per* Lord Wilberforce.

before it may be exercised. It does not permit the applicant or his solicitors to walk through an open door, much less to use force to gain entry; they must obtain the permission of the defendant or his representative. To facilitate service, the order may be specifically addressed to the defendant's servants and agents, as well as the defendant himself, and it may be provided that service on any apparently responsible person appearing to be in charge of the premises shall be deemed to be good service of the order.[78] The undertakings may require the applicant's solicitors to explain to the defendant, or his representative, in everyday language, the meaning and effect of the order,[79] and point out the desirability of obtaining legal advice before accepting service.[80] Once this has been done, or at least been attempted,[81] and service of the order has been accepted, the applicant may enter to carry out the terms of the order.[82]

(b) *Execution*

5.22   In *Columbia Picture Industries* v. *Robinson*,[83] Scott J. made a number of comments on the way in which orders should be executed. These arose out of concern about the circumstances of that case, but were stated in general terms, and so could well act as guidelines for the future.

Scott J. thought that no material should be taken from the defendant's premises unless clearly covered by the terms of the order. There should be no attempt to persuade the defendant to consent to the removal of additional material, at least in the absence of the defendant's solicitor.

A detailed record should be made of the material taken *before* it is removed from the defendant's premises.

Where material has been taken it should only be retained for as short a period as necessary. Once the plaintiff's solicitors have satisfied themselves as to what the material is, and have had a chance to take copies, it ought to be returned. Furthermore, it is inappropriate that material the ownership of which is in dispute should be retained by the plaintiff's solicitors pending the trial. If, for example, allegedly pirate tapes have been seized, they should, as soon as possible, be delivered to the defendant's solicitors, on their undertaking for safe custody, and production, if required, in court.

(c) *The role of the police*

5.23   The execution of an *Anton Piller* order, relying as has been seen on the permission of the defendant before it can be put into effect, ought to be a peaceful affair. In some cases, however, the applicant fears trouble, and informs the local police with a view to obtaining, if possible, the presence of a uniformed officer at the premises when the

---

[78] *e.g. Gates* v. *Swift* [1981] F.S.R. 57, 59.
[79] *V.D.U. Installations Ltd.* v. *Integrated Computer Systems and Cybernetics Ltd.*, *The Times*, August 13, 1988. Failure to fulfil this undertaking led to the solicitor being in contempt of court.
[80] See above, para. 5.14.
[81] *Columbia Picture Industries* v. *Robinson* [1986] 3 All E.R. 338, 357, 375–376.
[82] For the position if the entry is refused, see below, para. 5.34.
[83] [1986] 3 All E.R. 338, 371–372.

order is served, to forestall any breach of the peace. This was described as "normal practice" in *Columbia Picture Industries* v. *Robinson*.[84] The officer will remain outside the premises unless a breach of the peace does occur. Such a procedure received judicial approval from Warner J. in *ITC Film Distributors Ltd.* v. *Video Exchange Ltd.*[85] But he did not approve the rather different police involvement which in fact occurred in that case.

The police obtained a search warrant under the Obscene Publications Act 1959, s.3,[86] on the same day that the *Anton Piller* order was made. By arrangement, the applicant's representatives and the police went to the defendant's premises together. The police produced the search warrant, and 11 police officers, in plain clothes, entered the premises, together with the five representatives of the applicant permitted by the *Anton Piller* order. The defendant was cautioned by the police, and the *Anton Piller* order was then served. After taking advice from his solicitor, the defendant allowed the *Anton Piller* searches to take place.

It was clear that there was nothing inherently wrong with the procedure adopted **5.24** either as to the search warrant, or as to the *Anton Piller* order. But the fact that they were executed simultaneously inevitably led to some confusion as to who was who. At one stage the plaintiff's solicitor was thought to be a police officer. Warner J. felt that the presence of the police made the execution of the *Anton Piller* order more oppressive than it should have been. He also felt very strongly that the judge from whom the *Anton Piller* order was obtained should have been told of the plans to execute the order and the search warrant at the same time "so that he could, if he thought fit, have included in his order provisions to prevent it having an excessively oppressive result." The Court of Appeal agreed that the circumstances of the exercise of the order in this case were unfortunate and regrettable.[87] But they were not so serious as to warrant discharging the order, and Warner J.'s ruling to this effect was overturned.

So if the police are to be involved in more than a supervisory role when an *Anton Piller* order is executed, the applicant must inform the judge issuing the order. Such involvement should be avoided altogether, if possible.

(d) *Effect of irregularities in the execution of the order*

The irregularities in the case just discussed were, in the opinion of the judge, not **5.25** related to the execution of the order but to its granting. What if the execution is irregular because of the number of people who enter, or because property not covered by the order is removed, or because premises, or parts of premises, not covered by the order are entered? In *Fletcher Sutcliffe Wilde Ltd.* v. *Burch*[88] Peter Gibson J. had to consider the effect of more people than were mentioned in the order (six, instead of the permitted five) taking part in its execution. He had no doubt that

[84] [1986] 3 All E.R. 338, 353.
[85] *The Times*, November 18, 1981.
[86] For which see Chapter Four, para. 4.06.
[87] *The Times*, June 17, 1982.
[88] [1982] F.S.R. 65.

this amounted to a trespass on the part of those executing the order. But he was also of the view that the remedy for the defendant lay not in a counterclaim, nor in an attempt to enforce the applicant's undertaking as to damages,[89] but in a separate action for trespass. One of the main reasons for this was that the action would be brought in the Queen's Bench Division, where the courts would be far more used than the judges in the Chancery Division to dealing with claims for damages, in particular for such things as nervous shock, and personal distress and embarrassment.[90] In *Columbia Picture Industries* v. *Robinson*,[91] however, Scott J. had no doubt that because of the manner in which the order was obtained and executed, the defendants were entitled to substantial compensatory damages for the plaintiffs' breach of the cross-undertaking. Indeed, he was prepared to recognise that, if solicitors in executing an order outside its terms acted oppressively or excessively, exemplary damages would be available.

5. Challenging the order

5.26   In *Piller K.C.* v. *Manufacturing Processes*[92] Lord Denning, having made it clear that the *Anton Piller* order did not authorise forcible entry, but ordered the defendant to give permission to the applicant to enter, concluded, apparently with some diffidence: "with, I suppose the result that if they do not give their permission, they are guilty of contempt of court."[93] Later courts have had no doubt that such is the result of a simple refusal to comply with the order.[94] The defendant is not however expected just to lie down and be walked over. He is allowed to challenge the order.

(a) *Methods of challenging the order*

5.27   **(i) Appeal.** Although the Court of Appeal has power to hear an appeal against the grant of an *ex parte* order,[95] it has, in *WEA Records Ltd.* v. *Visions Channel 4 Ltd.*[96] set its face against doing so. This is because *ex parte* orders are by nature provisional, and the proper forum for their reconsideration is at an *inter partes* hearing before the judge who made the order, or another High Court judge; only after such a hearing was an appeal appropriate.

Thus the defendant has two options when faced with an *Anton Piller* order which he does not think should have been granted. He may either refuse permission to enter (thus risking contempt proceedings) and apply to the High Court for variation or the discharge of the order. Or, if he wishes to avoid being in contempt, he may

---

[89] See above, para. 5.14.
[90] Which the owner of the premises in the case was claiming.
[91] [1986] 3 All E.R. 338, 379.
[92] [1976] 1 Ch. 55 (C.A.).
[93] *Ibid.* 60.
[94] See, *e.g. Hallmark Cards Inc.* v. *Image Arts Ltd.* [1977] F.S.R. 150. But *cf. H.P.S.I. Ltd.* v. *Thomas and Williams* (1983) 133 New L.J. 598, below, para. 5.34.
[95] Supreme Court Act 1981, s.16(1).
[96] [1983] 2 All E.R. 589. N.B. that the plaintiff's right of appeal against refusal of an order is not affected by this case.

allow the order to be executed, but then take action on the undertaking as to damages given by the plaintiff when the order was made.[97]

(ii) Application for variation or discharge. The defendant, on giving notice to the applicant, or his solicitors, is entitled to go back to the court issuing the order and apply for its variation or discharge. The order itself should draw attention to this right.[98] He may even be able to persuade a court in an *ex parte* motion, to suspend the order until a hearing *inter partes*, but he will need to provide evidence in support of this request.[99] In any case, if the defendant obtains leave to move for the discharge of the order then, in effect the applicant will be unable to exercise it (since he relies on the defendant's permission), though the defendant will be, as we have seen, committing at least a technical contempt.[1]   **5.28**

There is no time limit for an application for variation or discharge of an order. Even a fully executed order can be discharged if it is established that it should never have been made.[2] But a judge is unlikely to accede to an application which is not made until the final trial of the action, when to do so would amount to an "empty gesture."[3] On the other hand, the view has been expressed that where the application for discharge is made solely for the purpose of enforcing the cross-undertakings in damages, it is preferable to wait for the full trial, rather than to use interlocutory proceedings.[3a]

(b) *Grounds for challenge*

In addition to simply controverting the evidence on which the order was made, there are two other grounds on which the defendant may apply to have the order discharged in whole or in part, or appeal against it.   **5.29**

(i) Non-disclosure of relevant information. If the applicant has not made full disclosure of relevant facts to the judge issuing the order the order may be discharged. Such facts may relate to the status of the defendants,[4] or to other circumstances arising out of its exercise: for example, the fact that the applicant knew that there was secret material on the defendant's premises which he would legitimately wish to keep from the applicant.[5]   **5.30**

The court may also discharge or vary if the applicant has failed to reveal relevant facts about the way in which he intends to execute the order.[6] The various factors must, however, either individually or cumulatively appear to the court to have been

---

[97] But not by means of an appeal, as suggested in *Bestworth Ltd.* v. *Wearwell Ltd.* [1979] F.S.R. 320 (Ch.D.), which must be regarded as having been overruled by the *WEA Records* decision.
[98] *C.B.S.* v. *Lambert* [1983] Ch. 37 (C.A.).
[99] *Hallmark Cards Inc.* v. *Image Arts Ltd.* [1977] F.S.R. 150 (C.A.).
[1] *Ibid.* 153, *per* Buckley L.J.
[2] *Booker McConnell plc* v. *Plascow* [1985] R.P.C. 425.
[3] *Columbia Picture Industries* v. *Robinson* [1986] 3 All E.R. 338, 378–379.
[3a] *Dormeuil Frères SA* v. *Nicolian International (Textiles) Ltd.* [1988] 3 All E.R. 197
[4] *Thermax Ltd.* v. *Schott Industrial Glass* [1981] F.S.R. 289, see above, para. 5.08.
[5] *Ibid.*
[6] *I.T.C. Film Distributors* v. *Video Exchange*, *The Times*, November 18, 1981. See above, para. 5.23.

sufficiently important to mean that the order should be discharged. Minor inaccuracies are not enough.[7] The duty of disclosure is owed to the court. Breach of it will not give rise to a tortious action.[8] It may, however, lead to evidence obtained from the order being excluded.[9]

5.31   **(ii) Self-incrimination.** As has been seen above, in situations falling outside the scope of section 72 of the Supreme Court Act 1981, the defendant will be able to apply for the variation or discharge of any order or part of an order which would involve a breach of the privilege against self-incrimination.[10]

6. Use of information

5.32   One of the undertakings which the plaintiff will normally be expected to give when seeking an *Anton Piller* order is not to use any information acquired as a result of the execution of the order except in the course of the current civil proceedings against the defendant. Any breach of this undertaking, even if it involves information which has been given in evidence in open court, will amount to a contempt of court.[11]

If the plaintiff wishes to use the information in other proceedings he must apply to the court for leave to do so. In *Sony Corporation* v. *Anand*[12] a request was made that information discovered in the exercise of an *Anton Piller* order be allowed to be used for the purpose of taking tortious, or criminal proceedings against third parties. This was not a surprising request, since one of the purposes of requiring the disclosure of information by the defendant in a copyright action, is to discover the names of others involved in the same unlawful activities. Browne-Wilkinson J., using the analogy of the discovery procedure approved by the House of Lords in *Norwich Pharmacal* v. *Commissioners of Customs and Excise*[13] agreed to modify the plaintiff's undertakings so as to allow him to use the information in this way. In *Crest Homes PLC* v. *Marks*[14] the plaintiff had obtained two *Anton Piller* orders. The execution of the second order revealed information which the plaintiff claimed should have been revealed on the first. The plaintiff sought leave to use this information in a contempt action against the defendant. The House of Lords, while reaffirming the importance of the undertaking not to use material for a collateral or ulterior purpose, felt that it could be relaxed if to do so would not cause injustice. Here the two orders could have been brought in the same action, and so the undertaking could be released. The argument that this relaxation would discourage defendants from making full and frank disclosure had little relevance in the circumstances, since the whole point of an *Anton*

---

[7] *Gallery Cosmetics Ltd.* v. *Number One* [1981] F.S.R. 556.
[8] *Digital Equipment Corporation* v. *Darkcrest Ltd.* [1984] 3 W.L.R. 617.
[9] *Guess? Inc.* v. *Lee* [1987] F.S.R. 125 (Hong Kong C.A.).
[10] See above, para. 5.17.
[11] *Home Office* v. *Harman* [1983] A.C. 280.
[12] [1981] Com.L.R. 55.
[13] [1974] A.C. 133.
[14] [1987] 2 All E.R. 1074.

Piller order is to gain possession of material without giving the defendant the opportunity of considering whether or not to disclose.[15]

In some circumstances it may be appropriate to allow a third party to have access to documents seized under an order. In *Customs and Excise Commissioners* v. *A. E. Hamlin*,[16] the Commissioners sought access to documents taken from a person they had been investigating in relation to the evasion of value added tax. Falconer J., while emphasising that such access should only be allowed with leave of the court (unless the person from whom the documents were seized consents), was prepared to grant the Commissioners access in this case. In *General Nutrition Ltd.* v. *Pradip*,[17] however, Warner J. was not prepared to allow the release of documents to the police simply because they might show that a criminal offence had been committed. In the previous case, the Commissioners' existing investigations had been hampered by the execution of the *Anton Piller* order, but that was not so here. This line was also taken by Browne-Wilkinson V.-C. in *E.M.I. Records* v. *Spillane*.[18] Disapproving of Falconer J.'s views in *Hamlin* he thought that as long as documents were held for the purpose of discovery it would be quite wrong to authorise their use in criminal proceedings under the tax laws which have no connection with the original cause of action.[19]

If the information relates to something not within the scope of the order it seems **5.33** that the undertakings will not apply to it. The decision in *Sony Corporation* v. *Time Electronics*[20] means that anything which is observed in the course of executing the order may be used as the basis for a new action. The case was only concerned with the result of the observation, and did not have to consider the use that might be made of items wrongfully removed from the defendant's premises. The rulings in *Fletcher Sutcliffe Wild Ltd.* v. *Burch*,[21] suggest that the defendant would have to challenge the seizure by a separate tort action. And the ruling of the Court of Appeal in *Helliwell* v. *Piggott-Sims*[22] means that the plaintiff will be able to use the items seized as evidence in any further action against the defendant or third parties. The plaintiff should, however, make full disclosure of how the evidence was obtained, and it must not concern trade secrets or be otherwise confidential.[23] It is submitted that the public policy grounds which may justify the absence of an exclusionary rule in relation to police activities and criminal prosecutions,[24] are much less pressing in relation to civil proceedings. Given the very exceptional power given to the private citizen under the *Anton Piller* order, it is a pity that the courts have not felt able to control its

[15] *Ibid.* 1081. N.B. the headnote in the All England report is inaccurate on this point, and should not be relied on.
[16] [1984] 1 W.L.R. 509.
[17] [1984] F.S.R. 403..
[18] [1986] 2 All E.R. 1016.
[19] *Ibid.* 1024.
[20] [1981] F.S.R. 333 (Ch.D.)—see above, para. 2.23.
[21] Para. 5.25, above.
[22] [1980] F.S.R. 582—see above, para. 2.21.
[23] *L.T. Piver S.A.R.L.* v. *S. & J. Perfume Co. Ltd.* [1987] F.S.R. 159.
[24] *i.e.* that the guilty should not be protected by someone else's wrongdoing—see above, para. 2.14.

exercise by firmer rules relating to information or other evidence obtained outside the strict scope of the order.

7. Failure to comply and contempt

5.34   There is no doubt that failure to comply with an order or undertaking contained in an *Anton Piller* order may amount to contempt, and lay the offender open to the penalties contained in the Contempt of Court Act 1981. This is so even if the order is subsequently discharged.[25] But courts often refer, as we have seen, to "technical" contempts in these circumstances, and this sympathetic approach, particularly as regards the defendant, was demonstrated in *H.P.S.I. Ltd.* v. *Thomas and Williams.*[26]

The two defendants were both brought before the court for alleged contempt—Thomas for initially refusing to give permission to enter his premises, and Williams for failing to comply with a direction in the order not to disclose the nature of the action to other persons. Woolf J. dismissed the application. He found that Thomas's refusal was largely attributable to the advice which he had received, and was not a matter of any significance, and that Williams' conduct was affected by the pressures resulting from the confusion and distress which were a necessary consequence of this sort of procedure being conducted at his house. There was no deliberate attempt on his part to interfere with the proper working of the order.

II. DISTRESS FOR RENT

5.35   As long ago as 1893 the remedy of distress for rent was described as surviving from "a primitive period when legal procedure still retained some of the germs of a semi-barbarous custom of reprisals."[27] The statutory restrictions which have been placed on it in modern times mean that it is not frequently used.[28] But is it by no means a defunct remedy.[29]

1. Sources

5.36   The law relating to what is essentially a common law remedy of self-help, is scattered among a number of statutes dating back to the seventeenth century, filled out by a quantity of authorities from the nineteenth century, when the remedy was employed far more frequently than at present. This diversity of sources means that the law in the area has become very complicated. The following discussion is an attempt to give the broad outlines of the remedy, with particular emphasis on the entry powers which attach to it, and the situations in which the power is in practice used at the present.

2. Essence of the remedy

5.37   The remedy is an alternative to an action for the recovery of rent, whereby the

[25] *Wardle Fabrics* v. *Myristis* [1984] F.S.R. 263, Ch.D.
[26] (1983) 133 New. L.J. 598. *cf. Crest Homes* v. *Marks* [1987] 2 All E.R. 1074.
[27] Bowen L.J. in *American Concentrated Must Corporation* v. *Hendry* (1893) L.J.Q.B. 388.
[28] See below, para. 5.38.
[29] See, *e.g.* its use by certain local authorities in recent years—D. Hoath, *Council Housing* (2nd ed.), p. 145; D. J. Hughes, *Public Sector Housing Law*, p. 122.

landlord seizes goods, and holds them as security for recovering the rent, or sells them to realise the sum owing to him.[30]

3. Limitations on availability

The landlord must in the following cases obtain the leave of the court before he may distrain. **5.38**

(a) *Protected or statutory tenancies*

Under the Rent Act 1977, s.147(1) if a dwelling-house is let on a protected or statutory tenancy,[31] he must seek the leave of the county court on the prescribed form. Any order granting leave may be adjourned, suspended, or postponed, or made subject to conditions.[32] The Rent (Agriculture) Act 1976 makes similar provisions as regards premises let on a protected occupancy, or on an agricultural statutory tenancy.

(b) *Company in liquidation*

Leave of the court is also required where an order has been made compulsorily winding up a company which is a tenant. This applies to both the initial exercise of the remedy, and proceeding with a distress which has already taken place. Again the court may impose conditions.[33]

4. Exercise of the remedy

(a) *Landlord or bailiff*

The distraint may be carried out by the landlord in person, or by a bailiff, who acts as his agent.[34] If a bailiff or other agent is employed he will normally be given a written authority, or "warrant," in order that the tenant may see that he has been duly authorised. A bailiff must be "certificated" by a county court judge.[35] His certificate may be a general one, or issued in relation to a particular distress. Procedure for the issue of a certificate is governed by the Distress for Rent Rules 1983.[36] A practising solicitor is *entitled* to a certificate on application, and payment of the required fee. **5.39**

(b) *Entry*

While at one time distress could only operate over goods which were seizable without entering the tenant's premises, it is now almost inevitable that the landlord **5.40**

---

[30] Distress for Rent Act 1689, s.1.
[31] As defined by the Rent Act 1977, ss.1 and 2.
[32] As for orders for possession: Rent Act 1977.
[33] Companies Act 1985, ss.523, 525(3).
[34] *Re Caidan, ex p. Official Receiver v. Regis Property Co. Ltd.* [1942] Ch. 90.
[35] Law of Distress Amendment Act 1888, s.7.
[36] S.I. 1983 No. 1917.

will need to be able to obtain entry in order to distrain. The rules relating to the manner in which he may obtain entry developed piecemeal during the latter part of the nineteenth century, and the result is a set of fairly clear, though not always coherent, rules.

(i) Time. The entry may be made at any time between sunrise and sunset,[37] but not on a Sunday.[38]

(ii) Use of force. The distrainor is expected to carry out the seizure of the goods peaceably. But if the tenant has some inkling of what he is after he is likely to refuse to let him in. Prima facie no "force" is allowed on the part of the distrainor, but force in this context was given a much narrower meaning in the nineteenth-century cases than is given in the modern law relating to police powers, etc.[39] It is perhaps more akin to "actual violence."

5.41   In *Eldridge* v. *Stacey*[40] the distrainor was unable to gain direct entry to the premises. He gained access to a neighbouring garden, climbed over a fence and entered the house through the back door, which was latched, but not locked. He then forced open the front door in order to admit his assistant. The court was of the opinion that climbing over the fence did not make the entry unlawful, nor did the entry through the latched back door. There was not any breaking open of doors, so the means used were acceptable. It was left to Lush J., four years later, in *Nash* v. *Lucas*,[41] to attempt to provide some explanation in principle for this decision. In this case the distrainor had pushed open a window,[42] which, like the door in *Eldridge* v. *Stacey* was shut but not locked. The court, in particular Cockburn C.J. (who clearly thought that *Eldridge* v. *Stacey* had gone too far), was not prepared to regard this as a lawful distress. In the course of argument Lush J. attempted to reconcile this with the earlier case in the following way[43]:

> "The ground of holding entry through a closed but unfastened door to be lawful, is, that access through the door is the usual mode of access, and that the licence from the occupier to anyone to enter who has lawful business may therefore be implied from his leaving the door unfastened. Entry through the window is not the usual mode of entry, and therefore no such licence can be implied from the window being left unfastened."

5.42   The idea of the implied licence is the same as that which was adopted in *Robson* v. *Hallett*,[44] but with rather different results. Its applicability to the bailiff who enters through an unlocked door was confirmed by the Court of Appeal in *Southam* v.

---

[37] *Tutton* v. *Darke* (1860) 5 H. & N. 647: 157 E.R. 1338; *Nixon* v. *Freeman* (1860) 5 H. & N. 562: 157 E.R. 1341.

[38] R.S.C., Ord. 65, r. 10; C.C.R. 1981, Ord. 7, r. 3.

[39] See, *e.g. Swales* v. *Cox* [1981] 1 Q.B. 849, above, para. 1.14.

[40] (1863) 15 C.B.(N.S.) 458.

[41] (1867) L.R. 2 Q.B. 590.

[42] In strict accuracy he had encouraged another of the landlord's employees who happened to have access to the window to do so.

[43] (1867) L.R. 2 Q.B. 590, 593.

[44] [1967] 2 Q.B. 939, see above, paras. 1.04, 1.14. The distress cases were not cited in *Robson* v. *Hallett*.

Smout.[45] The case concerned a bailiff's entry to arrest in connection with a judgment debt, but the court treated it as equivalent to entry for distress for rent. Lush J.'s approach in *Nash* v. *Lucas* was cited with approval. Lord Denning reformulated it in this way[46]:

> "where a man locks, bolts or bars his door, he makes it clear that no one is to come in. Whereas if he leaves it open, or if he just shuts it and all that is needed is to turn the handle or lift the latch or give it a push, then he gives an implied invitation to all people who have lawful business to come in."

This is clearly irreconcilable with the authorities on police powers, which it is suggested are to preferred in their analysis of the limits of any implied licence. The absurdity of the current analysis as regards distress can be seen by considering the effect of a notice saying "No entry to bailiffs." In *Robson* v. *Hallett* it was suggested that such a notice would be effective to remove the implied licence.[47] But the police have other powers, not available to a bailiff, which they may call upon if admission is refused. Is the tenant to be able to avoid distress being executed by this simple expedient?

The point is, of course, that without their power to pass through unlocked doors, **5.43** bailiffs would have much more difficulty in carrying out their duties. It would be better simply to specify (by statute) that certain powers of entry attached to a distrainor, provided no force was used, rather than to stretch the idea of the implied licence beyond the point where it has any contact with reality. And indeed in *Ryan* v. *Shilcock*,[48] which is generally cited as one of the main sources for the principles applicable in this area, the emphasis is not on any implied licence, but on whether the bailiff was employing a normal method of entry.

If the decisions in *Nash* v. *Lucas* and *Eldridge* v. *Stacey* seem a little odd nowadays, **5.44** the decision in *Crabtree* v. *Robinson*[49] goes even further down the path of absurdity. Here the bailiff entered by raising a *partly opened* window. The court said that this was distinguishable from opening a shut window, and held that the distress was lawful. In the absence of evidence that people habitually invite visitors to enter their homes through the windows, so that a licence could be implied from a window being left open, the decision is difficult to accept. It is submitted that it does not in fact follow the principles suggested by the court in *Eldridge* v. *Stacey*, and that as a decision of a two-man Divisional Court it should be regarded as very doubtful authority.[50] Unfortunately it received the approval of Lord Esher in *Long* v. *Clarke*,[51] though the specific point was not before the court.

(iii) Inner doors. The protection afforded to the tenant from forcible entry

---

[45] [1964] 1 Q.B. 308.
[46] *Ibid.* 323.
[47] In that case, to walk up to the front door.
[48] (1851) 7 Exch. 72.
[49] (1885) 15 Q.B.D. 312.
[50] Another possible approach might be to say, whatever aperture is used, that entry is lawful as long as nothing is broken, and no locks are picked.
[51] [1894] 1 Q.B. 119, 121.

applies only to the front or outside door to the premises. Once a peaceable entry has been made then any interior doors may be broken in order to effect the distress.[52] And this is so even where the interior door is in fact the entrance to the tenant's premises.[53]

(iv) Forcible re-entry. Once the distrainor has lawfully gained entry to the premises, he may use force to re-enter. This is so whether the distrainor leaves for his own purposes, or is ejected by the tenant. In *Banister* v. *Hyde*,[54] the distrainor left the house for the purpose of refreshment. He returned to find the door purposely locked against him. In *Eldridge* v. *Stacey*,[55] the person left in possession by the distrainor was forcibly expelled by the tenant on his return. In both cases the distrainor was allowed to use force to re-enter, the only condition being that the original distress must not have been abandoned. This is a question of fact, and the court did not demur from the finding of the jury in *Eldridge* v. *Stacey* that, despite a three-week delay there was no abandonment. Nor does the force used seem to be subject to any requirement of reasonableness. In *Eldridge* v. *Stacey* the distrainor was allowed to break down the front door with a sledge-hammer. The gross disparity between what is allowed on an initial entry and what is allowed to enforce a re-entry seems hard to justify.

(c) *Seizure of goods*

5.45   Once lawful entry to the premises has been obtained the distrainor will wish to seize goods to the value of the rent owing, plus expenses.[56] It is not necessary for the goods to be removed; they may be impounded on the premises. If they are left on the premises the tenant should be asked to sign a "walking possession agreement,"[57] to make it clear that the distress is not being abandoned. A bailiff is required to serve on the tenant, or leave on the premises, a notice listing the amount for which the distress is levied, and the authorised fees, charges and expenses.[58]

(d) *What may be seized?*

5.46   It has long been recognised that the landlord is not entitled to strip the tenant of all his property. A number of categories of possessions are recognised as being privileged from seizure. For example:

(i) Essentials of life:

(a) clothes and bedding belonging to the tenant and his family up to a total of £100;

---

[52] *Lee* v. *Gansel* (1774) 1 Cowp. 1: 98 E.R. 935.
[53] *e.g.* where he rents rooms within a larger house—*Lee* v. *Gansel*.
[54] (1860) 2 E. & E. 62: 121 E.R. 235.
[55] See above, para. 5.42.
[56] N.B. the limitations as regards undischarged bankrupts in the Insolvency Act 1986, s.347.
[57] See Distress for Rent Rules 1983 (S.I. 1983 No. 1917).
[58] *Ibid.*

(b) items connected with the tenant's trade or business, such as tools, account books, and business papers.[59]

(ii) Things which could not be returned in the same condition[60]:

(a) any perishable goods;
(b) loose money (*i.e.* not in a sealed bag or container).

(iii) To avoid possible breaches of the peace: *e.g.* things in actual use at the time of seizure.[61]

(iv) Third parties' goods:

(a) goods delivered to a person in the way of a public trade which he exercises, so that he possesses as bailee[62];
(b) goods falling within the Law of Distress Amendment Act 1908, s.1.[63]

Section 1 of the 1908 Act makes provision in relation to the goods of a sub-tenant, lodger or third party, which may be on the tenant's premises and therefore liable to be seized. The owner of the goods, before or after the distress has been levied, must serve a declaration in writing on the landlord setting out his rights over the goods. The details which must be supplied are laid down in section 1 of the Act.[64]

If the distress is levied after the declaration has been served, and the other requirements of section 1 have been complied with, the distress will be deemed "illegal,"[65] and the owner may apply to a justice of the peace for an order for the restoration of the goods.[66] The application will be heard before the stipendiary, or two magistrates, who will decide whether the order should be made. This is in addition to any other remedies which the owner may have against the landlord.[67]

The provisions of sections 1 and 2 do not apply to certain goods belonging to third **5.47** parties. These are specified in section 4 of the Act, and include goods belonging to the spouse or partner of the defaulting tenant, or subject to a hire-purchase agreement, or goods which are in the tenant's possession in circumstances which make him the "reputed owner" of them.[68]

Nor do they apply, by virtue of section 4(2)(c) to goods (other than goods belonging to a lodger) which either are goods in which the tenant and the sub-tenant

---

[59] *Gauntlett* v. *King* (1857) 3 C.B.(N.S.) 59.
[60] *Simpson* v. *Hartopp* (1744) Willes 512.
[61] *Simpson* v. *Hartopp*; *Field* v. *Adames* (1840) 12 Ad. & El. 649.
[62] *Swire* v. *Leach* (1865) 18 C.B.(N.S.) 479 (pawnbroker).
[63] Certain aspects of the 1908 Act were discussed in *Rhodes* v. *Allied Dunbar Pension Services Ltd.* [1988] 1 All E.R. 524, but the points do not seem to affect the operation of distress.
[64] See also *Sharpe* v. *Fowle* (1884) 12 Q.B.D. 385; *Rogers Eungblut & Co.* v. *Martin* [1911] 1 K.B. 19 (C.A.); *Druce & Co. Ltd.* v. *Beaumont Property Trust* [1935] 2 K.B. 257; *Godlonton* v. *Fulham and Hampstead Property Co.* [1905] 1 K.B. 431; *Lawrence Chemical Co. Ltd.* v. *Rubinstein, The Times,* November 27, 1981.
[65] See below, para. 5.55.
[66] s.2.
[67] See below, para. 5.61.
[68] This is a question of fact. See *Re Parker, ex p. Turquand* (1885) 14 Q.B.D. 636 (C.A.); *Chappell & Co. Ltd.* v. *Harrison* (1910) 193 L.T. 594.

have an interest, and which are on business premises, or are on premises used as offices or warehouses and the owner neglects to remove them for one month after notice to do so had been given.[69]

5.48   Finally, any goods belonging to, and in the offices of, a company or corporation on premises which are let to a director, officer, or employee of the company or corporation, are not protected.[70]

5. Sale

5.49   In most cases the distress will not take place unless the tenant is impecunious, so that almost inevitably the landlord will wish to sell the distrained property in order to pay off what is owed. The power to do so is governed primarily by the Distress for Rent Act 1689 (which first gave a right of sale). The power is permissive, not compulsory.[71]

The first requirement of exercising the power is that notice of the distraint, and the reason for it, must be left at the "chiefe mansion house or other most notorious place" on the premises in respect of which the rent is owed. The tenant or the owner of the goods then has five days to replevy the goods (or pay off the debt). It must be assumed, though there seems to be no authority on the point, that time should run from the serving of the notice, if that occurs at a later date than the distraint. The tenant or owner also has the power to obtain an extension of time up to a total of 15 days (including the initial five) by making a request in writing to the landlord or bailiff, and giving security for any additional cost which may result.[72] The landlord may sell within the period with the permission of the tenant or owner.[73] The periods of time should be calculated from the day following that on which the distress took place or the notice was given. So in *Robinson* v. *Waddington* goods seized on a Saturday morning could not lawfully be sold on the following Thursday afternoon.[74] The landlord should have waited until the Friday morning.

5.50   If a sale does take place the landlord is obliged to obtain the best price he can. It is not necessary for the goods to be appraised before sale, unless the tenant or owner gives written notice that this is required.[75] They may, in the same way, require the goods to be removed to a public auction room for sale.[76] In both cases the costs must be borne by the person making the request. If no request is made the landlord may sell in whatever manner he chooses, provided he does so within a reasonable time,[77] and always subject to the obligation to obtain the best price. This obligation means

---

[69] In the same manner as a notice to quit.

[70] The question as to whether goods belong to a partner, or fall within the above paragraph, may be determined by a stipendiary or two justices (as appropriate) on application by the superior landlord, under-tenant, or other third party having an interest in the property—s.4(2).

[71] *Philpott* v. *Lehain* (1876) 35 L.T. 885.

[72] Law of Distress Amendment Act 1888, s.6.

[73] *Ibid.*

[74] (1849) 13 Q.B. 753; 116 E.R. 1451.

[75] Law of Distress Amendment Act 1888, s.5.

[76] *Ibid.*

[77] *Pitt* v. *Shew* (1821) 4 B. & Ald. 208.

that the landlord may not buy the goods himself,[78] nor may he impose conditions on the sale which may affect the price.[79]

If the sale takes place on the tenant's premises, purchasers and prospective purchasers or their representatives, have the right to enter the premises in order to view, appraise, or buy the goods, and to remove any which they have bought.[80]

(a) *Proceeds*

Until the time of sale the property in the goods remains in the tenant or owner, **5.51** and the right to replevy subsists,[81] subject to the expenses which the bailiff is entitled to deduct from the proceeds.[82] As soon as the sale has taken place the proceeds become the property of the landlord to the extent of the debt owed to him.

(b) *Surplus*

If there is any surplus from the sale then the 1689 Act states that it should be left in **5.52** the hands of the sheriff, under-sheriff, or constable, for the owner's use. In practice it is easier for it to be paid direct to the owner, and the courts have given their approval to this procedure in a number of cases.[83] The tenant may dispute the amount which he receives, and it is a question of fact whether he took it in full satisfaction,[84] but the provision of statutory charges means that such disputes are very unlikely.[85]

(c) *Deficiency*

If the sale fails to realise the amount owing to the landlord, he may bring an action **5.53** for the balance of the debt.[86] However he may not generally levy distress again in respect of the same rent, unless there was insufficient property on the premises at the time of the first distress.[87]

(d) *Avoiding distress*

The 1689 and 1737 Acts contain a number of provisions dealing with attempts by **5.54** a tenant to avoid distress or its effects.

(i) Seized goods. Any improper dealing with seized or impounded goods will amount to "rescue" or "pound-breach" for which the distrainor may bring an action for treble damages.[88]

---

[78] *Moore & Nettlefold & Co.* v. *Singer Manufacturing Co.* [1903] 2 K.B. 168.

[79] *Hawkins* v. *Walrond* (1876) 1 C.P.D. 280—condition that the goods were to be consumed on the premises.

[80] Distress for Rent Act 1737, s.10.

[81] *Moore* v. *Pyrhe* (1809) 11 East 52; 103 E.R. 923; *Jones* v. *King* (1814) 5 Taunt. 451: 128 E.R. 765.

[82] The Distress for Rent Rules (S.I. 1983 No. 1917), set out in detail the amounts which the bailiff may claim.

[83] *e.g. Lyon* v. *Tomkies* (1836) 1 M. & W. 603; 150 E.R. 576, where Lord Abinger made the point that the tenant could only claim about irregularities in procedure if special damage could be shown.

[84] *Ibid.*

[85] See above, n. 82.

[86] *Philpott* v. *Lehain* (1876) 35 L.T. 855.

[87] *Dawson* v. *Cropp* (1845) 1 C.B. 961; *Wallis* v. *Savill* (1701) 2 Lut. 1532.

[88] 1689 Act, s.3.

(ii) Fraud. If a tenant "fraudulently or clandestinely" removes his goods from premises, to prevent distraint upon them, the landlord can, within 30 days, seize the goods wherever they may be found,[89] unless they have been sold to a bona fide purchaser for value.[90] Moreover, in contrast to the normal rules,[91] force may be used to gain entry to the premises where the goods have been concealed.[92] The Act requires the distrainor to call upon a constable to assist,[93] and, if the premises are a dwelling-house, to swear an oath before a justice of the peace, that there are reasonable grounds to suspect that the goods are on the premises. Entry may only be made during the day-time.[94]

The Law of Distress Amendment Act 1908 also contains a procedure, in section 6, whereby a landlord, in a situation where there is a sub-tenancy, can avoid using distress on the tenant by serving a notice on the sub-tenant that his rent is to be paid direct to the landlord. This does not, however, give the landlord any priority in respect of a mortgagee who has charge over debts owed to the tenant. In those circumstances the landlord will still have the remedy of distress.[95]

6. Remedies for improper distress

(a) *No right to distrain*

5.55   If the landlord did not in fact have any right to distrain, the distraint will be illegal, the person levying it will be a trespasser, and damages will be available without proof of any special damage.[96] If the goods are seized and sold when no rent was in fact due, the tenant is entitled to recover double the value of the goods.[97]

(b) *Improper entry*

5.56   If an entry is forced in a situation where this is not permitted, the distress will again be illegal, and the distrainor a trespasser.[98] The plaintiff will be entitled to recover the full value of the goods seized, without any deduction for any rent which may have been due.[99]

Alternatively, since a sale following an illegal distress confers no title on the purchaser, the plaintiff may sue the person in possession of the goods in conversion.

(c) *Privileged goods*

5.57   Seizure of privileged goods is an illegal distress (provided the procedures in the

---

[89] 1737 Act, s.1.
[90] 1737 Act, s.2.
[91] See above, para. 5.40.
[92] 1737 Act, s.7.
[93] And the constable must be present at the entry: *Cartwright* v. *Smith and Batty* (1833) 1 Mood. & R. 284.
[94] 1737 Act, s.7. N.B. there are special procedures for goods which do not exceed £50 in value—*ibid.* s.4.
[95] *Rhodes* v. *Allied Dunbar Pension Services Ltd.* [1988] 1 All E.R. 525.
[96] See above, para. 2.25.
[97] 1689 Act, s.4.
[98] See above, para. 5.41 for the situations when force may or may not be used.
[99] *Attack* v. *Bramwell* (1863) 3 B. & S. 520.

1908 Act have been followed).[1] If the goods are seized from a bailee, he is entitled to recover the full value of the goods in an action for damages, not simply the value of his own interest.[2] If, for example, he is a pawnbroker, having recovered the full value, he may retain from that the sum he advanced plus interest, and will be liable to hand over the surplus to the owner of the goods.[3]

(d) *1737 Act, ss.19 and 20*

Because of the disproportionate effect of categorising an otherwise lawful distress **5.58** as illegal as a result of some minor impropriety in the distrainor's subsequent action (such as selling within the five- or 15-day time limit), the 1737 Act limits the remedies for such irregularities. The plaintiff is entitled to recover only for special damage resulting from the irregularity,[4] and even this right is lost if the landlord makes a "tender of amends" before an action is brought.[5]

(e) *Excessive distress*

Simply taking goods of greater value than what is owed is not unlawful, even if it is **5.59** alleged to have been done maliciously.[6] If the difference is "excessive," however, the distress is irregular, but not illegal.[7] What amounts to excessive distress is a question of fact.[8] As Wilde C.J. put it in *Roden v. Eyton*[9]:

> "All that a landlord is bound to do is, to exercise a reasonable and honest discretion: he is authorised to protect himself by seizing what any reasonable man would think adequate to the satisfaction of his claim."

The issue should be judged on the basis of the difference between what was actually due and what was seized, notwithstanding any mistake in the warrant.[10]

(f) *Improper sale*

If the distrainor purports to sell the goods in a way which he has no power to use,[11] **5.60** *e.g.* by selling to himself, this brings the distraint to an end, and any subsequent dealings with the goods will not attract the protection of the 1737 Act, ss.19 and 20.[12] Such dealings will therefore amount to conversion of the goods.

(g) *Remedies*

These may be sought against the landlord or the bailiff. **5.61**

---

[1] See above, para. 5.46.
[2] *Swire* v. *Leach* (1865) 18 C.B.(N.S.) 479.
[3] *Ibid.* 492, *per* Erle C.J.
[4] 1737 Act, s.19.
[5] *Ibid.* s.20.
[6] *Stevenson* v. *Newnham* (1853) 13 C.B. 285.
[7] *Whitworth* v. *Smith* (1832) 1 M. & Rob. 193.
[8] *Crowder* v. *Self* (1839) 2 M. & Rob. 190.
[9] (1848) 6 C.B. 427, 430.
[10] *Crowder* v. *Self* (1839) 2 M. & Rob. 190.
[11] See above, para. 5.49.
[12] *Plasycoed Collieries Co. Ltd.* v. *Partridge, Jones & Co.* [1912] 2 K.B. 345.

(i) Damages. As we have seen, damages will generally be available in relation to both illegal and irregular distress.

(ii) Injunction. An injunction may be sought to prevent either an anticipated levy,[13] though the court may require the rent to be paid into court while the injunction continues, or a subsequent sale.[14]

(iii) Replevin. This is the traditional method of challenging an illegal distress. For the form of the remedy, see Chapter Two, para. 2.44.

III. EXECUTION AND ENFORCEMENT

A. High Court Judgments

5.62 The plaintiff in a civil action, having obtained judgment in the High Court, may find that he needs to enforce it by means of a writ of execution. Certain of these writs carry with them rights or powers of entry.

1. Issue of writs

5.63 The creditor obtains the issue of the writ by applying to the appropriate registry.[15] The writ is directed to the sheriff of the county where it is to be executed. The sheriff in turn issues a warrant to bailiffs, who actually execute the writ.

2. Writs of fieri facias, delivery, and specific delivery

5.64 As far as entry powers are concerned, these three writs are all governed by the same rules.[16] *Fieri facias* (or "*fi. fa.*") is used where damages have been awarded; delivery or specific delivery, where the court has ordered the transfer of property, with or without the alternative of damages, respectively.

3. Entry powers

5.65 The bailiffs have the power to enter the debtor's premises, or those of a third party to which property has been removed.[17]

4. Use of force

5.66 The bailiff is not generally allowed to use force. He has the same powers in relation to gaining access as does a person distraining for rent.[18] But force may be used in the following circumstances:

(a) once lawful entry has been obtained, in order to leave the premises, or remove

---

[13] *Shaw* v. *Earl of Jersey* (1879) 4 C.P.D. 120.
[14] *Walsh* v. *Lonsdale* (1882) 21 Ch.D. 9. See further on injunctions, Chap. Two, paras. 2.30–2.31.
[15] See R.S.C., Ord. 46, r. 6(1).
[16] *Cazet de la Borde* v. *Othon* (1874) 23 W.R. 110.
[17] *Semayne's Case* (1604) 5 Co.Rep. 91a; *Biscoe* v. *White* (1600) Cro.Eliz. 759.
[18] *Southam* v. *Smout* [1964] 1 Q.B. 308 (C.A.). And see above, paras. 5.40–5.44.

goods, if there is no one present to open the door, or those who are present refuse to do so[19];

(b) to re-enter, having been forcibly expelled[20];

(c) to enter premises where goods have been removed to avoid execution.[21] But in relation to the premises of a third party, the goods must actually be on the premises to justify entry without the owner's permission. Reasonable suspicion is not enough.[22]

5. Rights after entry

Inner doors, cupboards, trunks, etc., may be broken open,[23] and it is not necessary **5.67** for the bailiff to ask for them to be opened.

6. Property seizable on fieri facias

In relation to delivery, and specific delivery, the writ and warrant will specify the **5.68** property to be seized. In relation to *fieri facias* the goods must be those of the judgment debtor.[24] A third party's goods which happen to be on the premises may not be taken.[25] Any corporeal goods and chattels, including chattels real, such as leasehold interests and rentcharges (but excluding fixtures) can be seized. As regards leaseholds, the sheriff has a right to enter until it has been sold.[26] By virtue of section 12 of the Judgments Act 1838, money, cheques, bills of exchange, promissory notes, bonds. specialties, or other securities may be taken. Any money should be paid direct to the creditor, with any surplus (after deducting expenses) being returned to the debtor. Other cheques and securities may be held as security for the debt, and sued on by the creditor when the time for payment arrives.[27] Joint property may be seized, including partnership property where judgment is against the firm.

7. Exemptions

Clothes, and bedding up to a value of £100, and tools of the debtor's trade to a **5.69** value of £150, are excluded from seizure.[28]

8. Rights of third parties

As long as the debtor is entitled to *possession* of the goods the sheriff may seize them, **5.70**

[19] *Pugh* v. *Griffith* (1838) 7 Ad. & El. 827.
[20] *Aga Kurboolies Mohomed* v. *R.* (1843) 4 Moo.P.C.C. 239; *Banister* v. *Hyde* (1860) 2 E. & E. 627: 121 E.R. 235.
[21] *Semayne's Case* (1604) 5 Co.Rep. 91a.
[22] *Cooke* v. *Birt* (1814) 5 Taunt. 765; *Morrish* v. *Murrey* (1844) 13 M. & W. 52; *Southam* v. *Smout* [1964] 1 Q.B. 308 (C.A.). It is otherwise in relation to the house of the personal representatives, on a writ of *fi. fa.* against the deceased's estate—*Cooke* v. *Birt.*
[23] *R.* v. *Bird* (1679) 2 Show 87.
[24] *Glasspoole* v. *Young* (1829) 9 B. & C. 696.
[25] *cf.* distress, para. 5.46 above.
[26] *Playfair* v. *Musgrove* (1845) 14 M. & W. 239.
[27] 1838 Act, s.12.
[28] Protection from Execution (Prescribed Value) Order 1980 (S.I. 1980 No. 26), art. 2.

even though a third party may be the owner of them, or have an interest in them. Where the third party is the owner (as where the goods have been hired or pawned to the debtor), they may be seized and the debtor's interest sold.[29] Similarly, if the third party has rights over the debtor's goods (*e.g.* lien), the value of his interest will be met from the proceeds of the sale of the goods.[30]

If the goods are no longer in the debtor's possession, or the third party disputes his right to possession, then the sheriff will generally only be able to seize the goods which the debtor would be able to retain or recover in an action against the third party. But a claim by a third party which is based on a fraudulent transfer, or on a title later in date than the receipt of the writ by the sheriff (at which point it "binds" the debtor's property), will not prevent the sheriff from seizing goods.[31] Nor will the sheriff be affected by any estoppel which might bind the debtor.

The procedure for dealing with a claim by a third party in relation to goods which have already been seized, is to be found in R.S.C., Ord. 17. The claimant must give notice to the sheriff of the nature of his claim, and this will be passed on to the creditor. If the creditor accepts the claim the sheriff will withdraw from the seizure. If the claim is disputed the sheriff will seek relief through interpleader proceedings.[32] The court hearing the interpleader summons may either determine the issue between the parties there and then, or give directions for a trial of the dispute. In any case the sheriff will ask the court to make an order protecting him from further legal action.

The grounds on which the sheriff may claim that the court should give him such protection are based on his two possible defences to an action for conversion—the one under section 15 of the Bankruptcy and Deeds of Arrangement Act 1913 and the other under the common law.[33]

(a) *Bankruptcy and Deeds of Arrangement Act 1913, s.15*

5.71   This provides that where goods are seized from the possession of an execution debtor, and no claim is made to them prior to sale by the sheriff, the sheriff is immune from action in respect of the sale unless it is proved that he "had notice, or might by making reasonable enquiry have ascertained that the goods were not the property of the execution debtor." What is a reasonable inquiry will depend on the facts of each case. But in *Observer Ltd.* v. *Gordon*[34] it was accepted that "a sheriff would be ill-advised to seize without inquiry the goods on the premises of a tradesman whose business was the repair of other persons' goods: a cobbler or a motor repairer," but that "an ordinary retail shop would be quite different."[35] It was also pointed out that the sheriff is under a duty to execute the writ, and potentially liable

---

[29] *Pain* v. *Whittaker* (1824) Ry. & M. 99; *Jones Bros.* v. *Woodhouse* [1932] 2 K.B. 117; *Jelks* v. *Hayward* [1905] 2 K.B. 460.
[30] *Procter* v. *Nicholson* (1835) 7 C. & P. 67.
[31] *Imray* v. *Magnay* (1843) 11 M. & W. 207.
[32] R.S.C., Ord. 17, r. 2(3).
[33] See *Observer Ltd.* v. *Gordon* [1983] 2 All E.R. 945, 949.
[34] [1983] 2 All E.R. 945.
[35] *Ibid.* 950.

to contempt proceedings if he fails to do so. The sheriff should only be expected, therefore, to make such inquiry as could be concluded "within a reasonable time," and not unduly delay execution.[36]

(b) *Common law*

The common law defence is that the third party has no "substantial grievance" **5.72** against the sheriff. He may well, for example, have received the full value of his property from the proceeds of the sale. The claimant will need to show that he has a "fairly arguable" case against the sheriff.[37]

In *Neumann* v. *Bakeaway*[38] it was accepted by the Court of Appeal that, as well as "insolent and oppressive conduct" by the sheriff's officer,[39] a sale at a gross undervalue would be enough to amount to a substantial grievance.[40] The mere fact that the sale was by public auction will not be conclusive evidence in the sheriff's favour on this issue, but the claimant must produce some evidence of the true value of the goods *at the time of the sale*, as opposed to when he acquired them.[41] The Court of Appeal in *Neumann* v. *Bakeaway* also considered it relevant to this issue that the claimant had been very dilatory in putting forward his claim. There had in fact been a gap of about four months between seizure and sale, and the claimant had known of the seizure three months prior to the sale.[42]

9. Method of seizure

It is not necessary for there to be any physical seizure of the goods, provided **5.73** sufficient intimation of seizure is given to the debtor or his employees.[43]

The bailiff will need to make it clear what property is being seized. If seized goods are to be left on the debtor's premises, the bailiff will need to establish that he has not by his departure abandoned the seizure. This will generally be achieved by obtaining a signature on a "walking possession" consent form, which will list the goods being seized. The form does not have to be signed by the debtor himself, but simply by some responsible person on the premises.[44]

If such a document is not signed, then, whether or not there has been an abandonment is a question of fact to be decided in the light of all the circumstances. The sheriff may establish his continuing seizure by regular visits to the premises, and, where appropriate, starting interpleader proceedings.[45]

---

[36] *Ibid.* 951.
[37] See *Neumann* v. *Bakeaway Ltd.* [1983] 2 All E.R. 935, 943 (C.A.), and *Observer Ltd.* v. *Gordon* [1983] 2 All E.R. 945, 949.
[38] *Ibid.*
[39] *Cave* v. *Capel* [1954] 1 Q.B. 367.
[40] This was applied by Glidewell J. in *Observer Ltd.* v. *Gordon* [1983] 2 All E.R. 945, 952.
[41] *Neumann* v. *Bakeaway Ltd.* [1983] 2 All E.R. 935 (C.A.).
[42] *Ibid.* 938.
[43] *Bissicks* v. *Bath Colliery* (1877) 2 Ex.D. 459; (1878) 3 Ex.D. 174.
[44] *National Commercial Bank of Scotland Ltd.* v. *Arcam Demolition and Construction Ltd.* [1966] 2 Q.B. 593 (C.A.)—unauthorised signature by the debtor's wife held to be effective.
[45] *Lloyds and Scottish Finance Ltd.* v. *Modern Cars & Caravans (Kingston) Ltd.* [1966] 1 Q.B. 764.

10. Avoiding seizure

5.74   The sheriff is deemed to have authority to receive payment of the debt from the debtor, and to give a discharge.[46]

11. Effects of seizure

5.75   The sheriff does not by seizure obtain ownership of the property, but has a sufficient interest in it to entitle him to maintain an action for trespass or conversion.[47]

12. Sale

5.76   Once goods have been seized they must be sold. The sheriff is not entitled to hand them over to the creditor.[48] But the creditor, or indeed the debtor, may buy the goods at a sale.[49]

The sale should take place within a reasonable time of the seizure. There is no obligation to obtain the best price, simply a *reasonable* price,[50] but the sheriff must not act in such a way that the price is depressed. And if the debt is for more than £20, the sale must be by public auction publicly advertised on and during the three days next preceding the day of the sale.[51]

13. Writ of sequestration

5.77   This writ is used to enforce contempt proceedings, for example where a trade union refuses to comply with an injunction instructing it to call off illegal picketing. It gives the sequestrators control over all the contemnor's property and assets. This includes the power to enter on property in order to seize items, in much the same way as outlined above. In practice, however, control is usually achieved without the need for physical entry or seizure.

B. County Court Judgments

5.78   The enforcement of judgments of county courts is governed by Part VI of the County Courts Act 1984, together with the County Court Rules 1981, particularly Orders 25 and 26.

1. County Courts Act 1984, s.85

5.79   Section 85 of the Act provides that the party in whose favour a judgment or order

---

[46] *Rook* v. *Wilmot* (1590) Cro.Eliz. 209; *Taylor* v. *Baker* (1677) Freem K.B. 453; *Gregory* v. *Slowman* (1852) 1 E. & B. 360.
[47] *Wilbrahim* v. *Snow* (1670) 2 Wms. Saund. 47; *Giles* v. *Grover* (1832) 1 Cl. & Fin. 72 (H.L.).
[48] *Thomson* v. *Clerk* (1596) Cro. Eliz. 504.
[49] *Att-Gen.* v. *Fort* (1804) 8 Price 365; *Stratford* v. *Twynam* (1822) Jac. 418; *Cookson* v. *Fryer* (1858) 1 F. & F. 328; *Re Rogers, ex p. Villars* (1874) 9 Ch.App. 432. *cf.* the position in relation to distress for rent, above, paras. 5.49–5.50
[50] *Keightley* v. *Birch* (1814) 3 Camp. 521.
[51] Bankruptcy Act 1883, s.145.

for payment of money has been made, may apply to the registrar for a "warrant of execution in the nature of a writ of fieri facias."[52] The issue of the warrant will enable distress to be levied against any of the goods of the party against which the judgment or order was made, wherever they may be found within the district of the court.

A warrant may be issued in relation to debts payable by instalments, as long as the whole or part of any instalment which has become due remains unpaid.[53]

2. Execution of the warrant

As section 85 suggests, the warrant is to operate in much the same way as a writ of **5.80** *fi. fa.* The rules relating to the manner in which entry to premises may be obtained are the same, for example.[54] And the same exemptions apply as regards seizure of clothes, bedding, and tools of the debtor's trade.[55] A number of rules are peculiar to the warrant of execution, however, and these are dealt with below.[56]

3. Time when warrant takes effect

The warrant binds the property in the debtor's goods from the time when the application for the warrant was made to the registrar.[57] The registrar should indorse on the back of the warrant the hour, day, month, and year when he received the application.[58] He should also record the precise time of the application in the book prescribed for the purpose under section 12 of the Act.[59]

Despite the above rule, a purchaser in good faith and for valuable consideration, will obtain a good title to goods bought after the application has been received, provided that he did not have notice of the existence of an unexecuted warrant or writ.[60]

4. Manner of seizure—police presence

It is specifically provided that it is the duty of every constable to assist with every **5.81** execution of a warrant within his jurisdiction.[61]

5. What may be seized?

The rules as to what may or may not be seized are the same as for a writ of *fi. fa.* as **5.82**

---

[52] N.B. leave of the court is required in some cases before a warrant will be issued, *e.g.* where one of the parties has died—Ord. 26, r. 5.
[53] Ord. 26, r. 1.
[54] See above, paras. 5.64–5.66.
[55] County Court Act 1984, s.89. And see above, paras. 5.68–5.70.
[56] See also the special provisions concerning farmers—Ord. 26, r. 3.
[57] s.99(1). N.B. that if a warrant "pursues" the debtor's goods into another county court jurisdiction, it takes effect against those goods from the time when it was received by the registrar in that county court—s.103.
[58] s.99(3).
[59] s.85(3).
[60] s.99(2).
[61] s.85(4).

described in paras. 5.68–5.72 above. The debtor should be given an inventory of the goods seized and notice of the time of sale.[62]

6. Custody after seizure

5.83　　The seized goods should, pending sale:

(a) be deposited by the bailiff in some fit place; or
(b) remain in the custody of a fit person approved by the registrar to be put in possession by the bailiff; or
(c) be safeguarded in such other manner as the registrar directs.[63]

Any attempt to rescue, whether successful or not, gives rise to the possibility of a maximum penalty of one month's imprisonment, or a fine not exceeding level 4 on the standard scale or both, either as a result of a summary conviction, or simply by order of the county court judge.[64]

7. Sale

(a) *Time*

5.84　　There must be a gap of five clear days between the seizure of goods and their sale, unless either the goods are perishable, or the owner requests an earlier sale, in writing.[65]

(b) *Manner*

Any sale must be by brokers or appraisers appointed under the Act.[66]

Where the execution sum exceeds £20 (including legal and incidental expenses) the sale must be by public auction, advertised by the registrar for three days beforehand.[67] The court may authorise a private sale, on application, but such an application should not be entertained where there are other execution creditors until they have had a chance to be heard by the court.[68]

The debtor is entitled to a detailed account of the sale and the application of the proceeds.[69]

(c) *Third party's goods*

Where a third party's goods are sold before any claim has been made to them, the

---

[62] County Court Rules 1981, Ord. 26, r. 12.
[63] s.90.
[64] s.92.
[65] s.93.
[66] s.94. See s.95 for power of appointment. A bailiff may be appointed broker or appraiser—s.96.
[67] s.97.
[68] s.97(2). In *Crawshaw* v. *Harrison* [1894] 1 Q.B. 79, it was held that an unauthorised private sale is irregular rather than void. A claimant to the goods sold should first apply to the court for the sale to be set aside.
[69] County Court Rules 1981, Ord. 26, r. 13.

purchaser, the registrar, and anyone else acting under lawful authority, will be protected by section 98.

The purchaser will acquire a good title, and the registrar and other officers will be **5.85** immune from action by the third party, unless it is proved that they had notice, or might by reasonable inquiry have ascertained, that the goods were not the property of the execution debtor. In *Pilling* v. *Teleconstruction Co. Ltd.*[70] the judge ruled that what inquiries should be made depends on the circumstances of each case. Here the goods were all of such a nature as to be used in connection with the debtor's business, and were not of sufficient value to be likely to be subject to hire-purchase agreements.[71]

Section 98 operates subject to two provisos. First, that nothing in it affects the right of any claimant, who proves that at the time of sale he had a title to goods seized and sold, to any remedy against any person other than the registrar or other officer. Secondly it operates subject to sections 183, 184 and 436 of the Insolvency Act 1986, which deal with the rights of trustees in bankruptcy, official receivers, and liquidators over goods taken in execution.

Where a claim is made to goods which have been seized the bailiff is entitled to go ahead and sell the goods, paying the proceeds into court, unless the claimant follows certain procedures.[72] These involve depositing with the bailiff either the amount of the value of the goods claimed, or the sum which the bailiff is allowed to charge as costs for keeping possession of the goods until the decision of the judge can be obtained on the claim.[73]

It was held in *Miller* v. *Solomon*[74] that it is the value of the goods, and not the value of the judgment debt plus costs, which must be deposited. If the bailiff withdraws without receiving the full value, the court may order him to retake possession. But the bailiff will always be presumed to receive full value, so that he is not entitled to retain possession of the goods without specific authority from the court, even where the sum accepted does not in fact represent the goods' full value.[75]

7. Interpleader

Where there is a dispute over the ownership of goods, or their value, the issue may **5.86** be determined by interpleader proceedings initiated by the registrar.[76]

8. Execution and distress for rent

If there is a claim by a landlord for rent against a person subject to a judgment **5.87**

[70] (1961) 11 L.Jo. 424 (Ilford County Court).

[71] And *cf. Observer Ltd.* v. *Gordon* [1983] 2 All E.R. 945 (Q.B.D.), para. 5.71, above.

[72] s.100(3). This is subject to a discretion in the registrar to postpone sale until the determination of the claim—s.100(4).

[73] s.100(1).

[74] [1906] 2 K.B. 91.

[75] *Newsum Sons & Co. Ltd.* v. *James* [1909] 2 K.B. 384. See also *Wells* v. *Hughes* [1907] 2 K.B. 845 (C.A.); *Haddow* v. *Morton* [1894] 1 Q.B. 565; *Kotchie* v. *Golden Sovereigns Ltd.* [1898] 2 Q.B. 164; *Tellus Super Vacuum Cleaners* v. *Ireland* [1938] L.J.N.C.C.R. 54.

[76] s.101.

debt, the two claims may be satisfied from one distress levied by the bailiffs. The procedure for this is set out in section 102 of the County Courts Act.

9. Jurisdiction of the court

5.88   A warrant of execution may generally only be exercised within the jurisdiction of the county court from which it was issued. There is, however, a procedure in section 103 of the Act, which allows a warrant to be passed from the "home court" to another court in whose jurisdiction the goods of the debtor are believed to be. The warrant will bind those goods from the moment it is received by the registrar of that court.[77]

C. Crown Courts and Magistrates' Courts[78]

5.89   The enforcement of fines imposed by the Crown Court or magistrates' court, or of orders imposed by the magistrates' court,[79] is governed by sections 76–80 of the Magistrates' Courts Act 1980, and various of the Magistrates' Courts Rules 1981.[80]

1. Magistrates' Courts Act 1980, s.76

5.90   Under this section, where there is default in paying a sum adjudged to be paid on conviction, or by order of a magistrates' court,[81] the court may issue a warrant of distress or a warrant of committal.[82]

The basis on which the magistrates should decide whether to use distress or committal was considered in *R. v. Birmingham Justices, ex p. Bennett.*[83] In this case the magistrates, faced with a failure of the defendant who had been sentenced to 10 years' imprisonment to pay a £500 contribution to prosecution costs, committed him to prison for 60 days, to run concurrently with his existing sentence. The Divisional Court disapproved of this practice since "a concurrent prison sentence was no penalty at all on the defaulter, and, if applied generally, might result in the failure to collect substantial sums of money from those with the ability to pay." As long as there was evidence that there was a "reasonable likelihood" that the defendant had assets available to satisfy the sum owed, a warrant of distress rather than committal should be used.

2. Requirement of notice

5.91   A warrant for distress should not be issued unless the defendant has been

---

[77] s.103(2).

[78] The recovery of fines imposed by a Crown Court or magistrates' court, although in some ways part of the criminal process, is in effect simply the recovery of a civil debt. For this reason, and because "distress" is the one of the main methods available to obtain payment, it is appropriate to deal with this topic in this chapter.

[79] *e.g.* for maintenance.

[80] S.I. 1981 No. 552, as amended by S.I. 1983 No. 523.

[81] For this purpose a fine or order to pay costs or compensation imposed by a Crown Court is deemed to be a sum of this type—Powers of Criminal Courts Act 1973, s.32(1).

[82] A warrant of committal may also be issued where distress has not realised sufficient to satisfy the sum due plus costs, s.76(2)(a).

[83] [1983] 1 W.L.R. 114. (D.C.).

previously served with a copy of the minute of the order, or the order was made in his presence and the warrant is issued on that occasion.[84]

There is also a requirement of notice under rule 46. This applies where a magistrates' court is enforcing payment ordered by a Crown Court, where time is allowed for payment, where payment is to be made by instalments, or where the defendant was absent when the sum was adjudged to be paid. In these situations the clerk of the court should serve on the defendant a written notice stating the amount of the sum, and, if applicable, the amount of the instalments, and when and where they are to be paid. A warrant for distress or committal should not be issued until this had been done.

3. Form of the warrant

The contents of the warrant are to some extent governed by rule 54 of the Magistrates' Court Rules 1981. This requires the warrant to identify the person against whom distress is to be levied. It is not necessary for the warrant to be directed to a particular individual: it may be directed to all the constables of the police area in which the warrant is issued,[85] or to the authorised persons for the police area specified in the warrant. **5.92**

4. Execution of warrant

Any goods or money belonging to the person against whom the distress is levied may be seized, with the exception of: **5.93**

(a) clothes or bedding of any person or his family[86];
(b) tools and implements of a person's trade, up to the value of £150.[87]

If household goods are impounded, then unless the warrant itself says otherwise, or written consent is given by the person against whom the distress is levied, they should not be removed from the house until the day of the sale. Such goods should be identified by a conspicuous mark affixed to them.[88]

5. Sale

The warrant itself may specify the period (starting not earlier than the sixth day after the execution of the warrant) within which the goods are to be sold. If no period is specified then the sale should take place between the sixth and fourteenth day, inclusive, after the execution of the warrant.[89] Sale before the start of the specified period may not take place without the written consent of the debtor.[90] The sale **5.94**

---

[84] Magistrates' Court Rules 1981 (S.I. 1981 No. 552).
[85] A warrant in this form may be executed by any person under the direction of a constable.
[86] N.B. there is no maximum limit in this case—*cf.* distress for rent, and execution of High Court and county court judgments, paras. 5.46, 5.69, 5.80, above.
[87] r. 54(4), as amended by S.I. 1983 No. 523, r. 2, and Sched.
[88] r.54(8).
[89] r.54(5).
[90] r.54(5).

should be by public auction, again unless the debtor gives written consent to some other form.[91]

6. Disposal of proceeds

5.95 The proceeds of any sale, together with any money seized from the debtor, should be placed towards the payment of the debt and any costs of the distress and sale. Any balance should be returned to the owner.[92] The owner has a right to inspect a written account of the costs and charges which should be held by the clerk of the court.[93]

7. Avoiding distress

5.96 At any stage the debtor may halt the above processes by paying off the sum owed, plus costs.[94]

---

[91] r.54(6).
[92] r.54(9)
[93] r.54(10).
[94] r.54(7) and (11).

Chapter Six

TAXATION

The powers discussed in this chapter relate to taxation. All the powers of the Inland **6.01**
Revenue Commissioners (I.R.C.) are included, together with the powers of the
Commissioners of Customs and Excise in relation to value added tax (V.A.T.).
V.A.T. is discussed here rather than with the other Customs and Excise powers in
Chapter 7 because it is governed by a distinct set of rules which are in many ways
closer to the I.R.C.'s powers than to the other customs and excise powers.

This area of law has been the subject of detailed consideration by the Committee
on Enforcement Powers of the Revenue Departments, chaired by Lord Keith of
Kinkel.[1] The Committee was set up partly because of concern about the manner in
which some of the powers discussed in this chapter were being exercised.[2] It made a
number of proposals for reform, many of which have been implemented, particularly in relation to V.A.T.[3] The Finance Act 1988 contains further provisions based
on its recommendations.[4] The Committee's proposal for a general investigative
power of entry for the Inland Revenue[5] has not yet been acted on, however, and there
is still some way to go in harmonising the Inland Revenue's powers with those
applying to V.A.T.

A. Inland Revenue Commissioners

The I.R.C.'s powers of entry lie in three main areas—inspection, distress, and fraud. **6.02**

1. Inspection of documents

One of the main methods of control and enforcement used by the I.R.C. is the **6.03**
inspection of accounts and other documents related to the payment of tax. Where
the power is given to inspect the documents at particular premises, this will imply a
right to enter those premises, even if it is not expressly stated.

(a) *Income tax*

(i) **PAYE.** The main power here exists in relation to the PAYE scheme, and is **6.04**
contained in regulation 32 of the Income Tax (Employments) Regulations 1973.[6]

---

[1] The Committee issued its Report in four volumes, Vols. 1 and 2, Cmnd. 8822, Vol. 3, Cmnd. 9120
and Vol. 4, Cmnd. 9440. The Committee and its report are referred to in the rest of this chapter as the
"Keith Committee" and the "Keith Report."
[2] *Report*, Cmnd. 8822, paras. 1.3.1–1.3.3.
[3] See Finance Act 1985.
[4] See, *e.g.* s.10 (personal searches), and s.124 (examination of computers).
[5] *Report*, para. 4.5.21.
[6] S.I. 1973 No. 334.

Any authorised officer of the I.R.C. can require an employer to produce wage sheets and other documents relating to the payment of his employees. The officer may ask for all such documents relating to a specified period, or may specify particular items which he wishes to see. Production of documents is to take place at "the prescribed place,"[7] which means either a place agreed upon by the employer and the officer, or, in default of agreement, the place where the relevant documents and records are normally kept, or, as a last resort, the employer's principal place of business in the United Kingdom.

A similar power exists in relation to contractors and sub-contractors in the construction industry, under regulations 11(1) and (2) of the Income Tax (Sub-Contractors in the Construction Industry) Regulations 1975.[7a] Here the officer can call for the production of all documents and records relating to the calculation or payment of all sums paid to sub-contractors. Production is to take place at "the prescribed place," as defined above.[8] In relation to sub-contractors the power is only exercisable in respect of a person who is or has been within the preceding three years a sub-contractor, and who is not the user of a sub-contractor's tax certificate.[9] An identical power of inspection in relation to records concerning payments made without deduction of tax is given by regulation 26.[10]

In relation to all the above powers, the officer is entitled to take copies of, or make extracts from, any document. If it appears to him to be necessary he may remove a document, at a reasonable time, and for a reasonable period, but must give a receipt. Where a document which has been removed is reasonably required for the proper conduct of a business, a free copy must be provided by the officer within seven days.[11]

6.05   **(ii) Foreign dividends.** Schedule 3 to the Income and Corporation Taxes Act 1988 gives the I.R.C. powers in connection with the payment of foreign dividends.[12] Under paragraph 13 the I.R.C. may require any person entrusted with the payment of foreign dividends, and who is not in possession of an exemption certificate,[13] to make available at his premises for inspection by an authorised officer all books and other documents which the officer may reasonably require in order to determine whether any accounts delivered under paragraph 6 are complete and accurate.

(b) *Corporation tax—"transfer pricing"*

6.06   The only entry power which relates specifically to corporation tax appears to be that contained in section 772 of the Income and Corporation Taxes Act 1988. This is

[7] As defined in regulation 32(1A) (added by S.I. 1988 No. 637, reg. 6).
[7a] S.I. 1975 No. 1960.
[8] See reg. 11(2A), as added by S.I. 1988 No. 636, reg. 4.
[9] For which see Income and Corporation Taxes Act 1988, s.561. There is an obligation to retain documents of the type mentioned in regs. 11(1) and (2) for three years after the end of the year to which they relate, reg. 11(3).
[10] As amended by S.I. 1988 No. 636, reg. 6.
[11] See S.I. 1988 No. 636, regs. 4 and 6; S.I. 1988 No. 637, reg. 6.
[12] As defined in para. 6 of the Sched.
[13] Para. 13(2).

concerned with sales at an undervalue or overvalue between a United Kingdom company and a related overseas company—the practice commonly known as "transfer pricing." Section 772(6) of the Act provides that where it appears to the Board of the I.R.C. that a body of persons may be a party to a transaction or transactions with respect to which a direction under section 770 might be given, an inspector may be specifically authorised by the Board to enter any premises used in connection with the relevant trade carried on by that body of persons.

The entry must take place at a reasonable time, and the inspector must produce his authority on entry, if required. This should give the name of the inspector, and the name of the body of persons carrying on the trade in connection with which the premises are used.

Once on the premises the inspector may inspect any books, accounts, or other documents relating to the trade being carried on which he considers it necessary for him to inspect. He may also require the production of any such books, accounts, or documents, though he has no power to search for them.

(c) *Stamp duty*

Three statutes give the I.R.C. powers of entry in relation to its responsibility for the recovery of stamp duty.   **6.07**

(i) Stamp Act 1891. Section 16 of this Act is directed towards "public officers" having custody of any papers, documents, records, etc. inspection of which may lead to the recovery of duty, or prove or reveal any fraud or omission relating to it. Such officers are obliged to permit a person authorised by the I.R.C. to inspect the documents at any reasonable time, and to take notes and extracts from them as he considers necessary. No charge is to be made for allowing this.   **6.08**

"Public officer" has been widely defined as "an officer who discharges any duty in the discharge of which the public are interested, more clearly so if he is paid out of a fund provided by the public" (*e.g.* taxes).[14] The trustees and managers of unit trust schemes, and their servants and agents, are specifically designated "public officers" for the purposes of this section by virtue of the Finance Act 1946, s.56(1). It is in relation to such people that the most recent use of this power has been made.[15]

A refusal to permit inspection will lead to a fine of £10 for every offence.

(ii) Stamp Duties Management Act 1891. The strongest power in this area is given by section 18 of this Act. Where the I.R.C. have cause to suspect that a person has in his possession any forged stamps they may issue a warrant authorising the entry and search of premises belonging to the suspect. Doors (exterior or interior) which are not opened on demand may be forced. The entry must take place between nine a.m. and seven p.m.   **6.09**

The police may be called on to assist with the execution of the warrant.[16]

---

[14] *R.* v. *Whitaker* [1914] 3 K.B. 1283; see also *Henly* v. *Lyme Corporation* (1829) 5 Bing. 91, 107.
[15] Keith Report, para. 33.4.5.
[16] s.18(3).

Once on the premises *any* stamps found may be seized. The person from whom they are seized has a right to a receipt, on request, and to mark the stamps before they are removed.[17]

Refusing to permit entry, search or seizure, or assaulting, opposing, molesting, or obstructing, anyone exercising the powers under this section, is punishable with a fine of £50.[18]

6.10   **(iii) Stamp Duty Reserve Tax.** Sections 61, (but not 62), 111 and 114 of the Taxes Management Act 1970,[19] apply to stamp duty reserve tax[20] by virtue of the Stamp Duty Reserve Tax Regulations 1986.[21]

(d) *Inheritance tax*

6.11   Section 259 of the Inheritance Tax Act 1984 applies the powers contained in section 16 of the Stamp Act 1891 to inheritance tax.[22]

(e) *Petroleum revenue tax*

6.12   Paragraph 7(2) of Schedule 2 to the Oil Taxation Act 1975 empowers the I.R.C. to ask for accounts and documents related to oil fields to be made available for inspection, but there is no power to require that this should occur at any particular premises.

2. Inspection of land and other property

6.13   Various powers exist which enable the I.R.C. to value property for tax purposes. They are contained in the Taxes Management Act 1970 ("T.M.A.") and the Inheritance Tax Act 1984.

(a) *Income tax and corporation tax*

6.14   The determination of the annual value of land for the purposes of income tax or corporation tax is covered by section 110 of the T.M.A. The Board of the I.R.C. is empowered to authorise any person to enter and inspect such land, with a view to establishing its annual value. The entry must be made at a "reasonable time."[23]

The entrant must, if required to do so, produce evidence of his authority.

There is apparently nothing in the way of support powers in relation to this section. If the occupier refuses to admit a duly authorised inspector he commits no offence (unless, of course, he assaults the inspector). Nor does the inspector have any

---

[17] s.19.

[18] N.B. ss.16 and 17 also contain entry and search powers relating to forged and stolen stamps, but these are regarded as police powers, rather than I.R.C. powers—see Keith Report, para. 33.4.13.

[19] For which see para. 6.14 below.

[20] See Part IV of the Finance Act 1986.

[21] S.I. 1986 No. 1711.

[22] See para. 6.08 above.

[23] See above, para. 1.24.

right to use force,[24] though if he finds the entrance open, and is not challenged, it would seem that he may lawfully go on to the land.

By contrast, the powers relating to Capital Gains Tax under section 111 are backed up by an "obstruction" offence.[25]

(b) *Capital gains tax—Taxes Management Act 1970, s.111(1)*

For the purposes of the Capital Gains Tax Act 1979, the Board may authorise an **6.15** inspector, or other officer of the Board, to inspect any property in order to ascertain its market value. There is no express power of entry, but the person having custody or possession of the property is obliged to permit an authorised official to inspect it; where the property is immovable, or cannot be moved without great difficulty, this will mean in effect that the official must be allowed on to the land.

Time. The inspection is to take place "at such reasonable times as the Board may **6.16** consider necessary." The use of the plural suggest that more than one inspection of the same property may be made. It is also clear that the control of the inspections is ultimately in the hands of the Board rather than the individual inspector. As to "reasonable," see above, para. 1.24.

Obstruction. It is an offence wilfully to delay or obstruct a person carrying out **6.17** the powers under section 111, with a penalty on summary conviction of a fine not exceeding £5.[26] The meaning of "obstruction" is considered above in Chapter 1, paragraph 1.29. "Delay" would seem to widen the offence, perhaps even to include unhelpful inactivity.[27]

(d) *Inheritance tax*

A similar power exists in relation to inheritance tax under section 220 of the **6.18** Inheritance Tax Act 1984. The Board may authorise any person to inspect any property in order to value it for inheritance tax purposes. The person having custody or possession of the property is obliged to permit the inspection to take place at such reasonable times as the Board considers necessary.

Obstruction. It is a summary offence, attracting a fine not exceeding level 1 on **6.19** the standard scale, wilfully to delay or obstruct a person acting under the above power.[28]

3. Distress for taxes

The power to levy distress for the non-payment of taxes to the Inland Revenue is **6.20** governed by the T.M.A. s.61. The taxes for which distress may be levied are income

---

[24] See above, para. 1.13.
[25] s.111(2), below.
[26] s.111(2).
[27] *cf. Swallow* v. *London County Council* [1916] 1 K.B. 224.
[28] s.220(2). For meaning of "delay," see para. 6.17 above.

tax, corporation tax, capital gains tax, petroleum revenue tax, and supplementary petroleum duty.[29]

(a) *When does the power arise?*

6.21   The power arises when, following a demand by a collector,[30] the taxpayer neglects or refuses to pay the sum charged. He should be given a reasonable time to respond to the demand, particularly if it is not made directly to him.[31] A failure to respond at all may be evidence of a refusal.[32]

(b) *Procedure for levying distress*

6.22   The collector may of course levy the distress with the taxpayer's consent. This will be the normal situation.[33] If he meets resistance, however, he may obtain a warrant from the General Commissioners.[34] The warrant will empower the collector to break open the house or other premises where the distress is to be levied. The statute provides that the collector may call upon any constable to assist in the breaking and the levying, and indeed, in relation to a similar provision,[35] it was held that the breaking of the house *must* take place in the presence of a constable.[36] The Act is silent on any powers to use force once entry has been achieved, but there seems no reason why the powers should not be the same as for distress for rent, so that inner doors, cupboards, trunks, etc., may be broken.[37]

(c) *What property may be levied?*

6.23   The property which may be subject to a levy for taxes varies according to the nature of the charge. Where the charge is on a person or corporation,[38] the distress must be levied against goods belonging to the person charged. If goods belonging to a third party are found on the premises, they may not be taken. This includes trust property of which the taxpayer has possession, but only restricted use.[39] However, the Law of Distress Amendment Act 1888 does not apply to distress for taxes,[40] so that the exemptions which are provided by that Act (*e.g.* in relation to bedding, and tools of the debtor's trade) will not restrict the collector levying distress for taxes. Goods privileged from distress at common law, will, it seems, be protected.[41]

[29] Oil Taxation Act 1975, Sched. 3; Finance Act 1981, Sched. 16.
[30] *Gibbs* v. *Stead* (1828) 8 B. & C. 528; *Berry* v. *Farrow* [1914] 1 K.B. 632.
[31] See the T.M.A., s.115, Delivery and Service of Documents; and *Gibbs* v. *Stead*, note 30 above.
[32] *Ibid.*
[33] See Keith Report, para. 24.2.8.
[34] T.M.A., s.61(2). The Keith Committee found (Report, para. 24.2.15) that only one warrant had been applied for since 1960, and this had been refused. For the form of the warrant see, s.113(3), and also para. 6.28.
[35] 38 Geo. 3, c.5, s.17 (now repealed).
[36] *Foss* v. *Racine* (1838) 4 M. & W. 419. A constable may also be present in order to fulfil his general duty to keep the peace—see, *e.g. R.* v. *Clark* (1835) 3 Ad. & El. 287: 111 E.R. 422.
[37] See above, para. 5.44.
[38] Including a charge for Petroleum Revenue Tax or Supplementary Petroleum Duty.
[39] *Earl of Shaftesbury* v. *Russell* (1873) 1 B. & C. 666; 107 E.R. 244.
[40] *MacGregor* v. *Clamp & Son* [1914] 1 K.B. 288.
[41] See above, para. 5.46.

Where the tax is charged not on the taxpayer, but on property itself (*i.e.* income tax and corporation tax under Sched. A or B), then a third party's goods are not protected.[42] The collector does not have to worry about who is the owner of property or whether there is sufficient property of the taxpayer to cover the debt without touching that belonging to the third party; "it is enough for him that the goods are on the premises."[43]

(d) *Procedure after seizure*

There is no provision in the Act for "walking possession."[44] However, the courts **6.24** have recognised that this sort of arrangement may legitimately be made with the taxpayer.[45] Otherwise, the question of whether the collector has abandoned the distress is one of fact to be decided in all the circumstances.

Seized property is to be held for five days by the collector. Any costs involved in this will be charged to the debtor. At any time during this period the goods may be recovered by paying the tax owing, plus costs.[46]

If no such payment is made, the distress must be appraised, and then sold by public auction.[47] Any surplus, after the deduction of costs, must be restored to the owner of the goods distrained.[48]

(e) *Priority of claims*

By virtue of section 62 of the T.M.A. 1970, distress for taxes takes precedence over **6.25** all other claims to the taxpayer's goods or chattels, other than distress for rent by a landlord. A creditor seizing or receiving property in relation to some other debt may pay off the tax owing.[49] If he does not do so, the property which has been seized or transferred will be subject to distraint by the collector, as described above.[50]

Where distress for taxes is levied against a company within three months of an order for compulsory winding up,[51] the property distrained, or the proceeds of its sale, is subject to a first charge for the debts given priority by section 614 of the Companies Act 1985.[52]

(f) *Challenging distress for taxes*

(i) Defects in the warrant. By virtue of section 114 of the T.M.A. 1970 defects in **6.26** a warrant are not to lead to the warrant being quashed, or deemed void or voidable,

[42] *Juson* v. *Dixon* (1813) 1 M. & S. 601; 105 E.R. 225.
[43] *Ibid.* 606; 227, *per* Lord Ellenborough.
[44] See above, para. 5.45.
[45] *Berry* v. *Farrow* [1914] 1 K.B. 632; *Herbert Berry Associates Ltd.* v. *I.R.C.* [1977] 1 W.L.R. 1437.
[46] The Keith Committee found that during this period the defaulter "usually pays or comes to a suitable arrangement." (Report, para. 24.2.9.)
[47] s.61(5).
[48] Not necessarily the person from whose premises it was seized.
[49] Or one year's arrears, where more than two years are being claimed.
[50] s.62(2).
[51] But not a creditors' voluntary winding up—*Herbert Berry Associates Ltd.* v. *I.R.C.* [1977] 1 W.L.R. 1437 (H.L.).
[52] Companies Act 1985, s.614(4).

provided that the warrant is in substance and effect in conformity with, or according to the intent and meaning of, the Taxes Acts, and that the person or property which the warrant affects is "designated therein according to common intent and understanding."

Section 61 is silent as to the time for which a warrant is effective. Presumably this may be made clear on its face. In a case on previous legislation, *Elliott* v. *Yates*,[53] a warrant was challenged because it was used to levy distress after the end of the tax year in which it was issued. The Court of Appeal held that, although the warrant could only be used in relation to tax payable in the tax year of its issue, distress could be levied under it at any time until the collector had in effect closed his accounts, through being required to account for the monies collected to the Collector of Inland Revenue.

6.27   **(ii) Other defects.** If there are other defects in the carrying out of distress for taxes, such as lack of a warrant, or use of excessive force, or seizure of privileged goods, the distress will be wrongful, and the collector will be a trespasser. This will bring into play all the usual remedies,[54] including the possibility of obtaining an injunction to restrain the levy or sale, and damages for trespass. The defendant may be either the individuals involved, or the I.R.C.

4. Fraud

6.28   The powers of the I.R.C. in connection with suspected tax fraud are contained in section 20C of the T.M.A.[55] as interpreted by the House of Lords in *I.R.C.* v. *Rossminster.*[56]

(a) *The warrant*

6.29   An entry and search can only take place on the authority of a warrant. This is issued by a circuit judge, who must be satisfied as a result of information on oath given by an officer of the Board that there are reasonable grounds for suspecting that an offence has been committed, that evidence of it is to be found in the premises specified in the information, and that the officer has the approval of the Board.[57]

The offence must be one "involving any form of fraud in connection with, or in relation to, tax." This certainly includes false accounting,[58] forgery,[59] conspiracy to defraud,[60] perjury,[61] and false statements to income tax. It may go even further.[62] It seems to have been accepted by the I.R.C. in the Court of Appeal in *Rossminster,* that

[53] [1900] 2 Q.B. 370.
[54] See Chap. Two.
[55] Inserted by the Finance Act 1976, s.57(1), and Sched. 6.
[56] [1980] A.C. 952.
[57] The Board as a whole, not one of its officers: s.20C(2).
[58] Theft Act 1968, s.17.
[59] Forgery and Counterfeiting Act 1981.
[60] Criminal Law Act 1977, s.5.
[61] Perjury Act 1911, s.5.
[62] See, *e.g.* Lord Denning, *R.* v. *I.R.C., ex p. Rossminster* [1980] A.C. 952, 973.

the issuing judge would need to be told at least the general nature of the suspected offence or offences.[63] The House of Lords made it clear that such information need not appear on the face of the warrant, and could not be expected to be revealed prior to the conclusion of any proceedings against the taxpayer. Nevertheless the principle seems to remain unscathed, that in order to satisfy himself that reasonable suspicion exists the judge must have some idea of the type of offence which is suspected. It will be seen below that this in no way inhibits the scope of a search once the warrant has been granted.

The suspicion must relate to the fact that an offence has been committed: it is not enough that offences may be committed in the future. And the judge must also be satisfied that there are reasonable grounds for suspecting that relevant evidence is to be found on the premises specified in the information. It should be noted that the premises do not have to be those of the suspected perpetrator of the fraud; they may be any premises in relation to which there is a reasonable suspicion, *e.g.* those of the suspect's family, friends, business associates, accountant, or bank.

The form of the warrant has been discussed in Chapter One.[64] The House of Lords in *Rossminster* ruled that the statute requires very little information to be given in the warrant—simply the address of the premises to be searched, and the name of the officer or officers authorised to carry out the search.[65]

The warrant must be exercised within 14 days of the date of issue, but the entry may be at any time of the day or night.[66]

Force may be used, if necessary.[67]

(b) *What may be seized?*

The warrant itself is little more than the "key to the door."[68] It authorises the entry **6.30** and search of the premises. But the power to seize and remove property is given by section 20C(3).

There is an immunity for documents (which are partially defined in section 20D(3) as including "books, accounts and other documents or records whatsoever") in the possession of a barrister, advocate or solicitor with respect to which a claim to professional privilege could be maintained. Otherwise the officer may seize and remove anything which he had reasonable cause to believe may be required as evidence for the purposes of proceedings for tax fraud. Since the warrant does not have to specify the tax fraud, and the seizure is in any case not made under the authority of the warrant, the suspected offences in relation to which property is seized need not be the same as those for which the warrant was issued. This interpretation was adopted by the House of Lords in *Rossminster*. It has the effect of

---

[63] *Ibid. per* Browne L.J. at p. 978.
[64] Para. 1.20.
[65] In *Rossminster* 63 names were attached to the warrant—[1980] A.C. 952, 1003.
[66] See above, para. 1.24.
[67] See above, paras. 1.13–1.16.
[68] [1980] A.C. 952, 1023, *per* Lord Scarman.

making the reference in section 20C(4) to things seized "under the authority of the warrant" meaningless, but it is presumably too late now to argue for a contrary interpretation.

The suspicion under section 20C(3) must be objectively "reasonable"; an honest belief that there are reasonable grounds is not enough.[69]

The occupier of the premises, or a person having had possession or custody of seized items immediately before their seizure has the right to be provided, on request, with a list of what has been taken.[70]

If documents relating to a business are seized, a person who can show that access to them is required to enable him to continue to run the business has the right to be afforded reasonable access to them.[71] Of course, if large quantities of documents are taken it may be impossible for the business realistically to continue.[72]

(c) *Remedies*

6.31   As a result of the House of Lords decision in *Rossminster* it seems that a person must rely on tortious remedies, taken at the conclusion or abandonment of proceedings by the Revenue, unless there is some defect in the minimal formal requirements laid down by their lordships. Even then, it has been suggested that if documents seized were of the class that could have been seized, then, while the I.R.C. would be obliged to return the actual documents, they would be entitled to retain copies.[73]

B. Customs and Excise—Value Added Tax

6.32   The main entry powers of the Customs and Excise Commissioners in relation to V.A.T. are contained in the Value Added Tax Act 1983. The Commissioners also have powers under the Police and Criminal Evidence Act 1984, which could be used in relation to V.A.T. investigations. These powers are discussed further in Chapter Seven, para. 7.02. The powers under the Value Added Tax Act 1983 fall into two general categories—investigative, and enforcement.

1. Investigative

(a) *Value Added Tax Act 1983, Sched. 7*

6.33   **(i) Entry without warrant.** The most general power is given by paragraph 10(1), which empowers an authorised person,[74] to enter business premises for the purpose of exercising any powers under the Act relating to V.A.T.

The powers in respect of which paragraphs 10(1) is most likely to be used would

---

[69] See Lord Scarman, [1980] A.C. 952, 1024–1025, and paras. 1.17–1.19.

[70] s.20C(4).

[71] s.20C(5).

[72] See also the comments of Lord Salmon, [1980] A.C. 852. 1016, concerning the effects on the search on the Rossminster Group's business.

[73] *Per* Eveleigh L.J. [1980] A.C. 952, 967.

[74] "Any person acting under the authority of the Commissioners," V.A.T. Act 1983, s.48(1).

seem to be those under paragraphs 8 and 9. The former paragraph relates to the provision of information and the production and inspection of documents, and the latter to taking samples including the breaking open of gaming machines.[75]

A more specific power is provided by paragraph 10(2). This provides a power of entry where an authorised person had reasonable cause to believe that any premises are used in connection with the supply of goods under taxable supplies and that goods to be so supplied are on those premises. It may be used to inspect the premises themselves or the goods found on them.

In relation to paragraph 10(1) and (2) the entry must be made at a reasonable **6.34** time.[76] There is no power to use force to gain entry, nor does the occupier seem to commit any offence simply by refusing permission to someone seeking to exercise those powers. It may be however that a refusal would be sufficient to constitute a reasonable ground of suspicion under paragraph 10(3).

Neither paragraph 10(1) nor 10(2) gives any power to *search*. The distinction **6.35** between "inspection" and "search" was noted by the Keith Committee, which suggested that, in the absence of any clear judicial ruling, "inspection is by eye, search by hand," and that inspection would not allow the uncovering of anything not visible merely by walking round the premises.[77]

(ii) Entry under warrant. Paragraph 10(3) provides for the issue of a warrant by **6.36** a justice of the peace, where the justice is satisfied by information on oath that there are reasonable grounds for suspecting that a fraud offence[78] which appears to be of a serious nature is being, has been, or is about to be committed on any premises, or that evidence of the commission of such an offence is to be found there. The issue and exercise of the warrant will be subject to sections 15, 16 and 19 of the Police and Criminal Evidence Act 1984.[79] Where documents, or other items are in the possession of an innocent third party, however, the production order procedure under paragraph 10A (below, para. 6.39) should be used, if possible.

The warrant is to be issued to an "authorised person."[80] It will empower him to **6.37** enter the premises, search them, and seize any documents or other items on the premises which he has reasonable cause to believe may be required as evidence for the purposes of proceedings in respect of a fraud offence which appears to him to be of a serious nature. In addition, any person found on the premises and who is reasonably believed to be in possession of any such documents or items may be searched.[81]

---

[75] Para. 9A.
[76] See above, paras. 1.17–1.19.
[77] Report, para. 4.3.3.
[78] *i.e.* an offence under s.39(1)–(3) of the Value Added Tax Act 1983.
[79] For which see Chap. 3 (above), para. 3.07. For further discussion of the application of the P.C.E.A. to the Customs and Excise, see Chap. 7 (below), para. 7.02.
[80] See note 74, above. But the warrant itself may limit the number of "authorised persons" who may exercise it: para. 10(5)(*a*).
[81] A woman or girl must be searched by a woman.

6.38 The entry must take place within one month of the issue of the warrant. It can be at any time of day or night,[82] subject to any limitation which may be imposed by the warrant itself.[83] Force may be used to enter if necessary.

The person to whom the warrant is issued is specifically empowered to take with him such other persons as appear to him to be necessary. Presumably the most likely additional people would be police officers if a breach of the peace was anticipated. Indeed, paragraph 10(*c*) provides that the warrant may specify that it may only be exercised in the presence of a uniformed constable. But the power is expressed subjectively, and not in terms of reasonableness, so it would seem that the authorised person may take with him as many people as he wishes.

A copy of the warrant should be given to the occupier, or, in his absence a person appearing to be in charge of the premises. In default of either, a copy should be left in a prominent place on the premises.[83a]

There is nothing in the Act to say what should happen to property seized under paragraph 10(3), so it will fall to be dealt with under the general principles applying in this area.[84]

6.39 **Production orders.** A production order can be obtained from a justice of the peace who is satisfied by information on oath that there are reasonable grounds for believing that an offence in connection with V.A.T. is being or has been committed, and that recorded information which may be required as evidence is in the possession of any person.[85] The order will require the person in possession to give an authorised person access to it,[86] and to allow him to remove any of it which he reasonably considers necessary. If the information is held on a computer it must be produced in a visible, legible, and (if the authorised person wishes to remove it) removable form. The order must be complied with within seven days, or such longer period as specified in the order.

6.40 **Access to seized items.** Items have been removed under paragraph 10 or 10A, the occupier of the premises from which they were taken, or the person having custody or control of them prior to their removal, is entitled to a record of what was taken.[87] This must be provided within a reasonable time of being requested.

Access to items removed must be granted to a person having custody and control prior to the removal, or their representative. Access will be under supervision, and may be refused if there are reasonable grounds to believe that to grant it would prejudice the investigation, or criminal proceedings. A similar limitation exists in relation to the right to photograph or copy items.[88]

---

[82] *Bulloch* v. *H.M. Advocate* 1980 S.L.T. (Notes) 5.
[83] Para. 10(5)(*c*).
[83a] Para. 10(6). *cf.* Police and Criminal Evidence Act 1984, s.16(7)—above, para. 3.10.
[84] See above, paras. 2.37–2.53.
[85] Para. 10A(1).
[86] This includes the power to make copies, or take extracts.
[87] Para. 10B(1).
[88] Para. 10B(4), (5), (6).

(b) *Inspection of computers*

As a result of the increased use of computerised accounting systems, and the **6.41**
storage and handling of data electronically, the Commissioners were given a special
power in the Finance Act 1980 allowing the inspection of computers. This has now
been incorporated into Schedule 7 to the 1983 Act, under paragraph 3(3) of which
an authorised officer is entitled to have access to any computer and associated
apparatus used by a taxable person in connection with the production, delivery, or
receipt of tax invoices. The power must be exercised at a reasonable time. The officer
may inspect and check the operation of the computer, etc., and the taxpayer or other
person in charge of the equipment is required to give him any assistance he may
require. Obstruction of an officer, or failure, without reasonable excuse, to assist,
renders the offender liable to a fine not exceeding level 4 on the standard scale.[89]

2. Enforcement

In order to recover sums owing in respect of V.A.T. the commissioners are given **6.42**
the power in paragraph 6(4) to make regulations authorising the levy of distress on
the goods or chattels of the debtor.

The current regulations are contained in regulations 65 and 66 of the V.A.T.
(General Regulations) 1985.[90] Regulation 65 deals with England, Wales, and Northern Ireland; regulation 66 with Scotland. Only regulation 65 is dealt with here.

(a) *Conditions for exercise of the power*

There must have been a neglect or refusal to pay following a demand from a **6.43**
Collector of Customs and Excise, or an officer of rank not below that of Higher
Executive Officer. A Collector then has power to distrain on the goods and chattels
of the person to whom the demand was made, and may issue a warrant directing any
authorised person to levy such distress.[91] Where the tax is due under paragraph 4(a),
no distress shall be levied until 30 days after it became due.[92]

(b) *Mode of entry for distress*

There are no restrictions in the regulations on the time when distress may be **6.44**
levied. It is submitted that the court would apply the general rules relating to other
types of distress, and only allow it to be levied in the day time.

If it is necessary to use force to gain entry then a warrant for this must be obtained
from a Collector, and in this case entry is specifically limited to the day time.[93]

The levy or warrant to break open must be executed by or under the direction of
the authorised person to whom the warrant was issued.[94]

---

[89] Para. 3(4).
[90] S.I. 1985 No. 886.
[91] Reg. 65(1).
[92] *Ibid.*
[93] Reg. 65(2).
[94] Reg. 65(3).

(c) *What may be seized?*

6.45   Only goods or chattels belonging to the debtor may be seized, although they may be seized from any house or premises.[95] Goods belonging to a third party are immune under these regulations.

(d) *Procedure after seizure*

6.46   The property seized must be held for five days.[96] "Walking possession" may be agreed, though not provided for by the regulations.[97] During this period the debtor may redeem it by paying the sum due plus the costs of the distress.[98] If he does not do so, the property must be independently appraised, and sold by public auction. The proceeds of the auction are to be used for the payment of the debt, and the costs of the distress and auction. Any surplus should be restored to the owner of the property.[99] Breach of a walking possession agreement will render the person in default liable to a penalty equal to half the tax due, unless he can show that there was a reasonable excuse for the breach.[1]

The levying of distress does not itself extinguish any right to appeal in respect of assessments.[2] So an application for leave to appeal out of time will be considered notwithstanding that fact that distress has been levied. If the appeal is allowed this does not render the distress unlawful, since its legality must be judged at the time when it was levied. The result would simply be that the Commissioners would be required to account for the proceeds of the distress.[3]

---

[95] Reg. 65(1) and (2).
[96] Reg. 65(4).
[97] *P. J. Davies* v. *The Commissioners* [1979] V.A.T.T.R. 162.
[98] Reg. 65(5).
[99] Reg. 65(5).
[1] Finance Act 1985, s.16.
[2] *P. Davies* v. *The Commissioners* [1979] V.A.T.T.R. 162.
[3] *Ibid.*

CUSTOMS AND EXCISE

The powers of the Customs and Excise Commissioners other than those related to **7.01**
V.A.T. (for which see Chapter Six) were largely consolidated into a series of Acts in
1979, *viz.* the Customs and Excise Management Act, the Customs and Excise Duties
(General Reliefs) Act, the Alcoholic Liquor Duties Act, the Hydrocarbon Oil Duties
Act, the Matches and Mechanical Lighters Duties Act, and the Tobacco Products
Duty Act—cited collectively as the Customs and Excise Acts 1979. Under this
legislation the Commissioners have both general powers of entry, and specific
powers under a particular enactment, or in regulations made under them. The
Commissioners also have powers under the Police and Criminal Evidence Act 1984,
and powers connected with their responsibility for the collection of car tax. The
arrangement adopted in this chapter is to deal first with the general powers, and
then with the specific.

A. General Powers

1. Police and Criminal Evidence Act 1984

By virtue of regulations made under section 114 of the P.C.E.A. 1984,[1] certain **7.02**
provisions of that Act apply to the Customs and Excise, as regards investigations
into "assigned matters."[2] These include section 8, which means that Customs and
Excise officers have the same general power to obtain a search warrant for evidence
of a serious arrestable offence[3] as do the police.[4]

They also have the powers of entry without warrant under section 17(1)(*b*) (to
arrest a person for an arrestable offence),[5] and following arrest, under sections 18[6]
and 32.[7]

All powers of entry under a search warrant (whether under section 8 of the
P.C.E.A., or under one of the other powers outlined below) will be subject to sections
15 and 16 of the P.C.E.A.,[8] and also to section 9, which prevents search warrants

---

[1] S.I. 1985 No. 1800 (as amended by S.I. 1987 No. 439).
[2] Defined in the C.E.M.A. 1979, s.1, as "any matter in relation to which the Commissioners are for the
time being required in pursuance of any enactment to perform any duties."
[3] Provided it relates to an "assigned matter."
[4] See above, para. 3.26.
[5] See above, para. 3.25.
[6] Where the arrest is for an arrestable offence which relates to an "assigned matter": S.I. 1985
No. 1800, reg. 7.
[7] See above, para. 3.23.
[8] See above, para. 3.07.

obtainable under Acts passed prior to the P.C.E.A. being used to search for items subject to legal privilege,[9] or excluded as special procedure material. In the case of excluded and special procedure material, Schedule 1 to the P.C.E.A. must be used.[10] Paragraph 6 of the Regulations, however, has the effect of removing the protection for excluded and special procedure material from

> "Material in the possession of a person who acquired or created it in the course of any trade, business, profession, or other occupation or for the purpose of any paid or unpaid office and which relates to an assigned matter."

Sections 19 to 22 of the P.C.E.A., concerning the seizure and retention of items also apply, but the access and copying provisions in section 21 do not cover things seized as being liable to forfeiture.[11]

2. Customs and Excise Management Act 1979

7.03   The Keith Committee[12] recommended that there should be a general standardised provision for search under warrant where there are reasonable grounds for believing that evidence of an offence of fraud, including fraudulent evasion of a prohibition or restriction, is to be found on specified premises.[13] At the moment, however, apart from the powers under the P.C.E.A. outlined above, the only general power to search for property relates to items liable to forfeiture, and is given by section 161 of the Customs and Excise Management Act 1979 ("C.E.M.A."). It is exercisable under either a writ of assistance, or a magistrate's warrant.

(a) *Writ of assistance*

7.04   A writ of assistance is a kind of general search warrant, issued to an officer by the Queen's Remembrancer in the Central Office of the Supreme Court. It is valid for the reign in which it is issued and for six months thereafter.[14] By virtue of section 161(1) an officer holding a writ of assistance has the power to enter any building or place when there are reasonable grounds to suspect that anything liable to forfeiture under the Customs and Excise Acts [15] is kept or concealed there.[16]

The writ of assistance has attracted some criticism because of its wide scope, and the lack of time limit on it. The Law Reform Commission of Canada described the existence of the writ in that country as "an instrument of unconstitutional search and seizure, as an affront to common law traditions, and as an unnecessary instrument of search and seizure," and recommended its abolition.[17] Much the same kind of comments could be made of the existence of the writ in this country. The Keith

---

[9] As defined in the P.C.E.A., s.10. See above, para. 3.13.
[10] See above, para. 3.28.
[11] S.I. 1985 No. 1800, reg. 5.
[12] See above, para. 6.01.
[13] *Report*, para. 35.7.33.
[14] C.E.M.A., s.161(6).
[15] *i.e.* Customs and Excise Acts 1979, and any other enactment relating to customs and excise—s.1(1).
[16] The provisions relating to the exercise of these powers are dealt with below, para. 7.06.
[17] Law Reform Commission of Canada, Report 19, *Writs of Assistance and Telewarrants, 1983*, p. 44.

Committee, however, thought that in exigent circumstances there was a need for the Customs and Excise to have power to search premises where there are reasonable grounds to suspect that contraband is present, without the delay inevitable in obtaining a warrant. They regarded the writ of assistance procedure as preferable to the more extensive use of powers of search consequent upon arrest. They therefore recommended that the writ should be retained, subject to certain safeguards.[18]

(b) *Warrant*

7.05 The power of entry may also be given by an ordinary search warrant, issued by a justice of the peace, if he is satisfied by information on oath given by an officer that there are reasonable grounds to suspect that anything liable to forfeiture is kept or concealed in any building or place. The power is given to any officer, and any person accompanying an officer, and relates to any building or place named in the warrant. The warrant must be exercised within one month.

(c) *Powers on entry*

7.06 The officer has the same powers on entry whether he acts under a writ of assistance or a magistrate's warrant.[19]

The entry may take place at any time of the day or night,[20] but at night (*i.e.* between 11 p.m. and 5 a.m.—see section 1(1)) the officer must be accompanied by a constable.[21]

On entry the officer may search the premises for, and seize, detain, or remove, anything liable to forfeiture.[22] The provision is ambiguous as to whether it is enough that the officer reasonably suspects that what is seized is liable to forfeiture, but the more natural meaning of the words used is that the thing must actually be so liable. Seizure of items not liable to forfeiture, even on the basis of reasonable suspicion, will be an abuse of the powers under this section. There are however provisions in section 144 which provide some protection for the officer in this situation.[23]

Such force as is reasonably necessary for the purpose may be used either to effect the entry, or to carry out the search.[24]

(d) *Powers of a police constable*

7.07 A police constable has the power to obtain a warrant under section 161, and exercise it in the same way as a Customs and Excise officer where there are reasonable grounds to suspect that any equipment or materials for the manufacture of spirits is unlawfully kept or deposited in any building or place.[25]

---

[18] *Report*, para. 35.7.67.
[19] s.161(4).
[20] s.161(1)(*a*).
[21] s.161(2).
[22] s.161(1)(*a*). For what is forfeitable, see the C.E.M.A. ss.49, 140, 141, 142, and the more specific powers outlined in the rest of this chapter.
[23] See below, para. 7.41.
[24] s.161(1)(*b*). See Chap. One, para. 1.13.
[25] s.161(5).

(e) *Forfeiture procedures*

Once property liable to forfeiture has been seized the procedures set out under section 139 of and Schedule 3 to the C.E.M.A. must be followed.[26]

3. Revenue traders

7.08   The Customs and Excise Management Act 1979 gives general powers in relation to the premises of revenue traders. A "revenue trader" is any person carrying on a trade or business subject to:

(a) the provisions of the Customs and Excise Acts relating either to the protection, security, collection or management of the revenues derived from the duties of excise on goods produced or manufactured in the United Kingdom, or to an activity or facility for which an excise licence is required, or

(b) the provisions of the Betting and Gaming Duties Act 1972.

It also covers a person who is a wholesaler or an occupier of an excise warehouse, and includes a registered club.[26a]

(a) *General search power*

7.09   Power to enter, inspect, and search the premises of a revenue trader is given by section 112(1). It may be exercised by an officer at any time. At night (11 p.m. to 5 a.m.) the officer must be accompanied by a constable, unless the premises to be entered are those of a distiller, brewer or winemaker.[27]

There is no power to use force to enter unless the premises are those of a distiller, brewer or winemaker. In this case the officer must first demand admission, and declare his name and address. Then, if he is not immediately admitted, the officer, and anyone assisting him, may break open a door, or window, or break through a wall, in order to obtain admission.[28] This force may not be used at night, however, unless the officer is accompanied by a constable.[29]

Section 112 does not give any power to seize property. Note, however, the powers under section 117, below.

(b) *Enforcement powers against revenue traders*

7.10   Default by a revenue trader in the payment of excise duty (other than duty on imported goods) or of a penalty incurred under the revenue trade provisions of the

---

[26] Para. 7.33, below.

[26a] s.1(1).

[27] s.112(2). The Keith Committee recommended that police attendance should no longer be a matter of routine: *Report*, para. 34.5.9.

[28] s.112(3). Note that there is no need for a definite refusal to admit before force can be used: indeed it may be that the premises are empty.

[29] s.112(4). "At night" means between 11 p.m. and 5 a.m., s.1(1). s.112(1) also applies to vehicles, vessels, aircraft or structures in or from which tobacco products are sold or dealt in, or dutiable alcoholic drinks are sold by retail, s.112(5). The section applies to the occupier of a refinery, whether or not he is a revenue trader, as it applies to a distiller.

Customs and Excise Acts, renders certain property in the possession or custody of the trader[30] liable to be taken in execution.[31] The property at risk comprises;

"(a) all goods liable to a relevant excise duty [*i.e.* other than a duty on imported goods], whether or not that duty has been paid;

(b) all materials for manufacturing or producing any such goods; and

(c) all apparatus, equipment, machinery, tools, vessels and utensils for, or for preparing any such materials for, such manufacture or production, or by which the trade in respect of which the duty is imposed is carried on."[32]

The property need not be in the possession or custody of the trader (or of his agent or other person on his behalf) at the time it is taken as long as it was so at the time when the duty was charged, or became chargeable, or while it was owing, or, in relation to a penalty, at the time when the offence for which the penalty was charged was committed.[33] But goods which, after being charged with relevant excise duty, are sold in the ordinary course of trade to a bona fide purchaser for full and valuable consideration, and delivered into his possession before the issue of any warrant or process for distress or seizure, are not liable to be taken.[34] The burden of proof of immunity lies on the person claiming it.[35]

(c) *Distress*

The goods listed above are liable to be levied for distress once any relevant duty **7.11** has become payable. The officer may issue a warrant, signed by him, empowering any person to distrain, and sell the goods seized by public auction after six days notice of the sale. A distiller, brewer, licensed producer of wine or made wine or registered maker of cider may redeem anything seized at any time before the sale by paying to the officer the true value of the items removed towards the cost of the duty owed.[36]The proceeds of the distress are to be used to defray the duty owed, after payment of costs and expenses, with any surplus being paid to the trader.[37] Section 117 itself does not provide any detailed procedures for the distress, so the operation of this section would seem to be subject to the common law rules in this area.[38]

4. Pipelines[39]

Where a dutiable substance is carried by a pipeline, and the duty has not been **7.12**

---

[30] Or of his agent or any other person on his behalf.
[31] s.117(1).
[32] s.117(1).
[33] s.117(2).
[34] s.117(3).
[35] s.117(4).
[36] s.117(6). This is subject to ss.27(3) and (4) of the Alcoholic Liquor Duties Act 1979.
[37] s.117(7).
[38] See above, paras. 5.35–5.61.
[39] "Pipelines" are defined by the Pipelines Act 1962, s.65.

paid, section 162 of the C.E.M.A. 1979 provide a power of entry on to any land adjacent to the pipeline. The power is exercisable by an officer in order to enable him to get to the pipeline for the purpose of exercising any powers relating to it conferred by or under the Customs and Excise Acts 1979, or to get from the pipeline after the exercise of any such power.

5. Wharves and transit sheds

7.13 An officer may at any time enter an approved wharf or transit shed, and inspect it and any goods therein.[40]

6. Aircraft, aerodromes, etc.

7.14 Under section 33 of the C.E.M.A., an officer has a right of access at any time to any place to which he needs access to inspect an aircraft, and any goods loaded on it, or to inspect relevant documentation.[41]

An officer also has the right at any time to enter and inspect an aerodrome and all buildings and goods thereon. The person in control of the aerodrome has a duty to permit such inspection.[42]

In either case, failure to comply is a summary offence, punishable with a fine not exceeding level 4 on the standard scale, or imprisonment not exceeding three months.[43]

7. Powers to prevent smuggling

7.15 Any officer engaged in the prevention of smuggling may pass freely along and over any part of the coast, or of the shore or bank of any river or creek.[44] Gardens or pleasure grounds may not, however, be entered under this power.

Any officer (or constable, member of the armed forces or coastguard) who has reasonable grounds to believe that a signal or message connected with smuggling is being or is about to be made or transmitted from a house or place (or a ship, aircraft or vehicle), may enter and take reasonable steps to stop or prevent it.[45]

8. Examination and sampling

7.16 There are also implicit general powers to enter premises whenever an officer has the power to examine goods or to take samples, by virtue of sections 159 and 160 of the C.E.M.A.

B. Specific Powers

1. Alcoholic liquor

7.17 The powers of the Customs and Excise relating to the production and sale of

---

[40] C.E.M.A., ss.20 and 25, as amended by Finance Act 1987, s.6. See Keith Committee, *Report*, para. 34.5.10.
[41] s.33(1).
[42] s.33(2).
[43] s.33(4).
[44] C.E.M.A., s.82(2).
[45] *Ibid.* s.84(5).

alcoholic liquor were consolidated in the Alcoholic Liquor Duties Act 1979, and Regulations made under the Act.

(a) *Spirits*

The Spirits Regulations 1982,[46] contain provisions entitling Customs and Excise officers to examine plant and records used in or related to the manufacture of spirits.[47] As with many of the powers noted in this section, there is no power of entry attached to these regulations so the officer will have to rely on the consent of the occupier unless he enters under one of the more general powers.[48] Otherwise the only way of enforcing the power to examine is indirectly, through the obstruction offence.[49]

Methylated spirits. Under section 79 of the Alcoholic Liquor Duties Act 1979 there is a power for an officer to enter the premises of any person authorised under the Methylated Spirits Regulations 1983 to receive methylated spirits.[50] The power must be exercised in the day time.[51] It can be used to inspect and examine any methylated spirits on the premises, and to take samples of methylated spirits or any goods containing methylated spirits. A reasonable price must be paid for any samples taken.[52]

Regulation 28 requires a methylator or authorised user to produce records to an officer, and to allow him to copy, take extracts from, or remove (at a reasonable time, and for a reasonable period) such records. As with the Stills Regulations, there is no power of entry as such given by this regulation.

(b) *Beer*

An officer may at all reasonable times enter premises used for brewing beer under a limited licence (*i.e.* not for sale, but for domestic use, or consumption by the employees of the licensee). The premises may be inspected, equipment examined, and samples taken of worts, beer, or materials for brewing.[53]

2. Petrol and oil

Hydrocarbon Oil Duties Act 1979 (H.O.D.A.)

There are two main provisions under Regulations made under this Act which give powers of entry.

7.18

---

[46] S.I. 1982 No. 611.
[47] Regs. 7 and 16.
[48] *e.g.* the C.E.M.A. 1979, s.112.
[49] *Ibid.* s.16, below, para. 7.39.
[50] S.I. 1983 No. 252. Revenue traders dealing in methylated spirits are of course subject to the more general powers noted above.
[51] Does this mean the opposite of "at night," *i.e.* 5 a.m. to 11 p.m.? The Keith Committee recommended that this power should be exercisable at any reasonable time: *Report*, para. 34.5.9.
[52] See also the powers to search for secret equipment, below, para. 7.21.
[53] A.L.D.A. 1979, s.53(5).

(a) The Hydrocarbon Oil Regulations 1973.[54] Regulation 47(1) provides a very wide power of entry. It allows an "authorised person" (*i.e.* authorised by the Commissioners) to enter any premises, other than a private dwelling-house. The premises may be inspected. Any oil (or petrol)[55] on the premises or in, or on, or forming part of the fuel supply of, any vehicle on those premises, may be inspected, tested, or sampled. The vehicle does not have to be in the same ownership as the premises. The person carrying out the inspection is specifically empowered to bring any vehicle being used by him onto the premises. This provision is one which depends on sensible practice if its not to be oppressive. On its face it allows entry and inspection of any premises, even where there is no suspicion that there is oil on the premises. Moreover the entry is not limited as to time, and so would seem to be exercisable at any time of the day or night. It is to be hoped that when new Regulations are made under the 1979 Act, these points will be tightened up.

Once entry has been made, the person occupying or for the time being in charge of the premises is required, on request, to provide facilities for any inspection, testing or sampling.[56]

7.19   In addition, a person owning or in charge of a vehicle which an authorised person wishes to inspect, is required to assist by providing access to the fuel supply.[57] The person in charge of the vehicle must also produce on demand to an authorised person, all books or documents carried by him or on the vehicle, relating to the vehicle or to any oil in, or on, or forming part of the fuel supply of, the vehicle.[58]

(b) Road Fuel Gas.[59] A similar power to that under regulation 47 of the Hydrocarbon Oil Regulations 1973 (above) exists in relation to gas used as a fuel for road vehicles, under regulation 11 of the Gas (Road Fuel) Regulations 1972.[60] An authorised person is entitled to enter any premises other than a private dwelling-house. The entry must be made at a reasonable time. Otherwise there are no restrictions.[61] The person entering may examine any gas found on the premises, and require the occupier to provide such facilities as may be necessary for this purpose.

7.20   **(c) Horticultural producers.**[62] Where a horticultural producer makes an application for repayment of excise duty under the H.O.D.A., s.17, he may be required to permit an officer to inspect his premises or plant.[63] The result of a refusal to allow inspection is simply that the determination of the relevant facts is then left to the Commissioners to decide as they wish.[64]

---

[54] S.I. 1973 No. 1311, as amended by the Hydrocarbon Oil (Amendment) Regulations (S.I. 1981 No. 1134).
[55] See the H.O.D.A. s.1(2).
[56] Reg. 47(2).
[57] Reg. 47(4).
[58] Reg. 47(5). N.B. also the requirements in relation to production of records, in regs. 44 and 50.
[59] "Gas" is defined in H.O.D.A., s.5.
[60] S.I. 1972, No. 846.
[61] *cf.* para. 7.18 above, in relation to reg. 47.
[62] "Horticultural produce" is defined in the H.O.D.A. 1979, Sched. 2.
[63] s.17(5)(*c*).
[64] s.17(6).

3. Power to search for secret equipment

The premises of a revenue trader who holds a licence for the production of **7.21** alcoholic liquor, or the occupier of a refinery (whether or not a revenue trader), are subject to an additional entry power under section 113 of the C.E.M.A. 1979. The power arises when an officer has reasonable grounds to suspect that a secret pipe, cock, vessel, or utensil is kept or used by the revenue trader or occupier. The officer may break into the premises, and so far as is reasonably necessary, break up the ground in or adjoining those premises or any wall of the premises in order to search for secret equipment. The power may be exercised at any time, but at night (11 p.m. to 5 a.m.) the officer must be accompanied by a constable.[65]

Powers on entry

If the officer finds a pipe or something similar leading from the premises he may trace its course on to other premises into or from which it leads. So far as is reasonably necessary he may break up any part of the other premises to trace its course. The pipe itself may be cut, and any cock turned, to see if it conveys dutiable goods, or materials used in their manufacture, in such a manner as to prevent a true account thereof from being made.[66]

A successful search means that the equipment discovered, and any dutiable goods or materials for the manufacture of such goods, is liable to forfeiture. In addition the trader is liable on summary conviction to a fine not exceeding level 3 on the standard scale.[67] If the search is unsuccessful, any damage done must be made good by the Commissioners.[68]

4. Matches and mechanical lighters

(a) *Matches*

Under the Match Duty Regulations 1963,[69] which have effect under section 3(1) **7.22** of the Matches and Mechanical Lighters Duties Act 1979, a person holding an excise licence to manufacture matches is required to keep a stock book and a packing book.[70] These are to be kept at the factory while in use and for not less than 12 months after use. An officer of the Commissioners can demand their production at any reasonable time, together with any records or accounts required to check the accuracy of entries in the books.

A manufacture is also required to produce to an officer on demand all matches in his possession in order that the accuracy of the stock book can be checked.[71]

Where the manufacturer is claiming remission or repayment of duty for defective

[65] s.113(2).
[66] s.113(3).
[67] s.113(4).
[68] s.113(5).
[69] S.I. 1963 No. 1381.
[70] Reg. 2.
[71] Reg. 10.

matches, he must keep them intact, and apart from other matches in the factory until they have been examined by an officer.[72] Any matches in respect of which duty is to be remitted or repaid must be destroyed in the presence of an officer.

(b) *Mechanical lighters*

Section 7 of the Matches and Mechanical Lighters Duties Act 1979 gives a power to make regulations. The Regulations which currently have effect under this section are the Mechanical Lighters Regulations 1960.[73]

Under regulation 2 every manufacturer of mechanical lighters is required to keep a stock book, which must be produced for inspection at the request of an officer. In addition, the manufacturer must similarly produce such accounts and documents as will enable the officer to verify the account in the stock book.[74] The officer may make notes in, or take extracts from the stock book, and make copies of any other accounts or documents. There is also an obligation under regulation 5 to produce on demand all mechanical lighters in the manufacturers possession, so that the number can be checked against the stock book.

Where duty becomes repayable, or remittable, because a lighter has been destroyed, or is unfit for use, or otherwise defective, the manufacturer must produce it or evidence of its destruction to the proper officer. In the case of a lighter received back into the factory as defective, the manufacturer must destroy it in the presence of the officer, or otherwise deal with it to his satisfaction.[75]

It should be noted that none of the powers dealing with matches or mechanical lighters provide specifically for a power of entry.

5. Tobacco products

7.23   The Tobacco Products Regulations 1979,[76] which have effect under the Tobacco Products Duty Act 1979, impose an obligation on the occupier of premises registered for the purpose of manufacture or storage of tobacco products to keep records, and to produce them for the inspection of the proper officer at any reasonable time.[77] The production does not, however, have to take place at any particular premises, and there is no power here to inspect premises, or stocks.

6. Betting and gaming duties

7.24   The Betting and Gaming Duties Act 1981 gives Customs and Excise Officers a number of powers of entry in relation to various kinds of betting licences and duties. The Keith Committee found that this was the area where search warrants were most frequently used by the Customs and Excise.[78]

[72] Reg. 16.
[73] S.I. 1960 No. 1350.
[74] Reg. 2(4).
[75] Reg. 7.
[76] S.I. 1979 No. 904.
[77] Reg. 21.
[78] *Report*, para. 35.7.16.

(a) *Gaming licences*

Under section 15, a justice may issue a search warrant if satisfied by information on oath that there is reasonable ground for suspicion that gaming without a duly paid licence is taking place on any premises, or that evidence of such activity is to be found there. The warrant will authorise any office to enter the premises, by force if necessary, within one month of the issue of the warrant. The officer may search the premises, and any person found on them whom he has reasonable cause to believe to be concerned in the organisation or management of gaming. Records, accounts, documents, money, valuables, etc., reasonably believed to be required as evidence may be seized and removed.[79]

There is also a power of entry and inspection, without warrant, under paragraph 4 of Schedule 2 in relation to any premises currently licensed. The gaming licence must be produced, and information given on the gaming which is being or has been carried on.

(b) *General betting duty*

Under paragraph 10 of Schedule 1, an officer can enter any track or other premises on which he has reason to believe that bookmaking on events taking place there is being, or is to be carried on.[80] On entry the officer may require the provision of information, and the production of documents from the person carrying on the bookmaking, or any person who appears to have made a bet.

7.25

Paragraph 16 gives a power to obtain a search warrant in the same terms (*mutatis mutandis*) as in section 15, above.

(c) *Bingo duty and gaming machine licence duty*

Powers of inspection without warrant, and search under warrant, equivalent to those outlined above, are given by Schedule 3, paragraphs 13 and 17, in relation to bingo duty, and Schedule 4, paragraphs 4 and 17 in relation to gaming machine licence duty. In addition, however, paragraph 18 of Schedule 4 makes provision for the forfeiture of all gaming machines found on premises not properly licensed.

(d) *Distress*

Failure to pay general betting duty, bingo duty, or gaming machine licence duty, following a written demand by a proper officer, means that distress may be levied. The procedures for this are governed by section 28, which provides *inter alia* for the levy of distress on "club" premises, where appropriate, as well as against the individuals owing the duty.[81]

7. Prohibited imports

Any items which are imported in contravention of a prohibition are liable to

7.26

---

[79] s.15(3).

[80] The power covers "sponsored pool betting" and the operation of a totalisator, as well.

[81] s.28(2).

forfeiture. The general power to search for things liable to forfeiture (under the C.E.M.A. s.161) has been noted above, para. 7.03. Import prohibitions exist under a number of statutes and regulations. These are outlined below, according to subject-matter.

(a) *General controls*

The Import Export and Customs Powers (Defence) Act 1939 gives a general power to make Regulations controlling imports. The scope of this power was considered in *R.* v. *Secretary of State for Trade, ex p. Chris International Foods Ltd.*[82] Woolf J. ruled that although the Act was passed as part of emergency legislation, the powers given by it were not limited to security, but extended to control over imports and exports generally. This would include a power to control imports in order to protect Commonwealth suppliers. The current Regulations having effect under this Act are contained in the Import of Goods (Control) Order 1954.[83] Articles 1 and 2 of this Order provide that all imports are prohibited unless licensed. Licences may be specific or general. The current Open General Licence issued by the Department of Trade took effect on January 1, 1988. It allows all imports except for those covered by the Schedules to the licence, or by a specific statutory prohibition. The Schedules are mainly concerned with fabrics and clothing, metals, and certain foods.

(b) *Specific prohibitions*

7.27 **(i) Agricultural products.**

(1) Any agricultural products, by orders made under section 43(1) of the Agricultural Marketing Act 1958.

(2) Plants, trees, or bushes, by orders made under the Plant Health Act 1967, to control the introduction of pests into Great Britain: Plant Health Act 1967, s.2 (as amended by the European Communities Act 1972, s.4(1) and Schedule 4, paragraph 8 (1) and (2)).

(3) Under the Endangered Species (Import and Export) Act 1976, certain live or dead animals or plants, or parts or products of the same, unless licensed by the Secretary of State: section 1, and Schedules 1, 2, 3.

7.28 **(ii) Animals and fish.**

(1) Animals or carcases, and the carcases of poultry and eggs, and other things animate or inanimate which might carry or transmit disease: Regulations made under the Animal Health Act 1981, s.10.

(2) Musk rats, grey squirrels, rabbits: Destructive Imported Animals Act 1932, ss.1 and 10, and Regulations made thereunder. The Act gives power to make Regulations concerning any non-indigenous mammalian species of destructive habits.

(3) Docked horses, unless the importer has permission or is licensed: Docking and Nicking of Horses Act 1949, s.2.

[82] *The Times*, July 22, 1983.
[83] S.I. 1954 No. 23.

(4) Livestock imported from any of the Channel Islands, the Isle of Man, or the Republic of Ireland, by orders under the Agriculture Act 1957, s.6.

(5) Bees, bee products, hives, etc., by order under section 1 of the Bees Act 1980, to prevent the introduction or spread of diseases or pests affecting bees.

(6) Live fish, or live eggs of fish, of a species not native to England and Wales, by order of the Minister: Import of Live Fish (England and Wales) Act 1980, s.1.

(7) Live salmon or freshwater fish, or eggs of salmon or freshwater fish (unless under licence granted by the Minister): Diseases of Fish Act 1937, s.1 (as amended by the Diseases of Fish Act 1983, s.1).

(8) Sea fish caught in certain areas, as specified in orders made under the section: Sea Fish (Conservation) Act 1967, s.6.

(9) Skins of seals taken in contravention of an Order in Council under the Seal Fisheries (North Pacific) Act 1895: Seal Fisheries (North Pacific) Act 1912, s.4.

(iii) Copyright material. Infringing copies of literary, dramatic or musical **7.29** works, upon the owner of the copyright giving notice to the Commissioners: Copyright, Designs and Patents Act 1988, ss.111–112.

(iv) Drugs and medicines.

(1) Controlled drugs, unless licensed or excepted from control: Misuse of Drugs Act 1971, s.3.

(2) Vaccines, sera, toxins, etc., unless permitted or licensed by the Secretary of State: Therapeutic Substances Act 1956, s.3.

(3) Any medicinal product, except in accordance with a product licence: Medicines Act 1968, ss.7(3), 32(3).

(v) Explosives. All explosives, by virtue of the Explosives Act 1875, ss.40 and 43, and Regulations made thereunder.

(vi) Flick knives. Restriction of Offensive Weapons Act 1959, s.1.

(vii) Food, etc.

(1) Food intended for sale, or sold, for human consumption, contrary to orders made under the Food Act 1984, s.13(1) (*e.g.* the Public Health (Imported Milk) Regulations 1926[84]; and the Imported Food Regulations 1984.[85]

(2) Cocoa beans and cocoa, except under licence: International Cocoa Agreement Act 1973, s.1.

(3) Milk imported in breach of regulations under the Importation of Milk Act 1983, s.1.

(viii) Foreign prison-made goods. All such goods, unless in transit, or not imported for trade purposes, or of a type not manufactured in the United Kingdom: Foreign Prison-Made Goods Act 1897, s.1.

(ix) Forgeries and counterfeits. The following are "prohibited goods": **7.30**

---

[84] S.R. & O. 1926 No. 820.
[85] S.I. 1984 No. 1918.

(1) Counterfeit currency and "protected coins"[86]: Forgery and Counterfeiting Act 1981.

(2) All articles having any stamp, name, writing or other device implying, or intending to imply any sanction or guarantee by the Customs or by any other department of Government: Customs and Inland Revenue Act 1879, s.5.

(3) Any facsimile, imitation, or representation of a postage stamp (British or foreign), or any die plate instrument or materials for making such a facsimile, etc.: Post Office Act 1953, s.63(5).

7.31   **(x) Indecent or obscene articles**.
(1) Customs Consolidation Act 1876, s.42. All that survives of a long table of prohibited items in section 42 of the Customs Consolidation Act is the following:

> "Indecent or obscene prints, paintings, photographs, books, cards, lithographic or other engravings, or any other indecent or obscene articles."

"Indecent or obscene" are to be given their ordinary "dictionary" meanings here. In particular "obscene" means "lewd, disgusting, or offensive," rather than "having a tendency to deprave or corrupt" as under the Obscene Publications Act 1959.[87]
It was held in *Derrick* v. *Commissioners for Customs and Excise*[88] that films are within the scope of section 42. There is no authority on sound or video cassettes, tapes, or discs but in the light of the approach in *Derrick*, and in the *Attorney General's Reference (No. 5 of 1980)*[89] on the Obscene Publications Acts, it seems likely that they too would be held to be covered. In *R.* v. *Henn, R.* v. *Darby*,[90] the House of Lords held that these restrictions did not breach the rules against arbitrary discrimination or disguised restriction on trade under article 36 of the EEC Treaty, but were justified on grounds of public morality. In *Conegate Ltd.* v. *Customs and Excise Commissioners*,[91] however, the European Court held that the "public morality" exception could not be relied upon where the articles in question would not have been subject to restriction on sale, etc., if they had been produced in the United Kingdom. The articles in this case included inflatable "sex-dolls," which fell outside the scope of the Obscene Publications Acts, and similar legislation. This does not mean, however, that where articles would be subject to restriction, the 1876 Act has to be read as applying the standards, and incorporating the defences available, from the Obscene Publications Act.[92] For example the defence of "publication for the public good" under section 4 of the 1959 Act is irrelevant for the purposes of forfeiture proceedings based on the 1876 Act.

(2) Children and Young Persons (Harmful Publications) Act 1955. Under section 5 of this Act importation is prohibited of any work to which the Act applies, and any

---

[86] Defined in Forgery and Counterfeiting Act 1981, s.27(1).
[87] See *R.* v. *Anderson* [1972] 1 Q.B. 304 (C.A.); *R.* v. *Stanley* [1965] 2 Q.B. 327 (C.A.).
[88] [1972] 1 All E.R. 993.
[89] [1980] 3 All E.R. 816.
[90] [1980] 2 All E.R. 166.
[91] [1986] 2 All E.R. 688.
[92] *R.* v. *Bow Street Magistrates' Court, ex p. Noncyp Ltd., The Times*, January 21, 1989.

plate prepared for the purpose of printing copies of any such work and any photographic film prepared for that purpose.[93]

Computer tape which is used for typesetting would not seem to be covered under either (1) or (2).

(xi) Lotteries. Advertisements or other notices, which in the opinion of the **7.32** Commissioners, are imported for the purpose of publication in contravention of any Act relating to lotteries: Revenue Act 1898, s.1.

(xii) Matches made with white phosphorus. Factories Act 1961, s.77.

(xiii) Toxic substances.

(1) Certain carcinogenic substances: Carcinogenic Substances (Prohibition of Importation) Order 1967.[94]

(2) Radioactive substances. As specified in orders made by the Minister: Radioactive Substances Act 1948, s.2.[95]

(3) Goods infected, or likely to be infected with Anthrax: Anthrax Prevention Order 1971.

(xiv) Trade descriptions, marks, etc.

(1) Goods carrying a false indication of their place of manufacture, processing, etc. Trade Descriptions Act 1968, s.16.

(2) Goods which infringe a registered trade mark, following notice given by the registered user of the trade mark. Trade Marks Act 1938, s.64A.

C. Forfeiture Procedure

The procedures relating to items seized under the Customs and Excise Acts are **7.33** governed by the C.E.M.A. s.139 and Sched. 3.

1. C.E.M.A., s.139

If the property is seized by a constable,[96] rather than a customs and excise officer (*e.g.* under s.161(3) or (5) of the C.E.M.A.), the person seizing should normally deliver either the thing itself, or, if impracticable, notice of the seizure, to the nearest customs and excise office.[97] If the property is or may be required in connection with proceedings other than under the Customs and Excise Acts, the police may retain custody until the conclusion or abandonment of those proceedings.[98] The police must, however, give notice to that effect to the nearest customs and excise office, and allow customs and excise officers to inspect the property.[99] The Police (Property) Act 1897 does not apply to anything so held.[1]

[93] For the application of the Act, see para. 4.07 above.
[94] S.I. 1967 No. 1675.
[95] N.B. no orders have as yet been made.
[96] Or a coastguard, or a member of Her Majesty's armed forces: s.139(1).
[97] s.139(2).
[98] s.139(3).
[99] s.139(4).
[1] *Ibid.* and see above, paras. 2.54–2.57.

2. Schedule 3

Notice of seizure

7.34   Unless the property was seized in the presence of either the person whose offence or suspected offence occasioned the seizure, or the owner or his servant or agent, or the master or commander of a ship or aircraft from which the property was seized, the Commissioners must give notice of the seizure and of the grounds for it to any person who to their knowledge was at the time of the seizure the owner or one of the owners of the property.[2] The notice must be in writing, and served on him. Service may be achieved by delivery to his usual or last known place of abode or business, or to the registered or principal office of a body corporate. If he has no known United Kingdom address, notice may be given by publication in the London, Edinburgh, or Belfast Gazette. Any person wishing to challenge the forfeiture must give notice in writing of his intention at any customs and excise office, within one month of the seizure, or his receipt of the notice of seizure.[3]

7.35   If no such notice of claim is received, the property will be deemed to be duly condemned as forfeited.[4] Otherwise the Commissioners must take proceedings for condemnation by the court.[5] These proceedings may be instituted either in the High Court or a magistrates' court. If the court decides that the property was liable to forfeiture at the time it was seized, the court will condemn it as forfeited. If the proceedings are taken in a magistrates' court, there is a right of appeal to the crown court.[6]

There do not seem to be any rules as to how the Commissioners should deal with forfeited goods, but presumably they are free to dispose of them as they see fit. Certain powers in relation to the seized property are given by paragraph 16. This provides that, the Commissioners may at any time, if they see fit, whether or not the property has been condemned, either:

   (a) deliver it up to a claimant, upon his paying such sum as the commissioners think proper, being a sum not exceeding that which in their opinion represents the value of the thing, including any duty or tax chargeable thereon which has not been paid; or
   (b) if the thing is a living creature, or is in the opinion of the commissioners of a perishable nature, sell or destroy it.

If in later proceedings it turns out that the property should not have been

---

[2] Para. 1.
[3] Para. 3. N.B. the formal requirements in para. 4.
[4] Para. 5.
[5] Para. 6.
[6] Para. 11.

forfeited, paragraph 17 makes provision for compensating the claimant. Acceptance of such compensation precludes any further action against the commissioners.[7]

D. Car Tax

The Commissioners have responsibility for the collection of car tax on the sale of **7.36** cars. Entry powers in connection with this are given by paragraph 7 of Schedule 1 to the Car Tax Act 1983. There are powers to enter premises both with and without warrant.

1. Without warrant

Under paragraph 7(1) an authorised person may enter premises which are used in connection with the making, sale, import or export, of "chargeable vehicles."[8] This power may obviously be used in relation to offices used in connection with transactions related to chargeable vehicles, as well as to premises where the vehicles themselves are made or kept. The entry must be made at a reasonable time, but the paragraph does not specify any particular powers which may be used on entry.

A power more specifically concerned with searching for vehicles is given by paragraph 7(2). This provides that where an authorised person has reasonable grounds to believe that any premises are used in connection with (a) the making, sale, import or export, of chargeable vehicles, or (b) the storage of chargeable vehicles on which tax has not been paid, and that chargeable vehicles are on those premises, he may at any reasonable time enter and inspect those premises and take account of any vehicles or material found on them.

2. Under warrant

A warrant to enter any premises may be obtained from a justice of the peace, if he **7.37** is satisfied on information on oath that there are reasonable grounds for suspecting that an offence in connection with the tax is being, has been, or is about to be committed on the premises, or that evidence of the commission of such an offence is to be found there. The warrant will empower any authorised person to enter the premises at any time within one month of the issue of the warrant. Force may be used if necessary.[9]

3. Powers on entry under warrant

Any person entering under authority of the warrant may take with him such other persons as appear to him to be necessary, and, in addition to searching the premises, may seize and remove any documents or other items found on the premises which he has reasonable grounds to believe may be required as evidence for the purpose of proceedings for an offence relating to the tax. He may also search any person found

[7] Para. 17(3).
[8] As defined in ss.1 and 2 of the Act.
[9] Para. 7(3).

on the premises who he has reasonable grounds to believe to have committed or to be about to commit such an offence, or to be in possession of any such documents or other items. No woman or girl is to be searched except by a woman.[10]

4. Production of records, etc.

7.38   Makers and importers of chargeable vehicles are required to be registered under section 4 of the Act. All such registered persons, and any person who has chargeable vehicles on which tax has not been paid delivered to him as part of his business, is obliged to keep such records, etc., as the Commissioners may require, and produce them at a time and place specified by the Commissioners.[11]

The place specified might be the premises of the person required to produce the records, and although the paragraph gives no specific powers of entry, the general power under paragraph 7(1) noted above could presumably be used in these circumstances.

E. Obstruction

1. C.E.M.A., s.16

7.39   There is a general offence of obstruction in the C.E.M.A., s.16. It applies to any person engaged in the performance of any duty or the exercise of any power under any Act related to customs and excise. Any person who obstructs, hinders, molests or assaults such a person, or anyone assisting such a person, is guilty of an offence.[12] "Hinders" and "molests" seem to imply an interference less than actual obstruction, though given the fairly wide interpretation of "obstruction" their useful scope is not altogether clear.

In relation to searches, while they clearly fall within the above provision (s.16(1) (*a*)), there is also a specific provision in section 16(1)(*b*), whereby a person who does anything which impedes or is calculated to impede any search for things liable to forfeiture, or the seizure of such things, commits an offence. The subsection differs from section 16(1)(*a*) in that it will apply to actions in relation to goods, as much as to actions directed against the person carrying out the duty. Similarly section 16(1)(*c*) makes it an offence to rescue, damage, or destroy anything liable to forfeiture, or do anything calculated to prevent the procuring or giving of evidence as to whether or not anything is liable to forfeiture. It should be noted that section 16(1)(*b*) and (*c*) apply only in connection with the forfeiture powers. Interference with an officer entering under any other power will only be an offence if it falls within section 16(1)(*a*).

2. Penalty

7.40   The offences under section 16 are triable either way. On summary conviction the

---

[10] Para. 7(3).
[11] Para. 5(1) and (2).
[12] See *re* "obstructs," above, paras. 1.29–1.31, and *R.* v. *Forbes and Webb* (1865) 10 Cox C.C. 362; *R.* v. *Maxwell & Clanchy* (1909) 73 J.P. 176.

maximum penalty is a fine of £1,000 or three months' imprisonment, and on indictment a fine of any amount or two years' imprisonment.

F. Protection of Officers—C.E.M.A., s.144

It was noted above (para. 7.06) that the power to seize items liable to forfeiture **7.41** depends on the items in fact being so liable, and not on reasonable suspicion that they are so. Section 144 provides some protection for the Commissioners and their officers, however, in that if a court decides that seized items are not liable to forfeiture, it may nevertheless issue a certificate that there were reasonable grounds for the seizure. The result is that in any action arising out of an unlawful seizure, the defendant will not be liable to punishment or to pay damages.[13] If no certificate has been issued, the court hearing the action may itself decide that there were reasonable grounds for the seizure, which will have the same effect as the issue of a certificate.

Neither the issue of a certificate, nor a ruling by a court that there were reasonable grounds, affects the right of any person to the return of the seized property, or compensation in respect of any damage or destruction.[14] But damages to compensate simply for the unlawful removal of the property will not be available.

---

[13] s.144(2).
[14] s.144(3).

CHAPTER EIGHT

CENTRAL GOVERNMENT

8.01 A number of government departments employ inspectors to carry out certain of their statutory powers and duties. Such inspectors often have powers of entry.[1] They are dealt with in this chapter under the department which appoints them. The final section deals with the powers of the Commission of the European Economic Communities. In a number of cases, responsibility for supervision of a particular area of activity is shared between central and local government. The aim has been to confine this chapter to those powers which are more commonly used by central government officials. Local government powers are dealt with in Chapter Nine.

Apart from the powers which exist in relation to the collection and enforcement of taxes (dealt with in Chapters Six and Seven) the powers of entry are mainly given to enable simple "inspection." As has already been noted,[2] the distinction between "inspection" and "search" has been neatly stated by the Keith Committee[3];

> "[T]he general maxim is that inspection is by eye, search by hand, and that the power to inspect, while it covers walking round premises, and, for example, examining goods in packing cases, does not cover searching for things hidden, or rummaging through the contents of wastepaper baskets."

Of course there are going to be borderline cases. If the inspector is entitled to look into packing cases he may presumably lift the lid to do so. But if the lid is secured, can he demand that the occupier of the premises open it? It is suggested that he can, assuming that such an inspection is appropriate to the power under which he has entered, but that he is not entitled to force it open himself. That is where the distinction between use of the eyes, and use of the hands, comes into play.

THE POWERS

A. Ministry of Agriculture, Fisheries and Foods

8.02 This Ministry has the largest group of entry powers, under nearly 20 different statutes. It employs a number of groups of specialist inspectors. The largest of these

---

[1] The most recent (and most comprehensive) study of such "inspectorates" is Gerald Rhodes, *Inspectorates in British Government* (Allen & Unwin, 1981), which also contains some useful references to earlier work in this area—see in particular the notes on p. xiii.

[2] Para. 6.35, above.

[3] Report of the Committee on Enforcement Powers of the Revenue Departments (Cmnd. 8822), para. 4.3.3.

is the Horticultural Marketing Inspectorate (with about 150 officers), but there is also the Plant Health and Seeds Inspectorate, the Agricultural Wages Inspectorate, the Egg Marketing Inspectorate, the Sea Fisheries Inspectorate, and the Veterinary Service. The Forestry Commission and the Meat and Livestock Commission, for which the Ministry is responsible, also have inspection powers. The powers of these and other inspectors employed by the Ministry are grouped here according to subject-matter.

1. Animals

(a) *Animal Health Act 1981*

This Act consolidated the existing legislation relating to disease in animals.[4] **8.03** General enforcement powers are given in Part V of the Act to both Ministry and local authority inspectors, but there are also some more specific powers in other sections. Unless otherwise stated, the word "inspector" in this section includes local authority inspectors.[5]

(i) General powers—Part V. By virtue of section 63 of the Act, an inspector has the power to enter any land or shed to which the Act applies, or other building or place where he has reasonable grounds for supposing that:

(a) disease exists, or has within 56 days existed[6]; or
(b) the carcase of a diseased or suspected animal is or has been kept, or has been buried, destroyed, or otherwise disposed of; or
(c) there is to be found any pen, place, vehicle, or thing in respect of which any person has on any occasion failed to comply with the provisions of the Act, or of any order of the Minister, or of a regulation of a local authority; or
(d) the Act or an order of the Minister or a regulation of a local authority has not been or is not being complied with.[7]

The entry may take place at any time,[8] but if required to do so by the owner, occupier or person in charge, the inspector must state his reasons for entry in writing.[9]

In addition there are two other powers which are not subject to the requirements of section 63(4). An inspector may at any time enter any land, building or other place, on or in which he has reasonable grounds for supposing that there is being or has been kept any animal or other thing which has been imported contrary to an order under section 10 (which provides for import controls to prevent the spread of

---

[4] As defined (fairly restrictively) in s.87.
[5] For the power to appoint local authority inspectors, see s.52 of the Act.
[6] "Disease" means cattle-plague, pleuro-pneumonia, foot and mouth disease, sheep-pox, sheep scab, swine fever, and in relation to poultry, fowl pest, Newcastle disease, fowl plague, fowl cholera, infectious bronchitis, infectious laryngo tracheitis, pullorum disease, fowl typhoid, fowl pox, and fowl paralysis, together with any other disease specified by the Minister by order—s.88.
[7] s.63(2).
[8] *Ibid.*
[9] s.63(4).

disease).[10] And an inspector of the *Minister* may at any time enter any land, building or other place, where he has reasonable grounds for supposing that animals are or have been kept, for the purpose of ascertaining whether any disease exists, or has within 56 days existed there.[11]

8.04   *Poultry.* Similar powers to those contained in section 63 are given in relation to poultry under section 64. An inspector of the Minister, or, if so authorised, an inspector of a local authority, may at any time enter any pen, shed, land, or other place in which he has reasonable grounds for suspecting that poultry is being or has been kept, for the purpose of ascertaining whether disease exists or has existed in them.[12]

There is an additional power where an order has been made for protecting poultry from unnecessary suffering.[13] In order to enforce such an order, an inspector may enter any premises in which he has reasonable grounds for supposing that there is poultry:

(a) exposed for sale; or
(b) in course of conveyance; or
(c) packed for conveyance or exposure for sale.

The power is one of examination of the poultry itself, and any receptacle or vehicle used for conveyance or exposure for sale.

8.05   **(ii) Specific powers.** *Expenditure for eradication of disease.* Section 3 of the Act gives the Minister a power to spend money for the eradication of disease in animals (including horses). In order to obtain information relevant to the exercise of this power the Minister may authorise in writing any veterinary inspector or other officer of the Minister to inspect animals. Such a person may for this purpose enter any land or premises and take such samples as he may consider necessary. The entry must be at a reasonable time, and the officer must produce his authority on demand. Obstructing or impeding an inspector is an offence, subject to a fine not exceeding level 3 on the standard scale, or imprisonment for one month, or both.[14]

8.06   *Wild animals.* In order to prevent the spread of disease, it may be necessary to destroy wild animals in a particular area.[15] Section 22 empowers an "authorised officer,"[16] who has reasonable grounds for suspecting that there exists among the wild members of a species in the area a disease to which section 21 applies, to enter any land in the area and

[10] s.63(6).
[11] s.63(9) as amended by the Animal Health and Welfare Act 1984.
[12] s.64(1). "Disease" is defined in section 88; see above, n. 6.
[13] See, *e.g.* the Conveyance of Live Poultry Order 1919 (S.R. & O. 1919, No. 933).
[14] s.4(2).
[15] See s.1(*a*) and s.21.
[16] Which means an officer of the appropriate Minister (Minister of Agriculture in England; Secretary of State in Wales), a veterinary inspector, or some other person authorised by the Minister to exercise the powers—s.22(1).

(a) take samples of animals, or excreta, or materials with which wild members of that species may have been in contact;
(b) carry out any other investigation which he considers necessary for the purpose of determining whether an order under section 21 should be made in respect of the whole or part of the area in question.[17]

Where an order has been made under section 21, an authorised officer has the further power to enter any land in the areas to which the order applies at any time, in order to:

(a) carry out the destruction of the wild members of a species to which the order relates; or
(b) take measures, such as erecting fences, to prevent the movement of animals in or out of that area, or to prevent recolonisation by the wild species following destruction[18]; or
(c) ascertain whether destruction has been effectively carried out.[19]

A power to enter continues for two years after the revocation of an order of destruction, in order to take samples (as under s. 22(2)) for the purpose of ascertaining whether the land has been or is being recolonised, and whether the disease exists among the recolonists.[20]

None of the powers given by section 22 entitles the officer to enter a dwelling-house.[21] And if the owner, occupier, or person in charge of the land requires it, the officer must show his authority, and state in writing the reasons for his entry.[22]

Control of zoonoses. In connection with the control of zoonoses (animal diseases **8.07** which can be transmitted to man) a power of entry is given by section 30 of the Animal Health Act. Where a veterinary inspector has reason to believe that an animal which is afflicted with a designated disease, or which is the carrier of a designated organism is on any land, he may enter the land and make such tests and take such samples of any animal, feeding stuff, litter, dung, vessel, pen, vehicle, or other thing whatsoever which is on or forms part of the land, as he considers appropriate for the purpose of ascertaining whether such an animal is or has been on the land.[23]

The inspector must, if so required, produce evidence of his authority. He also has the power to require the owner, or person having charge of the animals on the land,

---

[17] s.22(2).
[18] See s.21(7).
[19] s.22(3).
[20] s.22(4).
[21] s.22(5).
[22] s.22(6). There is an additional requirement as regards nature reserves that seven days' notice of any entry must be given to the Nature Conservancy Council, and the officer must on entering follow the Council's reasonable requirements for minimising the damage to flora, fauna, geological, or physiographical features, s.22(7).
[23] s.30(2). For "designated disease" or "organism" see Animal Health Act 1981, s.29; Zoonoses Order 1975 (S.I. 1975 No. 1030); and the Importation of Processed Animal Protein Order 1981 (S.I. 1981 No. 677), Art. 4.

to take such reasonable steps as he may specify for the purpose of collecting or restraining animals on the land in order to facilitate the exercise of his testing and sampling powers. Failure to comply amounts to an offence under the Act.[24] A person found guilty is liable on summary conviction to a fine not exceeding level 5 on the standard scale, or if the offence is committed with respect to more than 10 animals, to a fine not exceeding level 3 on the standard scale per animal.[25]

8.08   *Destruction of foxes, etc.—rabies infection.* Under section 19 the Minister has the power to make orders for the destruction of foxes (or other wild mammals) not held in captivity in an area declared to be infected with rabies.[26] The order may authorise any person to enter land (other than a dwelling-house) for the purpose of carrying out, or deciding whether to carry out, the destruction of animals. In addition the order may deal with the erection of fences, disposal of carcases, and authorise methods of destruction which would otherwise be unlawful.

No order has been made under this section but the Rabies (Control) Order 1974,[27] has effect as if so made. Article 10 of the order authorises an officer of the Ministry, and any other person authorised in writing by the Minister for the purpose, to enter land to destroy foxes (within the limits outlined above) in accordance with the requirements of section 19(3). The order imposes an obligation on the Minister, before destruction commences, to notify in writing (or by any other appropriate method) the occupier of the land and any other person who may be on it, of the proposal to carry out the destruction, and the methods to be used.

8.09   *Powers under statutory instruments.* Under section 28 (seizure of diseased or suspected animals), section 32 (slaughter), and section 35 (seizure and disposal of carcases, etc.) the Minister has power to make regulations. The orders mentioned below, which have been made or have effect under the Animal Health Act 1981, all contain entry powers generally given to veterinary inspectors. The older orders included provisions such as that in the Cattle Plague Order of 1928,[28] Article 4(2) of which provides:

> "For the purposes of this Article the Veterinary Inspector may enter on any part of the premises and the occupier and the persons in his employment shall render such reasonable assistance to the Inspector as may be required for all or any of the purposes of this Article."

The more recent orders, however, tend to have provisions in the form exemplified by Article 7(1) of the Tuberculosis (England and Wales) Order 1984[29]:

> "Where by reason of information received . . . there is reason to believe that there is on any premises an affected animal . . . a veterinary inspector shall, with

---

[24] s.30(3).
[25] s.75(1).
[26] See s.17.
[27] S.I. 1974 No. 2212.
[28] S.R. & O. 1928 No. 206.
[29] S.I. 1984 No. 1943.

all practicable speed, take such steps as may be necessary to establish the correctness of that information. For the purpose of carrying out his duties under the foregoing provisions ... a veterinary inspector may examine any bovine animal or carcase on the premises and take such samples as may be required for the purpose of diagnosis from any such bovine animal or carcase."

As will be seen, the power of entry under this provision is implied rather than express. The owner of the relevant animals is, however, under a duty to assist the inspector,[30] and there seems little doubt that in appropriate circumstances an inspector would be entitled to go on to premises without the occupier's permission.

Orders containing entry powers.   **8.10**

(A) UNDER SECTION 28.
Cattle Plague Order of 1928 (S.R. & O. 1928 No. 206) (as amended).
Sheep-Pox Order 1938 (S.R. & O. 1938 No. 229) (as amended).
Importation of Animals Order 1977 (S.I. 1977 No. 944).
Importation of Equine Animals Order 1979 (S.I. 1979 No. 1701).
Importation of Birds, Poultry and Hatching Eggs Order 1979 (S.I. 1979 No. 1702).
Warble Fly (England and Wales) Order 1982 (S.I. 1982 No. 234) (as amended).
Tuberculosis (England and Wales) Order 1984 (S.I. 1984 No. 1943).
Infectious Diseases of Horses Order 1987 (S.I. 1987 No. 790).

(B) UNDER SECTION 32 (SLAUGHTER).
Sheep-Pox Order of 1938, as above.
Brucellosis Mellitensis Order of 1940 (S.R. & O. 1940 No. 1251).
Swine Vesicular Disease Order 1972 (S.I. 1972 No. 1980) (as amended).
Rabies Control Order 1974 (S.I. 1974 No. 2212).
Enzootic Bovine Leukosis Order 1980 (S.I. 1980 No. 79).
African Swine Fever Order 1980 (S.I. 1980 No. 145).
Aujesky's Disease Order 1983 (S.I. 1983 No. 344)
Infectious Diseases of Horses Order 1987, as above.

(C) UNDER SECTION 35 (SEIZURE OF CARCASES, ETC.). None of the orders having effect under this section specifically grants powers of entry. The Diseases of Animals (Seizure of Carcases, etc.) Order 1964[31] gives a power to *seize* but it is not backed up by a power of entry. The proposed entrant must presumably rely on the general entry power under section 63 of the Act.[32]

Obstruction. Section 66 of the Act provides a fairly comprehensive obstruction   **8.11**
offence. It is committed by

"(*a*) refusing any inspector or other officer admission to any land, building,

[30] See Art. 8(1).
[31] S.I. 1964 No. 1255, as amended by S.I. 1972 No. 2041.
[32] See above, para. 8.03. N.B. the amendment of s.35 by the Animal Health and Welfare Act 1984, s.1.

place, pen, vessel, or boat, aircraft, or vehicle of any other description which the inspector or officer is entitled to enter or examine; or

(*b*)   obstructing or impeding him in so entering or examining; or
(*c*)   otherwise in any respect obstructing or impeding an inspector or other officer in the execution of his duty, or assisting in any such impeding or obstructing."[33]

There is a defence of "lawful authority or excuse," with the burden of proof on the accused.

On summary conviction the penalties are a fine not exceeding level 5 on the standard scale for a first offence, and a fine or one month's imprisonment for the second and any subsequent offence.[34]

(b) *Pests Act 1954*

Under this Act the Minister of Agriculture[35] has power to designate "rabbit clearance areas."[36] In relation to this, a person authorised in that behalf by the Minister has the power to enter any land at any reasonable time. The power is to be used to inspect the land for the purpose of determining whether, and if so in what manner, the powers conferred by section 1 are to be exercised in relation to the land, or whether, and if so in what manner, any requirement imposed under this section has been complied with.[37]

(c) *Agriculture Act 1967*

Under section 23 of this Act an authorised officer of the Meat and Livestock Commission has the power to enter any premises (other than a building used solely as a private dwelling-house) which he has reasonable cause to believe to be premises used for the slaughter of livestock or for the storage, processing, grading, classification, packing, cutting, or sale of meat.[38] The entry, which must be at a reasonable time, is to be for the purpose of obtaining information with respect to any matter which is of concern to the Commission. The officer may take with him such other persons as may appear to him to be necessary,[39] and may inspect any livestock or meat, or if meat is retailed on the premises, any price lists, price labels, etc., or other displays of prices. It is a summary offence, subject to a fine not exceeding level 1 on

---

[33] s.66(1).
[34] s.75.
[35] In Wales, the Secretary of State.
[36] s.1(1).
[37] s.1(8). N.B. ss.100, 106(2)–(7) of the Agriculture Act 1947 apply, see below, para. 8.13.
[38] s.23(1).
[39] s.23(2).

the standard scale, wilfully to obstruct an officer or other person in the exercise of powers under this section.[40]

(d) *Agriculture Act 1970; Eradication of brucellosis—s.106(8)*

For the purpose of obtaining information in connection with a scheme for the **8.12** eradication of brucellosis (s.108(1) and (2)) certain powers of entry are given to the Ministry of Agriculture officers, authorised in writing by the Minister (or in Wales the Secretary of State) to exercise the powers of this subsection. After production of his authority, if required, he may enter any land or premises, at any reasonable time, in order to inspect any animal; apply any test; take any sample; examine and take copies of or extracts from any document. The officer is given the discretion to decide what information is needed in connection with the scheme. It is a summary offence to obstruct or impede an officer acting in the exercise of his powers under this section, punishable with a fine not exceeding level 3 on the standard scale, or one month's imprisonment.

2. Agriculture—land

(a) *Agriculture Act 1947*

There is a general power to enter land for the purpose of determining whether, **8.13** and if so, in what manner, any of the powers conferred by the Act are to be exercised in relation to any land, or whether, and if so in what manner, any direction given under such a power has been complied with.[41] This covers such things as the provision of guaranteed prices and assured markets, compulsory acquisition of land by the Minister, and pest and weed control. In general terms it is concerned with encouraging efficient agricultural production, and proper agricultural conditions.

The entry power is given, under section 106, to any person authorised by the Minister (in Wales the Secretary of State). If requested, he must produce some duly authenticated document showing his authority, before entering. Entry may take place at any reasonable time, but if the power is being used to determine whether land is to be compulsorily purchased under Part IV or V of the Act, or if the land is being used for residential purposes, 24 hours' notice of entry must be given to the occupier.[42] For any other purposes the occupier must be notified that it is intended to enter during a period, not exceeding 14 days, starting at least 24 hours after the giving of the notice. If the entry is to take measures to secure compliance with a direction or requirement under Part V of the Act, then notice need only be given on the first occasion.[43] If the direction or requirement was imposed on someone other than the occupier, then that person must be given notice of the entry as well.[44] There

---

[40] N.B. The powers apply to stalls or vehicles as well as to "premises"—but there is no power to *stop* a vehicle on a highway.

[41] The long title of the Act describes it simply as an "Act to make further provision for agriculture."

[42] s.106(3).

[43] s.106(4).

[44] s.106(5). For provision as to service of notices, see s.107.

is a summary "obstruction" offence,[45] for which the penalty is a fine not exceeding level 2 on the standard scale.

(b) *Hill Farming Act 1946*

8.14   This Act is concerned with the rehabilitation of livestock rearing land, the control of keeping of rams and ram lambs, and the regulation of the burning of grassland heather. Under section 34 of the Act, an officer of the Minister of Agriculture has powers of entry and inspection in connection with the above purposes. The officer must be authorised by general or special directions from the Minister, and must, if so required, produce written evidence of his authority before entering. Twenty-four hours' notice to the occupier is required before admission can be demanded as of right, and the entry must take place at a reasonable time.

The land to which the section applies is any land which the officer has reason to believe to be used, or to be capable of being used, for livestock rearing purposes; and any land which he has reason to believe to be used in connection with the use for livestock rearing purposes of other land. It is an offence to obstruct or impede an officer, punishable on summary conviction with a fine not exceeding level 2 on the standard scale.

(c) *Agriculture Act 1967; Rural Development Boards*

8.15   There is a power under section 45 of the Agriculture Act 1967 for the Minister (or in Wales the Secretary of State) to appoint Rural Development Boards in connection with the special problems of development, and the special need of areas of hills and uplands.[46] A person duly authorised in writing by a Board has power, under section 55 of the Act, to enter on any land in the Board's area for the purpose of determining whether, and if so in what way, any of the functions of the Board should be exercised in relation to the land.

All entries must take place at a reasonable time. If so required the officer must produce a duly authenticated document showing his authority. If the land is occupied 48 hours of notice must be given before entry may be demanded as of right. If the land is occupied for residential purposes the period of notice is seven days. If the land is unoccupied, or the occupier is temporarily absent, the officer must leave the land as effectively secure against trespassers as when he entered. It is a summary offence wilfully to obstruct an officer, punishable with a fine not exceeding level 1 on the standard scale.

(d) *Land Drainage Act 1976*

The entry powers under this Act are dealt with in Chapter Nine, paras. 9.110–9.111.

---

[45] s.106(7). The offence does not require "wilful" obstruction.
[46] At the time of writing there do not seem to be any Boards in existence.

3. Agriculture—plants and produce

(a) *Agriculture and Horticulture Act 1964*

In connection with the grading of "horticultural produce,"[47] a person authorised **8.16** in that behalf by the Minister (or the Secretary of State in Wales) has a power of entry, and in some circumstances a power to obtain a warrant to enter.

(i) Without warrant—section 13(1). The officer must produce, if so required, a duly authenticated document showing his authority. He has the right thereupon to enter any premises (other than a building used solely as a private dwelling-house) which he has reasonable cause to believe to be premises where regulated produce is grown for sale, graded, or packed, or on which regulated produce is to be found.

The entry must be at a reasonable time. On entering, the authorised person may inspect and take samples of any regulated produce found on the premises. He may seize and detain any label, together with any container to which the label is affixed, used in connection with such produce. If produce is found incorrectly labelled (*i.e.* the produce is of an inferior grade to that indicated) then, under section 13(2), the authorised person may relabel it in the prescribed manner.[48]

(ii) Warrant—sections 13(2) and (3). If:

(a) entry is refused, or refusal is apprehended, and notice of the intention to apply for a warrant has been given to the occupier; or

(b) application to admission, or notice of it would defeat the object of the entry; or

(c) the premises are unoccupied, or the occupier is temporarily absent,

then a magistrate, being satisfied by a sworn information in writing of one of the above, may issue a warrant to an authorised officer to enter the premises, by force if necessary. The warrant continues in force for one month.

(iii) Both powers. In relation to entry under section 13(2) or section 13(3), the **8.17** officer may take with him such other persons and equipment as may appear to him to be necessary.[49] If the premises are unoccupied they must be left as secure as they were on entry.[50] It is an offence to disclose information relating to any manufacturing process or trade secret obtained as a result of the entry.[51] Any person who wilfully obstructs, or fails to assist, an officer commits an offence under section 15 of the Act, punishable on summary conviction with a fine not exceeding level 3 on the standard scale.[52]

(b) *Plant Health Act 1967*

This Act is a consolidating Act, dealing with the control of pests and diseases

---

[47] Defined in s.24.

[48] For which see the Grading of Horticultural Produce (Amendment) Regulations 1973 (S.I. 1973 No. 22), and the Grading of Horticultural Produce (Forms of Labels) Regulations 1982 (S.I. 1982 No. 387).

[49] s.13(4).

[50] s.13(5).

[51] s.13(6).

[52] N.B. both powers apply to stalls and vehicles, as well as to premises: s.13(7).

injurious to agricultural and horticultural crops, trees and bushes. It is essentially an enabling Act, and a number of orders have been made, or continue to have effect under it.

Section 3 empowers the Forestry Commissioners (as regards the protection of forest trees and timber from attack by pests) and the Minister of Agriculture (in all other cases) to make such orders as the authority thinks expedient for preventing the spread of pests.[53] Such orders may direct or authorise entry on any land for the purpose of removing or destroying any crop, seed, plant (or any part thereof) or any substance, which has on it or is infected with a pest, or to or by means of which, a pest is in the opinion of the competent authority likely to spread. Entry may also be authorised for the purpose of carrying out examinations or inquiries authorised by the orders, or for any other purpose of the orders.[54]

8.18   **Execution of the Act.** The orders having effect under the Act may give powers of entry to inspectors authorised by the Minister of Agriculture.[55] Such inspectors, as well as being able on entry to destroy or remove any pest-infected crop, plant, etc.,[56] may also be given power generally to take such steps as the inspector may think expedient in connection with any crop, seed, plant, or part thereof, for preventing the spread of the pest.[57]

Compensation. Under section 4(2) of the Act, the Minister may pay compensation in respect of any crop, etc., which is removed or destroyed by or under the instruction of an inspector authorised by him. Compensation is to be based on the value of what was taken or destroyed at the time of taking or destruction; if the Minister so requires, that value is to be ascertained either by his officers, or by arbitration.

Orders. The following orders, having effect under this Act, give entry powers.
Colorado Beetle Order of 1933 (S.R. & O. 1933 No. 830).
Red Core Disease of Strawberry Plants Order 1957 (S.I. 1957 No. 753).
Fire Blight Disease Order of 1958 (S.I. 1958 No. 1814).
Potato Cyst Eelworm (Great Britain) Order 1973 (S.I. 1973 No. 1059).
Wart Disease of Potatoes (Great Britain) Order 1973 (S.I. 1973 No. 1060).
Watermark Disease (Local Authorities) Order 1974 (S.I. 1974 No. 768).
Prevention of Spread of Pests (Seed Potatoes) (Great Britain) Order 1974 (S.I. 1974 No. 1152).
Mediterranean Carnation Leaf Roller (Great Britain) Order 1975 (S.I. 1975 No. 1842).
Plum Pox (Sharka Disease) Order 1975 (S.I. 1975 No. 2225).
Beet Cyst Nematode Order 1977 (S.I. 1977 No. 988).
Dutch Elm Disease (Local Authorities) Order 1984 (S.I. 1984 No. 687).

[53] s.3(1).
[54] s.3(2).
[55] s.4(1).
[56] Or crops, etc., to or by means of which the pest is likely to be spread.
[57] s.4(1).

Dutch Elm Disease (Restriction on Movement of Elms) Order 1984 (S.I. 1984 No. 686).

Progressive Wilt (Disease of Hops) Order 1978 (S.I. 1978 No. 505).

Import and Export (Plant Health) (Great Britain) Order 1980 (S.I. 1980 No. 420).

Tree Pests (Great Britain) Order 1980 (S.I. 1980 No. 450).

Plant Pests (Great Britain) Order 1980 (S.I. 1980 No. 499).

Restriction on Movement of Spruce Wood Order 1982 (S.I. 1982 No. 1457).

(c) *Plant Varieties and Seeds Act 1964*

Part II of this Act is concerned with sale of seeds and seed potatoes, both as **8.19** regards the information which is provided with seeds which are offered for sale, and the condition of the seeds themselves.[58]

Section 25 gives a power of entry to any person duly authorised by the Minister. The power arises where the person has reasonable cause to believe that the premises which he proposes to enter are used for any purpose of a business in the course of which seeds are sold (wholesale or retail, whether by principal or agent).[59] The powers are not available in respect of premises which are used exclusively as a private dwelling.[60] The entry must take place at a reasonable hour, and the entrant must, if so required, produce his authority. The powers may be used for the purpose of exercising powers under seeds regulations in relation to the inspection or copying of records or other documents, or to determine whether there has been a contravention of Part II of the Act, or of seeds regulations. In addition, sections 25(5) and (6) give specific powers which may be exercised on entry. Under section 25(5) there is a power to examine any seed found on the premises, and to take samples (without payment). Section 25(6) provides that the owner, or authorised seller, of any seed offered or exposed for sale, or stored for the purposes of sale, may be required to deliver to a person duly authorised by the Minister such statement as the seller of the seeds would be obliged by the seeds regulations to deliver to a purchaser, within the time limit imposed for delivery of such a statement. Failure to comply with this requirement constitutes a summary offence, with a fine not exceeding level 3 on the standard scale.[61] Obstructing or impeding any person acting in the exercise of powers conferred by section 25 also constitutes a summary offence, with the same penalty.[62] Section 26 provides for specific rules for the handling of samples taken as the result of the exercise of such powers, and for the use of samples in any subsequent criminal proceedings.[63] It specifically excludes samples taken other than in the manner prescribed from being used as evidence of an offence under Part II of the Act.

---

[58] See s.16.
[59] s.25(4).
[60] s.25(2).
[61] s.25(7).
[62] s.25(9).
[63] See s.16 and the seeds regulations made under it.

(d) *Weeds Act 1959*

This Act is concerned with preventing the spreading of "injurious weeds."[64] Under section 4 any person authorised by the Minister in that behalf, may, for the purpose of carrying the Act into effect, enter and inspect any land. The occupier must be served with a notice of the date on which the inspection is to take place, and the authorised person must, if so required, produce his authority at the time of entry.[65] Any person who prevents or obstructs an authorised entry is liable on summary conviction to a fine not exceeding level 3 on the standard scale.

4. Agriculture—fish

(a) *British sea-fishery officers*[66]

8.20　These officers, whose main duties relate to fishing boats and their activities, do also have powers of entry on to land under the Sea Fish (Conservation) Act 1967, and the British Fishing Boats Act 1983.

(i) Sea Fish (Conservation) Act 1967. Under section 15 of this Act (as amended by the Fisheries Act 1981, s.25), which gives British sea-fishery officers the power to seize nets and fish, such an officer also has the power to enter any premises (other than a dwelling-house) used for carrying on any business in connection with the operation of fishing boats, or with the treatment storage or sale of sea fish.

8.21　*Powers on entry.* The officer may require any person on the premises to produce any documents in his custody or possession relating to the catching, landing, transshipment, sale or disposal of any sea fish, and take a copy of any such document.[67] In addition, if the officer has reason to suspect that an offence under the Act has been committed, he may search the premises for any such document, and require any person on the premises to do anything which appears to the officer to be necessary to facilitate the search. Any document found or produced may be seized and detained to be used in evidence in proceedings for the offence.

Offences. A person who without reasonable excuse fails to comply with a requirement of the officer, or assaults or wilfully obstructs an officer in the exercise of his powers, is liable on summary conviction to a fine not exceeding £5,000, or on conviction on indictment, to a fine.[68]

(ii) British Fishing Boats Act 1983. This Act attempts to ensure that British fishing boats exploiting fishery resources satisfy certain conditions with respect to

---

[64] See s.1—this phrase includes spear thistle, creeping or field thistle, curled dock, broad-leaved dock, and ragwort, together with any others prescribed by the Minister by Regulations (at the time of writing no such Regulations had been made).

[65] s.4(1).

[66] See the Sea Fisheries Act 1968, s.7, as amended by the Fisheries Act 1981, s.26, for the definition of who is a "sea-fishery officer."

[67] s.15(2A).

[68] s.15(2C).

the nationality of members of the crew. Under section 3 a search warrant may be obtained to look for documentary evidence of an offence under section 1 of the Act. The warrant can be obtained from a justice of the peace who is satisfied by information on oath that such an offence has been committed, and that a relevant document is to be found on the premises specified. The premises must be used for carrying on a business in connection with the operation of fishing boats, or ancillary activities, but may not be a dwelling-house. The warrant will remain in force for one month.

Powers on entry. The officer named in the warrant may enter the premises, with or without a constable, and search them for relevant documents. He may also require any person on the premises to do anything which appears to him to be necessary for facilitating the search, and in particular to produce any relevant document in his possession. The officer may copy any document so produced, and may seize for use as evidence any document found or produced.

Offences. Failure to comply with an officer's requirement, preventing or attempt- **8.22** ing to prevent another from so complying, or assaulting or wilfully obstructing an officer, renders the offender liable on summary conviction to a fine not exceeding £5,000, and on indictment to a fine.[69]

Protection of officers. A British sea-fishery officer purportedly acting under his section 3 powers, is not as a result to be liable in any civil or criminal proceedings, provided that the court is satisfied that he was acting in good faith, with reasonable skill and care, and that there were reasonable grounds for so acting.[70]

(b) *Other officials*

(i) Diseases of Fish Act 1937. This Act is designed to provide powers to prevent **8.23** the spread of disease among salmon and freshwater fish. A power of entry is given both under a warrant and without warrant.

a. *Warrant.* If a justice of the peace is satisfied on information on oath that there is reasonable cause to suspect that an offence under this Act has been committed, he may issue a warrant.[71] The warrant should specify the person authorised to enter, the land to be entered, and the times at which entry may take place. The warrant remains in force for one week only.

Once on the land, the entrant has the power to seize any fish, eggs of fish, or foodstuff or article, which he suspects to have been imported or brought into Great Britain, or to have been, or to be about to be, removed or otherwise dealt with in contravention of this Act or of any licence granted, order made, or notice served thereunder.

b. *Without warrant.* An inspector appointed by the Minister has the power to enter

[69] s.4(1).
[70] s.4(2).
[71] s.6(1).

(upon production on demand of his authority) any land in order to carry out an inspection and to take samples.[72] If none of the sample is found to be infected the Minister must pay the market value for it.[73]

Any person authorised in writing by a fishery board may, on production on demand of his authority, enter any land within the district of the board (not being part of a fish farm), to perform any duties imposed on him by the board in the exercise of their functions under the Act. The powers in the Act apply to the diseases mentioned in section 13 of the Act, and in the Diseases of Fish Orders of 1973 and 1978.[74] Refusal to admit an inspector, or intentional obstruction of him, is an offence punishable on summary conviction with a fine not exceeding level 4 on the standard scale.

(ii) Sea Fisheries (Shellfish) Act 1967. Where a fishery is subject to rights granted under section 1 of the Act there is a power to enter any land within the limits of the fishery.[75] The power is exercisable by a person authorised by the Minister of Agriculture on giving notice.[76] Twenty-four hours' notice must be given to the occupiers and to the grantees.[77] Written evidence of authorisation must be produced if so requested, before entry.

Entry may be sought in order to carry out an inquiry and examination into whether the grantees are properly cultivating the ground for shellfish, or otherwise complying with the requirements of a section 1 order. Obstruction is a summary offence, subject to a fine not exceeding level 3 on the standard scale.

8.24   *Deposit of shellfish.* The Minister has power under the Act to prohibit the deposit of shellfish in certain areas.[78] An inspector authorised by the Minister has the right to enter any land subject to such a prohibition at any reasonable time, where either the inspector has reasonable grounds to believe that the prohibition is being or has been contravened; or entry is required to remove shellfish.[79]

The inspector must give 24 hours' notice of the entry to the occupier (if any), and must produce written evidence of his authority if so required.[80] On entry the inspector has the right to take away samples of shellfish, and to dispose of them as he thinks fit.[81] Obstruction of an inspector is an offence punishable on summary conviction with a fine not exceeding level 3 on the standard scale.

5. Agriculture—eggs

8.25   There are two statutory instruments which give powers of entry in relation to the

[72] s.6(2).
[73] s.6(3).
[74] S.I. 1973 No. 2093; S.I. 1978 No. 1022.
[75] s.5(4).
[76] s.2.
[77] s.5(5).
[78] s.12.
[79] See ss.12(5) and 14(3).
[80] s.14(4).
[81] s.14(3).

production and marketing of eggs. These are the Eggs (Protection of Guarantees) Order 1973, and the Egg (Marketing Standards) Regulations 1985.[82]

The former was made under sections 5, 9(4) and 35(3) of the Agriculture Act 1957, and section 70 of the Agriculture Act 1967. Article 6 empowers any authorised officer of the Minister (in Wales the Minister and the Secretary of State jointly) at all reasonable times to enter upon land used for the production, storage, grading, packing, or sale, other than sale by retail, of eggs, and may inspect and take samples of any eggs found upon the land so used.

The latter Order, which was made under section 2 of the European Communities Act 1972, and the European Communities (Designation) Order 1972,[83] also gives power, under Article 4, to authorised officers to enter, inspect, and take samples from any land or premises (other than premises used solely as a dwelling) on which any activity regulated by a Community provision is being, or is reasonably suspected of being, carried on. Certain additional powers are attached to this power, such as the right to demand the production of documents,[84] and the specific right of the officer to take with him such other persons as appear to him to be necessary.[85]

Wilful obstruction, failure to comply with properly made requirements, or failure to give reasonable assistance when required, amount to an offence punishable on summary conviction by a fine not exceeding £2,000.

6. Agriculture—contamination of food

Part I of the Food and Environment Protection Act 1985 gives powers to the Minister of Agriculture and the Secretary of State for the Environment to make emergency orders where food may have been contaminated as a result of an escape of substances. Investigating officers and enforcement officers may be appointed,[86] who will have powers of entry under section 4. **8.26**

There are three main situations in which an officer may enter land.[87] First, where an investigating officer has reasonable grounds to suspect that food unfit for human consumption, or things from which such food might be derived, is on the land. Secondly, an enforcement officer may enter where a direction under section 2 has been given in relation to the land or things on it, or there are books, documents, etc., which may help to find things covered by a direction, or if he has reasonable grounds to suspect that entry is necessary to perform any of his functions under Part I of the Act. Thirdly, if an emergency order under section 1 is in force, an investigating or enforcement officer may enter any land in the area designated in the order. He may also enter any land on which he has reasonable grounds to suspect that there is present food, or anything from which food could be derived which has been in the designated area, or any document, etc., which might assist in locating such items.

---

[82] S.I. 1973 No. 591, S.I. 1985 No. 1271.
[83] S.I. 1972 No. 1811.
[84] Art. 4(1).
[85] Art. 4(2).
[86] s.3; British sea-fishery officers, see para. 8.20, are deemed to be "investigating officers" for these purposes.
[87] Or any vehicle, vessel, aircraft, hovercraft, or marine structure.

The above powers are all subject to Schedule 2 to the Act.

This provides that the officer must enter at a reasonable hour, unless it appears to him that his purpose might be frustrated by so doing.[88] He must, if requested, show his authorisation, and identify himself, his purpose, and his grounds for performing it.[89] He may take with him any other person, and any equipment or materials.[90] He may use reasonable force, if necessary.[91]

Premises used only as a dwelling may only be entered under a warrant issued by a justice of the peace.[92] The justice must be satisfied that the officer has reasonable grounds for believing that there is something in the dwelling relevant to the officer's functions, and also that it is not practicable to communicate with any person entitled to grant entry, or entry has been unreasonably refused, or such refusal is likely in the absence of a warrant, or the purpose of the entry may be frustrated or seriously prejudiced unless an officer arriving at the dwelling can secure immediate entry.

Sections 15 and 16 of the Police and Criminal Evidence Act 1984 apply to warrants issued under this Schedule.[93]

Intentional obstruction is a summary offence punishable with a fine not exceeding level 5 on the standard scale.[94]

7. Agriculture—pesticides

8.27   Part III of the Food and Environment Protection Act is concerned with the control of pesticides. The Ministers have powers under section 16 to make regulations prohibiting, or controlling, the use of pesticides. Enforcement powers are contained in section 19. Under these an authorised person[95] may enter any land if he has reasonable grounds to believe that any pesticide is being or has been applied to or stored in it, and that it is necessary for him to enter for any of the general purposes of Part III.[96]

This power is subject to the provisions of Schedule 2 to the Act, which are dealt with above, para. 8.26.

8. Agriculture—other powers

(a) *Agricultural Wages Act 1948*

8.28   Under section 12 of the Act, the Minister has the power to appoint officers to investigate complaints and to secure the proper observance of the Act. These officers have the power to enter any premises or place for the purpose of enforcing the Act

---

[88] Para. 6.
[89] Para. 5.
[90] Para. 2.
[91] Para. 8.
[92] Para. 7.
[93] Para. 7(4); for ss.15 and 16, see above, para. 3.07.
[94] Para. 10, and s.21(5).
[95] s.19(1).
[96] s.19(2). Note also the power to enter vehicles, vessels, aircraft, hovercraft, or marine structures, under s.19(3).

generally, and in particular inspecting wage sheets, or other records of wages paid to agricultural workers, and records of their terms and conditions of employment.[97] The entry must take place at a reasonable time, and in respect of a dwelling-house, reasonable notice of the entry must be given. The officer may be required to produce his certificate of employment, issued by the Minister. It is an offence (punishable on summary conviction with a fine not exceeding level 3 on the standard scale or three months' imprisonment) to "hinder or molest" an officer acting in the exercise of his powers.[98] It is also an offence (punishable on summary conviction with a fine not exceeding level 5 on the standard scale or three months' imprisonment) to produce false records or information.[99]

(b) *Farm and Horticultural Development Regulations 1981*[1]

These Regulations, made under section 2(2) of the European Communities Act 1972, provide for grants to be made for approved development plans for agricultural business. Regulation 19 provides that for the purposes of the Regulations, and in particular to ensure that grants are only made in proper cases, any person duly authorised in that behalf by the Minister may enter upon and inspect any land, and inspect any premises, plant, equipment or livestock, in respect of which a grant under the Regulations has been made or claimed. The entry must be at a reasonable time, and the entrant must, if so required, produce his authority.

(c) *Hops Certification Regulations 1979*

These Regulations implement the EEC hop certification system.[2]

Regulation 5 empowers the Minister to appoint inspectors. Such inspectors have the following powers, which may be exercised at all reasonable times, upon production, if so required, of their authority:

(a) to enter and inspect any certification centre, or place where records are kept in accordance with the Regulations;

(b) to require any person having control of any such centre, premises or place, and any certifying officer, to give the inspector such assistance and afford him such facilities as the inspector may reasonably ask for;

(c) to require any person to produce and permit the inspector to inspect any documents in that person's possession or control, being documents which are required to be prepared or maintained by the Regulations, or other Community provisions.

Intentional obstruction is an offence, as is failure (without reasonable excuse) to provide facilities or assistance, or to produce or permit the inspection of any document. The offence is punishable on summary conviction with a fine not exceeding £200.

---

[97] s.12(3)(*b*).
[98] s.12(7)(*a*).
[99] s.12(7)(*d*).
[1] S.I. 1981 No. 1707.
[2] S.I. 1979 No. 1095. They were made under s.2(2) of the European Communities Act 1972.

(d) *Milk (Cessation of Production) Act 1985*

This Act creates a scheme for the compensation of milk producers who cease, or reduce, milk production. Under section 2 a duly authorised officer of the Minister may, at all reasonable times, enter on any land occupied by a person to whom a payment has been made under the Act. The purpose of the entry is to determine whether that person is involved, or has a substantial financial interest in the production of milk. On entry the officer may require any person who is or has been engaged in the production of milk to produce any accounts or records in his possession or under his control. The officer may inspect them, copy or take extracts from them, or remove them for a reasonable period.

B. Education

Education Act 1944

8.29 Under section 77 of this Act the Secretary of State for Education has a duty to cause inspections at appropriate intervals of every educational establishment. For this purpose he has the power to recommend the appointment of inspectors by Her Majesty, and may also himself authorise others to assist, or act as additional inspectors.[3]

The powers of inspectors seem to be simply to inspect: the Act is silent as to any more detailed powers.

Local authorities also have powers of inspection under this section in respect of educational establishments maintained by the local authority, using its own officers.[4]

Religious instruction in voluntary schools is subject to inspection by the governors, and not by Her Majesty's inspectors, or local authority inspectors. Obstruction of an inspector is a summary offence, punishable with a fine not exceeding level 4 on the standard scale, or three months' imprisonment, or both.

C. Employment

1. Health and safety

8.30 The main powers of entry in relation to employment arise in connection with health and safety at work, and are governed by section 20 of the Health and Safety at Work etc. Act 1974.

Powers under the Act are divided, as far as enforcement is concerned, between the Health and Safety Executive and the local authorities. The division of responsibilities is governed by the Health and Safety (Enforcing Authority) Regulations 1977.[5]

---

[3] An "educational establishment" is defined in s.77(1) (as amended) as a school, an institution within the P.C.F.C. funding sector, or an institution which is maintained or assisted by a local education authority and provides higher education or further education (or both) and any institution which requests an inspection.

[4] s.77(3).

[5] S.I. 1977 No. 746.

The main areas assigned to local authorities under Schedule 1 to the Regulations are (with some exceptions) shops, premises used for wholesale storage or distribution, office activities, catering services, and the provision of residential accommodation.[6]

The following discussion is related to the powers of the Executive; local authority powers are considered in Chapter Nine.

The power to appoint inspectors is given by section 19 of the 1974 Act. This power **8.31** is part of the Executive's general responsibility for enforcing the "relevant statutory provisions." This phrase means the provisions of Part I of the 1974 Act, the provisions of any health and safety regulations, or of any agricultural health and safety regulations, and the provisions of the Acts mentioned in the first Schedule to the 1974 Act, and any regulations made or having effect under them.[7] Inspectors covered by this section include: the Factories Inspectorate, the Mines and Quarries Inspectorate, the Alkali and Clean Air Inspectorate, the Explosives Inspectorate, and the Nuclear Installations Inspectorate.

Section 19 requires that the appointment of an inspector should be in writing, specifying which of the powers under the relevant statutory provisions are to be exercisable by the inspector. The inspector will only be entitled to exercise the powers specified in the instrument, unless these are varied by the Executive.

Within these limits the powers of an inspector are governed by the general provisions of section 20. This section gives the inspector the power to enter any premises which he has reason to believe it is necessary for him to enter for a purpose for which he has been appointed. The entry must normally take place at a reasonable time. If, however, in the opinion of the inspector (which does not in this instance have to be based on reasonable grounds) the situation is, or may be, dangerous, the entry may take place at any time. The section does not give any specific power to use force to obtain entry.

If the inspector has reasonable cause to apprehend any serious obstruction in the execution of his duty he may take a constable with him, and in any case he may take any other person duly authorised by the Executive, and any equipment or materials he may require.

Powers on entry

Section 20(2)(d)–(m) specifies a number of powers which an inspector will have on **8.32** obtaining entry to any premises under this section. As well as general powers of examination and investigation (s.20(2)(d)) he has the following powers.

(1) To direct that the premises, part of them, or anything in them, shall be left undisturbed for as long as is reasonably necessary for such examination or investigation.[8]

---

[6] The main exceptions arise where toxic or dangerous materials are used or present on the premises, *e.g.* petrol, gas, or sewage.

[7] 1974 Act, s.53(1). A complete list of all the current relevant statutory provisions is given in App. 1.

[8] s.20(2)(e).

(2) To take measurements, photographs, and make recordings as he considers necessary for the examination or investigation.[9]

(3) To take samples of any articles or substances found in the premises, and of the atmosphere in or in the vicinity of the premises.[10]

(4) To dismantle, or subject to any process or test, any article or substance which appears to him likely to cause danger to health or safety. The article may not, however, be destroyed, unless this is necessary as part of carrying out the statutory provisions under which the inspector is authorised to act. Before taking any action the inspector should consult, as seems to him appropriate, as to the dangers of doing what he proposes.[11] A person present at the time and having responsibilities in relation to the premises may demand to be present when any action is taken under this power, unless the inspector considers that the person's presence would be prejudicial to the safety of the State.[12]

(5) To take possession of a dangerous article for as long as is necessary in order to examine it, to deal with it under (4) above, to ensure that it is not tampered with before such examination is complete, or to ensure that it is available for use in evidence in subsequent proceedings.[13] An inspector taking possession of any article or substance under this subsection is obliged to leave either with a responsible person, or if that is impracticable, fixed in a conspicuous position, a notice giving particulars of that article or substance. The notice should identify what has been taken and state the power that is relied on (*i.e.* s.20(2)(*i*)). Moreover, if it is practicable, the inspector must take a sample of what has been taken, and give a portion to a responsible person on the premises.

(6) To obtain information by requiring any person who the inspector has reasonable cause to believe to be able to give any information relevant to any examination or investigation to answer such questions as the inspector thinks fit to ask, and to sign a declaration of the truth of his answers. The person has a right to nominate a person whom he wishes to be present during the questioning: the inspector has the power to control who else, if anybody, is present.[14] Any answer given will not be admissible evidence against the person or his or her spouse.[15]

8.33   Two Scottish cases have considered the relationship between the two subsections, *i.e.* 20(2)(*g*) and 20(2)(*i*), which give a power to remove material from premises which have been inspected (powers (3) and (5) above). Both cases concerned the removal by an inspector of material suspected of containing asbestos. In *Skinner* v. *John McGregor (Contractors) Ltd.*[16] the sheriff held that whenever the inspector suspects that the material is dangerous he should be regarded as acting under subsection 20(2)(*i*) in removing it. This brings into play the provisions of subsection

---

[9] s.20(2)(*f*).
[10] s.20(2)(*g*). The Secretary of State has power to make Regulations—s.20(3).
[11] s.20(5).
[12] s.20(4).
[13] s.20(6).
[14] s.20(2)(*j*).
[15] s.20(7).
[16] [1977] S.L.T. 83 (Sh. Ct.).

20(6) as regards providing notice and samples of the material removed to a responsible person at the premises. In *Skinner* v. *McGregor* these procedures had not been followed, and the sheriff ruled the material inadmissible as evidence against the accused. This approach was rejected by the High Court in *Laws* v. *Keane*,[17] where the court disapproved *Skinner* v. *McGregor*, taking the view that the distinction between subsections 20(2)(*g*) and (*i*) relates not to whether the substance is dangerous or not, but to whether a sample of the substance was taken or the entire quantity. If only a sample is taken there is no need for the protective provisions of subsection 20(6), because the occupier will retain material on which to conduct his own tests.

Although *Skinner* v. *McGregor* cannot therefore be regarded as good law on the question of the applicability of of subsections 20(2)(*g*) and (*i*), the decision in *Laws* v. *Keane* does not affect the argument that failure to comply with subsection 20(6) (where this is required) will render any material taken inadmissible in subsequent proceedings. It is perhaps open to question whether the exclusionary approach adopted by the Scottish court would be followed in an English court, where defects in the procedures for obtaining evidence have not generally been regarded as rendering relevant evidence inadmissible.[18]

By virtue of subsection 20(8), a person cannot be compelled to produce a document which he would be entitled to withhold on discovery on grounds of legal privilege.

"Imminent danger"

One other section of the 1974 Act gives a power of seizure to an inspector, in addition to those discussed under section 20. This is section 25. It empowers an inspector who finds in any premises which he has power to enter, an article or substance which he has reasonable cause to believe is, in the circumstances, a cause of imminent danger of serious personal injury, to seize the article and cause it to be rendered harmless. This may be by destruction. If it is practicable to do so, the inspector should take a sample of the dangerous material and give a portion of it to a responsible person at the premises where it was found.[19] After the event the inspector has an obligation to prepare a written report of the incident, and provide a signed copy to a responsible person at the premises, and to the owner of the material. If the owner's name or address cannot be ascertained by reasonable enquiry, the owner's copy may be served by delivery to the person at the premises who received the other copy.[20]

8.34

Offences

The powers of inspectors discussed above are backed up by a number of offences contained in section 33 of the Act. The most general offence is subsection 33(1)(*h*) which makes it an offence intentionally to obstruct an inspector in the exercise or

8.35

[17] [1983] S.L.T. 40.
[18] See above, paras. 2.14–2.19.
[19] s.25(2).
[20] s.25(3).

performance of his powers or duties. It is also an offence to contravene any requirement imposed by an inspector under section 20,[21] or to prevent or attempt to prevent
any other person from appearing before an inspector, or from answering any
question to which the inspector may by virtue of section 20(2) require an answer.[22]
All the above offences are triable summarily, with a maximum penalty of a fine not
exceeding level 5 on the standard scale.[23]

Two other offences relevant to the powers under discussion are triable either way.
These are contravening a requirement imposed by an inspector under section 25,
and knowingly or recklessly making a statement which is false in purported compliance with a requirement to furnish information.[24] The penalties for these offences
are, on summary conviction, a fine not exceeding £1,000, and on indictment an
unlimited fine.[25]

2. Wages Act 1986

8.36   The Secretary of State can appoint officers under section 20 of the Act. Currently
there are about 70. Most of their investigations are conducted by post and question-
naire,[26] but there is a power of entry under section 20(3)(c). This arises where an
officer has reasonable cause to believe that an order under section 14 (minimum
wages) applies to an employer. The officer may enter the employer's business
premises (including premises used to give out work to homeworkers, or to provide
living accommodation for workers). On entry the officer may presumably exercise
any of his other powers under section 20(3), which include inspecting wage sheets,
lists of homeworkers, etc., and examining workers covered by a section 14 order.

Intentional obstruction of an officer is an offence punishable on summary conviction with a fine not exceeding level 3 on the standard scale.[27]

3. Docks and Harbours Act 1966

8.37   Where a "welfare amenity scheme" is in force in a port,[28] a health and safety
inspector may enter and inspect any place in the port where welfare amenities are
required by the scheme to be provided and maintained, and exercise such other
powers as may be necessary for carrying into effect Part II of the Act, which is
concerned with the establishment of such schemes.[29] The power is to be exercised for
the purpose of ascertaining whether the requirements of the scheme are being
complied with. The entry may take place at any reasonable time, day or night, but
the inspector must produce his instrument of appointment, or an authenticated

---

[21] s.33(1)(e).
[22] s.33(1)(f).
[23] s.33(2).
[24] s.33(1)(k).
[25] s.33(3).
[26] See the annotations to section 20 in *Current Law Statutes*, and H.L.Debs., Vol. 478, No. 136,
cols. 249–250.
[27] s.21(2).
[28] For which see s.25.
[29] s.32(1).

copy, if required by the occupier or any other person holding a responsible position of management at the premises.[30] Obstruction of an inspector is a summary offence, subject to a fine not exceeding level 1 on the standard scale.

4. Explosives Act 1875

Under section 74 of this Act, a health and safety inspector has the same powers to enter premises to seize explosives or ingredients of them, as does a police constable. This power is described in Chapter Four above (paragraph 4.24). **8.38**

D. Energy

Energy Act 1976

The enforcement powers which are detailed in Schedule 2 to this Act include powers of entry with or without warrant. **8.39**

(a) *Without warrant*

Under paragraph 3 of Schedule 2, a person duly authorised by, or on behalf of the Secretary of State, may enter any premises other than those used only as a dwelling.[31] The entry may be made at all reasonable hours, though the entrant may be required to produce his authorisation. The purposes for which the entry power may be used are, (i) securing compliance with orders and directions of the Secretary of State under the Act, and (ii) checking estimates and forecasts or verifying returns and information provided in response to directions under paragraph 1 of the Schedule. Once on the premises the authorised person has the power to make such inquiries and inspections, and purchase or take such samples of any substance, as are allowed by the terms of his authorisation or he thinks necessary for those purposes.[32]

(b) *With warrant*

The power to enter premises with a warrant is governed by paragraph 4 of the Schedule. It may not be used against premises used only as a dwelling. The warrant is issued by a justice of the peace who has received a sworn information in writing submitted on behalf of the Secretary of State, but the grounds on which the warrant may be issued vary, according to whether or not an Order in Council under section 3 of the Act is in force. An Order in Council under section 3 may be made to implement reserve powers under the Act, either to deal with an emergency in fuel or electricity supplies in this country, or to implement international treaty obligations to take emergency measures in connection with a reduction in fuel supplies. **8.40**

(i) When no Order in Council is in force. In this case the circumstances in which a warrant can be issued are as follows:

[30] s.32(2).
[31] Para. 3(3).
[32] N.B. the limitations on this power noted below, para. 8.41.

(a) admission to the premises has been refused after seven days' notice of the intention to enter had been given to the occupier; or

(b) application for admission would defeat the object of the entry, or the premises are unoccupied.

(ii) When an Order in Council is in force. In this case the warrant may be issued in the same circumstances as above, but, as regards (a) there is no requirement of notice, and the apprehension of a refusal after notice has been given is sufficient. As regards (b) additional grounds for issue of a warrant exist where the case is one of urgency, or where the occupier is temporarily absent.

8.41 *Force.* In any case where the entry is by warrant, force may be used to enter the premises, if necessary.

Time limit. The warrant may be executed at any time, but it expires at the end of one month from the date of issue.

Powers on entry. Once entry has been obtained under a warrant the person entering may search the premises and take possession of any documents which he finds there which appear to him to be relevant for the purposes for which the warrant was obtained. Any documents so seized may be held for three months, or until the conclusion of any proceedings for an offence under the Act started within that time to which they are relevant. If the premises are unoccupied, or the occupier is temporarily absent, the premises are to be left as effectively secured against trespassers as they were before entry.

Limitations on both powers. There are two limitations on the availability of these entry powers. First, they may not be used simply for the purpose of securing compliance with orders under section 15 of the Act, which gives the Minister of Transport the power to make regulations for the official testing of the fuel consumption of passenger cars. Secondly, unless an Order in Council under section 3 is in force, the powers may not be used only for the purpose of securing compliance with orders under section 1(1), which gives the Secretary of State a general power to make orders regulating or prohibiting the production, supply, acquisition or use of any substance used as a fuel, such as petrol, gas, or electricity.

Obstruction. It is an offence wilfully to obstruct any person exercising a power conferred by or under the Energy Act 1976.[33] A person found guilty of such an offence is liable on summary conviction to a fine not exceeding level 5 on the standard scale.[34]

E. Environment

1. National Parks and Access to the Countryside Act 1949

8.42 Under section 108 of this Act a power of entry on to land is given to a person duly

---

[33] s.18(2)(*b*).
[34] s.19(1).

authorised in writing by the Secretary of State for the Environment (in Wales the Secretary of State for Wales), or by any other authority having power compulsorily to acquire land, or to make an access order. The purpose for which the power may be used is to survey land in connection with either (a) purchase of the land, compulsorily or by agreement, or (b) making an access order in respect of it. There is also a power to enter in connection with surveying or valuing the land where there is a claim for compensation under the Act. The power here is given to Officers of the Valuation Office of the Inland Revenue Department, or to any person duly authorised in writing by the authority from which the compensation is claimed.[35] In respect of the above powers, if the land is occupied, at least 14 days' notice in writing of the proposed entry must be given to the occupier. The proposed entrant must, if so required, produce evidence of his authority before entering.[36] Wilful obstruction of a person exercising these powers is a summary offence, subject to a fine not exceeding level 1 on the standard scale.

2. Radioactive Substances Act 1960

This Act set up a system of registration of users of radioactive material (other than the United Kingdom Atomic Energy Authority). Authorisation is required for the disposal of radioactive waste. The Secretary of State for the Environment is assisted in the execution of the Act by inspectors appointed under section 12, which also gives the inspectors powers of entry. These powers may be exercised with or without warrant, but certain general provisions cover both cases. **8.43**

General provisions. (1) The powers may be exercised by an inspector alone, or together with other persons.[37]

(2) Unoccupied premises must be left as effectively secured against trespassers as they were found.[38]

(3) Before carrying out a test on the premises the inspector must consult with such persons having duties on the premises as the inspector considers appropriate to make sure that the test does not create any danger.[39]

(4) "Emergency"—several of the powers mentioned below are available for use in an "emergency." This is defined for the purposes of the Act in section 12(9). A case of emergency is a case where a person requiring entry to premises has reasonable cause to believe that circumstances exist which are likely to endanger life or health, and that immediate entry is necessary to verify the existence of those circumstances, or to ascertain their cause, or to effect a remedy.

(5) Force may only be used where the entry is under warrant, or in an emergency.[40]

Powers of entry. *(a) Without warrant.* An inspector, having shown, if so required, **8.44**

---

[35] s.108(2).
[36] s.108(3).
[37] Sched. 2, para. 8.
[38] Sched. 2, para. 5.
[39] Sched. 2, para. 6.
[40] Sched. 2, para. 7.

written evidence of his authority,[41] may, at any reasonable time, enter any premises in respect of which:

(i) a person is for the time being registered under section 1 of the Act;

(ii) a person is exempted from registration by section 2(1) or (2);

(iii) an authorisation under section 6(1) or 7 is in force[42];

(iv) an inspector has reasonable grounds to believe that radioactive material is being kept there, or on or from which such material has been or is being accumulated or disposed of (and the premises do not fall within (i), (ii), or (iii), above.) In this case the power may only be used with the consent of the occupier, or in an "emergency," or under a warrant.

On entry under the above powers the inspector may take with him such equipment as he may require; carry out such tests and inspections, and take such samples of waste, as he considers expedient; and require the occupier, or any person with duties on or in connection with the premises to provide such information or allow the inspector to inspect such documents, relating to the use of the premises, as the inspector may specify. An inspector may also enter without warrant, at any reasonable time, and on showing written evidence of his authority if so required, in order to dispose of radioactive waste in accordance with the Secretary of State's powers under section 10(4) of the Act. This power may only be exercised with consent, or in an "emergency," or under a warrant.

8.45   (b) *With warrant.* A warrant for entry for one of the purposes listed above may be obtained from a justice of the peace who is satisfied by a sworn information that admission to specified premises is reasonably required, and that one of the following conditions is satisfied:

(i) that admission was sought after not less than seven days' notice had been given (or in the case of premises falling within categories (i), (ii) or (iii) in para. 8.45 above, 24 hours' notice); or

(ii) that admission was sought in an emergency, and was refused; or

(iii) that the premises are unoccupied; or

(iv) that application for admission would defeat the object of the entry.

Such a warrant continues in force until the purpose for which entry was required is satisfied.

Obstruction. Obstructing an inspector is an offence, as is refusing or without reasonable excuse, failing to provide information or to permit any inspection reasonably required under section 12. The penalty on summary conviction is a fine not exceeding £100, and on indictment, a fine.[43]

3. Countryside Act 1968

8.46   The powers under the National Parks and Access to the Countryside Act 1949

---

[41] Sched. 2, para. 1.
[42] s.12(3). But no entry may be made of "prohibited places" under the Official Secrets Act 1911.
[43] s.13(5).

(above, para. 8.42) apply also to the exercise of powers under the Countryside Act 1968, by virtue of section 46 of that Act.

4. Conservation of Seals Act 1970

Under section 11 of this Act, the Secretary of State for the Environment, or the **8.47** Minister of Agriculture, may, after consultation with the Natural Environment Research Council, authorise in writing any person to enter upon any land. The purposes for which entry may be authorised (and the authorisation must itself specify the purpose) are:

(a) obtaining information relating to seals;
(b) killing or taking seals for the purpose of preventing damage to fisheries by them.

The authorisation may impose conditions on the exercise of the power, and must also specify the land to be entered, the period (not exceeding eight weeks) during which the power may be exercised, and the number, species, and age of seals that may be killed or taken (where this is the purpose of the entry).

Notice. As regards entry for purpose (a) above, not less than 48 hours' notice, and for purpose (b) 28 days' notice, of the intention to issue an authorisation, and its purpose, must be given to the occupier. If the authorisation is for purpose (b) above, then the Secretary of State (or the Minister) must have regard to any representations that might be made by the occupier. If the occupier can show that he has killed or taken the required number of seals before the expiry of the notice, the authorisation shall not be issued.

Powers on entry. The authorised person may take with him such other persons as may be necessary, but he must, if so required by the occupier, produce his authority. Any seals taken or killed by an authorised person shall belong to the Secretary of State, and may be disposed of as he thinks fit.[44]

Obstruction. Wilful obstruction of an authorised person exercising a power of entry under section 11 is a summary offence, subject to a maximum fine not exceeding level 4 on the standard scale.

5. Ancient Monuments and Archaeological Areas Act 1979

This Act contains a wide range of powers concerned with the discovery, inspec- **8.48** tion, and preservation of ancient monuments and sites of archaeological interest. These powers include a number of powers of entry exercisable by persons appointed by the Secretary of State for the Environment. Under the National Heritage Act 1983, the powers are exercisable in relation to sites and monuments in England by the Historic Buildings and Monuments Commission for England (referred to in the rest of this section as "the Commission").

(a) *General provisions—section* 44. This section sets out a number of general provisions which apply to all the powers under the Act.

[44] s.11(5).

(i) Dwelling-houses.[45] Except in relation to section 43 (below), there may not be entry of any building or part of a building occupied as a dwelling-house, without the consent of the occupier.

(ii) Notice. Except in relation to section 5 (below), which has its own notice provisions, admission as of right may only be demanded where the occupier of the land has been given at least 24 hours' notice. If the purpose of the entry is to carry out works on the land (other than excavations under ss.26 or 38), the period is extended to 14 days.[46] In addition, the entrant must, if so required, produce evidence of his authority before entering.[47]

(iii) Additional powers. Any power of entry is to be construed as including power for the entrant to take with him any assistance or equipment reasonably required for the purpose of the entry, and to do anything on the land reasonably necessary for that purpose.[48] If the entry is for the purpose of carrying out any archaeological investigation or examination of the land, the entrant may take and remove such samples of any description as appear to him to be reasonably required for the purpose of archaeological analysis.

(iv) Restrictions. Where work is going on on land in respect of which a power of entry is exercisable, the entrant must comply with any reasonable requirement or conditions imposed by the person carrying out the work for the purpose of preventing interference with or delay to the work.[49] However, this does not apply where the work is being carried on in contravention of section 2(1) or (6) or section 35 of the Act, or where the requirement or conditions would in effect frustrate the purpose of the entry.

(b) *Specific powers*

8.49   **(i) Section 5—urgent works.** If it appears to the Secretary of State that work is urgently necessary for the preservation of a scheduled monument, he may either enter the site to execute the work, or, if the site is in England, authorise the Commission to do so. In either case the owner and the occupier must be given at least seven days' written notice. Any compensation payable under section 35 of the Powers of the Criminal Courts Act 1973 in respect of the damage to the monument becomes payable (in so far as not already paid) to the Secretary of State, or the Commission, as appropriate.

(ii) Sections 6 and 6A—inspection of scheduled monuments, etc. These sections contain a number of powers. They may be exercised by a person authorised in writing (by the Secretary of State or the Commission as appropriate), and, unless otherwise stated, at any reasonable time. The powers of the Commission only apply to land situated in England.

[45] s.44(1).
[46] s.44(2).
[47] s.44(3).
[48] s.44(4).
[49] s.44(6).

Purpose of entry. (1) A person authorised by the Secretary of State may enter to inspect any scheduled monument in, on, or under any land with a view to ascertaining its condition, and whether it is or has been or is likely to be damaged (by any works being carried on in contravention of section 2(1), or otherwise). A person authorised by the Secretary of State of the Commission may enter to ascertain whether any works in contravention of section 2(1) are being carried out, or, as regards the Commission, have been carried out.

(2) A person authorised by the Secretary of State may enter for the purpose of inspecting any scheduled monument in, on, or under land, in connection with an application for scheduled monument consent for works affecting the monument, or in connection with any proposal by the Secretary of State to modify or revoke such a consent.

(3) A person authorised by the Secretary of State or the Commission may enter to observe the execution of scheduled monument consent works, and to inspect the condition of the land and the monument after their completion, in order to ensure that the works are or have been executed in accordance with the consent and any conditions attached to it.

(4) A person authorised by the Secretary of State may enter any land on which works to which a scheduled monument consent relates are being carried out to inspect the land (and any buildings or structures on it) with a view to recording any matters of archaeological or historical interest, and to observe the works with a view to recording such matters, and to examine and record any objects or other material of archaeological or historical interest discovered during the works.[50]

(5) If the Secretary of State thinks it is expedient to modify or revoke a scheduled monument consent as regards a monument in England he should consult with the Commission. The Commission may then authorise an entry for the purpose of inspecting the monument.

(6) A person authorised by the Secretary of State or the Commission may enter land in, on, or under which a scheduled monument is situated, with the consent of the owner and the occupier, for the purpose of erecting and maintaining on or near the site of the monument such noticeboards and marker posts as appear to the Secretary of State or the Commission to be desirable with a view to preserving the monument from accidental or deliberate damage.

(iii) Section 26—land believed to contain an ancient monument. A person **8.50** authorised by the Secretary of State may enter any land in, on, or under which the Secretary of State knows or has reason to believe, there is an ancient monument. The power may be used simply to inspect the land and any buildings or structure on it, with a view to recording matters of archaeological or historical interest, or to carry out excavations. Such excavations, however, may only take place with the consent of "every person whose consent to the making of the excavation would be required

---

[50] s.6(4).

apart from this section,[51] (*i.e.* presumably, the owner, occupier, or anyone else having an interest in the land).

(iv) Section 38—sites covered by an operations notice. The Secretary of State has power under section 34 to appoint an "investigating authority" for an area of archaeological interest. In default of such appointment, the Secretary of State, or the Commission (in England), will be the investigating authority.

The investigating authority has the right, where an operations notice has been served,[52] to enter at any reasonable time the site of the operation, and any land giving access to it, to inspect the site (and any buildings or structures on it) with a view to recording any matters of archaeological or historical interest and determining whether it would be desirable to carry out any excavations,[53] or to observing the operations and examining and recording any objects of such interest, and recording anything else of such interest, discovered during the operations.

If the authority decides to excavate, there is an additional power of entry (at any reasonable time) to the site or any land giving access to it, to carry out the excavations. It should be noted that the authority has a limited period in which to serve notice of an intention to excavate, amounting to four weeks from the date of the service of the operations notice.[54] It is also limited as to the time which may be taken over the excavations.[55]

The powers of the authority are under the general supervision of the Secretary of State, who may give directions to the authority limiting or removing its powers under section 38.[56] The Secretary of State should consult with the Commission before giving such a direction with respect to land situated in England.[57]

8.51   **(v) Section 40.** Where an operations notice has been served the Secretary of State may at any reasonable time enter the site for the purpose of inspecting the site (including any building or other structure on it) and recording any matters of archaeological or historical interest. The Royal Commission on Historical Monuments may also enter to inspect any building or structure, and to record any such matters.

(vi) Section 43—survey and valuation. Where there is a proposal to acquire land under the Act, or a claim for compensation in respect of such an acquisition, or for any damage, an "authorised person"[58] may in that connection enter any land (not necessarily the land to be acquired or the subject of the claim), for the purpose of surveying it, or estimating its value. The power to survey includes a power to

---

[51] s.26(3).

[52] For which see s.35.

[53] The investigating authority also has this power where it has been notified that operations are to be carried out by an authority possessing compulsory purchase powers. The power to enter lasts for a month from the date on which it was first exercised; s.39(1) and (2).

[54] s.38(3).

[55] See ss.38(4) and (5).

[56] s.38(8).

[57] s.38(10).

[58] *i.e.* a Valuation Officer of the Inland Revenue, a person duly authorised in writing by the Secretary of State or other authority proposing to make the acquisition, or liable for the compensation, s.43(2).

search and bore to ascertain the nature of the subsoil or the presence of minerals.[59] But notice of the intention to exercise this power must be given in the notice of intended entry.[60] Moreover, if the land is held by statutory undertakers, and they object on the grounds that the work would be seriously detrimental to the carrying on of their undertaking, the Secretary of State must authorise the work.

(c) *Compensation*

Where damage to land or other property on the land results from the exercise of the powers under sections 6, 6A, 26, 38, 39, 40, or 43, compensation is payable to any person having an interest in the land or property. The compensation is recoverable from the Secretary of State, the Commission, or other authority by or on whose behalf the power was exercised. As regards areas of archaeological importance liability lies with the Secretary of State or the Commission rather than the investigating authority.[61] Disputes as to the amount of any compensation are to be determined by the Lands Tribunal.[62] **8.52**

(d) *Obstruction*

Intentional obstruction is a summary offence, carrying a fine not exceeding level 3 on the standard scale.

6. Wildlife and Countryside Act 1981

Section 51 of this Act gives various authorities powers of entry. The person exercising them must in every case be authorised in writing, and produce evidence of his authority, if required to do so, before entering. Entry may take place at any reasonable time, and may be of any land other than a dwelling. **8.53**

The powers are given to:

(1) The Nature Conservancy Council;
    (a) to ascertain whether an order should be made under section 29 (which deals with areas of special scientific interest), or if an offence under that section is being, or has been committed on that land,
    (b) to ascertain the amount of any compensation to be paid in respect of a section 29 order.

(2) The Secretary of State or the relevant authority within section 34, to ascertain whether an order should be made, or whether an offence is being or has been committed, under section 34 (which concerns limestone pavements).

(3) The Ministers (*i.e.* the Secretary of State, the Minister of Agriculture, Fisheries and Food, and in Wales the Secretary of State) or the local planning authority, to ascertain whether an order should be made or whether an

[59] s.43(3).
[60] s.44(9).
[61] s.46(2).
[62] s.47.

offence is being or has been committed under section 42 (which concerns agricultural operations on moors and heaths in National Parks).

In relation to all the above, if the purpose is to see whether an order should be made, or to assess compensation, entry to occupied land may not be demanded as of right unless 24 hours' notice has been given to the occupier.[63]

Obstruction. Intentional obstruction is a summary offence, carrying a fine not exceeding level 3 on the standard scale.

7. Food and Environment Protection Act 1985

8.54   Part II of the Food and Environment Protection Act is concerned with the licensing of the deposit of substances, articles, etc., in the sea, and the incineration of them at sea.[64] Enforcement powers are contained in section 11. A person authorised by one of the Ministers[65] may, *inter alia*, enter any land or vehicles in the United Kingdom if he has reasonable grounds for believing that any substances or articles intended to be deposited in the sea or under the sea-bed or incinerated on a vessel or marine structure at sea are or have been present there.[66]

Schedule 2 to the Act applies to this powers,[67] with the exception that there is no power to enter premises used only as a dwelling.[68]

F. Home Office

1. Aviation Security Act 1982

8.55   This Act gives the Home Secretary power to make directions connected with the security of aircraft and aerodromes. As part of the exercise of this power he may authorise a person in writing to enter and inspect any aerodrome or aircraft.[69] Force may not be used to gain entry, and the inspector must, if required, produce his authority.[70] The purposes for which entry may be authorised are to determine whether a direction should be made under the Act, or, when such a direction has been made, to determine whether it is being or has been complied with. Wilfully obstructing or impeding an inspector is an offence, punishable on summary conviction with a fine of up to £1,000, and on indictment with a fine, or up to two years' imprisonment, or both.

2. Immigration

8.56   Note that the powers of entry in relation to immigration are given to police officers

---

[63] s.51(3).
[64] s.6.
[65] *i.e.* the Secretary of State for the Environment, or the Minister of Agriculture, Fisheries and Food.
[66] s.11(2). Note also the power to enter foreign vessels, aircraft, etc., in the U.K., and British vessels, etc., anywhere.
[67] For which, see above, para. 8.26.
[68] s.11(4).
[69] ss.20(1) and (3). See also, above, para. 4.22.
[70] s.20(4).

rather than immigration officials, and these powers are therefore dealt with in Chapter Four, paragraph 4.27.

3. Protection of personal data

This area is under the general supervision of the Home Office, although the Data Protection Registry, and Data Protection Registrar which were created by the Data Protection Act 1984 are independent of the Government.   **8.57**

The Act establishes a system of registration for users of personal data which is processed automatically (*e.g.* on a computer). The system is under the supervision of the Data Protection Registrar. He has powers of entry under warrant by virtue of section 16 and Schedule 4.

The warrant is obtained from a circuit judge, who must be satisfied by information on oath that there are reasonable grounds for suspecting that an offence has been or is being committed, or that the "data protection principles" set out in Schedule 1 have been or are being contravened by a registered user. In either case, he must also be satisfied that evidence of this is to be found on specified premises, and that one of the following conditions is fulfilled:

(a) the Registrar has given seven days' written notice to the occupier demanding access, but access was unreasonably refused when demanded at a reasonable hour, and the occupier has subsequently been notified of the intention to apply for a warrant, and given an opportunity to be heard by the judge on the question of whether or not it should be issued[71]; or

(b) the case is one of urgency; or

(c) compliance with the requirements of (a), above, would defeat the object of the entry.[72]

If the judge decides to issue the warrant, it will authorise the Registrar or any of his officers or servants to enter and search the premises; inspect, examine, operate and test any data equipment found there; and inspect and seize any documents which may be evidence of an offence or contravention.[73] The powers are not exercisable in respect of data exempt from Part II of the Act, *e.g.* pension and payroll data, domestic records, club membership lists, and mailing lists.[74] Nor may they be used in relation to communications in the hands of a professional legal adviser, made between the adviser and his client in connection with the giving of advice on the Act, or with proceedings arising out of the Act, unless held with the intention of furthering a criminal purpose.[75]

The warrant must be executed within seven days of its issue,[76] and reasonable force may be used.[77] It may be executed at any time, but should be executed at a

[71] Sched. 4, para. 2.
[72] *Ibid.*
[73] Sched. 4, para. 1.
[74] Sched. 4, para. 8.
[75] Sched. 4, para. 9.
[76] Sched. 4, para. 1.
[77] Sched. 4, para. 4.

reasonable hour unless it appears to the person executing it that there are reasonable grounds for suspecting that the evidence would not then be found.[78] If the occupier is present he should be shown the warrant and given a copy; if not, a copy should be left in a prominent place on the premises.[79] A receipt should be given for seized items, if requested.[80]

Anything seized may be retained for as long as necessary, but the occupier should, on request, be given copies, provided that the person executing the warrant considers that this can be done without undue delay.[81] In addition, there is provision in paragraph 10 for an occupier who claims that partly exempt material is being inspected or seized, to supply, at the request of the person executing the warrant, copies of so much of the material as is not exempt.

Intentional obstruction, or failing without reasonable excuse to give assistance, is an offence punishable on summary conviction with a fine not exceeding level 5 on the standard scale.[82]

After execution, or the expiry of the time for execution, the warrant should be returned to the issuing court, with an indorsement as to the powers exercised under it.[83]

G. Department of Health

1. Medicines Act 1968

8.58   The enforcement of the licensing provisions, etc., of this Act is entrusted to the Secretary of State for Health, and operated through inspectors appointed by him. Powers of entry, etc., are contained in section 111, which provides for entry with or without warrant. A person entering under a section 111 power may take with him such other persons and equipment as may appear to him to be necessary. If property which is unoccupied, or from which the occupier is temporarily absent, is entered under warrant, it must be left as effectively secured against trespass as it was found.[84]

(a) *Without warrant*

An inspector, duly authorised in writing by the Secretary of State, has a right to enter any premises, at any reasonable time. He must produce his authority if so required.

(i) Reasons for entry. The reasons for which entry may be sought are:

(a) to ascertain whether there is or has been on or in connection with those premises, any contravention of any provision of the Act, or of any regulation

---

[78] Sched. 4, para. 5.
[79] Sched. 4, para. 6.
[80] Sched. 4, para. 7.
[81] *Ibid.*
[82] Sched. 4, paras. 12, and s.19(3).
[83] Sched. 4, para. 11.
[84] s.114(1).

or order made under it which the Secretary of State is required or empowered to enforce.[85]

(b) generally for the purpose of the performance by the Secretary of State of his functions under the Act or under any such regulations or order.[86]

Entry in the above way may also be made of any stall or place other than premises.[87]

A specific power of entry on the same terms as mentioned above, is given in relation to any premises occupied by an applicant for a licence or certificate under Part II of the Act (which provides for product licences, manufacturer's licences, wholesale dealer's licences, clinical trial certificates, and animal test certificates) for the purpose of verifying any statement contained in the application for the licence or certificate.

(ii) Private dwelling-house. Under the above provisions, entry to premises used **8.59** only as a private dwelling-house may not be demanded as of right unless 24 hours' notice has been given to the occupier.[88]

(b) *With warrant*

A warrant authorising entry may be obtained for any of the purposes outlined above, provided that a justice of the peace is satisfied, on sworn information in writing that there are reasonable grounds for entry for such a purpose.[89] He must also be satisfied that one of the following further conditions is fulfilled:

(a) that admission to the premises has been refused, or that a refusal is apprehended, and (in either case) notice of the intention to apply for a warrant has been given to the occupier; or
(b) that an application for admission, or the giving of such notice would defeat the object of the entry; or
(c) that the case is one of urgency; or
(d) that the premises are unoccupied, or the occupier is temporarily absent.

(i) Force. Entry under a warrant may be by force if necessary.

(ii) Time. The section contains no restrictions on the time at which the warrant **8.60** may be executed, but entry must take place within one month of its issue.[90]

(c) *Powers on entry*

All the following powers may only be exercised on the production, if so required, of the authorised person's authority.[91]

---

[85] s.111(a).
[86] s.111(b).
[87] s.111(2)(b).
[88] s.111(4).
[89] s.111(5).
[90] s.111(7).
[91] s.112(8).

Section 112 gives an authorised person various powers of inspection, sampling and seizure. These powers are not dependent on an entry under section 111, but once such an entry has taken place, they are clearly available to be used.

(i) Inspection. The power of inspection arises in relation to:

(a) any substance or article appearing to the authorised person to be a medicinal product[92]; or

(b) any article appearing to him to be a container or package used or intended to be used to contain any medicinal product, or to be a label or leaflet used or intended to be used in connection with a medicinal product; or

(c) any plant or equipment appearing to him to be used in connection with the manufacture or assembly of medicinal products; and any process of manufacture or assembly of any medicinal products; and the means employed, at any stage in the process of manufacture or assembly, for testing the materials after they have been subjected to those processes.

8.61 The purpose for which inspection is permitted is simply to ascertain whether there is or has been a contravention of the Act, or of any regulation or order made under it which the Secretary of State is required or empowered to enforce. For these purposes the authorised person may also require any person carrying on a business which consists of or includes the manufacture, assembly, or supply of medicinal products, and any person employed in connection with such a business, to produce any books or documents relating to the business which are in his possession or under his control. Copies may be taken of any such books or documents, or any entries therein.[93]

8.62 **(ii) Sampling.** For the same purposes as for inspection (above), an authorised person has the right to take a sample of any substance or article appearing to him to be:

(a) a medicinal product sold or supplied or intended to be sold or supplied, or

(b) a substance or article used or intended to be used in the manufacture of a medicinal product.[94]

The person who obtains the sample on behalf of the Secretary of State (the "sampling officer") must follow the procedures set out in Schedule 3 to the Act. This requires him to divide the sample into three parts, each part to be marked and sealed or fastened up in such manner as its nature will permit.[95]

8.63 One part is to be retained for future reference and one part submitted for

---

[92] As defined in s.130.
[93] s.112(3).
[94] s.112(3).
[95] Sched. 3, para. 2. If the sample consists of unopened containers, and it appears to the sampling officer that to open the containers and divide the contents is either not reasonably practicable, or might affect the composition or impede the proper analysis or other examination of the sample, the three parts may be obtained by dividing the containers into three lots, unopened—para. 11.

analysis.[96] The third part is to be handed over by the sampling officer to the person who is in effect the person against whom any subsequent action may be taken, but whose identity is determined by the following rules (to be found in paragraphs 3–8):

(a) Where the sample was purchased; the seller.
(b) Where the sample was obtained from an automatic machine:
    (i) the owner of the machine, if his name and an address in the United Kingdom are stated on it; or
    (ii) if no such name or address is given: the occupier of the premises on which the machine stands, or to which it is affixed.
(c) If the goods from which the sample was taken were in transit from outside the United Kingdom, and had not been delivered: the consignee.
(d) If the goods were otherwise in transit: the consignor.
(e) In any case not falling within the above: the person appearing to the sampling officer to be the owner of the substance or article from which the sample was taken.

The sampling officer must, if requested, pay the value of the sample to the person mentioned in (c), (d), or (e), above (as appropriate).[97] In the event of disagreement as to the value, the issue must be decided by arbitration.[98] In each case, as well as supplying the sample, the officer should inform the person to whom it is delivered that the sample has been obtained for the purpose of analysis, or other appropriate examination.[99] If after reasonable inquiry the sampling officer is unable to ascertain the name and address of the person to whom the part of the sample should be supplied, he may retain it instead of supplying it.[1]

Further notice. It may well be that a substance or article which has been taken for sampling has on it the name and address of its manufacturer or assembler. If so, and the address is a United Kingdom address, the sampling officer is required to serve a notice on the person so named (unless of course it is a person to whom a sample must be supplied under the above provisions). The notice should state that the sample has been obtained, and specify the person from whom it was purchased, or the place where it was obtained.[2] It should be served within three days of the sample being obtained.[3]

(iii) Seizure. The power of seizure under section 112(4) relates to any substance or article which an authorised person has reasonable cause to believe to be something in relation to which, or by means of which, an offence under the act is being or has been committed. It also covers any document which an authorised person has   **8.64**

---

[96] Para. 10.
[97] Para. 28(1).
[98] Para. 28(2).
[99] Para. 9.
[1] Para. 13.
[2] Para. 14(1).
[3] Para. 14(2).

reasonable cause to believe to be a document which may be required as evidence in proceedings under the Act.

The Act requires that where anything is seized under section 112(4) the person from whom it was seized should be informed. There is no requirement for this information to be given in writing, nor for any receipt to be supplied.

In the case of vending machines, the information should be given either to the person whose name and address appears on the machine, or in the absence of this, the occupier of the premises on which the machine stands, or to which it is affixed.[4]

The person who is informed of the seizure under the above provisions has a right, within 21 days of being informed, to request that a sampling procedure should be applied to any substance or article (other than a document) which has been seized. On receipt of this request the authorised officer must (provided that the nature of the substance or article makes it reasonably practicable to do so) either set aside a sample of the substance or article, or treat the substance or article itself as a sample, whichever he considers more appropriate, having regard to the nature of the substance or article.

The sample thus obtained must then be divided into three parts, each part marked and sealed or fastened up in such manner as its nature will permit, and one part supplied to the person making the original request under section 113(2).

The procedure to be followed then follows paragraphs 10, 11, 12, and 15 to 27 of Schedule 3 to the Act.[5]

(d) *Obstruction, etc.*

8.65   Three offences are created by section 114(2). All are punishable on summary conviction with a fine not exceeding level 3 on the standard scale. The offences are:

(a) wilfully obstructing a duly authorised person acting in pursuance of the Act;
(b) wilfully failing to comply with a requirement properly made by such a person acting under section 112;
(c) failing, without reasonable cause, to give a person so acting any other assistance or information which that person may reasonably require of him for the purpose of the performance of his functions under the Act.

Thus there is a positive duty to assist, as well as the negative duty not to hinder. Moreover, giving false information constitutes a more serious offence, punishable on summary conviction with a fine of up to £1,000, and on indictment to a fine or imprisonment for up to two years, or both.[6] A person's duty to give information, or answer questions, ceases, however, when to do so might incriminate the person, or his or her spouse.

(e) *Restrictions on disclosure*

8.66   Where a person enters premises under section 111, and obtains in those premises

---

[4] s.112(6).
[5] Above, paras. 8.62–8.63.
[6] s.114(3).

information relating to any manufacturing process or trade secret, or in any case where he obtains or is furnished with information in pursuance of the Act, disclosure of the information to another (other than in the performance of his duty) constitutes an offence.[7] The penalties are on summary conviction, a fine not exceeding £1,000, and on indictment, a fine, or up to two years' imprisonment, or both.[8]

(f) *Animal feeding stuffs*

Section 117 of the Act gives power to the Minister of Agriculture to make regulations modifying the provisions of sections 112 and 113 of the Act in their application to animal feeding stuffs. This power has been exercised in the Medicines (Animal Feeding Stuffs) (Enforcement) Regulations 1976.[9]

These Regulations basically make the provisions of sections 112 and 113 apply to animal feeding stuffs, whether or not they are medicinal products. The modified versions of the sections are set out in Schedule 1 to the Regulations. There are also very detailed provisions dealing with the taking of samples in Schedule 2. These are not dealt with here.

(g) *Protection of officers*

Provided that an officer of an enforcement authority acts within the scope of his employment, and in the honest belief that he is doing only what his duty under the Act requires or entitles him to do, he is protected from personal liability by section 119(1). Any action by a person aggrieved by the actions of someone purportedly acting under the authority of the Act should therefore be pursued against the Secretary of State, rather than the individual officer.

2. Registered Homes Act 1984

(a) *Nursing homes*

Under this Act the Secretary of State has power to make regulations with respect to the inspection of premises used or reasonably believed to be used as a nursing home.[10] The current powers are contained in the Nursing Homes and Mental Nursing Homes Regulations 1984.[11] These regulations are concerned with the registration of nursing homes, the facilities which they provide, and the records, etc. which they should keep. A power of inspection is given by regulation 10. This says that any person authorised by the Secretary of State may enter and inspect any premises which are used, or which he reasonably believes to be used as a nursing home. The inspector must, if requested, produce at the time of entry a duly authenticated document establishing his authority.

8.67

---

[7] s.118(1).
[8] s.118(2).
[9] S.I. 1976 No. 30, as amended by the Medicines (Feeding Stuffs Limits of Variation) Order 1976 (S.I. 1976 No. 31). See also the Animal Health and Welfare Act 1984, s.15.
[10] s.26.
[11] S.I. 1984 No. 1578, as amended by S.I. 1986 No. 456.

(i) **Powers on entry.** On entry the inspector may require the person who is registered under the Act in respect of the home to produce records, and provide information which is reasonably required for the purpose of the inspection. Unless he is a medical officer an inspector is not entitled to inspect any clinical record relating to a patient in a home.[12]

(ii) **Frequency of inspection.** The Secretary of State is obliged to cause an inspection of each home at least twice a year, though he may do so more frequently if he decides to.[13]

(iii) **Obstruction.** Refusal, without reasonable cause, to allow the inspection of any premises, register, or record, is an offence under the regulations,[14] punishable on summary conviction with a fine of not more than level 4 on the standard scale.[15]

(b) *Mental nursing homes*

8.68   There is here a power of entry under section 35 of the Act itself. This provides that a person authorised in that behalf by the Secretary of State may, at any time, after producing if asked to do so, some duly authenticated document showing that he is authorised, enter and inspect any premises which are used, or which that person had reasonable cause to believe to be used, for the purposes of a mental nursing home.[16] He may also inspect any records kept pursuant to section 27(*b*).

(i) **Additional powers on entry.** The person may also interview in private any patient who is or appears to be suffering from mental disorder. This may be done for the purpose of investigating complaints as to the patient's treatment, or in any case where the inspector has reasonable cause to believe that the patient is not receiving proper care. If the inspector is a medical practitioner, he may also *examine* the patient in private, and require the production of any medical records relating to the patient's treatment in that home.[17]

(ii) **Obstruction, etc.** As well as a general offence of obstruction sections 35(5) and (6) create a number of specific offences. These are, refusing to allow an inspection, refusing without reasonable cause to let the inspector interview or examine a patient, refusing without reasonable cause to produce documents or records, and insisting on being present at a private examination or interview. All these offences are triable summarily, with a penalty of a fine not exceeding level 4 on the standard scale, or three months' imprisonment.

3. Anatomy Act 1984

8.69   Under section 9 of this Act the Secretary of State has power to appoint inspectors of anatomy. The current practice is for there to be but one such inspector, who will

[12] Reg. 10(3).
[13] Reg. 11.
[14] Reg. 15(2).
[15] Registered Homes Act 1984, s.49.
[16] s.35(1).
[17] s.35(2).

be a medical practitioner. In connection with his general supervisory function in respect of places licensed to practise anatomy, he has a power of entry under section 10. He may, at any reasonable time, enter any such place on which he has reasonable cause to believe that an offence has been or is being committed, by an unauthorised anatomical examination (s.11(1)(a)), or by a breach of the terms of a licence (s.11(2)), or by a breach of regulations. The inspector must be duly authorised in writing by the Secretary of State for this purpose. Intentional obstruction of an inspector is an offence punishable on summary conviction with a fine not exceeding level 3 on the standard scale, or imprisonment for up to three months (s.11(5)).

H. Department of Social Security

Social Security Act 1986

The enforcement powers under this Act give the Secretary of State the power to appoint inspectors.[18] These inspectors have the power to enter premises where an inspector has reasonable grounds for supposing that   **8.70**

(a) any persons are employed; or
(b) there is being carried on any agency or other business for the introduction or supply to persons requiring them of persons available to do work or perform services; or
(c) a personal or occupational pension scheme is being administered.[19]

The power does not extend to private dwelling-houses which are not used by, or by permission of, the occupier, for the purposes of a trade or business.

Every inspector must have a certificate of appointment, which is to be produced, if so required, on applying for admission to the premises.[20]

(a) Powers on entry

The powers exercisable by an inspector on entry are put in fairly wide and general terms. The inspector may enter to: **8.71**

(1) make such examination and inquiry as may be necessary;

  (a) for ascertaining whether the provisions of the benefit Acts are being or have been complied with in any such premises, or
  (b) for investigating the circumstances in which any injury or disease which has given or may give rise to a claim for industrial injuries benefit was or may have been received or contracted:

(2) examine, or to require to be examined, every person whom he finds in the premises, or whom he has reasonable cause to believe to be or to have been a person liable to pay contributions under the Social Security Act 1975 (or a state scheme premium). The examination, which may relate to any matters under the benefit Acts on which the inspector may reasonably require information, may take place with or without the presence of any other person as the inspector thinks fit:

---

[18] s.58.
[19] s.58(3).
[20] s.58(4).

(3) exercise such other powers as may be necessary for carrying the benefit Acts into effect.[21]

The "benefit Acts" are the Social Security Act 1973, the Social Security Acts 1975 to 1986, the Industrial Injuries and Diseases (Old Cases) Act 1975, and the Child Benefit Act 1975.[22]

(b) *Duty to submit to inspection*

8.72   In addition to making it an offence to obstruct an inspector (see below), section 58 imposes a positive duty on certain people to provide information and to produce documents. The people subject to this duty are:

(a) the occupier of any premises liable to inspection under the Act;

(b) any person who is or has been an employee;

(c) any person carrying on an agency or other business for the introduction or supply to persons requiring them of persons available to do work or to perform services;

(d) any person who is or has at any time been a trustee or manager of a personal or occupational pension scheme;

(e) any person who is or has been liable to pay any contributions under the Social Security Act 1975, or any state scheme premium;

(f) the servants or agents of any such person as specified in paragraphs (*a*) to (*e*) above.

The information or documents to which the duty applies are those which the inspector reasonably requires for the purpose of ascertaining,

(*a*) whether any contributions under the Social Security Act 1975 or any state scheme premiums are or have been payable, or have been duly paid, by or in respect of any person; or

(*b*) whether any benefit is or was payable to or in respect of any person.[23]

But no one can be required to answer any questions or to give any evidence tending to incriminate himself, or his spouse.[24]

(c) *Obstruction*

8.73   Wilfully delaying or obstructing an inspector in the exercise of his powers under the Act, or refusing or neglecting to answer questions, furnish information, or produce documents, when so required, is a summary offence punishable with a fine of not more than level 3 on the standard scale.[25]

Rather unusually there is also a continuing offence in section 58(a), whereby if the refusal or neglect to provide information, etc., is continued after a conviction under

[21] s.58(2).
[22] s.84(1).
[23] s.58(6).
[24] s.58(7).
[25] s.58(8).

section 145(3), the person is guilty of a further offence, and liable on summary conviction to a fine of not more than £40 for each day on which the refusal or neglect continues. The first conviction must, however, have been for "refusal or neglect," and not for "delay or obstruction."

I. *Department of Trade and Industry*

1. Companies Act 1985

Wide powers of investigation into the affairs of companies are given to the **8.74** Department by the 1985 Act. Section 447 gives a power to conduct a preliminary investigation into a company where the Department thinks that there is good reason to do so. Books and papers may be ordered to be produced. Failure to comply with such an order paves the way for the use of the power of entry under warrant, given by section 448.

Section 448

The warrant (which remains in force for one month) is obtained from a justice of the peace, who must be satisfied by information on oath,[26] that there are reasonable grounds for suspecting that there are on any premises any books or papers of which production has been required under section 109, and which have not been produced in compliance with that requirement. It will authorise any constable, together with any other person named in the warrant (*i.e.* the Department's officers) and any other constables, to enter the premises specified in the information. Force may be used to the extent that it is reasonably necessary.

(i) Powers on entry. The premises may be searched, and books and papers which appear to be those which were ordered to be produced may be seized. Alternatively the entrants may take any other steps which appear necessary to preserve, or prevent interference with the books and papers. Property seized should be returned within three months, or at the conclusion of criminal proceedings of the type mentioned in section 449(1)(*a*) or (*b*)[27]

(ii) Obstruction. Obstruction of either the entry or the seizure of property is an offence punishable on summary conviction by a fine of up to £1,000, and on indictment by an unlimited fine.[28]

2. Financial Services Act 1986 ("F.S.A.")

The F.S.A. gives powers of entry under warrant in section 199. The warrant is **8.75** obtainable from a justice of the peace in three main situations. First, on information on oath laid by the Secretary of State or the Securities and Investments Board ("S.I.B.") that there are reasonable grounds for believing that certain offences have

---

[26] Laid by an officer of the Department, or on the Department's authority.
[27] s.448(4).
[28] s.448(5); Sched. 24.

been committed under the F.S.A. or the Company Securities (Insider Dealing) Act 1985.[29]

Secondly, on information on oath laid by the Secretary of State or the S.I.B. that there are reasonable grounds for believing that documents[30] whose production has been required under section 105 of the F.S.A.[31] (and which have not been produced) are on premises owned or occupied by a person whose affairs are being investigated under section 105. The person must be an "authorised person,"[32] a person whose authorisation has been suspended or who is subject to a direction under section 33(1) of the F.S.A., or an appointed representative of an authorised person.

Thirdly, on information on oath laid by an inspector appointed under section 94 of the F.S.A.[33] that there are reasonable grounds for believing that documents whose production has been required under section 94, and which have not been produced, are on any premises owned or occupied by the manager, trustees or operator of a scheme which is being investigated, or by a manager, trustee or operator whose own affairs are being investigated.

A warrant issued under section 199 will authorise a constable, together with any other person named in it, and any other constable, to enter premises using such force as is reasonably necessary. Once on the premises the constable may search them, seize or copy documents appearing to be those which should have been produced, or take steps to preserve or prevent interference with them. He may also require any person named in the warrant to provide an explanation of the documents or state where they may be found. Failure, without reasonable excuse, to comply with such a request is equivalent to obstruction.[34]

The warrant, which will be subject to sections 15 and 16 of the Police and Criminal Evidence Act 1984, but not to section 9,[35] will remain in force for one month.

Documents seized may be held for three months, unless proceedings are instituted within that time, in which case they may be held until the conclusion to the proceedings.[36]

Obstruction is an offence punishable on summary conviction with a fine not exceeding the statutory maximum, and on indictment with a fine.

3. Civil Aviation Act 1982

8.76   This Act gives the Secretary of State for Trade and Industry a number of powers

---

[29] Namely, ss.4, 47, 57, 130, 133, 171(2) or (3) of the F.S.A. (which are concerned with the authorisation and control of investment and insurance businesses, and the offer of unlisted securities), and ss.1, 2, 4, or 5 of the Company Securities (Insider Dealing) Act 1985.

[30] "Documents" in this section includes information recorded in any form. If documents are to be produced, this means "in legible form": s.199(9).

[31] Which concerns the investigation of investment businesses.

[32] s.207(1).

[33] Investigation of unit trust schemes, and other collective investment schemes.

[34] s.199(6).

[35] See above, para. 3.28.

[36] s.199(5).

of entry in connection with the operation of aerodromes, airfields, and airports, some of which are exercisable in conjunction with the Civil Aviation Authority.[37]

(a) *Section 44: Power to obtain rights over land*

The Secretary of State may make an order creating rights over land:

(a) to secure safe and efficient use for civil aviation purposes of any land which is vested in a relevant authority,[38] or which such authority proposes to acquire; or

(b) to secure provision of any services in relation to any such land; or

(c) to secure that civil aircraft may be navigated in safety and efficiency.[39]

Such an order may include a power to enter land to carry out, install, maintain, or remove any works, structures or apparatus.[40] Seven days' notice of entry must be given, except in cases of emergency, or to carry out routine maintenance.[41] Compensation is payable if land is damaged as a result of an entry under section 44, disputes over the amount payable being settled by the Lands Tribunal.[42]

Obstruction. Wilful obstruction is a summary offence, punishable with a fine not exceeding level 3 on the standard scale. Control of prosecutions is in the hands of the Secretary of State or the Director of Public Prosecutions, unless the Civil Aviation Authority was the authority in whose favour the order was made, in which case the control is in the hands of that authority.

(b) *Section 47: Warning of presence of obstructions near licensed aerodromes*

The Secretary of State may by order authorise the authorised proprietor of a licensed aerodrome, or a person acting under his instructions, to enter land in the vicinity in order to install, repair, or maintain, warnings of obstructions from buildings, structures, or erections, which are a danger to aircraft. The power of entry may include land which it is necessary to cross in order to get to the obstruction.[43] **8.77**

The Secretary of State must give notice (in the way he considers best for the purpose of informing those concerned) of his intention to make an order. Two months at least must be allowed for making representations by those having an interest in the land affected by the order. The draft order should be available for inspection free of charge; details of its availability being given in the notice.[44]

Once the order has been made, the initiative passes to the proprietor of the aerodrome. Except in a case of emergency, he is obliged to give 14 days' notice of an

---

[37] N.B. s.18, which limits rights to enter "prohibited places" under the Official Secrets Act 1911, s.3; this does not apply to constables, Inland Revenue or Customs and Excise officers, or central government officers specially authorised for the purpose.

[38] *i.e.* the Secretary of State, Eurocontrol (for which see s.24 of the Act), or the Civil Aviation Act.

[39] s.44(1).

[40] s.44(3).

[41] ss.44(4) and (5).

[42] s.44(6).

[43] s.47(1).

[44] s.47(3).

intention to carry out works to the owner of the land, and everyone known to the proprietor to have an interest in it. The notice must be in writing, and served in the manner specified in the order. If written objection is received from such a person within 14 days of the notice being served, and the grounds for the objection specified, no further action may be taken without the Secretary of State's sanction.[45]

(i) Compensation. The obligation to pay compensation resulting from any loss or damage arising as a consequence of the order falls on the proprietor of the aerodrome. In the event of a dispute as to the amount payable, the issue is to be determined by an arbitrator appointed by the Lord Chief Justice.[46]

(ii) Obstruction. Wilful obstruction of a person exercising any of the powers conferred by an order is a summary offence, punishable with a fine not exceeding level 3 on the standard scale.[47]

(iii) Statutory undertakers. There are special provisions in section 47(9) relating to land held by statutory undertakers. These provide that the order should be framed so as not to interfere with the proper carrying on of the undertaking; that the undertakers should be given at least three days' clear notice of an intention to enter; that the entrant should comply with any reasonable direction of the undertakers given to prevent interference with the undertaking; and that the undertakers should be entitled to compensation in respect of the cost of any safety precautions taken in respect of people acting under the order.

(c) *Section 50: Entry for the purposes of survey*

8.78   This section gives a power of entry in connection with the compulsory purchase of land by the Civil Aviation Act, the creation of rights over land, or the declaration that land shall be subject to control by directions.[48] In any of these circumstances a person duly authorised by the Secretary of State may enter upon any of the land in question to make a survey.[49]

(i) Timing and notice. The entry may take place at any reasonable time, but occupied land may not be entered as of right unless the required amount of notice has been given. Where the Secretary of State is acting through the Civil Aviation Act the period is eight days; where he acts directly it is 24 hours.[50] In any case the authorised person must produce his authority, if so requested, at the time of entry.[51]

(ii) Compensation. If land is damaged as the result of the exercise of the power of entry under this section, compensation is payable. Disputes as to whether compen-

---

[45] s.47(4).
[46] s.47(4). See also s.47(5) for what is included within "loss or damage."
[47] s.47(7).
[48] See s.50(1).
[49] s.50(2). The survey must be "relevant" to the purposes for which the power of entry arose under s.50(1).
[50] s.50(4).
[51] s.50(2).

sation is payable, and if so how much, and to whom, are to be settled by the Lands Tribunal.[52]

(iii) Obstruction. It is an offence to obstruct an authorised person in the exercise of his powers of entry and survey. The offence is punishable on summary conviction with a fine not exceeding level 2 on the standard scale. Proceedings may not be instituted without the consent of the Secretary of State, or the D.P.P., or where the power is being exercised by or on behalf of that body, the C.A.A.

J. Department of Transport

The Department of Transport employs vehicle examiners to carry out safety checks **8.79** on virtually all motor vehicles. In some situations these examiners have powers of entry.

1. Transport Act 1968—large goods vehicles[53]

Section 82 of the Act gives two powers of entry. First, where an examiner has reason to believe that a large goods vehicle is kept on any premises, or that any documents required to be carried by a driver or preserved are to be found there, he may enter the premises at any time which is reasonable having regard to the circumstances. He must produce his authority if required to do so. Once on the premises he may inspect any such vehicle, and inspect and copy (but not remove) any such document, which he finds there.[54]

Secondly, an examiner may, at any time which is reasonable in the circumstances, enter premises of an applicant for, or holder of an operator's licence, and inspect any facilities on those premises for maintaining the authorised vehicles in a fit and serviceable condition.[55]

Obstruction of an examiner is a summary offence, carrying a fine not exceeding level 3 on the standard scale.[56]

2. Road Traffic Act 1988—goods vehicles

The Secretary of State has power to appoint "goods vehicle examiners" under **8.80** section 68 of this Act. Such examiners may at any time which is reasonable having regard to the circumstances of the case, enter any premises on which they have reason to believe that a goods vehicle is kept.[57]

Obstruction is a summary offence, carrying a fine not exceeding level 3 on the standard scale.[58]

---

[52] s.50(7).
[53] As defined in s.71 of the Act.
[54] s.82(2)(*b*).
[55] s.82(4).
[56] s.82(5). Note also that there is a limited power to seize documents or articles under s.82(6), and that by virtue of s.82(9) a police officer can exercise the powers under this section.
[57] s.68(3)(*b*).
[58] s.68(4).

3. International Carriage of Perishable Foodstuffs Act 1976

8.81   As part of the controls over the enforcement of regulations under this Act, there is a power to appoint examiners.[59] An examiner may enter any premises on which he has reason to believe transport equipment in respect of which a certificate of compliance or a certification plate is in force is kept. He must produce his authority if so required, and may enter at any reasonable time, in the circumstances. He may then inspect the equipment, and in the case of a goods vehicle, or any containers carried by it, detain the vehicle or container for as long as is necessary to inspect it.[60]

Wilful obstruction is a summary offence, carrying a fine not exceeding level 3 on the standard scale.[61]

4. Public Passenger Vehicles Act 1981

8.82   Under section 7 the Secretary of State can appoint certifying officers, and public service vehicle examiners. Such an officer or examiner may at any time which is reasonable in the circumstances enter any premises on which he has reason to believe there is a public service vehicle. He must produce his authority if so required.[62]

Intentional obstruction is a summary offence, carrying a fine not exceeding level 3 on the standard scale.[63]

K. The EEC Commission

1. Competition

8.83   As part of the enforcement of the EEC's competition law, as expressed in Articles 85 and 86 of the Treaty of Rome, the European Commission has investigatory powers under the Council Regulation 17 (February 6, 1962). These include, under Article 14, a power for "officials authorised by the Commission" to enter any "premises, land and means of transport."

The Commission has power to compel entry by making a formal decision to that effect under Article 14(3). Although in some cases such a decision will only be taken where the officials have not obtained all that they were seeking by consent,[64] there is no need for this preliminary stage to take place. It is entirely in order for the Commission's officials to arrive unannounced, and demand entry there and then.[65]

There are, however, some formalities which have to be complied with. The "competent authority" of the Member State (in this country the Office of Fair Trading) in which the power is to be exercised must be consulted before a decision is

---

[59] s.6(1).
[60] s.6(2)(*b*).
[61] s.6(3).
[62] s.8(1)(*b*).
[63] s.8(2).
[64] *e.g.* as in *A.M. & S. Europe Ltd.* v. *Commission of the European Communities* [1983] 1 All E.R. 700.
[65] *National Panasonic (U.K.) Ltd.* v. *Commission of the European Communities* [1981] 2 All E.R. 1.

taken under Article 14(3).[66] This authority should be informed in good time that an investigation is to be made, and of the identity of the officials authorised to carry it out.[67] Officials of the competent authority may accompany and assist the Commission's officials.[68]

It should be noted that the power relates to the premises, land, etc., of "undertakings and associations of undertakings." Private houses would thus seem to be excluded from the scope of this power.

Once at the premises the officials must produce their written authority, which **8.84** should specify the subject-matter and the purpose of the investigation, and the penalties for incomplete production of the required books and other business records. They may then examine and take copies of, or extracts from the books and business records. They may not, however, remove them from the premises. "Oral explanations" may be sought from those on the premises. This has been taken to mean requests for information on specific questions arising from the books and records which the officials are examining.[69]

In the *A.M. & S.* case the issue arose as to the extent (if at all) that the person subject to the search could claim legal privilege for documents which the officials wished to examine. The court held that, although the wording of Article 14 was wide enough to include within its scope relevant communications between lawyer and client, certain of such communications were immune from disclosure. These were written communications "made for the purposes and in the interests of the client's rights of defence" which "emanate from independent lawyers, that is to say lawyers who are not bound to the client by a relationship of employment."[70]

The requirement that the papers relate to the client's rights of defence does not apparently mean that they have to relate to a particular case or dispute, or to be of recent origin. A number of the documents in the case dated from the time of the United Kingdom's accession to the Community, and were principally concerned with avoiding conflict with the Community provisions on competition. Nevertheless, the court held that these should be protected from disclosure.[71]

An undertaking wishing to claim the benefit of legal privilege must provide the Commission's officials with relevant material (*e.g.* selected passages, or headings) which will demonstrate that the material is protected.[72] If the Commission is not prepared to accept the claim to privilege, the issue must be brought before the court itself.[73]

2. Transport

Council Regulation 11 (June 27, 1960) on Abolition of Discriminatory Transport **8.85**

---

[66] Art. 14 (4).
[67] Art. 14 (2).
[68] Art. 14(5). This occurred in both the *National Panasonic* and the *A.M. & S.* cases.
[69] *National Panasonic (U.K.) Ltd.* v. *Commission of the European Communities* [1981] 2 All E.R. 1, para. 15.
[70] *A.M. & S. Europe Ltd.* v. *Commission of the European Communities* [1983] 1 All E.R. 705, para. 21.
[71] *Ibid.* para. 34.
[72] *Ibid.* para. 29.
[73] *Ibid.* paras. 31 and 32.

Rates, implementing Article 79 of the Treaty of Rome, gives the Commission powers to ensure compliance with the rules established by the Article. Under Article 14, authorised representatives of the Commission have the right to be given access to all premises, land and vehicles of undertakings.

Details of a proposed inspection, and the status of those responsible for carrying it out, should be given to the relevant Member State beforehand, and officials of that State may assist the Commission's officials.

Officials should carry a pass, stating that they are empowered to carry out inspections, which should be produced before entry. They must also carry a written authority naming the undertaking to be inspected, and the purpose of the inspection.

Once on the premises the officials may check, and take copies and extracts (on the spot) from the books and business records of the undertaking. They may also require explanations on all points relating to such books and records. Article 14(3) requires them to observe "professional secrecy," in accordance with Article 214 of the Treaty of Rome. This is a wider concept than "legal privilege," covering anyone whose occupation leads him to be entrusted with confidential information. In addition, the Commission must ensure that all facts made known to them as a result of the exercise of Article 14 powers remain confidential.[74] Information obtained in this way may only be used for the implementation of Regulation 11, unless the Council unanimously decides otherwise.[75]

3. Other powers

8.86   In certain other situations Commission officials have the power to make "spot checks" on premises, but these do not specifically grant powers of entry.[76]

---

[74] Art. 15 (1).
[75] Art. 15 (2).
[76] See, *e.g.* Reg. 724/75/EEC, March 18, 1975, Establishing Regional Development Fund, Art. 9 (3); and Dir. 72/462/EEC, December 12, 1972, on Inspection of Imported Meat, Art. 5.

CHAPTER NINE

LOCAL GOVERNMENT AND PUBLIC UTILITIES

This chapter deals with the powers of local government officials, employees of the **9.01** electricity boards, public gas suppliers, the water authorities, and those working in the Post Office and telecommunications. Within the category of local government powers, the chapter has been divided into subject areas. Not all of these are self contained and exclusive. They are adopted for ease of exposition only. Some of the powers are exercised by specific categories of inspectors, *e.g.* weights and measures inspectors, but many are exercisable simply by "a duly authorised person" who might be employed in one of several of the local authority's departments. In particular, environmental health inspectors may well exercise powers listed under other headings, *e.g.* "Public Entertainments."

Throughout the first part of this chapter the phrase "local authority" is used. The majority of the powers discussed are exercisable by district councils, or their equivalent, although a number are given to county councils. The subject-matter of the power being exercised will, of course, determine who is entitled to use it, the local authority having responsibility for that subject-matter in any particular area will be the one which authorises its officers to enter premises.

The powers described below show that local authority officers have very wide **9.02** powers of entry. It is clear, however, that much of the time local authority officers rely on the consent of the landowner in order to gain entry. There is not very often any need as far as these officers are concerned to rely on any more formal powers. The result is that most entries will be made on the basis of a licence to enter. This means, of course, that the landowner can terminate the licence at any time, and demand that the officer should leave his property. At this stage it may be too late for the officer to try to bring into play any rights of entry which he may possess under statute. In general, then, it would seem to be preferable for the officer to make clear from the outset that he is entering under a particular statutory power even where the entry takes place with the occupier's consent. This will make the lawful basis of the entry the statutory power rather than simply a licence, so that any subsequent withdrawal of consent by the occupier will not automatically terminate the lawfulness of the officer's presence on the property.

I. LOCAL AUTHORITY POWERS

A. Environmental Health

1. General powers

Section 287 of the Public Health Act 1936 gives local authority officers a general **9.03** power of entry in connection with the enforcement of the provisions of the Act.[1] Specifically the power may be used:

(a) to discover contraventions of the Act, or of byelaws made under it;
(b) to discover whether circumstances exist which would authorise or require the council to take action, or execute works under the Act, byelaws. This has been held to be wide enough to allow the authority to enter premises in order to carry out work on neighbouring premises[2];
(c) to carry out any such work or action as mentioned in (b);
(d) to perform any other functions of the council.

The entry may take place at any reasonable time, but the officer must produce some authenticated document showing his authority if so required. Twenty-four hours notice must be given before entry may be demanded to premises other than a "factory, workshop, or workplace."[3] The notice must be in writing,[4] and must be specifically worded.[5] A general indication of an intention to proceed under a section which empowers the authority to carry out work on private land is not sufficient.

Entry under warrant

9.04   In certain circumstances there is a power to obtain a warrant to enter. A justice of the peace must be satisfied by a sworn information in writing that admission to the premises has been refused, or that refusal is apprehended, or that the premises are unoccupied or the occupier is temporarily absent, or that the case is one of urgency, or that an application for admission would defeat the object of the entry. In addition the justice must be satisfied that there is reasonable ground for entry to the premises for one of the authorised purposes.

Where the reason for seeking the warrant is a refusal or apprehended refusal, notice of the intention to apply for a warrant must be given to the occupier, and the justice should be satisfied of this before issuing it.

The form of the warrant is that it will authorise the authority to enter the premises, through the agency of an authorised officer, by force if necessary.

On leaving premises entered under a warrant, the officer is obliged to leave them as secure against trespass as they were found.[6]

Disclosure of information relating to a manufacturing process or trade secret acquired as a result of entry to a factory, workshop, or workplace is an offence, punishable on summary conviction with a fine not exceeding level 3 on the standard scale or up to three months imprisonment.[7]

---

[1] The following provisions are treated for the purposes of this section as coming under the Act: Clean Air Act 1956, s.31, and Sched. 3, Pt. I, para. 1; Public Health Act 1961, ss.67, 75, 77; Local Government (Miscellaneous Provisions) Act 1976, s.35.
[2] *Senior* v. *Twelves* (1958) 56 L.G.R. 239.
[3] As defined in s.343(1).
[4] s.283.
[5] *Stroud* v. *Bradbury* [1952] 2 All E.R. 76 (D.C.).
[6] s.287(3).
[7] s.287(5).

Wilful obstruction is a summary offence, punishable with a fine not exceeding level 1 on the standard scale, and a further fine of £5 per day for continuing offences.[8]

2. Acupuncture, tattooing, ear-piercing, and electrolysis

Part VIII of the Local Government (Miscellaneous Provisions) Act 1982 allows local authorities to set up systems of registration for those practising (other than medical practitioners or dentists) any of the above activities, and to make byelaws concerning the cleanliness and hygiene of premises used by those registered. The provisions of the Act will only have effect where the council has passed a resolution that it will apply in their area. If such a resolution has been passed, then section 17 gives a power of entry.   **9.05**

The power is exercisable by an authorised officer of the local authority, who will have to obtain a warrant from a justice of the peace. The justice must be satisfied that there are reasonable grounds to suspect that an offence under section 16, involving breach of the provisions as to registration, or contravention of the byelaws, is being committed on certain premises. The justice must also be satisfied that admission to the premises has been refused, or refusal is apprehended, and that notice of the intention to apply for a warrant has been given to the occupier, or that the case is one of urgency, or that application for admission would defeat the object of the entry. Subject to these requirements the warrant may be sought in relation to any premises in the local authority's area. It will remain in force for seven days, or until executed, whichever is the shorter.[9]

The officer executing the warrant must produce his authority if required to do so by the occupier.[10] The section gives no specific powers to the officer other than entry, so presumably he is limited to such investigations as are necessary to confirm or dispel his suspicions. Whether this would extend to being able to search the premises is doubtful, but the power seems of little use if it does not allow, for example, cupboards to be opened, to look for hidden equipment.

Obstruction

Refusal, without reasonable excuse, to permit an authorised officer to enter is a summary offence, subject to a fine not exceeding level 3 on the standard scale. Each refusal is a separate offence.[11]   **9.06**

3. Animals

(a) *Boarding kennels*

A local authority may authorise in writing any of its own officers, or any veterinary surgeon or veterinary practitioner, to inspect any premises in its area licensed   **9.07**

[8] s.288.
[9] s.17(5).
[10] s.17(6).
[11] s.17(7).

under the Animal Boarding Establishments Act 1963.[12] The entry will be subject to compliance with precautions specified by the authority to prevent the spread of disease among animals. It may be exercised at any reasonable time, on production of the inspector's authority, if required. The premises, and any animals or other things found there, may be inspected for the purpose of ascertaining whether any offence under the Act has been or is being committed. It should be noted that the word "animal" in this Act means "any dog or cat" unless the context otherwise requires.

Wilfully obstructing or delaying a person exercising the above powers is a summary offence punishable with a fine not exceeding level 2 on the standard scale.[13]

(b) *Breeding of dogs*

Establishments for the breeding or rearing of dogs are required to be licensed by the local authority under section 1 of the Breeding of Dogs Act 1973.[13a] The local authority may authorise in writing its own officers, or any veterinary surgeon or practitioner to inspect any premises so licensed in their area. The authorised person may, on producing his authority if required, enter the premises at any reasonable time, and inspect them and any animals found on them, to ascertain whether an offence under the Act has been or is being committed.[14]

Wilful obstruction or delay of the exercise of the entry or inspection powers is a summary offence subject to a fine not exceeding level 3 on the standard scale.

(c) *Pet shops*

9.08   Under section 1 of the Pet Animals Act 1951, pet shops are required to be licensed by the local authority. Licensed premises may be entered by an authorised officer of the local authority, or a veterinary surgeon, for the purpose of inspecting the premises and any animals or other things on them, in order to discover whether an offence against the Act has been or is being committed.[15]

The power must be exercised at a reasonable time, and the entrant must produce his authority if required. Wilful obstruction or delay of entry or inspection is a summary offence subject to a fine not exceeding level 2 on the standard scale.[16]

(d) *Riding establishments*

Premises used for keeping a riding establishment, *i.e.* where horses are kept for hire, or for instruction for riding in return for payment, are subject to a power of entry under the Riding Establishments Act 1964, s.2. Any person keeping such an establishment is required to be licensed by the local authority.

The power of entry is available to a person authorised in writing by the local

---

[12] s.2.
[13] s.2(1), s.3(2).
[13a] But note the exception under the Animals (Scientific Procedures) Act 1986, s.27(3).
[14] s.2.
[15] s.4(1).
[16] ss.4(2) and 5(2).

authority, being an officer of the local authority, or some other local authority, or a veterinary surgeon or practitioner.[17] It may be used to inspect, at any reasonable time, any premises in respect of which a licence is in force or has been applied for, or where the authorised person has reason to believe that a person is keeping a riding establishment.[18] Once on the premises, the entrant may inspect the premises themselves, and any horses or other things found on them, for the purpose of making a report to the local authority, or, if a licence has been granted or applied for, ascertaining whether an offence has been or is being committed against the Act.[19]

Inspection and report by a vet is a necessary preliminary to a prosecution for a contravention of or failure to comply with the conditions of a licence.[20]

Wilful obstruction or delay of entry or inspection is a summary offence punishable with a fine not exceeding level 2 on the standard scale.

(e) *Wild animals*

The Dangerous Wild Animals Act 1976 makes it an offence to keep a "dangerous **9.09** wild animal" (as defined in the Schedule to the Act), except under a local authority licence. Animals kept in zoos, circuses, pet shops, or in a place which is a designated establishment within the meaning of the Animals (Scientific Procedures) Act 1986, are exempt from this requirement by section 5.

When an application is made for a licence section 3 empowers a local authority to authorise a veterinary surgeon or practitioner, or other person whom it deems competent, to inspect the premises where any animals are to be kept. Premises where an animal is or may be kept under an existing licence may also be inspected. The authorised person may enter the premises, on production, if required, of his authority, at all reasonable times, and inspect them and any animals on them, to decide whether a licence should be granted or varied, or whether an offence under the Act has been or is being committed. Note that this power only exists where a licence is held, or has been applied for. It does not authorise entry and inspection where it is suspected that an animal is being kept without a licence. There is a power to seize such an animal, or one held where there is a breach of a licence, under section 4. But this section confers no power of entry.

The applicant or licensee may be required to pay the reasonable costs of an inspection (s.3(3)). Wilful obstruction of an entry or inspection under section 3 is an offence punishable on summary conviction with a fine not exceeding level 5 on the standard scale (s.3(4)).

(f) *Zoos*

The Zoo Licensing Act 1981 established a system of licensing zoos (as defined in **9.10** section 11(2)) to which the public have access. Inspection powers are given to local

---

[17] Taken from a list drawn up jointly by the Royal College of Veterinary Surgeons and the British Veterinary Association—s.2(3).
[18] s.2(1).
[19] s.2(2).
[20] s.5(2).

authorities under sections 10, 11, and 12, and are divided into "periodical," "special," and "informal" inspections. Some or all of these powers may be dispensed with as regards "small" zoos.[21]

(i) Periodical. Licensed zoos must be inspected during the first year in which a licence is first granted to the zoo, and not later than six months before the end of the fourth year of such a licence.[22] The licence period is four years for an initial licence, and six years for a renewal, or granting of a fresh licence to an existing holder.[23] In the case of a renewed licence, or a fresh licence granted to an existing holder, an inspection must be made during the third year of the licence, and not later than six months before the end of the sixth year of the licence.[24] Section 10(4)(a) and (b) lays down who should conduct a periodical inspection. Up to three inspectors can be appointed by the local authority. At least one of them must be a veterinary surgeon or practitioner. A further two inspectors must be nominated by the Secretary of State, after consultation with the local authority, from the list which he is required to keep under section 8. The list is in two parts and there must be one nomination from each part.[25] The first part consists of veterinary surgeons and practitioners who have experience of animals of the kinds which are kept in zoos or which in the Secretary of State's opinion might be so kept.[26] The second part contains the names of persons who are, in the Secretary of State's opinion, competent to inspect animals in zoos, advise on keeping them and their welfare, and advise on the management of zoos generally.[27] A person's name may appear on both parts of the list.[28] The operator is entitled to be consulted about the date of the inspection, and must be given 28 days notice of the proposed date.[29] In addition the names of all the inspectors must be notified to the operator of the zoo, who may object to any or all of the names. The local authority and the Secretary of State may if they think fit give effect to the objection, but they are under no obligation to do so.[30]

(ii) Conduct of the inspection. Up to three representatives of the operator may accompany the inspector. In addition the inspectors may require the attendance of any vet employed or retained by the zoo. The inspection must cover all features of the zoo directly or indirectly relevant to the health, welfare and safety of the public and the animals, including measures for the prevention of the escape of animals.[31] All records required to be kept under the conditions of the licence must be produced to the inspectors.[32]

---

[21] See s.14.
[22] s.10(3).
[23] s.5(1) and (2), and s.6(2).
[24] s.10(3)(b).
[25] s.10(4)(a)(ii).
[26] s.8(2).
[27] s.8(3).
[28] s.8(4).
[29] s.10(2).
[30] s.10(4)(b).
[31] s.10(4)(d).
[32] s.10(4)(e).

The inspectors' report must be sent to the local authority, and the local authority must within a month of receiving it send a copy to the operator, giving him an opportunity to comment.[33] Disagreement between inspectors may be referred to the Secretary of State.[34] As the result of a report the local authority may wish to exercise its power to vary or revoke a licence.[35]

(iii) Special Inspections. A local authority may at any time carry out an inspection of a licensed zoo as a result of the report of a periodical or informal inspection, representations of a properly constituted body concerned with zoo management, or the welfare of animals, or some other circumstances which in their opinion call for investigation.[36] Such an inspection will be conducted by persons authorised by the local authority, who appear to them to be competent. There are no detailed provisions here as there are for periodical inspections, but if the inspection relates to the health of animals at least one inspector (who may be the only inspector) must be a vet with experience of animals of kinds kept in zoos.[37]

The local authority is not obliged to give notice of a special investigation, but on appointing the inspector(s) both they and the operator must be notified of the scope of the inspection.[38] The conduct of the inspection will be limited by its stated scope, but otherwise it will proceed in exactly the same way as a periodical inspection.[39]

(iv) Informal inspections. A licensed zoo which has not been the subject of a periodical inspection or a special inspection in any year should receive an informal inspection.[40] The local authority is given a fairly free hand to arrange for such inspections. The wording of the section implies that there should be just one inspector, being a person appearing to the local authority to be competent for the purpose, but otherwise there are no special procedures, and no obligation for a report to be submitted.

(v) Obstruction. None of the above provisions specifically refer to a power of entry, which probably means that forcible entry is never permitted,[41] unless perhaps the licence conditions provide for such a power. Co-operation between inspectors and operators is clearly encouraged, but a refusal to allow an inspection will amount to obstruction of the inspector, and if done intentionally this is an offence, punishable on summary conviction with a fine not exceeding level 3 on the standard scale.

4. Building Act 1984

The powers and duties of local authorities as regards buildings and building **9.11**

---

[33] s.10(5) and (7).
[34] s.10(6).
[35] ss.16 and 17. As regards local authority zoos the Secretary of State has this power—s.13(4).
[36] s.11(1).
[37] s.11(5).
[38] s.11(4).
[39] s.11(5).
[40] s.12(1).
[41] See above, para. 1.15.

regulations are consolidated in the Building Act 1984. Section 95 and 96 contain powers of entry and inspection in the same terms as section 287 of the Public Health Act 1936,[41a] with the references to "byelaws" being replaced by references to "building regulations." Otherwise the powers are identical.

Wilful obstruction is an offence under section 112, punishable on summary conviction with a fine not exceeding level 1 on the standard scale.

5. Caravan sites

9.12   Section 26 of the Caravan Sites and Control of Development Act 1960 gives authorised local authority officers powers of entry with or without warrant.

Without warrant

The right applies to any land which is used as a caravan site or in respect of which an application for a site licence has been made. It must be exercised at a reasonable hour, and the officer must, if required, produce documentary evidence of his authority before entering. Twenty-four hours notice of an intended entry must be given to the occupier before entry can be demanded as of right.

The purposes for which entry may be made are:

(a) determining conditions to be attached to a site licence (or if existing conditions should be altered);

(b) ascertaining whether there is or has been on or in connection with the land any contravention of the provisions of Part I of the Act;

(c) ascertaining whether or not circumstances exist which would authorise the local authority to take any action, or execute any work, under Part I of the Act;

(d) taking action, or executing work, authorised by Part I of the Act.

The authorised officer may take with him such other persons as may be necessary.[42]

Under warrant

A warrant may be issued if a justice of the peace is satisfied that there is reasonable ground for entry on to the land for one of the above purposes. In addition he must be satisfied that one of the following conditions is fulfilled:

(a) permission to enter has been refused, or is apprehended and notice of the intention to apply for a warrant has been given;

(b) that the occupier is absent and the case is one of urgency; or

(c) application for admission would defeat the object of the entry.

The warrant will continue in force until the purpose for which entry is necessary is satisfied.

[41a] See above, para. 9.03.
[42] s.26(3).

In all other respects entry under warrant is to be treated in the same way as entry without warrant, and it is in either case an offence wilfully to obstruct any person acting in execution of the powers under section 26. The offence is punishable on summary conviction with a fine not exceeding level 1 on the standard scale.

Evidence obtained as a result of an unlawful entry purported to be made under section 26 may well still be admissible.[43]

6. Excavations

Section 25 of the Local Government (Miscellaneous Provisions) Act 1976 gives **9.13** local authorities power to carry out works in relation to excavations on any land which is accessible to the public and dangerous because inadequately enclosed. The local authority may also be obliged to maintain or remove works which have been carried out. Powers of entry are given by section 26 to a person authorised in that behalf by the local authority.[44] They may be used to decide whether works should be carried out, to carry out the work, or to decide whether work which has been carried out should be or has been removed, repaired, or maintained.

There is no requirement that the entry be at a reasonable time, but the authorised person must, if so required before or after entering, produce evidence of his authority.[45] He may take with him such other persons and equipment as are necessary for his purpose.[46] Unoccupied land must be left as secure against trespassers as it was found.[47]

Compensation

Compensation is payable to any person having an interest in or right over land which suffers damage in consequence of the carrying out, maintenance, repair, or removal of works by the local authority, or as a result of a failure to leave land secure against trespassers.[48] No compensation under this section is payable to a person having an interest in the site of the excavation in respect of damage attributable to the presence of permanent works on the land, other than damage attributable to interference with an easement or profit.[49] Disputes as to compensation are to be determined by the Lands Tribunal.

Obstruction

Wilful obstruction of the exercise of the entry power under section 26(1) or the power to take other persons or equipment on to the land under section 26(2), is an offence, as is the wilful obstruction of the doing of things in connection with works on

---

[43] *Cameron v. Charles Simpson Motors* [1980] C.L.Y. 2630—see above, para. 2.19.
[44] N.B. the power does not apply to operational land of statutory undertakers, or any British Coal Corporation land—s.26(6).
[45] s.26(2)(*a*).
[46] s.26(2)(*b*).
[47] s.26(2)(*c*).
[48] s.26(3).
[49] s.26(4).

the land. It is an offence to interfere with or remove, without the agreement of the local authority, works which have been carried out. In each case the penalty on summary conviction is a fine not exceeding level 3 on the standard scale.[50]

7. Infectious Diseases

9.14   The legislation connected with the control of spreading and infectious diseases has now been consolidated into the Public Health (Control of Disease) Act 1984. Section 61 gives a general power of entry, with or without warrant, in the same terms as section 287 of the Public Health Act 1936.[51] Section 63 of the 1984 Act contains the same additional provisions as section 287(3) to (5) of the 1936 Act. The 1984 Act also provides for specific powers of entry in relation to "common lodging-houses" (s.40), and canal boats (s.50).

8. Nurses agencies

9.15   Premises used to carry on an agency for the supply of nurses are required to be licensed by the Nurses Agencies Act 1957, s.2. Section 3 gives a power of entry to any registered and qualified nurse authorised by the local authority, or any other duly authorised officer. The power must be exercised at a reasonable time, and the entrant must, if required, produce some duly authenticated document showing his authority. The power may be exercised in relation to any premises specified in a licence or an application for a licence, or any premises which are used, or which the entrant has reasonable cause to believe to be used, for the purposes of or in connection with an agency for the supply of nurses.

Once on the premises the entrant may inspect them, and any records kept in connection with an agency carried on on those premises.

Section 3 states that "no person shall obstruct" an authorised entrant in the execution of his duty, but fails to make this an offence. If this phrase is itself apt to create an offence, then section 4(5) makes the penalty a fine, on summary conviction, not exceeding level 1 on the standard scale.

9. Pests

9.16   The Prevention of Damage by Pests Act 1949 imposes a duty on local authorities to keep their district free from rats and mice, as far as practicable,[52] and, if delegated to them by the Minister of Agriculture, to control infestation of food by rats, mice, insects, or mites.

In respect of both these duties a power of entry is given by section 22 of the Act. It is exercisable by any person duly authorised in writing, at any reasonable time, on production of evidence of his authority, if so required.[53] Admission as of right to occupied land must be preceded by 24 hours notice to the occupier.

---

[50] s.26(5).
[51] Above, para. 9.03.
[52] s.2.
[53] s.22(4).

The entry may be used, as regards the general duty under section 2:

(a) to carry out an inspection required by Part I of the Act;
(b) to ascertain whether there is or has been any failure to comply with Part I, or a notice served under it;
(c) to take steps authorised by sections 5 or 6, which allow the local authority to take direct action against infestations in certain situations.

In respect of infestations there is no general power to inspect, but the power may be used to check on compliance with the Act, or to take authorised action. In addition, a person entering to check compliance may take samples of any food found on the premises.

Compensation

Compensation for damage to land arising out of the exercise of the above powers is recoverable from the local authority.[54]

Offences

(i) Disclosure. Information relating to any manufacturing process or trade secret obtained in a factory, workshop, or workplace, to which a person is admitted under section 22, must not be disclosed, other than in the course of duty in connection with the purpose of the entry. To do so is a summary offence, punishable with a fine not exceeding level 3 on the standard scale, or imprisonment for up to three months.

(ii) Obstruction. Wilful obstruction is a summary offence, subject to a fine not exceeding level 1 on the standard scale.

10. Petrol

The Petroleum (Consolidation) Act 1928 gives local authorities a power to grant "petroleum spirit" licences. Section 17 gives officers of the local authority power to inspect and sample petrol kept for trade or industry, but gives no power of entry. However, refusing to show an officer where such petrol is kept is an offence, as is refusing to give assistance in inspection, or wilful obstruction of an officer. In each case the offence is punishable on summary conviction with a fine not exceeding level 2 on the standard scale.[55]

9.17

Search warrant

The power to obtain a warrant under section 18 is primarily directed towards the seizure of petrol suspected of being sold in contravention of the Act. The warrant has to be obtained from a court of summary jurisdiction on a sworn information on oath that there are reasonable grounds for suspecting that petroleum spirit is being "kept,

---

[54] s.22(6).
[55] s.17(5).

sent, conveyed, or exposed or offered for sale" in contravention of the Act.[56] The warrant will authorise any person named in it to enter and examine any place, vehicle,[57] named in the warrant, to search for and take samples of petrol, and to seize and remove it if it is being dealt with in contravention of the Act. The power to seize depends on an actual offence, not on reasonable suspicion.[58] If the petrol is in a vehicle, that vehicle may be used to remove it, for 24 hours after the seizure. The owner of the vehicle must be paid reasonable compensation. In the absence of agreement as to the amount, this is to be determined by the court which decides on whether the petrol is to be forfeited. It may be recovered in the same way as a fine under the Act.[59]

Procedure after seizure

Once petrol has been seized, proceedings should be started forthwith before a court of summary jurisdiction to determine whether it is to be forfeited. The person seizing it is not liable for any loss or damage resulting from the seizure, unless due to some wilful act or neglect during the detention.[60]

Obstruction

If a person, or his employee, or any person acting by his direction or with his consent, refuses or fails to admit a person authorised by a warrant, or obstructs or prevents him from making a search, examination, or seizure, or from taking samples, that person commits an offence, punishable on summary conviction with a fine not exceeding level 5 on the standard scale.[61]

11. Pollution and refuse

(a) *Control of Pollution Act 1974*

9.18 This Act gives local authorities wide powers to deal with the disposal of waste on land (Pt. I), and "noise pollution" (Pt. III). A general power of entry in connection with these powers is given by section 91.[62] It may be exercised with or without warrant. In either case the person entering must, if required, produce evidence of his authority before he enters.[63] He may take with him such other persons and equipment as he may think necessary.[64] Unoccupied land should be left as secure against trespassers as it was found.[65]

---

[56] Section 18 does not apply to any carriage covered by the Road Traffic (Carriage of Dangerous Substances in Packages, etc.) Regulations 1986 (S.I. 1986 No. 1951: s.18(4)).
[57] Or ship.
[58] s.18(1).
[59] s.18(2)(c).
[60] s.18(2)(b).
[61] s.18(3).
[62] s.9 (supervision of licensed activities), and s.16 (removal of waste deposited in breach of licensing conditions) are particularly mentioned by local authorities as being powers in respect of which entry powers might need to be used.
[63] s.92(1).
[64] s.92(2).
[65] s.92(3).

Without warrant. The official entering must be authorised in writing by the local authority. He may enter at any reasonable time, for the purpose of:

(i) performing any function conferred on the authority or that person by virtue of the Act; or

(ii) determining whether, and if so in what manner, such a function should be performed; or

(iii) determining whether any provision of the Act, or of an instrument made under it, is being complied with.

Notice of the intended entry is required in certain cases. Where the land is used for residential purposes, or the official wishes to take heavy equipment on to the land, the occupier must have been served with notice of the intended entry at least seven days previously before entry may be demanded as of right. No notice is required if the land is unoccupied, or in an "emergency."[66] An "emergency" is defined in section 92(7) as arising

"where a person requiring entry ... has reasonable cause to believe that circumstances exist which are likely to endanger life or health and that immediate entry ... is necessary to verify the existence of those circumstances or to ascertain their cause or to effect a remedy."

With warrant. A warrant may be obtained to enter land which a person is entitled to enter without warrant where a justice of the peace is satisfied by a sworn information in writing that admission has been refused or refusal is apprehended, or that the land is unoccupied or the occupier temporarily absent, or the case is one of emergency (as defined above), or that an application for admission would defeat the object of the entry.[67] He must also be satisfied that there are reasonable grounds for entering for the purpose for which it is required, and that one of the following four conditions is satisfied:

(i) admission was sought not less than seven days after notice of the intended entry; or

(ii) admission was sought in an emergency and was refused by or on behalf of the occupier; or

(iii) the land is unoccupied; or

(iv) an application for admission would defeat the object of the entry.[68]

The warrant will authorise the use of force to enter, if necessary,[69] and will continue in force until the purpose for which the entry was required is satisfied.

Powers on entry. The precise powers available on entry depend on the purpose   **9.19**
for which entry is required, and reference must therefore be made to the other Parts of the Act to determine this. Section 91(1)(b), however, states generally that the

---

[66] s.92(3).
[67] s.91(2)(a).
[68] s.92(3).
[69] s.91(2).

official may carry out inspections, measurements, and tests of the land or of any articles on it to the extent which he considers appropriate for the purpose for which he entered.

Compensation. Where damage is suffered by any person as a result of the exercise of the above powers, or as a result of the failure to leave the property secure (as required by s.92(4)), the local authority is under a duty to make full compensation. This duty does not arise where the damage is attributable to the default of the person who sustained it. Disputes as to a person's entitlement to, or the amount of, any compensation, are to be determined by arbitration.[70]

Offences. It is an offence, punishable on summary conviction with a fine not exceeding level 5 on the standard scale, to disclose information relating to any trade secret obtained by virtue of the Act.[71] The offence is not committed where the disclosure is in the course of a person's duty, is authorised by Regulations, or is made with the written consent of a person having right to disclose it, or relates to air pollution.[72] Section 79 contains its own protection as regards trade secrets and air pollution.[73]

It is an offence punishable on summary conviction with a fine not exceeding level 3 on the standard scale, wilfully to obstruct a person exercising powers under section 91 or 92.

(b) *Refuse Disposal (Amenity) Act 1978*

Local authorities have power under this Act to enter land in the open air to remove motor vehicles,[74] or other items,[75] which have been abandoned without lawful authority, or to decide whether these powers should be exercised.[76] The power is to be exercised at any reasonable time by a person duly authorised in writing by the local authority.[77] It is subject to the provisions of section 281(1) to (5) of the Town and Country Planning Act 1971.[78] The local authority is also required to give notice to the occupier (if any) of land on which the vehicle or other item is abandoned of their intention to remove it. In the case of a vehicle which the local authority think should be destroyed because of its condition, a notice to that effect must be displayed on it.[79]

12. Protection of buildings

9.20   Section 29 of the Local Government (Miscellaneous Provisions) Act 1982 applies

[70] s.92(5).
[71] s.94(1).
[72] s.94(2).
[73] s.79(5) and (6).
[74] s.3.
[75] s.6.
[76] s.8.
[77] Or the Secretary of State.
[78] See below, para. 9.50.
[79] s.3(5).

to buildings,[80] which are unoccupied or from which the occupier is temporarily absent. If it appears to the local authority that the building is not effectively secure against trespassers, or is likely to become a danger to the public health, it may undertake work to remedy the situation.[81] Unless the local authority considers that it is necessary to carry out the work immediately, or that it is not possible to contact an owner or occupier, each owner and occupier of the building should be given 48 hours notice of the intention to carry out the work. Appeals against such a notice may be made to the county court.[82]

Subject to this, any person duly authorised in writing by the local authority may enter the building, any land that appears to the local authority to be appurtenant to it, and any other land if it appears to the local authority to be unoccupied, and it would be impossible to undertake the work without entry to it. There is no power to enter occupied land not appurtenant to the building, even if the work would be impossible without entry to it. Nor is there any obstruction offence in respect of this section.

The local authority is entitled to recover expenses reasonably incurred in carrying out the work from the person to whom notice was, or could have been, given.[83] Proceedings to recover expenses are heard in the county court. If no notice of the works was given, they may be challenged as being unnecessary or unreasonable.[84]

13. Scrap metal dealers

Local authorities are required to maintain a register of scrap metal dealers in their area under the Scrap Metal Dealers Act 1964. A local authority officer, authorised in writing, has a right to enter, at any reasonable time, and on production of evidence of his authority, if required, any place not registered which he has reasonable grounds to believe to be being used as a scrap metal store, in order to confirm or allay his suspicions. No force may be used. The officer may also obtain a warrant from a justice of the peace, which will be valid for one month, and will give a right to use force to enter.[85] Obstruction is an offence punishable on summary conviction with a fine not exceeding level 1 on the standard scale.[86]

9.21

14. Sports grounds

The Safety of Sports Grounds Act 1975 gives local authorities controls over any sports stadium designated by the Secretary of State as requiring a "safety certificate." A power of entry and inspection is given by section 11. It applies to all sports grounds, and may be exercised by any person authorised by the local authority.[87] He

9.22

---

[80] Including "structures"—s.29(3).
[81] s.29(2). Note that there are separate provisions relating to "operational land" of the British Rail Board or statutory undertakers.
[82] s.31.
[83] s.29(11).
[84] s.32.
[85] s.6(3).
[86] s.6(5). Note also the slightly wider powers given to the police under this Act—see above, para. 4.52.
[87] Or the chief officer of police, or the Secretary of State.

must produce his authority, if required. He may then enter the ground at any reasonable time, and make such inspection, and inquiries relating to it as he considers necessary. In particular he may examine records of attendance, and records relating to the maintenance of safety at the ground, and take copies of them.

15. Trees

9.23   Section 23 of the Local Government (Miscellaneous Provisions) Act 1976 gives local authorities powers to serve notices requiring work to be done to make trees which are likely to cause damage to persons or property safe. In certain situations the local authority may itself carry out the work.[88]

Section 24 supports section 23 by giving powers of entry. They may be exercised by a person having authority in writing in that behalf from the local authority in order to decide whether any action should be taken in respect of a tree situated on the land entered, or to carry out work. There is no requirement that the entry be at a reasonable time, but the person entering must, if so required before or after entering the land, produce evidence of his authority.[89] He may take with him such other persons and equipment as is necessary.[90] Unoccupied land must be left as secure against trespassers as it was found.

Compensation

A person interested in any land which suffers damage by reason of the exercise of the powers of entry, or the taking on to the land of other persons or equipment, or the failure to leave unoccupied land secure, is entitled to compensation from the local authority.[91] There is no right to compensation for damage arising simply from action being taken to make the tree safe, even if, for example, the damage is to property not situated on land belonging to the person on whose land the tree is sited. Thus, if in felling or lopping a tree, council workmen damage a neighbouring greenhouse, the owner must sue in tort, and cannot rely on the statutory rights to compensation. Disputes as to the entitlement or amount of compensation is to be determined by the Lands Tribunal.[92]

Obstruction

Wilful obstruction of a lawful entry on to land, or of the taking on to land of other persons or equipment, is an offence, as is the wilful obstruction of carrying out work on the land. In each case the offence is punishable on summary conviction with a fine not exceeding level 3 on the standard scale.

B. Fire

9.24   The main entry powers given to local fire brigades are contained in the Fire Services

[88] s.23(1) and (2).
[89] s.24(2)(a).
[90] s.24(2)(b).
[91] s.24(4).
[92] s.24(5).

Act 1947. These enable fire officers to enter premises to obtain information (s.1) and extinguish fires (s.30). The powers of fire officers in relation to clubs, cinemas, and theatres dealt with below (paras. 9.58–9.61) should also be noted.

1. Obtaining information

Under section 1 of the Fire Services Act 1947 a fire authority has a duty to make efficient arrangements for obtaining information for fire fighting purposes with respect to the character of the buildings and other property in their area, the available water supplies and the means of access to them, and other "material local circumstances." The information may be obtained by inspection, and accordingly any member of a fire brigade, authorised in writing by the authority, has the same powers of entry as a local authority officer under section 287 of the Public Health Act 1936.[93]

2. Extinguishing fires

The power of entry under section 30 of the 1947 Act relates to any premises or place in which a fire has, or is reasonably believed to have broken out, or which it is necessary to enter for the purpose of extinguishing a fire or of protecting it from acts done for fire-fighting purposes. The power is given to any member of a fire brigade who is on duty, or acting under a "reinforcement scheme,"[94] or any constable. He may break into the premises, if necessary, without the consent of the owner or occupier. Once on the premises the officer may do anything which he deems necessary for extinguishing the fire, for protecting the premises from the fire or acts done for fire-fighting purposes, or for rescuing any person or property.[95]

Wilful obstruction of, or interference with, a member of a fire brigade engaged in fire-fighting, is a summary offence, punishable with a fine not exceeding level 3 on the standard scale.[96]

3. Fire precautions

The Fire Precautions Act 1971 was passed to strengthen and rationalise the law **9.25** relating to fire precautions. Certain classes of premises are required to have a "fire certificate," and as part of the procedures for the issue of the certificate, and the general enforcement of the Act, the fire authority has a duty to appoint inspectors, and cause premises to be inspected. In performing these duties the authority must act in accordance with any guidance issued by the Secretary of State.[97] These inspectors have entry powers under section 19. The powers may also be exercised by fire inspectors appointed by the Secretary of State under the Fire Services Act 1947, and by any officer of a fire brigade duly authorised in writing by a fire inspector under section 20 of the 1971 Act.

[93] For which see above, para. 9.03.
[94] See s.2.
[95] s.30(1).
[96] s.30(2).
[97] s.18, as amended by the Fire Safety and Safety of Places of Sport Act 1987.

Scope of the power

The power of entry exists wherever it is necessary for the purpose of carrying the Act and any Regulations made under it into effect. It must be exercised at a reasonable time, and on production, if required, of the officer's authority.[98] twenty-four hours notice of the intended entry must be given before the power to enter may be exercised as of right on premises used as a dwelling.[99] The power applies to the following premises:

(a) any premises requiring a fire certificate or about which regulations concerning fire precautions have been made under section 12 of the Act, or in respect of which there is in force an exemption under section 5A of the Act from the requirement of a fire certificate;

(b) any premises (other than premises used solely or mainly for public religious worship, or consisting of or comprised in a house which is occupied as a single private dwelling) which are:

   (i) used as, or for any purpose involving the provision of, sleeping accommodation;

   (ii) used as, or as part of, an institution providing treatment or care;

   (iii) used for the purposes of entertainment, recreation or instruction, or for the purposes of any club, society or association;

   (iv) used for purposes of teaching, training, or research;

   (v) used for any purpose involving access to the premises by members of the public, whether on payment or otherwise;

   (vi) used as a place of work[1];

(c) any premises which have been, are being, or are to be used as a dwelling, where:

   (i) a room is, or is to be, used as living accommodation, and that room is below the ground floor of the building, or two or more floors above the ground floor, or six metres or more above the surface of the ground on any side of the building; or

   (ii) explosive or highly flammable materials have been, are being, or are to be kept anywhere under, in or on a building which constitutes or comprises the premises, in a quantity greater than that prescribed by regulations as the maximum in relation to materials of that kind[2];

(d) any premises not falling within (a), (b), or (c), but which form part of a building comprising any premises so falling;

(e) any premises which the inspector has reasonable cause to believe to be premises falling within paragraphs (a) to (d).

---

[98] s.19(1) and (4).

[99] s.19(5). The same notice is required as regards other premises specified in Regulations made for the purpose of s.19(5). At the time of writing no such Regulations have been made.

[1] s.10(1)(*a*) and s.1(2).

[2] s.3(1). At the time of writing no Regulations have been made, and indeed s.3 has not been brought into force.

Powers on entry

The inspector may inspect the whole or any part of the premises entered, and **9.26** anything on the premises.[3] He may also make inquiries to ascertain whether premises fall within categories (a) to (d) above, to identify the owner or occupier of such premises, or to ascertain whether the provisions of the Act or Regulations, or of a fire certificate, are being complied with. If there is a fire certificate in force with respect to the premises, the inspector may require the production of it, or a copy of it.[4]

In respect of any of his powers of entry or on entry the inspector is entitled to require any person having responsibilities in relation to premises in respect of which a power of entry exists (whether or not the owner or occupier) to give such facilities and assistance (within the scope of his responsibilities) as is necessary to enable the inspector to exercise his powers.[5]

Offences

(i) Disclosure. It is an offence to disclose any information (not just trade secrets, **9.27** etc.) obtained in premises entered under the above powers, unless the disclosure is in the course of the person's duty, or for the purpose of legal proceedings (including arbitration) or a report of such proceedings.[6] The offence is punishable on summary conviction with a fine not exceeding level 3 on the standard scale. Disclosure of information to an enforcing authority (as defined by section 18(7) of the Health and Safety at Work Act 1974) in order to enable it to discharge its functions is specifically excluded from this provision.[7]

(ii) Obstruction. Intentional obstruction of an inspector in the exercise of his powers or duties, or failure, without reasonable excuse, to comply with a requirement of an inspector, is an offence punishable on summary conviction with a fine not exceeding level 3 on the standard scale.[8]

4. Gaming premises

Under the Gaming Act 1968, s.43, a person duly authorised in writing by a fire **9.28** authority may at any reasonable time enter premises in the authority's area which are licensed under the Act, to see whether appropriate fire precautions are being sufficiently observed.[9]

C. Food

1. General powers

The main power here is under the Food Act 1984, s.87. Local authority officers **9.29**

---

[3] s.19(1)(*a*).
[4] s.19(1)(*c*).
[5] s.19(1)(*d*).
[6] s.21.
[7] s.21(2), (3)—as added by the Fire Safety and Safety of Places of Sport Act 1987, s.11.
[8] s.19(6).
[9] For the obstruction offence related to this section see s.43(3).

must be duly authorised in writing.[10] An officer entering premises may take with him such other persons as may be necessary.[11] The power may be used either to discover whether there is or has been on or in connection with the premises entered, a contravention of the Act or byelaws made under the Act, or generally, for the performance of the authority's functions under the Act or byelaws.[12] There are powers of entry both with and without warrant.

Entry without warrant

The right to enter at all reasonable hours applies as regards any premises, except that 24 hours notice must be given to the occupier of premises used only as a dwelling-house.[13] The officer must produce his authority, if required, before entry.

Entry under warrant

A warrant may be obtained if a justice of the peace is satisfied by a sworn information in writing, both that there are reasonable grounds for entering for one of the purposes mentioned above, and that one of the following conditions is fulfilled[14]:

(a) admission has been refused, or refusal is apprehended, and notice of the intention to apply for a warrant has been given to the occupier;
(b) application for admission, or the giving of notice, would defeat the object of the entry;
(c) the case is one of urgency (not further defined);
(d) the premises are unoccupied or the occupier is temporarily absent. Such premises must be left as secure against trespassers as they were found.[15]

The warrant will be valid for one month, and will authorise entry by force if necessary.[16]

Offences

(a) Disclosure. Any person who enters a factory or workplace under the above powers commits an offence by disclosing, other than in the course of his duty, any information obtained there relating to any manufacturing process or trade secret. The offence is punishable on summary conviction with a fine not exceeding level 3 on the standard scale, or with imprisonment for a term not exceeding three months.[17]

(b) Obstruction. Wilful obstruction is a summary offence subject to a fine not exceeding level 5 on the standard scale.[18] It is also an offence to fail to give assistance

[10] s.89 gives the same powers of entry to inspectors of the Ministry of Agriculture, and the Ministry of Health.
[11] s.87(3).
[12] s.87(1).
[13] *Ibid.*
[14] s.87(2).
[15] s.87(3).
[16] s.87(4), (2).
[17] s.87(5).
[18] s.91(1).

or information which is reasonably required or requested, or knowingly to give false information. The privilege against self-incrimination is specifically preserved.[19]

2. Slaughterhouses

The Slaughterhouses Act 1974 provides for the licensing of slaughterhouse and knackers yards by local authorities. Local authority officers have entry powers in the same terms as under the Food Act 1984 (above).[20] The only difference is that the penalty for wilful obstruction is a fine not exceeding level 3 on the standard scale or imprisonment for up to one month, and for failure to give assistance, a fine not exceeding level 1 on the standard scale.[21]

9.30

3. Poultry

The Slaughter of Poultry Act 1967 attempts to provide for the humane slaughter, for commercial purposes, of turkeys, domestic fowl, guinea fowl, ducks, and geese.[22] A person authorised by the local authority (or the Minister of Agriculture, or the Secretary of State) may enter premises to ascertain whether there is, or has been, a contravention of, or failure to comply with the Act or regulations made under it.[23]

9.31

The premises which may be entered are those on which the slaughter of poultry is, or appears to be, in progress, or to have been in progress within 48 hours of the entry, or on which poultry is, or appears to be, kept for the purpose of such slaughter.[24]

Obstruction is a summary offence, subject to a fine not exceeding level 2 on the standard scale.

4. Fertilisers and feeding stuffs

The Agriculture Act 1970, Part IV, which concerns fertilisers and feeding-stuffs, gives a local authority certain duties, together with a power to appoint inspectors.[25] These inspectors have powers to enter premises and take samples under section 76.

9.32

The power may be exercised by an inspector at all reasonable times, on production if required of written evidence of his authority. The inspector may take with him such other persons and equipment as may appear to him to be necessary. The power may be used in relation to;

(a) any premises on which the inspector has reasonable cause to believe that there are any fertilisers or feeding stuffs which are kept there for the purpose of being sold in the course of trade and are ready for sale;

(b) any premises (not used only as a dwelling) on which he has reasonable cause to believe that there is any fertiliser or feeding stuff which the occupier of the premises has purchased.

---

[19] s.91(3).
[20] Slaughterhouses Act 1974, s.20.
[21] s.21(1).
[22] s.1, s.7, and the Slaughter of Poultry Act 1967 Extension Order (S.I. 1978 No. 201).
[23] s.4(1), as substituted by the Animal Health and Welfare Act 1984, s.4.
[24] s.4(1). Where slaughter is, or appears to be in progress the entry may be at any time; otherwise it must be at a reasonable hour.
[25] s.67.

Powers on entry

The inspector may take a sample of any material on the premises (including material in a vehicle) which he has reasonable cause to believe to be fertiliser or feeding stuff, as above. The manner of taking samples is specified in Regulations— namely the Fertilisers (Sampling and Analysis) (Amendment) Regulations 1980,[26] and the Feeding Stuffs (Sampling and Analysis) Regulations 1982.[27]

Offences

Disclosure, other than in the course of duty, of information relating to a manufacturing process or trade secret obtained in premises entered under this power is an offence punishable on summary conviction with a fine not exceeding level 5 on the standard scale.

Wilful obstruction of an inspector is also a summary offence, punishable with a fine not exceeding level 3 on the standard scale.

5. Poisons

9.33
As part of the controls over the use of substances included in Part II of the poisons list, other than in a registered pharmacy,[28] a local authority has a duty to appoint inspectors. The inspector will have the power at all reasonable times to enter premises on which he has reasonable cause to suspect that a breach of the law has been committed in relation to such substances, or on which a person whose name is entered in the local authority's list carries on business.[29] On entry the inspector may make examinations and inquiries, and do anything else (including buying samples) which may be necessary for his inspection. Wilful obstruction or delay of an inspector is a summary offence, as is refusing to allow a sample to be taken, or failing, without reasonable excuse to give information.[30] In each case the offence is punishable on summary conviction with a fine not exceeding level 2 on the standard scale.

D. Health and Safety at Work

9.34
The main powers of local authority inspectors in this area are contained in the Health and Safety at Work Act 1974. The areas of responsibility of local authorities for health and safety at work are set out in the Health and Safety (Enforcing Authorities) Regulations 1977, as follows[31]:

"1. The sale or storage of goods for retail or wholesale distribution other than—
(*a*)   on premises controlled or occupied by a railway undertaking;

---

[26] S.I. 1980 No. 1130.
[27] S.I. 1982 No. 1144.
[28] Which will be subject to inspection by the Pharmaceutical Society of Great Britain—Poisons Act 1972, s.9(3).
[29] *Ibid.*s.9(6). For the local authority's "list," see ss.5 and 6.
[30] s.9(8).
[31] S.I. 1977 No. 746, Sched. 1.

(*b*) in warehouses or other premises controlled or occupied by the owners, trustees or conservators of a dock, wharf or quay;

(*c*) at container depots;

(*d*) water and sewage and their by-products;

(*e*) natural gas and town gas;

(*f*) solid fuel or other minerals at any mine or quarry or at premises controlled from a mine or quarry;

(*g*) petroleum spirit in premises where motor vehicles are maintained or repaired by way of trade;

(*h*) wholesale distribution of flammable, toxic, oxidizing, corrosive or explosive substances or petroleum spirit.
    2. Office activities.
    3. Catering services.
    4. The provision of residential accommodation.
    5. Consumer services provided in shop premises except dry cleaning or radio and television repairs or the maintenance or repair of motor vehicles.
    6. Dry cleaning in coin-operated units in launderettes and similar premises.
    6A. The keeping of wild animals for exhibition to the public (otherwise than for the purposes of a circus) at premises to which members of the public have access with or without a charge for admission."

"Office activities" and "shop premises" are further defined in Part II of the Schedule. This makes it clear, *inter alia*, that the premises of wholesalers, and coal merchants, are within the definition of shop premises.

The local authority has the responsibility for enforcing the "relevant statutory provision" related to the above areas. A complete list of these is set out in Appendix 1. The powers of local authority inspectors under the 1974 Act are exactly the same as those of inspectors employed by the Health and Safety Executive: these are dealt with in Chapter Eight, paragraph 8.30.

In addition to the 1974 Act, local authorities have duties and powers under two other Acts which relate to Health and Safety at Work and which contain their own entry powers.

1. Shops

Local authorities have a duty to appoint inspectors to enforce the Shops Act **9.35** 1950.[32] As a result of the decision of the Divisional Court in *Rotherham Borough Council*

---

[32] s.71(2).

v. *Tutin*,[33] these inspectors operate not under the Health and Safety at Work Act 1974 but under the otherwise repealed provisions of section 146 of the Factories Act 1961. The reason why this section is not repealed for the purposes of the Shops Act is that the statutory instrument repealing it could only affect "relevant statutory provisions" under the 1974 Act. The Shops Act 1950 was not such a provision,[34] so section 146 continues to have effect for this limited purpose. While accepting this line of reasoning, Donaldson L.J. commented that he was "appalled at the complexity of the legislation, which was an offence to good government," and that "citizens should not be exposed to the possibility of being prosecuted for an offence [*i.e.* obstructing a Shops Act inspector] when the question of whether that offence exists can only be the subject of very advanced legal crossword puzzles."[35]

The effect of this decision is that an inspector appointed under the Shops Act continues to have the power to enter a shop when he has reasonable cause to believe that any person is employed there. The power may be exercised at any reasonable time, by day or night. On entry the inspector may inspect and examine every part of the shop.[36] There is also a power to enter, by day, any place which the inspector reasonably believes to be a shop, and any part of a building of which a shop forms part, and in which he has reasonable cause to believe that explosive or highly inflammable materials are being stored or used. In either case the inspector may take with him a constable if he has reasonable cause to anticipate serious obstruction.[37]

The inspector may, in addition, require the production of registers, certificates, notices, and documents kept in accordance with the Shops Act, and may inspect and copy them. He may make inquiries as to the compliance with public health legislation, and the employment of young persons.[38] Any person found in the shop may be questioned (alone or in the presence of another person, as the inspector thinks fit) and required to sign a declaration of the truth of the matters about which he is questioned. The privilege against incriminating oneself or one's spouse is specifically preserved.[39] A person found in a shop may also be required to give information concerning the occupier of the shop. Wilfully withholding such information will be deemed "obstruction."[40] Finally, the inspector may exercise such other powers as may be necessary for carrying the Act into effect.[41]

Obstruction of an inspector is a summary offence subject to a fine not exceeding £20. Moreover the occupier of a shop in which the offence took place may be charged with it. Certain behaviour will be deemed to amount to obstruction,[42] namely:

---

[33] (1981) 27 *Inspector Journal*, (No. 1), 17.

[34] See 1974 Act, s.15(1) and Sched. 1.

[35] I am grateful to the Director of Legal and Administrative Services at Rotherham Borough Council for providing some of the details of this case.

[36] Factories Act 1961, s.146(1).

[37] s.146(1)(*b*).

[38] s.146(1)(*d*).

[39] s.146(1)(*f*).

[40] s.146(3).

[41] s.146(1)(*h*).

[42] s.146(3).

(a) wilfully delaying an inspector;

(b) failure to comply with a requisition;

(c) failure to produce any required register, certificate, notice or document;

(d) concealing or preventing, or attempting to conceal or prevent, a person from appearing before, or being examined by an inspector.

2. Filling materials

The manufacture, use, or storage of the filling materials specified in the Rag Flock **9.36** and Other Filling Materials Act 1951,[43] may take place only on premises registered (as regards use), or licensed (as regards manufacture or storage), by the local authority. Powers of entry and inspection are contained in section 13.

The power is exercisable at all reasonable times by an authorised officer of the local authority, on production, if required, of documentary evidence of his authority. It is available in respect of any premises:

(a) registered or licensed under the Act; or

(b) on which the authorised person had reasonable ground to believe that materials to which the Act applies, or articles filled with such materials are being held for sale, or offered or exposed for sale; or

(c) which the authorised person has reasonable grounds to believe ought to be registered; or

(d) on which he has reasonable grounds for believing that rag flock is manufactured with a view to its use, or sale for use, on premises which ought to be registered; or

(e) in respect of which an application for the grant or renewal of a licence has been made, or which (not being a private dwelling) are in the same building as such premises.[44]

Powers on entry

Entry of premises under (e), above, is simply to enable the inspector to decide **9.37** whether the licence should be granted. In respect of the other premises the inspector may inspect them and any materials found there. He may also require the production of records required to be kept under section 9 of the Act, or, if the premises are unlicensed and unregistered, or the section 9 records are not produced, the production of any books, account, or records relating to any business carried on at the premises, and information relating to materials or articles to which the Act applies found on the premises. He may take copies of, or extracts from, any documents so produced.[45]

If the inspector (entering premises under (a) to (d) above) finds filling material or articles on the premises in respect of which he has reasonable grounds for believing that an offence has been committed under the Act, he may require the occupier to

[43] Or in Regulations made under it—see s.33.
[44] s.13(1) and (2).
[45] s.13(4).

keep them intact on the premises. This obligation will last for one month, unless proceedings in respect of them have been instituted, in which case it will last until those proceedings have been finally disposed of. If the owner of the material is convicted of an offence in relation to it, the court may order it to be forfeited to the local authority.[46]

The inspector entering under any of the powers, or simply by permission of the occupier, may take samples of any materials which appear to be covered by the Act.[47] The samples should be divided into three, with the occupier being provided with one part (if he asks for it), and the samples being tested as provided by section 15.

Offences

9.38   **(i) Disclosure.** No information relating to a trade or business obtained as a result of entry under the above powers may be disclosed, except with the consent of the person carrying on the trade or business, or in connection with the execution of the Act or any proceedings under it. To do so is an offence punishable on summary conviction with a fine not exceeding level 3 on the standard scale, or up to six months imprisonment, or both.[48]

(ii) Obstruction. Wilful obstruction of a person acting in execution of the Act is an offence punishable on summary conviction with a fine not exceeding level 1 on the standard scale or imprisonment for up to three months, or both.[49]

It is also an offence to fail to give any assistance which such a person may reasonably request, or any information which the person is authorised to ask for, or may reasonably require, or in response to such a request, knowingly to make a false statement.[50] The penalty in this case is simply a fine not exceeding level 1 on the standard scale. The privilege against self-incrimination is specifically preserved.

E. Highways

9.39   The powers of entry of a highway authority are contained in sections 289 to 294 of the Highways Act 1980. As part of the exercise of their general functions a highway authority has powers to enter to survey land, or to maintain, alter or remove, structures or works.

1. Survey

Section 289 gives a power to enter to survey in respect of land which the local authority needs to survey in connection with any of their functions as a highway authority. The power allows the authority to enter any other land in order to carry

---

[46] s.20.
[47] s.14.
[48] s.18.
[49] s.17(1).
[50] s.17(2).

out the survey, as well as the actual land to be surveyed. Seven days notice of an intended entry must be given to the occupier (except in the case of a highway of which the authority is itself the highway authority),[51] before entry may be demanded as of right.[52] In any case the entry must be at a reasonable time, and the entrant, who must be authorised in writing by the authority,[53] must, if required, produce his authority before or after entering on the land.[54] He may take with him such other persons, vehicles and equipment, as he may consider necessary.[55]

Powers on entry

Provided that notice of an intention to do so was included in the notice of the intended entry (where such notice was required), the power to enter includes the power to do the following things in addition to actually carrying out the survey:

(a) place and leave on or in the land any apparatus for use in connection with the survey of that or any other land (whether from the air or on the ground) and to remove such apparatus[56];
(b) search and bore for the purpose of ascertaining:
   (i) the nature of the subsoil or the presence of minerals in it;
   (ii) whether any damage to a highway which is maintainable at public expense and for which the authority is responsible is being caused, or is likely to be caused by mining operations or other activities taking place under the highway, or in or under land adjoining, or in the vicinity of the highway.

The British Coal Corporation and statutory undertakers have special rights of notice and to object, if the second of the above powers is to be used in a way which will affect their interests.[57] Ministerial approval for the work may be required in the event of such objections.[58]

2. Maintenance, etc.

A highway authority has the power or right in certain circumstances to maintain, **9.40** alter, or remove "structures" or "works" on land not belonging to the authority, or forming part of a highway for which they are the highway authority.[59] Section 291 provides that, if necessary, a person duly authorised in writing by the authority may at any reasonable time enter land for that purpose. The provisions as to notice, production of authority, and entry of other people and equipment, etc., are the same as for section 289 (above).

[51] s.290(6).
[52] s.290(3).
[53] s.289(1).
[54] s.290(1).
[55] s.290(2).
[56] s.289(2). Notice of the intention to use this power must be given to the owner as well as the occupier.
[57] s.290(5).
[58] s.290(7).
[59] s.291. "Structure" includes a bridge, fence, barrier or post; "works" include tunnels, ditches, gutters, watercourses, culverts, drains, soakaways or pipes—s.291(4). See, *e.g.* s.80 (fences) and ss.91–92 (bridges).

Compensation

A person whose land, or other property on the land, has been damaged, or has been disturbed in his enjoyment of such land or property, as a result of the exercise of powers under section 289 or 291, may recover compensation from the authority.[60] Disputes as to the amount of compensation are to be settled by the Lands Tribunal.[61]

Offences

(i) **Disclosure.** If as a result of the exercise of powers under section 289 or 291 a person admitted to a factory, workshop or workplace obtains information relating to any manufacturing process or trade secret, disclosure of such information (unless in the performance of his duty in connection with the purposes of the entry) is an offence, punishable on summary conviction with a fine not exceeding £1,000 and on indictment with up to two years imprisonment or a fine, or both.[62]

(ii) **Obstruction.** Wilful obstruction, or removal or interference with apparatus left in the exercise of powers under sections 289 and 291 is a summary offence subject to a fine not exceeding level 3 on the standard scale.

3. Footpaths and bridleways

9.41   Land may need to be surveyed in connection with the making of orders of creation, extinguishment, or diversion of public paths. A person authorised in writing by the Secretary of State or other authority may enter the land in question (but not any other) for this purpose.[63] In addition, where a claim for compensation has been made as a result of a path creation order, a person who is an Officer of the Valuation Office of the Inland Revenue, or who is duly authorised in writing by the authority from whom the compensation is claimed, may also enter upon the land.[64] In both cases the entrant must, if required, produce evidence of his authority before entering, and as regards occupied land at least seven days notice must be given to the occupier before admission may be demanded as of right.[65] Wilful obstruction is a summary offence, with a penalty of a fine not exceeding level 3 on the standard scale.[66]

4. Premises

9.42   A highway authority may in the discharge of any of its functions need to "enter, examine or lay open" premises for the purpose of:

(a) surveying;
(b) making plans;

[60] s.292(1).
[61] s.307.
[62] s.292(4).
[63] s.293(1).
[64] s.293(2).
[65] s.293(3).
[66] s.293(4).

(c) executing maintaining or examining works;
(d) ascertaining the course of sewers or drains;
(e) ascertaining or fixing boundaries;
(f) ascertaining whether any hedge, tree or shrub is dead, diseased, damaged, or insecurely rooted.[67]

The functions in respect of which these powers may be used are those under section 101 (filling roadside ditches), section 154 (cutting or felling overhanging trees), and the provisions listed in Schedule 22 to the Act.

If the owner or occupier refuses to allow this to be done, the authority may, having given notice of their intention to do so, make a complaint to a magistrates court for an order authorising them to "enter, examine or lay open" the premises.[68] The complaint is heard *inter partes*, and if "no sufficient cause" is shown against it, the magistrates will make an order for entry, etc., in the terms outlined below. The phrase "no sufficient cause" was considered in *Robinson* v. *Corporation of Sunderland*,[69] in relation to a similar provision under the Public Health Act 1875, ss.36 and 305. The appellant had tried to challenge the application before the magistrates by showing that the local authority were incorrect in their assessment of the need to enter his premises to provide a water closet, etc., since he alleged that he was already adequately provided for. The Divisional Court ruled that the magistrates had been right to refuse to hear evidence on this issue. They felt that "sufficient cause" might relate to errors in the local authority's procedures, such as the absence of an inspector's report on which to base their decision, or to things which would make entry dangerous or inconvenient, such as illness in the house, but could not relate to the specific issue of the need to exercise the power.[70] This was based on the fact that section 36 was expressed in terms of a subjective approach on the part of the local authority to the need for the facilities in question. It is to be assumed that the same approach would be taken as regards section 294 of the Highways Act 1980.

The order, if made, will empower any authorised officer of the local authority to enter, examine, or lay open the premises described in the order for the purposes specified in the order. No entry must take place, or works begin (except in an emergency, which is not defined in the Act) unless at least seven days notice has been given to the occupier.[71] Subject to this the entry may be at any reasonable time between 9 a.m. and 6 p.m.[72]

Compensation is payable by the local authority in respect of damage or disturbance of enjoyment of the land, or other property.[73] Disputes as to the amount are to be settled by arbitration, if the parties agree to this, or by the county court.[74]

[67] s.294(1).
[68] *Ibid.*
[69] [1899] 1 Q.B. 751.
[70] *Ibid.* 755, *per* Lawrence J., and 757, *per* Channell J.
[71] s.294(3).
[72] s.294(2).
[73] s.294(4).
[74] s.308.

5. Traffic signs

Under section 71 of the Road Traffic Regulation Act 1984, a highway authority may enter land in connection with its powers and duties in relation to traffic signs, or the removal of signs under section 69.

F. Housing

9.43 The main Act in this area is the Housing Act 1985. Many of the local authorities' responsibilities under the Act are backed up by entry powers, and these are dealt with below according to their subject matter.

1. Survey and examination

The Act contains a number of virtually identical provisions allowing a person authorised by a local authority (or the Secretary of State) to enter premises for the purposes of survey and examination where it appears necessary in order to determine whether any powers under the relevant part of the Act should be exercised, or to survey, examine or value, as appropriate, where the local authority has the power to purchase compulsorily. The relevant sections are 54 (Part II, Provision of Housing), 197 (Part VI, Repair Notices), 222 (Part VII, Improvement Notices), 260 (Part VIII, Area Improvement), 319 (Part IX, Slum Clearance), 340 (Part X, Overcrowding), 395 (Part XI, Houses in Multiple Occupation), and 600 (Part XVII, Compulsory Purchase and Land Compensation). In each case the authorisation must be in writing and state the particular purpose for which entry is authorised. The entry must be at a reasonable time, and 24 hours notice must be given to the occupier, and the owner (if known). Each provision is backed up by the immediately subsequent section (*i.e.* sections 55, 198, etc.) which makes obstruction a summary offence, punishable with a fine not exceeding level 2 on the standard scale.

In addition to these general powers, a local authority also has entry powers in the following circumstances.

2. Inspection of local authority houses

9.44 As part of the local authority's control over its housing stock, all houses owned by it are to be at all times open to inspection by the local authority.[75] This is a particularly wide power. Presumably it is not in practice abused, but there seems no reason why the power should not be exercisable only at reasonable times, or why a local authority officer should not be required to show his authority before entering.

3. Homeless persons

Where a local housing authority has reason to believe that an applicant for

---

[75] s.21(1). "House" includes any yard, garden, outhouses, and appurtenances belonging to the house, or usually enjoyed with it": s.56.

accommodation is homeless, or threatened with homelessness, and that there is a danger of loss of, or damage to, the applicant's personal property, there is a power of entry under section 70. The power applies to the usual, or last usual, place of residence of the applicant, and may be exercised at any reasonable time in order to deal with the applicant's personal property, in particular by storing it, or arranging for its storage. The power extends to personal property of any person who might reasonably be expected to reside with the applicant.

4. Repair notices

A local authority has power under section 189 of the Act to require work to be done, *e.g.* to render a house fit for human habitation. If the notice is not complied with then the local authority has the power to execute the work itself, and to enter the house for this purpose.[76] The local authority does not appear to be required to give any further notice before entering, though if the original notice is the subject of an appeal they must wait 21 days from the determination of the appeal (or for a longer period if the court so specifies). If, however, they do give notice, in writing, to the person having control of the building (and the owner, if they think fit) of their intention to enter and carry out the work, then, if after seven days from the service of the notice, any person on whom the notice was served, or anyone employed by him, is in the building for the purpose of carrying out work, at the same time as the local authority workman is trying to carry out the specified works, this will be deemed to be obstruction of the local authority. There is a specific defence if the person can prove that the work he was doing was urgently necessary to obviate danger to the occupants of the house. Obstruction is a summary offence, subject to a fine not exceeding level 2 on the standard scale. In addition the local authority may recover any expenses incurred.

9.45

5. Demolition order—vermin

Where a demolition order under Part IX of the Act has been made in relation to any premises, and it appears to the local authority that the premises require to be cleansed from vermin, they may serve a notice in writing on the owners of the premises that the authority intends to cleanse the premises before demolition.[77] Once such a notice has been served, and the demolition order has become operative and the premises have been vacated, the local authority may enter to carry out the cleansing work. The owner cannot start or continue the demolition until the local authority serve a further notice authorising him to do so.[78] However, the owner may in his turn serve notice on the local authority requiring them to carry out the cleansing work within 14 days. At the expiry of that period the owner is entitled to proceed with the demolition whether the cleansing work is completed or not.

9.46

6. Overcrowding

As part of its powers to control overcrowding, a local authority has a power of

9.47

[76] ss.193, 194.
[77] s.273(1).
[78] s.273(2).

entry under section 337, in order to measure rooms, so as to determine the number of persons permitted to sleep in the dwelling. The entrant must be authorised in writing, stating the purpose for which entry is authorised. The entry must be at a reasonable time, and 24 hours notice must be given to the occupier (and the owner, if known).

7. Multiple occupation

(a) *Control orders*

9.48   Section 379 gives the local authority powers to make a "control order" to take into its management certain houses in multiple occupation. Section 387 gives a power of entry in relation to such premises for the purpose of survey and examination, or to carry out any works. The power may be exercised at any reasonable time by the local authority, or a person authorised in writing by the local authority. If a person refuses to allow works to be carried out the local authority may obtain an order from a magistrates court ordering him to permit the local authority to do everything it considers necessary. Failure to comply renders a person liable on summary conviction to a fine not exceeding level 3 on the standard scale, and to a further fine of £20 for every day or part of a day during which the failure continues.

(b) *Warrants*

As a supplement to the general powers of entry under sections 387 and 395, noted above, section 397 enables the authority to obtain a warrant from a justice of the peace. The justice must not grant the warrant unless satisfied that admission has been refused following at least 24 hours' notice,[79] or that application for admission would defeat the purpose of the entry.

Force may be used if necessary, and the person obtaining the warrant may be accompanied by others. Unoccupied premises, or those from which the occupier is temporarily absent, must be left as secure against trespassers as they were found.

The warrant remains in force until the purpose for which entry was required is satisfied. This would seem to imply that more than one entry may be made using the same warrant.

8. Common lodging houses

In connection with its powers under Part XII of the Act in relation to common lodging houses, a local authority has a power of entry under section 411. This power is in the same terms as section 287 of the Public Health Act 1936.[80] Wilful obstruction is a summary offence under section 412, punishable with a fine not exceeding level 1 on the standard scale.

9. Enforcing covenants

9.49   Section 33 of the Local Government (Miscellaneous Provisions) Act 1982

[79] Notice is not needed if an offence listed in s.395(2) is suspected.
[80] Above, para. 9.03.

empower a local authority to enforce covenants in connection with the development, etc., of land against successors in title to the land. One method of enforcement of the covenant is to enter the land, carry out any work necessary to comply with the covenant, and recover expenses from the person against whom the covenant is enforceable.[81] The local authority must give at least 21 days notice of their intention to enter to any person having an interest in the land, or against whom the covenant is enforceable. Sections 283, 288, and 291 of the Public Health Act 1936 apply to this power.[82]

G. Planning

1. General planning powers

The most widely used powers of entry in the planning field are contained in **9.50** section 280 of the Town and Country Planning Act 1971, which authorises entry for a wide range of purposes, including survey, inspection, and valuation. In relation to all the powers the person entering must be duly authorised in writing by the local authority, and the entry must take place at a reasonable time. In addition all the powers are subject to the restrictions contained in section 281, which are dealt with below.

(a) *Survey*

A local planning authority may authorise entry to survey land in connection with[83]:

(a) the preparation, approval, adoption, making or amendment of a structure plan or local plan[84];
(b) any application for planning permission,[85] a tree preservation order,[86] or permission to display advertisements.[87] The land entered does not have to be the land in relation to which the application is made.
(c) any proposal to make, issue, or serve any order or notice relating to the general planning controls under Part II (other than s.44), or the powers under Part IV (which provides special control in relation to listed buildings, trees, advertisements, waste land, industrial and office development), or Part V (enforcement of controls under Parts III and IV).

(b) *Inspection*

A local planning authority may authorise entry:

[81] s.33(3).
[82] s.33(6)—see above, paras. 9.03–9.04.
[83] s.280(1).
[84] For which see Pt. II of the Act.
[85] Pt. III of the Act.
[86] s.60.
[87] s.63.

(a) to any land to ascertain whether in respect to any building on the land, an offence has been or is being committed under section 55 or Schedule 11 (demolition, alteration, or extension of listed buildings), or section 98 (non-compliance with listed building enforcement notice), or whether the building is being maintained in a proper state of repair;

(b) to any land for the purpose:

    (i) of ascertaining whether any offence appears to have been committed under section 57 (damage to listed buildings);

    (ii) of exercising the authority's powers to carry out urgent works in an unoccupied listed building (section 101) or to require the replacement of trees (s.103) or to ascertain whether those powers should or may be exercised;

(c) to any land in respect of which an order or notice under section 280(1)(c) (*i.e.* (c) of "Survey," above) has been made or served, for the purpose of ascertaining whether the order or notice has been complied with.

(c) *Valuation*

9.51   Where a local authority may be subject to a claim for compensation resulting from planning restriction (Pt. VIII of the Act) other than the replanting of trees under section 175, or from an order extinguishing a right to use a highway (s.212(5)), or from statutory undertakers (Pt. XI, except s.237(2) or s.238(1)(c)), it may authorise entry to any land (not necessarily the land in relation to which compensation is to be paid) to survey it, or estimate its value.

Similarly, in connection with its power to acquire land (ss.112, 113, and Pt. VI), the local authority may authorise entry to any land to survey it or estimate its value in connection with the acquisition, or the payment of compensation in respect of the acquisition.[88]

(d) *Other powers*

Placards and posters. Local authorities have power under section 109A to remove or obliterate placards or posters in their area which, in their opinion, contravene the advertisement regulations. It is particularly directed against fly-posting. The authority may authorise entry on to any unoccupied land to exercise these powers if it would be impossible to exercise the power without entering the land.[89]

Search and bore. Any power to survey given by section 280 is to be construed as including a power to search and bore on the land for the purpose of ascertaining the nature of the subsoil or the presence of minerals therein.[90] Notice of an intention to exercise this power must be given at the same time as notice of an intended entry (for which see below). If the land is held by statutory undertakers, and they object on the

[88] *cf.*compulsory purchase powers—see below, para. 9.54.
[89] s.280(4A).
[90] s.280(9).

grounds that it would be seriously detrimental to the carrying out of their undertaking, Ministerial approval must be obtained before the power may be exercised.[91]

(e) *Controls over entry powers*

General controls over all the above entry powers are provided by section 281.

At the time of entry. Any person entering under section 280 must, if required produce evidence of his authority to do so. Admission as of right to occupied land cannot be demanded unless 24 hours notice has been given to the occupier.[92]

After entry. Where entry has been made to a factory, workshop, or workplace, the unauthorised disclosure of information thus obtained concerning any manufacturing process or trade secret, is an offence punishable on summary conviction with a fine not exceeding £400, or on indictment with imprisonment for up to two years, or a fine, or both.[93]

Compensation for any damage caused by an entry or survey may be recovered by any person interested in the land from the authority on whose behalf the entry was effected. Claims are subject to section 179 of the Act, which requires disputes over compensation to be determined by the Lands Tribunal.

(f) *Obstruction*

Wilful obstruction of a person exercising powers under section 280 is an offence punishable on summary conviction with a fine not exceeding level 2 on the standard scale.[94]

In *R.* v. *Chief Constable of Devon and Cornwall, ex. p. Central Electricity Generating Board,*[95] the Court of Appeal held that the C.E.G.B. was entitled to rely on the use of self-help to remove protesters who were obstructing the exercise of their powers of entry and survey under section 280.[96]

2. Coastal protection

Local authorities who are "coastal protection authorities"[97] have powers of entry under section 25 of the Coast Protection Act 1949, in connection with their duties to protect the land against erosion and encroachment by the sea. There is power to obtain a warrant if necessary.[98] In either case the person entering may take with him such other persons as may be necessary, and must leave unoccupied land as secure against trespassers as it was found.[99]

9.52

---

[91] s.281(5).
[92] Some local authority officials have indicated to me that in their opinion the notice requirement often defeats the object of the power. N.B. also s.283, service of notices.
[93] s.281(3).
[94] s.281(2).
[95] [1981] 3 All E.R. 826.
[96] See further, above, para. 1.29.
[97] See s.1 of the Coast Protection Act 1949.
[98] s.25(4).
[99] s.25(5).

(a) *Entry without warrant*

9.53   A person authorised by a coastal protection authority has, on production if required, documentary evidence of his authority, a right of entry at all reasonable hours. In respect of land used for residential purposes 24 hours notice must be given to the occupier.[1] Subject to this the person may enter,

   (i) any land on which the authority has power to carry out work under the Act[2];

   (ii) any land which it is reasonably necessary to enter to gain access to land on which the authority has power to carry out work under any provision of the Act;

  (iii) any land, to inspect and survey it in order to decide whether, and if so how, any functions of the authority are to be exercised, or whether there is compliance with any orders, etc., under the Act (or any other enactment);

  (iv) any land to estimate compensation payable under the Act, or the value of any interest in the land.[3]

The power under (i) or (ii) includes the power to authorise the entry of necessary persons, vehicles, plant, and materials, and to carry out works to facilitate their passage.[4]

(b) *Entry under warrant*

A warrant may be obtained from a justice of the peace, on sworn information in writing, if the justice is satisfied that there is reasonable ground for the entry, and that one of the following circumstances exists;

   (i) admission has been refused or refusal is apprehended, and notice of the intention to apply for a warrant has been given to the occupier; or

   (ii) the land is unoccupied, or the occupier temporarily absent; or

  (iii) the case is one of urgency (not further defined)[5];

The warrant will authorise entry for the purposes listed above, by force if necessary, and will continue in force until the purpose for which entry is necessary has been satisfied.[6]

(c) *Offences*

Disclosure. Information obtained in a factory or workplace entered under this Act, which relates to any manufacturing process or trade secret, may not be disclosed, other than in the course of duty, by the person obtaining it, or any coastal protection officer to whom it is disclosed. To do so is an offence punishable on

---

[1] s.25(3).
[2] Other than a power under s.4.
[3] s.19 contains provisions as to compensation.
[4] s.25(6).
[5] s.25(4).
[6] s.25(7).

summary conviction with a fine not exceeding level 3 on the standard scale, or up to three months imprisonment.[7]

Obstruction. Wilful obstruction is an offence punishable on summary conviction with a fine not exceeding level 3 on the standard scale.

3. Compulsory purchase

A general power to enter and survey land in which a local authority proposes to **9.54** acquire an interest, or over which it proposes to acquire a right is given by the Local Government (Miscellaneous Provisions) Act 1976, s.15.[8] The power is exercisable by a person authorised in writing in that behalf, at any reasonable time. The person must produce his authority, if required, before or after entry. In addition, if land is occupied, entry may not be demanded unless 14 days notice has been given.[9] The authorised person may take with him such other persons and such equipment as is necessary for the survey.

As well as the general power to survey, the authorised person may search and bore, in order to ascertain the nature of the subsoil or the presence of minerals.[10] Equipment for this purpose may be taken on to the land, but may only be left on or in the land, or removed, if not less than 14 days notice has been given to the owner of the land, and the occupier, if any.[11] If the land is unoccupied it must be left as secure against trespassers as it was found.

If as a result of a survey, a person interested in any land suffers damage, from the survey itself, the taking on to the land of persons or equipment, or the leaving of the land insecure against trespass, he is entitled to compensation from the local authority.[12] Disputes as to compensation are to be determined by the Lands Tribunal.[13]

Offences

Disclosure. Any person who discloses, other than in the course of his duty arising **9.55** out of the entry, any information obtained during the entry about a manufacturing process or trade secret, commits an offence, punishable on summary conviction with a fine not exceeding £1,000, and on indictment with a fine, or up to two years imprisonment, or both.[14]

Obstruction. It is an offence wilfully to obstruct the entry on to any land or the conduct of a survey under the above powers. It is also an offence to remove or

---

[7] s.25(9).

[8] This power does not apply where the local authority has a power to enter the land by virtue of s.64(1)(*d*) of the Highways Act 1971, or s.280(7) of the Town and Country Planning Act 1971 (see above, para. 9.50) or para. 20(1) of Sched. 4 to the Community Land Act 1975.

[9] s.15(3)(*c*).

[10] s.15(2).

[11] N.B. there are special provisions relating to land held by statutory undertakers s.15(3)(*e*)(ii), 15(3)(*f*), and 15(4).

[12] s.15(5).

[13] s.15(6).

[14] s.15(8).

interfere with apparatus left on or in land under this section. In each case the penalty on summary conviction is a fine not exceeding level 3 on the standard scale.[15]

Survey after compulsory purchase order made

Under section 11(3) of the Compulsory Purchase Act 1965 an acquiring authority, on giving between three and 14 days notice to the owners or occupiers, may enter any land subject to compulsory purchase, for the purpose of surveying it and taking levels. The compulsory purchase order must have taken effect for this power to arise, for it is only then that an authority becomes an "acquiring authority" under the Act.[16] Compensation for any damage must be paid by the authority, disputes being decided by the Lands Tribunal.

Urban development corporations

A person authorised in writing by an urban development corporation or an Officer of the Valuation Office of the Inland Revenue has power, on production if required of his authority, to enter land which the corporation proposes to purchase compulsorily, in order to survey or value it.[17] The power must be exercised at a reasonable time, and admission as of right to occupied land cannot be demanded unless 28 days notice is given. Similar notice is required if it is intended to use the powers under the section to search and bore (to ascertain the nature of the subsoil, or the presence of minerals) or to place or leave apparatus on the land (or remove it).[18] Unoccupied land must be left as secure against trespassers as it was found. Compensation for any damage is payable by the corporation,[19] with disputes going to the Lands Tribunal.[20]

National parks

A local authority has entry powers in relation to compulsory purchases under the National Parks and Access to the Countryside Act 1949, which is dealt with above, in Chapter Eight, para. 8.43.

4. Contravention of war-time regulations

9.56   Where land was outside a local planning authority's control during the war period by reason of a Crown interest in or on the land, a power of entry exists under the Building Restrictions (War-Time Contraventions) Act 1946 for five years after the disposal of the Crown's interest.[21] The power is exercisable by any officer of the authority authorised to act for the purposes of the section, and may be used,

---

[15] s.15(7).
[16] s.1(3).
[17] Local Government, Planning and Land Act 1980, s.167. Note that there are special provisions for land held by a local authority or statutory undertakers.
[18] s.167(3) and (4).
[19] s.167(8).
[20] s.167(9).
[21] s.5.

(a) to discover if there was a contravention of planning control or the building laws during the war years, or an unlawful use which dates from then; or

(b) to obtain information where an application has been made under section 2 of the Act for the local authority's sanction for war-time non-compliance with building laws or planning controls.

The entry may take place at all reasonable hours, but in relation to occupied premises 24 hours notice must be given before entry can be demanded as of right. The officer must, if required, produce some documentary evidence showing his authority to act for the purposes of the section.

Unauthorised disclosure of information on any manufacturing process or trade secret obtained in a factory, workshop, or workplace entered by an officer under this section is a summary offence punishable with a fine not exceeding level 3 on the standard scale, or imprisonment for up to three months. Wilful obstruction is a summary offence subject to a fine not exceeding level 1 on the standard scale.

5. Mineral Workings Act 1985

Under section 89 of the National Parks and Access to the Countryside Act 1949, a local authority has powers to reclaim or improve land that has been used for underground mining (other than for coal). An entry power in relation to this is given by section 7 of the Mineral Workings Act 1985.   **9.57**

The power is exercisable by any person duly authorised in writing by the local authority, in order to survey the land,[22] or carry out works on it.[23] Entry as of right may only be demanded if 10 clear days written notice of the intended entry has been given to every person who is an owner or occupier of the land.[24]

Alternatively a warrant may be obtained from a justice of the peace who is satisfied that there is reasonable ground for the entry, and that, either admission cannot, or will not be able to be, obtained, or that an owner or occupier entitled to notice cannot be identified or traced.[25] The justice must also be satisfied that the authority has taken all reasonable steps to inform all owners and occupiers of the intention to apply for a warrant. The warrant will authorise entry by force, if necessary, and will remain valid until the purpose for which entry is required has been satisfied.[26]

A person entering under section 7 must produce his authority if so required before entering, and may take with him such other persons and equipment as may be necessary.[27]

---

[22] Including the power to search and bore for the purpose of ascertaining the nature of the subsoil: s.7(4).

[23] s.7(3).

[24] s.7(5). The notice shall specify the purpose for which entry is required, and, if practicable, the nature of any intended works: s.7(6).

[25] s.7(7).

[26] s.7(8). More than one entry under the same warrant thus seems permissible.

[27] s.7(9).

The local authority must pay compensation for damage to land or chattels, or disturbance of their enjoyment, with disputes going to the Lands Tribunal.[28]

Intentional obstruction of a person entitled to enter land under section 7 is a summary offence, punishable with a fine not exceeding level 3 on the standard scale.[29]

H. Public Entertainments

1. Cinemas

9.58   The Cinemas Act 1985 applies to

> "any exhibitions of moving pictures which is produced otherwise than by the simultaneous reception and exhibition of—
>
> (a)   television programmes broadcast by the British Broadcasting Corporation or the Independent Broadcasting Authority, or
>
> (b)   programmes included in a cable programme service which is, or does not require to be, licensed under section 4 of the Cable and Broadcasting Act 1984."

Virtually all such exhibitions which are made for gain are subject to various controls. The Act does not, however, apply to "video games," because an "exhibition" here means something shown to an audience, not the display of moving objects on a television screen.[30] Powers of entry are given by section 13. In all cases the entrant must produce his authority if required to do so.

(a) *Entry without warrant*

An authorised officer of the local licensing authority or of the fire authority,[31] has power to enter and inspect premises if he has reasonable cause to believe that one of three circumstances exists:

(i)   that the premises are licensed under the Act, and are about to be used for an exhibition for which a licence is required; or

(ii)   that the premises are licensed under section 1 and are being used or are about to be used for a non-commercial exhibition within section 6; or

(iii) that notice in respect of the premises has been given under section 7 (occasional exhibitions), or section 8 (exhibitions in moveable buildings or structures), and that they are being or are about to be used for an exhibition which would otherwise have required a licence under section 1 of the Act.

---

[28] ss.7(11), (12), and (13).
[29] s.7(10).
[30] *British Amusement Catering Trades Associationv. Westminster City Council*[1988] 1 All E.R. 740 (H.L.). It would, however, appear to cover video cassettes or discs, shown on an ordinary television or projected, provided there was an "audience."
[31] Or a constable.

The power exists simply to enable the entrant to determine whether the relevant provisions of the Acts, regulations made under them, and any licence are being complied with.

In addition an authorised officer of a fire authority may enter any premises in respect of which, either a licence is in force, or notice has been given under section 7 or 8 of the Act, in order to inspect them to ensure that there are adequate fire precautions, and that any fire precautions required by statute or licence are being complied with. Twenty-four hours notice of the intention to exercise this power must be given to the occupier.

(b) *Entry under warrant*

An authorised officer of a licensing authority (or a constable) may obtain a warrant from a justice of the peace to enter and search any premises in respect of which he has reason to suspect that an offence under section 10(1) of the Act has been, is being, or is about to be committed. Section 10(1) is concerned with the use of premises without, or in breach of, any licence, consent, or other Regulations under the Act. Section 9(2) of the Police and Criminal Evidence Act 1984 applies to this power.[32]

Once on the premises the officer may seize and remove any apparatus, equipment, or other thing whatsoever, found there which he has reasonable cause to believe may be liable to be forfeited under section 11(2).[33] Section 11(2) allows a court to order the forfeiture of anything produced to it which relates to an offence under the Act.

(c) *Obstruction*

Intentional obstruction of the exercise of any of the above powers is a summary offence, subject to a fine not exceeding level 3 on the standard scale.

2. Clubs

A club supplying intoxicating liquor on club premises is required to be registered **9.59** under the Licensing Act 1964 (unless a justices' licence is held for the premises).[34] When there is a first application for a registration certificate, or an application for renewal in respect of different, additional, or enlarged premises,[35] the local authority has a power to enter and inspect under section 45. It is to be exercised by an authorised officer, not more than 14 days after the making of the application.[36] Forty-eight hours notice of the intended entry must be given to the person signing the application. The entry must take place at a reasonable time on the day specified in the notice. The officer must produce his authority on entry. Obstruction is a summary offence, subject to a fine not exceeding level 1 on the standard scale.

---

[32] See above, para. 3.28.
[33] s.14(2).
[34] s.39.
[35] s.45(4).
[36] This time limit may be extended by a magistrates court: s.45(3).

Fire authority

A fire authority has the right to inspect premises as regards fire risk on the same basis as outlined above. The fire authority's power, however, exists both on first registration and *any* subsequent renewal, not simply those renewals falling within section 45(4), above.[37]

3. Dancing and music

9.60   Schedule 1 to the Local Government (Miscellaneous Provisions) Act 1982 provides a licensing scheme as regards public dancing or music, or other entertainment "of a like kind."[38] Sports events to which the public are invited are also covered. But music in a place of public religious worship, or performed as an incident to a religious meeting or service, is outside the Act. Open air entertainments are generally outside the scheme, except that local authorities can resolve that the scheme should apply to musical events held on private land, presumably to enable them to deal with such things as "pop festivals."[39]

Powers of entry both with and without warrant are given by the schedule. Local authority officers, and fire officers, must in all cases produce their authority if required to do so by the occupier.[40]

(a) *Without warrant*

Under paragraph 14 of the Schedule, where an authorised officer of a local authority,[41] has reason to believe that an entertainment to which the Schedule applies is being or is about to be given, at a place for which an entertainment licence is in force, he may enter to check compliance with the licence.[42] Similarly, an authorised officer of a fire authority has a right to enter a place for which a licence is in force to inspect it to ensure that fire precautions are adequate, and that there is compliance with any terms of the licence relating to such precautions.[43] The fire officer must give not less than 24 hours' notice to the occupier before making such an entry.

(b) *Warrant*

A local authority officer (or a constable) may obtain a warrant from a justice of the peace to enter any place where he has reason to suspect that an offence under paragraph 12 of the Schedule is being committed. This paragraph concerns failure to have a licence when required, and breaking the terms of any licence. No powers

---

[37] s.46.

[38] Sched. 1. para. 1. In Greater London the similar provisions contained in the London Government Act 1963, s.52(3) and Sched. 12, apply.

[39] s.1(2), and Sched. 1, para. 3.

[40] s.14(4).

[41] Or an authorised officer of a fire authority, or a constable.

[42] This power has to be exercised at a reasonable time in London—London Government Act 1963, Sched. 12, para. 12.

[43] Para. 14(2). This power does not exist under the London Government Act 1963.

are given once entry has been obtained, *i.e.* there is no power to search the premises, or, unless by implication, to inspect them.

(c) *Obstruction*

Refusal to permit entry or inspection under the above powers is a summary offence, subject to a fine not exceeding level 3 on the standard scale.

4. Theatre

An authorised officer of a licensing authority, or a fire authority, on production if **9.61** so required of his authority, may at all reasonable times enter any premises licensed under the Theatres Act 1968 on which he has reason to believe that a performance of a play is being or is about to be given.[44] The premises may be inspected with a view to seeing whether the terms of the licence are being complied with.[45]

Wilful obstruction of such an officer is a summary offence, punishable with a fine not exceeding level 3 on the standard scale.[46]

I. Rates

The general method of recovering rates is by means of distress. They are not **9.62** recoverable simply by action.[47] The rules governing distress for rates are contained in the General Rate Act 1967, ss.96 to 107.

Once a demand for rates has been issued, the power to seek a distress warrant from the magistrates will arise after seven days.[48] There are special provisions for rates payable by instalments, which will be recoverable only as each instalment becomes due.[49] The application for a distress warrant must be made within six years of the date of the demand.[50]

Distress for rates may be levied on the occupier of a hereditament for which the owner is liable to pay rates, but only if the rates have been demanded in writing from the occupier, and the occupier has failed to pay within 14 days.[51] The amount which may be raised by the distress is limited to the amount due in rent by the occupier at the time of the distress, and the occupier is entitled to deduct the amount of rates for which distress is made, and the costs for the distress, from the rent payable to the owner.[52]

The local authority institutes proceedings by making a complaint before a justice of the peace for the issue of a summons to the person liable for the rate to appear before the magistrates. The person summoned may raise a number of objections,

---

[44] s.15(4). See s.12 for the licensing provisions, and s.18 for the definition of a "play."
[45] s.15(2).
[46] s.15(5). See also above, para. 4.46, for the police power of entry under s.15(3).
[47] *Liverpool Corporation* v. *Hope* [1938] 1 K.B. 751.
[48] s.96(1).
[49] s.96(2).
[50] *China* v. *Harrow U.D.C.* [1954] 1 Q.B. 178.
[51] s.62.
[52] *Ibid.*.

including a claim that he was not the person liable for the rates. This may be done even though he did not appeal against the initial assessment. In *Verrall* v. *London Borough of Hackney*,[53] the appellant was closely associated with, and an officer of, an unincorporated association which used certain premises. The Court of Appeal ruled that, although he had not appealed against the original demand for rates, the magistrates hearing the local authority's application for a distress warrant could listen to arguments that he was not liable. On the facts the court did not think that there was any real possibility that the appellant could be held to have been the exclusive occupier of the relevant property, and so no distress warrant was issued.

9.63   Apart from this, the grounds on which a person may object to the issue of a warrant seem to be governed by no discernible principle. There is authority, however for the following objections being allowable:

    (a) the property is not in the rating area[54];

    (b) the property is exempt for rates[55];

    (c) more than is due is being demanded[56];

    (d) the rates have already been paid[57];

There is no appeal against a decision to issue a distress warrant, except by way of case stated.[58]

The warrant, once issued, may be directed to the rating authority, the constables of the police area, and such other persons as the court may think fit. It will normally be executed by bailiffs employed by the rating authority, rather than the police. It may be executed anywhere in England and Wales. One warrant of distress may be issued against a number of persons in default.[59]

The manner in which the warrant is to be executed is not dealt with by the Act. It must be assumed that the bailiff (or whoever executes the warrant) will have the same powers of entry as with a distress for rent.[60] Once on the ratepayer's property the bailiff may seize any goods and chattels in the ratepayer's possession. The common law and statutory restrictions relating to tools, clothing, etc.,[61] do not apply here.[62] Goods which have been hired by a tenant may not, however, be taken.[63]

"Walking possession" is impliedly recognised by section 101, which provides for the making of charges for such possession.[64]

If the distress is insufficient to produce the sums directed to be levied under the

[53] [1983] 1 All E.R. 277, C.A.

[54] *Baglan Bay Tin Plate Co. Ltd.* v. *John* (1895) 72 L.T. 805.

[55] *Evans* v. *Brook* [1959] 2 All E.R. 399.

[56] *Pigg* v. *Tow Law Overseers (Weardale) Union* (1923) 22 L.G.R. 17 (D.C.).

[57] General Rate Act 1967, Sched. 12, forms C(1), C(2), and D.

[58] s.98.

[59] s.99(4). Sched. 12 contains a form of warrant appropriate to this situation, as well as one for a single distress.

[60] See above para. 5.35.

[61] See, *e.g.* para. 5.46.

[62] *Potts* v. *Hickman* [1941] A.C. 212.

[63] *Prudential Mortgage Company* v. *St. Marylebone B.C.* (1910) 8 L.G.R. 901.

[64] *cf.* para. 5.45.

Act, this may lead to the issue of a warrant for commitment.[65] The Act, however, makes no provision for the manner of disposal of property seized, other than that it is to be sold. There is no obligation to have the property valued,[66] to sell by auction, or to obtain the best price. Provided the property is disposed of in good faith there seems to be no way of challenging the authority's actions. Any surplus after payment of the sums owed should be returned to the person from whom the property was seized.

Of course, the distress can be avoided at any stage by paying the sums due, which may include costs and charges incurred up to that time.[67] If the distress is levied, however, the person aggrieved may appeal to the Crown Court (from which there is no further right of appeal).

If the distress was unlawful, there is also the possibility of an action for trespass. A defect or want of form in the rate, assessment, or warrant will not make the distress unlawful.[68] And an irregularity in the execution of the warrant, will not make the bailiff a trespasser *ab initio*, though any special damage caused by the irregularity itself may be recovered.[69]

J. Social Services

As a provider of social services, a local authority has entry powers in three areas, children, mental health, and residential homes. At times these powers will link in with those of the Departments of Health and Social Security dealt with in Chapter Eight. **9.64**

1. Children

(a) *Nurseries and Child-Minders Regulation Act 1948*

Control of nurseries and child-minders, as defined in section 1 of the Act, is given to the local social services authority,[70] and nurseries and child-minders must register with it. An authorised officer of the authority may at any reasonable time enter premises used as a nursery, or the home of a child-minder, and inspect it, the children, the arrangements for their welfare, and any records kept there.[71] **9.65**

Failure to register a nursery, or as a child-minder, is an offence, as is breach of the terms of registration.[72] If an authorised officer has reasonable cause to believe that children are being received into unregistered premises, or an unregistered home, he may obtain a warrant from a justice of the peace, who must have a similar belief, authorising entry and inspection of the premises or home.[73]

---

[65] ss.102 and 103. But see *R.v. Poole Justices*[1983] 2 All E.R. 897.
[66] Unless the ratepayer asks for it.
[67] s.105—and see *Brintons Ltd.* v. *Wyre Forest District Council* [1977] Q.B. 178.
[68] s.99(6).
[69] s.99(7).
[70] See Local Authority Social Services Act 1970.
[71] s.7(1).
[72] s.4.
[73] s.7(2).

In relation to both the above powers, the officer must produce documentary evidence of his authority if so requested.[74] Obstruction is a summary offence, punishable with a fine not exceeding level 2 on the standard scale.[75]

(b) *Adoption Act 1976*

Any officer of a local authority authorised to visit "protected children,"[76] may, on producing documentary evidence of his authority if required, inspect any premises in the area of the authority in which such children are, or are to be, kept.[77] A refusal to allow the officer to exercise this power is a summary offence, punishable with a fine not exceeding level 5 on the standard scale, or imprisonment for up to three months, or both.[78]

(c) *Child Care Act 1980*

9.66 **(i) Section 15 Orders.** The entry powers under section 15 of this Act apply in relation to children who are in care of a local authority (under s.2) or the subject of a resolution under section 3 (assumption by the local authority of parental rights and duties). A justice of the peace has power to order the production of such children before a magistrates' court.[79] Failure to comply with an order without reasonable excuse is a summary offence punishable with a fine not exceeding level 3 on the standard scale.

The justice of the peace may also, if satisfied by information on oath that there are reasonable grounds for believing that such a child is in specified premises, issue a warrant authorising a named officer of the local authority to search the premises for the child. If found, the child must be placed in accommodation provided by the local authority.[80]

(ii) Visiting children in voluntary homes. Local authorities have a duty to visit children in "voluntary homes" (other than community homes) in their area.[81] These homes are basically children's homes supported by voluntary contributions or endowments.[82] For this purpose an authorised person may enter any such home in the authority's area. There is also a power to enter homes outside the authority's area, in order to visit children who are in the care of the authority under section 2 of the Act, or section 23 of the Children and Young Persons Act 1969. The power does not apply to homes subject to inspection by a government department.[83] The officer must, if required, produce documentary evidence of his authority.[84] Obstruction of

[74] s.7(3).
[75] s.7(4).
[76] As defined in s.32.
[77] s.33(2). The Local Authority is under a duty to arrange such visits "from time to time"—s.33(1).
[78] N.B. also the Secretary of State's power under the Children and Young Persons Act 1969, s.58.
[79] s.15(2).
[80] s.15(3). N.B. also the powers of a constable under s.16.
[81] s.68(1).
[82] See s.56.
[83] s.68(3).
[84] s.68(4).

entry or inspection is a summary offence subject to a fine not exceeding level 2 on the standard scale.[85]

(d) *Foster Children Act 1980*

There are two powers of entry under this Act, enabling a local authority to inspect premises where foster children are living.

First, under section 8, an officer of a local authority authorised to visit foster children, on producing documentary evidence of his authority if required, may inspect any premises in the local authority's area, in the whole or part of which foster children are to be or are being kept.

Secondly, if a justice of the peace is satisfied on sworn information that there are reasonable grounds for believing that a foster child is being kept on any premises, and that a duly authorised officer has been refused admission to the premises (or the part where the child is kept), or such a refusal is apprehended, or the occupier is temporarily absent, he may issue a warrant authorising the local authority officer to enter the premises for the purpose of inspecting them. Force may be used, if necessary, but the entry must take place within 48 hours of the issue of the warrant, and at a reasonable time.[86]

Refusal to allow an inspection under section 8, or wilful obstruction of entry under a warrant, is an offence punishable on summary conviction with a fine not exceeding level 5 on the standard scale, or up to six months imprisonment, or both.[87]

2. Mental health

Under the Mental Health Act 1983 a local authority has responsibilities for the mentally disordered living in its area. Thus, if an approved social worker,[88] of a local social services authority has reasonable cause to suspect that a mentally disordered patient is not under proper care, he may, at any reasonable time, and on production if required of documentary evidence of his authority, enter and inspect any premises (other than a hospital) in the local authority's area in which the patient is living.[89] Refusal, without reasonable cause, to allow such an inspection is an offence, punishable on summary conviction with a fine not exceeding level 4 on the standard scale, or imprisonment for up to three months, or both.

9.67

The power of a police constable to enter under warrant, under section 135, is dealt with in Chapter Four, paragraph 4.28.

3. Residential homes

Section 17 of the Registered Homes Act 1984 contains entry powers in respect of "residential care homes," which are defined as,

9.68

   "residential accommodation with both board and personal care for persons in

[85] s.68(5).
[86] s.13(1).
[87] s.16(3).
[88] For which see s.114.
[89] s.115.

need of personal care by reason of old age, disablement, past or present dependence on drugs or alcohol or past or present mental disorder."[90]

A local authority, being a "registration authority,"[91] may authorise a person to enter and inspect at any time any premises in the area of the authority which are used, or which the authorised person has reasonable grounds to believe to be used, as a "residential care home."[92] The officer must produce documentary evidence of his authority if required, before entry or inspection.[93] The power to inspect specifically covers records required to be kept by Regulations.[94] The Secretary of State may by Regulations require inspections on certain occasions or at certain intervals.[95]

Obstruction is a summary offence, punishable with a fine not exceeding level 4 on the standard scale.[96]

K. Trading Standards

9.69 After environmental health inspectors, trading standards inspectors possess the most widely used entry powers among local authority officers. In this section the Weights and Measures Act 1985 is dealt with first, and then the other Acts under which entry powers are given, in chronological order.

1. Weights and Measures Act 1985

The power to enter premises under this Act is given by section 79. There are powers to enter both with and without warrant. They are given primarily to local weights and measures inspectors, but an inspector may take with him such other persons and equipment as may appear to him to be necessary.

(a) *Entry without warrant*

An inspector may, within the area for which he was appointed inspector, at all reasonable times enter any premises (other than premises used solely as a private dwelling-house) on which he has reasonable cause to believe there are certain items. These items are any weighing or measuring equipment which is, or which the inspector has reasonable cause to believe to be used for trade, and any goods to which any of the provisions of the Act (or any instrument made under it) apply.[97] The inspector must, if so required, produce his credentials before entry.

(b) *Entry under warrant*

In certain circumstances an inspector can obtain a warrant to enter premises from

---

[90] s.1.
[91] As defined in s.20(1).
[92] s.17(2). The Secretary of State may also authorise similar entry and inspection.
[93] s.17(5).
[94] s.17(3).
[95] s.17(4).
[96] s.17(6).
[97] s.79(1).

a justice of the peace. The inspector must provide a sworn information in writing and the justice must be satisfied that there is reasonable ground to believe that there are on the premises goods or equipment of the type mentioned above, or articles liable to forfeiture under the Act, or documents or goods which may be required as evidence in proceedings for an offence under the Act. The justice must also be satisfied of the existence of one of the following circumstances:

(i) that admission to the premises has been refused, or is expected, and that notice of the intention to apply for a warrant has been given to the occupier;

(ii) that an application for admission, or the giving of such notice, would defeat the object of the entry;

(iii) that the case is one of urgency;

(iv) that the premises are unoccupied, or the occupier temporarily absent.

The warrant will be valid for one month, and will permit the use of force to enter the premises, if necessary.[98] Premises entered under a warrant must be left as secure against trespassers as they were found.[99]

(c) *Powers on entry*

(i) Inspection and testing. The inspector may inspect and test any weighing or measuring equipment which is, or which he has reasonable cause to believe to be, used for trade, or in the possession of any person or upon any premises for such use.[1] He may also inspect any goods which are, or which he has reasonable cause to believe to be, goods to which any of the provisions of the Act, or any instrument made under it, applies.[2]   **9.70**

An inspector also has the power under section 38 to require a person making representations as to the quantity of goods which he is offering or exposing for sale, or having in his possession goods which have been sold but not delivered, to weigh or measure the goods, or the containers in which the goods are made up, or to allow the inspector to do so. The inspector may also require goods to be sold to him.

Containers or vending machines may be broken open, if necessary.[3] If the breaking of a container does not reveal any breach of the Act, and it is not resealed, or cannot be resealed without injury to the contents, the inspector may be required to buy the goods on behalf of the weights and measures authority.[4]

(ii) Seizure. Under section 79 the inspector, on production if required of his credentials, may seize and detain any article which he has reasonable cause to believe to be liable to forfeiture under the Act, and documents or goods which he has reason to believe may be required as evidence in proceedings for an offence under the Act.

[98] s.79(3).
[99] s.79(6).
[1] s.79(1)(*a*).
[2] s.79(1)(*b*).
[3] s.38(1).
[4] s.38(2). None of the powers under s.38 may be used in relation to milk, except while the milk is on premises for the time being registered in pursuance of Milk and Dairies Regulations made under the Food and Drugs Act 1955.

Under section 39 an inspector has power to require the production of, and to seize and detain, certain documents. First, where any document is required by or under the Act to be associated with any goods, the inspector may, on production of his credentials, require the person in charge of the document to produce it for inspection.[5] If, when the document is produced, the inspector has reasonable cause to believe that it contains any inaccurate statement, he may seize and detain it. If he does so he must give in exchange a copy, signed by him, certifying the seizure, and specifying the alleged inaccuracy.[6] Alternatively he may endorse the document with details of the inaccuracy, without seizing it.[7]

(d) *Offences*

9.71   **(i) Disclosure.** A person who enters a workplace under section 79 commits an offence if he discloses to any person, other than in the performance of his duty, information obtained by him in the workplace with regard to any secret manufacturing process or trade secret. The penalty is, on summary conviction a fine not exceeding £1,000, or on indictment a fine, or up to two years imprisonment, or both.[8]

(ii) Obstruction. An offence is committed by a person who wilfully obstructs an inspector, wilfully fails to comply with a requirement under sections 38, 39, or 40, or fails, without reasonable cause, to give any other assistance or information which the inspector may reasonably require of him.[9] The privilege against self-incrimination is specifically preserved,[10] but otherwise a person commits an offence if he provides information which he knows to be false.[11] The penalty for an offence under section 80 or 81 is, on summary conviction, a fine not exceeding level 5 on the standard scale.

2. Trade Descriptions Act 1968

9.72   Section 28 of this Act gives powers of entry, with or without warrant, to duly authorised officers of local weights and measures authorities or of Government departments. In practice the powers are almost exclusively used by local officials. They may take with them such other persons and such equipment as may appear to them to be necessary.[12]

(a) *Entry without warrant*

The power exists in relation to any premises which are not used only as a

---

[5] s.39(1).
[6] s.39(2).
[7] N.B. The power to "check-weigh" goods loaded on road vehicles, under s.40. An inspector has no power to stop a vehicle on a highway—s.79(9).
[8] s.84(5).
[9] ss.80, 81.
[10] s.81(3).
[11] s.81(2).
[12] s.28(4).

dwelling.[13] It must be exercised at a reasonable hour, and the officer must produce his credentials, if so required. The purpose for which the power is given is to ascertain whether any offence under the Trade Descriptions Acts 1968 and 1972 has been committed. There is no need for "reasonable suspicion," so the power may quite legitimately be used for "spot-checks."

(b) *Entry under warrant*

A justice of the peace, on sworn information in writing, may issue a warrant authorising an officer to enter any premises, provided he is satisfied either that there are reasonable grounds to believe that items which the officer has power to inspect are on the premises, and that their inspection is likely to disclose evidence of the commission of an offence, or that some offence under the Act has been, is being, or is about to be committed on the premises. He must also be satisfied of the existence of one of the four circumstances outlined in paragraph 9.69 (above). The warrant remains valid for one month. Premises unoccupied, or from which the occupier is temporarily absent at the time of the entry under warrant, must be left as secure against trespassers as they were found.[14]

(c) *Powers on entry*

(i) **Production of documents, etc.** A person carrying on a business may be **9.73** required to produce books or documents relating to it.[15] This power is dependent on the officer having reasonable cause to suspect that an offence under the Trade Descriptions Acts has been committed. Items produced may be copied, but this section does not give any power to remove originals.[16] Legal privilege justifying the non-production of documents held by a solicitor is specifically recognised.[17]

(ii) **Seizure of goods and documents.** Where an officer has reasonable cause to believe that an offence under the Act has been committed, he may seize and detain any goods for the purpose of ascertaining by testing, or otherwise, whether this is so.[18] He may also seize goods or documents which he has reason to believe may be required as evidence in proceedings under the Act.[19]

The relationship between the power to demand production of documents (under s.28(1)(*b*)) and seizure (under s.28(1)(*d*)) was carefully considered by the Divisional Court in *Barge* v. *British Gas Corporation*.[20] As part of a "low-key" investigation, a trading standards officer wished to remove some documents, leaving copies with the defendants. The defendants refused to comply with this request, and were charged with obstruction. The Divisional Court ruled, however, that section 28(1)(*b*) gave

---

[13] s.28(1).
[14] s.28(4).
[15] s.28(1)(*b*).
[16] *Barge* v. *British Gas Corporation* (1982) 81 L.G.R. 53.
[17] s.28(1).
[18] s.28(1)(*c*).
[19] s.28(1)(*d*).
[20] (1982) 81 L.G.R. 53.

no power to demand the handing over of the documents so that they could be removed, and that the power of "seizure" under section 28(1)(*d*) required something more than a mere request to hand the document over. An attempt, at least, to take physical possession of the item (though this need not involve the use of any "excessive degree of force")[21] was necessary to indicate that the officer was exercising his seizure powers. Consequently the defendant in the case was not wilfully obstructing the officer in refusing to hand over the documents, nor was he failing to comply with a requirement properly made, since there was no power to "require" anything more than the "production" of the documents.

Section 28 gives an additional power as regards containers, or vending machines. In order to exercise his powers to seize goods the officer may, if reasonably necessary, require any person having authority to do so to break open any container or vending machine. If the person fails to do so, the officer may break it open himself.[22]

The officer has a duty to inform any person from whom items are seized. In the case of a vending machine, the person whose name and address is stated on the machine as being the proprietor should be informed, or in default, the owner of the premises on which the machine stands or to which it is affixed.[23]

(d) *Testing of goods*

9.74 If goods which have been seized are submitted to a test, the officer must inform the person mentioned in the preceding paragraph of the result of the test. Where as a result of tests proceedings are instituted against any person, that person must be allowed to have the goods tested on his own behalf, if practicable.[24]

(e) *Compensation*

The owner of goods who suffers loss because of the seizure and detention of them, or because of their consequent loss, damage, or deterioration, is entitled to compensation, unless convicted of an offence under the Act in relation to the goods.[25] Disputes as to the amount of any compensation are to be determined by arbitration.

(f) *Offences*

9.75 **(i) Disclosure.** It is an offence for a person to disclose information obtained in pursuance of the Act, and for a person entering premises under section 28 to disclose any information relating to any manufacturing process or trade secret obtained in the premises, unless the disclosure was made as part of his functions under the Act,[26] or for a purpose specified in section 174(3) of the Consumer Credit Act 1974.[27] This provision was added to protect officers giving evidence in proceedings to which they

---

[21] *Ibid.* 59.
[22] s.28(1)(*e*).
[23] s.28(2).
[24] s.30(1).
[25] s.33(1).
[26] s.18(5).
[27] s.28(5A).

were not a party. The penalty for this offence is on summary conviction a fine of up to £1,000, or on indictment, a fine or up to two years imprisonment, or both.

(ii) Obstruction. It is an offence under section 29(1) wilfully to obstruct an officer, or wilfully to fail to comply with a requirement properly made under section 28, or to fail without reasonable cause to give an officer any assistance or information which he may reasonably require for the performance of his functions under the Act.

The penalty is a fine not exceeding level 3 on the standard scale.

It is also an offence knowingly to make a false statement in giving information,[28] though the privilege against self-incrimination is specifically preserved.[29] In this case the penalty is, on summary conviction a fine not exceeding £1,000, or on indictment, a fine, or up to two years imprisonment, or both.

(g) *Motor fuel*

Sections 27 to 30, and 33 of the Trade Descriptions Act 1968 are specifically applied by section 75 of the Control of Pollution Act 1974, which relates to the content and composition of motor fuel. **9.76**

(h) *Video recordings*

By virtue of section 162 of the Criminal Justice Act 1988, local weights and measures officers can use the powers in sections 27 to 33 of the Trade Descriptions Act 1968 to enforce the provisions of the Video Recordings Act 1984.

3. Fair Trading Act 1973

Local trading standards officers have a power of entry under section 29 of the Fair Trading Act in relation to the control of offences under section 23 of the Act. Sections 29 to 32 are virtually identical to sections 28 to 30 and 33 of the Trade Descriptions Act 1968, and are therefore not discussed in detail again. The only change of significance is the substitution throughout of references to offences under section 23 of the Fair Trading Act for references to offences under the Trade Descriptions Act. **9.77**

4. Consumer Credit Act 1974

Section 162 of this Act gives power of entry, with or without warrant, to trading standards officers, in very similar terms to section 28 of the Trade Descriptions Act 1968. In a limited number of situations, mainly concerned with bank records, the permission of the Director General of Fair Trading is required.[30] In 1982 only four such applications were made, and only one granted.[31] An officer entering under this section may take with him such other persons and equipment as he thinks necessary. **9.78**

(a) *Entry without warrant*

An officer may, at all reasonable hours, enter any premises other than those used **9.79**

---

[28] s.29(2).
[29] s.29(3).
[30] s.162, and the Consumer Credit (Entry and Inspection) Regulations 1977 (S.I. 1977 No. 331).
[31] Ninth Annual Report of the Director General, Pt. 2.

only as a dwelling. He must if required produce his credentials. The power is given in order to ascertain whether there has been a breach of the Act, but, as with the Trade Descriptions Act (above, paragraph 9.72) its availability does not depend on the officer having a suspicion, reasonable or otherwise, of any offence.

(b) *Entry under warrant*

The power of entry under warrant is given in identical terms to the Trade Descriptions Act 1968, s.28(3), with the substitution of references to the Consumer Credit Act for the Trade Descriptions Act.[32] There is a similar obligation to leave unoccupied premises secure against trespassers.[33]

(c) *Powers on entry*

Once lawfully on the premises the officer has the following powers:

(i) Inspection. He may inspect any goods to ascertain whether there has been a breach of the Act.[34]

(ii) Production of documents etc. If he has reasonable cause to suspect that a breach of the Act has been committed, in order to ascertain whether this is so, he may require any person carrying on or employed in connection with a business to produce any books or documents relating to it. Where information relating to a business is recorded otherwise than in a legible form (*e.g.* electronically on disks, or tape) the person in control of the information may be required to provide a document containing a legible reproduction of the whole or any part of the information.

Any books or documents produced may be copied, in whole or in part, but this subsection does not entitle the officer to take away originals.

(iii) Seizure. The officer, if he has reasonable cause to believe that a breach of the Act has been committed, may seize and detain any goods in order to ascertain, by testing or otherwise, if this is so.[35] He may also seize and detain any goods, books, or documents which he has reason to believe may be required as evidence in proceedings for an offence under the Act.[36]

If necessary for securing that the Act is duly observed, the officer may, in connection with his power to seize, require any person having authority to do so to break open any container. If that person fails to comply, the officer may break it open himself.[37]

Nothing may be seized without informing the person from whom the goods, etc.,

---

[32] See above, para. 9.72
[33] s.162(4); *cf.* Trade Descriptions Act s.28(4), above, para. 9.72.
[34] s.162(1)(*a*).
[35] s.162(1)(*c*).
[36] s.162(1)(*d*).
[37] s.162(1)(*e*).

are seized.[38] Legally privileged documents held by a solicitor or barrister cannot be required to be produced, nor seized.[39]

(d) *Testing of goods*

Any goods seized may be tested, and the person from whom they were seized must **9.80** be informed of the results.[40] If the test leads to proceedings, the defendant must be allowed to have the goods tested on his behalf, if it is reasonably practicable to do so.[41]

(e) *Compensation*

The owner of goods which have been seized or detained under the Act is entitled, unless convicted of an offence under the Act in relation to the goods, to compensation for any loss resulting from the seizure, or from loss, damage, or deterioration of the goods during detention. Any dispute as to compensation is to be determined by arbitration.[42]

(f) *Obstruction*

It is an offence, punishable on summary conviction with a fine not exceeding level 4 on the standard scale,

(i)   wilfully to obstruct an officer;
(ii) wilfully to fail to comply with a requirement properly made under section 162;
(iii) without reasonable cause to fail to give an officer any other assistance or information he may reasonably require.

It is also an offence knowingly to give false information,[43] but the privilege against self-incrimination is specifically preserved.[44] The penalty for giving false information is, on summary conviction a fine of up to £1,000, and on indictment, a fine, or up to two years imprisonment, or both.

5. Aerosol Dispensers (EEC Requirements) Regulations 1977[45]

These Regulations, made under the European Communities Act 1972, s.2(2), are **9.81** intended to give effect to the Council Directive No. 75/324/EEC. They give entry powers, both with and without warrant, to local weights and measures officials, in a form similar to those outlined above under the Weights and Measures Act, etc. In all

---

[38] s.162(2).
[39] s.162(7).
[40] s.164(3).
[41] s.164(4)(*b*).
[42] s.163.
[43] s.165(2).
[44] s.165(3).
[45] S.I. 1977 No. 1140.

cases the official entering may take with him such other persons and equipment as may appear to him to be necessary.[46]

(a) *Entry without warrant*

An official, authorised in writing by the local weights and measures authority in that behalf, may enter any premises on which he has reasonable cause to believe unfilled containers marked or intended to be marked with a reversed epsilon in accordance with the Regulations, are being filled, or that aerosol dispensers so marked which have previously been sold in the United Kingdom are being stored with a view to sale. The power may be used for the purpose of determining whether an offence has been committed under the Regulations.[47] It does not extend to premises used as a private dwelling. The exclusion is not limited in this case to premises used *only* as a private dwelling; premises used partly for business, but also used as living accommodation would seem to be excluded.[48] The entry under this provision may take place at all reasonable hours, on production, if required of the official's authorisation.

(b) *Entry under warrant*

To issue a warrant, a justice of the peace must be satisfied, on sworn information in writing, that there is reasonable ground to believe:

(i) that any goods liable to inspection and test under regulation 5 are on any premises, and that their inspection or testing is likely to disclose evidence of the commission of an offence under the Regulations; or

(ii) that an offence under the Regulations has been, is being, or is about to be committed on the premises.[49]

The justice must also be satisfied of one of the other conditions, as specified in the Weights and Measures Act 1985, s.79.[50] Force may be used, if necessary, to effect entry, but unoccupied premises must be left as secure against trespassers as they were found.[51]

(c) *Powers on entry*

9.82   The official may inspect any aerosol dispensers or any article which he has reasonable cause to believe to be an aerosol dispenser.[52] As part of his investigation into whether an offence has been committed he may inspect any goods, and test aerosol dispensers and unfilled containers, which are marked, or which he has reasonable cause to believe will be marked, with the reversed epsilon. He may also

---

[46] Reg. 5(5).
[47] Reg. 5(1).
[48] See above, para. 1.28.
[49] Reg. 5(4).
[50] See above, para. 9.69.
[51] Reg. 5(5).
[52] Reg. 5(1).

select batches of such containers or dispensers, to test samples in accordance with section 6.2.1. of the Annex to the Directive. The officer can require the filler of the containers, or the person on whose premises they are stored for sale, to provide such reasonable facilities as appear to the officer to be necessary to determine whether dispensers or containers comply with the Regulations.[53] To fail to do so is an offence, punishable on summary conviction with a fine not exceeding £400.[54]

The official may remove the containers in order to conduct the tests elsewhere, if he considers that there are inadequate facilities on the premises. Wherever the tests are carried out, the officer must, as soon as reasonably practicable, notify the person on whose premises the containers were found of the results of the tests. Until then, no container from the batch being tested may be filled, sold or supplied.[55] To do so is an offence, as is to fill, sell or supply any container marked with a reversed epsilon taken from a batch which has failed a test.[56] In each case the offence is summary. On first conviction the penalty is a fine not exceeding £2,000, with the alternative, or the addition, of up to three months imprisonment.[57]

(d) *Offences*

(i) Disclosure. Disclosure by any person, other than in the performance of his **9.83** duty, of any information obtained in a workplace which the person entered under these Regulations, relating to any manufacturing process or trade secret, is an offence, punishable as the offence under the preceding paragraph.[58]

(ii) Obstruction. Wilful obstruction of an officer is an offence, as is failing, without reasonable cause, to give the officer any assistance or information he may reasonably require in the exercise of his powers.[59] It is punishable on summary conviction with a fine not exceeding £20.[60] Unlike most of the other provisions relating to Trading Standards officers, legal privilege, and the privilege against self-incrimination, are not covered here.

6. Energy Conservation Act 1981

Part I of this Act gives the Secretary of State a power to make orders concerning **9.84** heat generators and gas appliances. Local weights and measures authorities are given the job of enforcing such orders.[61] An enforcement officer (*i.e.* a weights and measures officer, or a duly authorised officer of a government department) may, on production if required of his credentials, enter any premises not used only as a dwelling. Entry may be at any reasonable time, in order to ascertain whether an

---

[53] Reg. 5(1)(ii).
[54] Reg. 11(1).
[55] Reg. 5(2).
[56] Reg. 11.
[57] Reg. 11(2).
[58] Reg. 11(2).
[59] Reg. 6.
[60] Reg. 11(1).
[61] s.20.

offence under an order has been committed.[62] On entry, the officer may inspect any appliance, and relevant instructions or documents. If he has reasonable cause to believe that an offence has been committed, or that the items may be required as evidence, he may seize them. In this connection he may, if reasonably necessary, require containers to be broken open, and if this is not done, break them open himself.

The Officer may also demand the production of and take copies from, books or documents relating to a trade or business, in order to confirm or negate his reasonably held suspicion that an offence has been committed. Barristers and solicitors cannot be compelled to produce privileged communications, nor can such items be seized, under the powers in this section.

There is also a power of entry under warrant where a justice of the peace is satisfied by a sworn information in writing that an offence has been, is being, or is about to be committed on any premises, or that there is reasonable ground to believe that examination of appliances, etc., on any premises is likely to disclose evidence of the commission of an offence. The justice must also be satisfied that admission has been or is likely to be refused, and that notice of the intention to apply for a warrant has been given, or that an application for admission or giving notice would defeat the object of the entry, or that the premises are unoccupied, or that the occupier is temporarily absent and it would defeat the object of the entry to await his return. The warrant will be valid for one month, and will authorise entry by force, if necessary.

An officer entering with or without a warrant, may take with him such other persons and equipment as may appear to him to be necessary. Unoccupied premises entered under a warrant must be left as secure against trespassers as they were found.

Disclosure (other than in the performance of functions under the Act) of trade secrets or other information obtained through the above powers, is an offence punishable on summary conviction with a fine not exceeding the statutory maximum, or on indictment, with imprisonment for up to two years, or a fine, or both.

It is an offence under section 22, punishable on summary conviction with a fine not exceeding level 3 on the standard scale, wilfully to obstruct an officer, wilfully to fail to comply with a requirement properly made by an officer, or without reasonable cause to fail to give an officer any other assistance or information which he may reasonably require for the performance of his duties.

If a person giving information as mentioned above under section 20, knowingly or recklessly makes a statement which is false in a material particular, he is guilty of an offence punishable on summary conviction with a fine not exceeding the statutory maximum, and on indictment with a fine. The privilege against incrimination of oneself or one's spouse is specifically preserved.

Section 24 provides that the owner of seized goods who suffers loss because they are lost, damaged, or deteriorate during detention, may obtain compensation from

---

[62] The Secretary of State has entry powers in respect of Part II Orders (On-site testing), under s.21.

the local authority, unless he is convicted of an offence in relation to the goods. Disputes as to compensation are to be determined by arbitration.

7. Consumer Protection Act 1987

9.85

This Act is the United Kingdom government's attempt to give effect to the European Commission's Directive on Product Liability.[63] Part II is concerned with safety, and Part III with misleading price indications. The enforcement provisions in Part IV, which will generally be exercised by local trading standards officers, include powers of entry both with and without warrant. In either case, the officer entering the premises may take with him such other persons and such equipment as may appear to him to be necessary.[64]

(a) *Entry without warrant*

Under section 29 an officer may enter any premises other than premises occupied only as a person's residence. The entry may take place at any reasonable hour, on production, if required, of the officer's credentials. The purpose for which entry is permitted is to ascertain whether there has been any contravention of any safety provision, or any provision made by or under Part III of the Act (hereinafter "the relevant provisions").

(b) *Entry under warrant*

A warrant to enter premises may be issued if a justice of the peace is satisfied by information on oath that there are reasonable grounds for believing that goods or records which an officer has power to inspect under section 29 are on the premises, and that such inspection is likely to disclose evidence of a contravention of the relevant provisions, or that such a contravention has taken place, is taking place, or is about to take place, on the premises. He must also be satisfied that:

(i) admission to the premises has been or is likely to be refused, and that notice of intention to apply for a warrant has been given to the occupier; or
(ii) an application for admission, or the giving of notice, would defeat the object of the entry; or
(iii) the premises are unoccupied; or
(iv) the occupier is temporarily absent and it might defeat the object of the entry to await his return.

The warrant will authorise entry by force if necessary, and will continue in force for one month. Premises entered under a warrant must, if unoccupied or if the occupier is temporarily absent, be left as secure against trespassers as they were found.

[63] 85/374/EEC.
[64] s.30(3).

(c) *Powers on entry*

9.86

    (i) **Inspection and examination.** The officer may inspect any goods to ascertain whether the relevant provisions have been contravened.[65] He may also examine any procedure (including any arrangements for carrying out a test) connected with the production of goods to see if there has been any contravention of a safety provision.[66]

    (ii) **Production and seizure.** If the officer has reasonable cause to suspect that relevant provisions have been contravened he has two further powers. First he may require any person carrying on a business or employed in connection with a business to produce any books or documents relating to it.[67] The officer may take copies of any books or documents produced, or of any entry therein. Secondly, the officer may seize and detain any goods for the purpose of ascertaining, by testing or otherwise, if the provisions have been contravened.

A further seizure power exists as regards goods and documents which the officer has reason to believe may be required as evidence in proceedings for an offence in respect of a contravention of the relevant provisions.[68] The person from whom items are seized must be informed of this fact by the officer seizing them.[69]

An appeal against the detention of seized goods can be made to the magistrates court.[70]

(d) *Tests*

Where seized goods are subjected to a test the officer must inform the person from whom they were seized of the result of that test. If proceedings are instituted as a result of the test, the defendant must be allowed to have the goods tested, if it is practicable.[71]

(e) *Compensation*

Any person having an interest in seized goods, who suffers loss because they are lost or damaged as a result of the exercise of powers under section 29, may obtain compensation from the authority, provided there has been no contravention of the relevant provisions in relation to the goods, and the exercise of the power is not attributable to the fault or neglect of the claimant.[72] Disputes as to compensation are to be determined by arbitration.

(f) *Offences*

    (i) **Unlawful entry.** Any person who is not an officer of an enforcement

---

[65] s.29(2).
[66] s.29(3).
[67] s.29(5).
[68] s.29(6).
[69] s.30(1).
[70] s.33.
[71] s.30(6).
[72] s.34.

authority, who purports to act as such under section 29 or 30 commits a summary offence, punishable with a fine not exceeding level 5 on the standard scale.[73]

(ii) **Obstruction.** It is an offence punishable on summary conviction with a fine not exceeding level 5 on the standard scale intentionally to obstruct an officer, intentionally to fail to comply with a requirement properly made by an officer, or without reasonable cause to fail to give an officer any other assistance or information which he may reasonably require for the performance of his functions.[74]

If a person giving information as mentioned above, knowingly or recklessly makes a statement which is false in a material particular, he is guilty of an offence punishable on summary conviction with a fine not exceeding £1,000, and on indictment with a fine.

II. PUBLIC UTILITIES

A. Electricity

All powers of entry of the Electricity Boards are regulated by the Rights of Entry (Gas and Electricity Boards) Act 1954.[75] The effect of the Act is that no right or power of entry may be exercised in respect of a building or part of a building except with the consent of the occupier, or under a warrant granted under the Act, or in an emergency.[76] An "emergency" arises for the purposes of the Act when a person attempting to exercise a lawful right of entry to which the Act applies has reasonable cause to believe that circumstances exist which are likely to endanger life or property, and that immediate entry to the premises is necessary to verify the existence of those circumstances or to ascertain their cause or to effect a remedy.[77] A simple refusal of admission to a person who seeks to exercise a right of entry to which the Act applies without a warrant is deemed not to be "obstruction."[78]

9.87

Section 2 of the Act provides a procedure for obtaining a warrant. A justice of the peace must be satisfied, on sworn information in writing, that admission to specified premises is reasonably required for the purpose stated in the information, that the Board would, apart from the Act, be entitled to exercise a power of entry, and that any requirements of the Act giving the power of entry have been complied with.[79] In addition the justice must be satisfied that notice of the intended entry has been given to the occupier under the Act giving the power of entry, or that admission was sought after not less than 24 hours notice, or was refused in a case of emergency, or that the

[73] s.30(5).
[74] s.32(1).
[75] Passed in response to the decision in *Grove* v. *Eastern Gas Board* [1952] 1 K.B. 77, see above, para. 1.15.
[76] s.1(1).
[77] s.3(3).
[78] s.1(3).
[79] s.2(1).

premises are unoccupied, or that an application for admission would defeat the object of the entry.[80]

A warrant issued under section 2 will authorise entry by force if necessary, and will continue in effect until the purpose for which entry is required has been satisfied.[81] Unoccupied premises must be left as secure against trespassers as they were found.[82] Compensation and obstruction provisions under the Act granting the right of entry for which the warrant is sought have effect in relation to entry under the warrant.[83]

Two statutes give powers of entry to Electricity Boards, the Electric Lighting Act 1882 and the Electricity Act 1957.

1. Inspection

9.88   The most general power is given by section 24 of the Electric Lighting Act 1882. This empowers any officer appointed by the Board to enter at all reasonable times any premises to which electricity is or has been supplied by the Board. The purposes for which the power may be used are:

(a) to inspect lines or meters belonging to, or let by hire by, the Board;
(b) to ascertain the quantity of electricity consumed or supplied (*e.g.* by reading meters);
(c) to remove items, where supply is no longer required, or the Board is authorised to cut off the supply.

As regards the last purpose, section 53 of the Schedule to the Electric Lighting (Clauses) Act 1899 requires that 48 hours written notice of an intention to disconnect a meter be given. Failure to do so is a summary offence, punishable with a fine not exceeding level 2 on the standard scale. All damage caused by an entry and inspection under section 24 must be made good by the Board.

2. Survey

9.89   Section 35 of the Electricity Act 1957 gives a person duly authorised in writing by an Electricity Board the power to enter, at all reasonable times, any land, and survey it for the purpose of ascertaining whether the land would be suitable for the purposes of any functions of the Board. The power may not be used in respect of land covered by buildings or used as a garden or pleasure ground.[84]

Sections 280(9) (power to search and bore), 281(1) (production of authority and notice of entry), 281(2) (obstruction), and 281(6) (notice of intention to bore) of the Town and Country Planning Act 1971 apply to this power.[85] In the requirements for notice, however, under section 281(1), a period of 28 days is substituted for 24 hours,

---

[80] s.2(2). Notice under this section must be given according to the procedures in s.63 of the Electricity Act 1947 (or s.44 of the Gas Act 1972 in the case of the British Gas Corporation).
[81] s.2(4).
[82] s.2(5).
[83] s.2(6).
[84] So the Rights of Entry (Gas and Electricity Boards) Act 1954 will not in practice apply to this power.
[85] See above, para. 9.50.

and the power to bore relates only to the nature of the subsoil, and not to the presence of minerals.

It was an attempt by the Central Electricity Generating Board to exercise this power which lead to the case of *R.* v. *Chief Constable of Devon and Cornwall, ex p. Central Electricity Generating Board.*[86]

B. Gas

All the powers of entry of public gas suppliers are subject to the Rights of Entry (Gas and Electricity Boards) Act 1954, which is discussed above (paragraph 9.87) in relation to electricity. It applies in exactly the same way here, with the substitution of references to "a public gas supplier" for references to the Boards. Public gas suppliers have more powers of entry than the Electricity Boards, but they cover similar areas. **9.90**

Schedule 5 to the Gas Act 1986 constitutes the "Public Gas Supply Code," and various entry powers are given under it. All the powers are subject to paragraph 18.[87] These state that an officer may be accompanied by such persons as may be necessary or expedient, and that premises entered must be left as secure as they were found. Damage must be made good, or compensation paid.

Intentional obstruction is a summary offence, punishable with a fine not exceeding level 3 on the standard scale.

1. Inspection

Under paragraph 15 of Schedule 5 to the Gas Act 1986, any officer authorised by a public gas supplier may at all reasonable times enter any premises in which there is a service pipe connected with the supplier's gas main. The officer must produce some documentary evidence of his authority.[88] The purposes for which this power may be used are the inspection of meters, fittings, and works, and ascertaining the quantity of gas consumed or supplied, *e.g.* by reading a meter. The power of entry lapses if the occupier has applied in writing for the disconnection of the pipe and the supplier has failed to disconnect it within a reasonable time. Paragraph 15 may also be used to enter in order to maintain service pipes,[89] alter burners, remove, inspect and re-install meters,[90] remove, test, and replace appliances required to be kept in use,[91] or inspect premises where the supplier has reason to believe that a compressor, compressed air or extraneous gas is being used.[92] **9.91**

2. Disconnections

A supplier is given power under paragraph 17 of Schedule 5 to disconnect a gas **9.92**

---

[86] [1982] Q.B. 458. See para. 1.29.
[87] As well as the 1954 Act.
[88] Unless there is no one to whom it may be produced: *Grove* v. *Eastern Gas Board* [1952] 1 K.B. 77.
[89] Paras. 1 and 2.
[90] Para. 4(3).
[91] Para. 8(7).
[92] Para. 15(1)(*e*).

supply for non-payment. Seven days written notice of their intention to do so must be given. A power of entry to enable them to carry out a disconnection is given by paragraph 16. It may also be used to disconnect a supply at the consumer's request, or to remove pipes, metres, fittings, or apparatus belonging to the supplier from premises where gas has been supplied, but a person entering occupation does not take a supply.

The power may be exercised by an officer authorised by the supplier. He must give 24 hours written notice to the occupier, or the owner or lessee of unoccupied premises. If the owner or lessee is unknown and unascertainable by diligent inquiry, the notice must be fixed to a conspicuous part of the premises, not less than 48 hours before entry.[93]

3. Safety

9.93   Paragraph 13 of Schedule 5 also has an entry provision related to safety. Paragraph 13(4) empowers an authorised officer to enter any premises in which the supplier has reasonable cause to suspect that gas is escaping, or may escape. The officer may inspect the gas fittings and carry out any work necessary to prevent the escape, and take any other steps necessary to avert danger to life or property. Where the supplier has reasonable cause to believe that escaped gas has entered, or may enter, any premises, an officer may enter those premises and take similar steps to safeguard life or property. The provision of paragraphs 26 and 27 of the Schedule concerning compensation and obstruction, dealt with above, apply to these powers as well.

The main provisions concerning safety, however, are contained in the Gas Safety (Rights of Entry) Regulations 1983,[94] having effect under section 18 of the Gas Act 1986.[95] The Regulations empower a duly authorised officer, on production of documentary evidence of his authority, to enter any premises in which there is a service pipe connected to gas mains.[96] He may take with him such other persons as may be necessary. The purpose for which the power may be used is the inspection of gas fittings, flues, ventilator systems, or other things used for the supply of gas or connected with gas mains.[97] Accordingly, on entry, the officer may examine any of these things to see whether there is compliance with regulations made under section 31 of the 1972 Act, or whether they are likely to constitute a danger to any person or property.[98] If he thinks it necessary to do so to avert danger to life or property he may disconnect and seal off any gas fitting, or all or part of the gas supply.[99] If there is at the time no supply he may signify the refusal of the supplier to give or allow a supply. The officer taking action under regulation 2(2) must at the same time fix a notice prominently to the fitting or part of the system sealed off, or to the meter if the whole

---

[93] Para. 25(2).
[94] S.I. 1983 No. 1575.
[95] As substituted by the Oil and Gas (Enterprise) Act 1982, s.14.
[96] Reg. 2.
[97] Reg. 2(*a*).
[98] Reg. 2(*b*).
[99] Reg. 2(*c*).

supply is sealed off or a supply is refused, or, if there is no meter, in a conspicuous place.[1] The notice should indicate the effect of regulations 7 and 8, which make it an offence to re-connect a fitting or supply.

The supplier must then, within five clear working days (*i.e.* excluding Saturdays, **9.94** Sundays, and public holidays) give the consumer written notice, setting out the action taken and the reasons for it, together with information about the consumer's right of appeal.[2] Appeals must be made to the Secretary of State, within 21 days of the service of the notice (or longer at the Secretary of State's discretion) on the basis that the action was unjustified, or the defects or circumstances specified in the notice do not exist, or have ceased to exist.[3]

As with the other powers dealt with above, the officer must leave the premises as secure as they were found, and the supplier is obliged to make good, or pay compensation for, any damage caused.[4] Intentional obstruction of an officer is a summary offence, punishable with a fine not exceeding level 3 on the standard scale.[5]

One other provision related to safety appears in Schedule 5 to the Gas Act 1965, which is concerned with inquiries into accidents, under section 17 of the Act. Paragraph 4 of the Schedule gives a tribunal set up to inquire into an accident power to enter and inspect any place or building, if the tribunal considers it necessary for the purpose of the inquiry.

4. Survey

The powers of entry of a gas supplier in relation to survey are contained in **9.95** Schedule 6 to the Gas Act 1965. The Rights of Entry (Gas and Electricity Boards) Act 1954 applies to these powers, even where they are concerned with entry to land rather than buildings.[6] Any of the powers may be exercised by an authorised person alone, or with others, and together with any vehicles apparatus or materials required.[7] The powers relate to gas storage. The Minister may designate land to be prospected for finding a site for underground gas storage.[8] The designated land, and any other land which it is necessary to enter to gain access to the designated land, may then be entered at any reasonable time by a person authorised in writing by the supplier, for the purpose of finding or proving a site for underground storage of gas. Once on the land the person may survey it, carry out trial borings, and remove specimens, solid or fluid taken from boreholes.[9] Twenty-eight days notice must be given to the owner and occupier before admission may be demanded as of right.[10]

---

[1] Reg. 4(1).
[2] Reg. 3.
[3] Reg. 5.
[4] 1986 Act, s.18(5).
[5] *Ibid.*s.18(7).
[6] Para. 5.
[7] Para. 10.
[8] Para. 1.
[9] Para. 2(1). There must be no interference with a public right of way, or contravention of any statutory prohibition or restriction.
[10] Para. 2(2).

The same notice must be given of an intention to survey, make borings, or remove specimens.[11] The power does not authorise entry to buildings.[12]

There is also a power for a person authorised as above to enter and survey any land in order to prepare documents to be submitted to the Minister at any stage of proceedings for making a storage authorisation order, or to make estimates in connection with a claim for compensation under Part II of the Act.[13] Again, 28 days notice of the entry must be given to the owner and occupier before admission may be demanded as of right.

Once an area has become a "storage area," a power of entry is given to any person authorised in writing by the Corporation or the Minister to supervise the carrying out of certain controlled operations on the land or in the "protective area."[14] Any land in the storage or protective area can be entered, together with any land to which entry is required in order to obtain access, and any land from the surface of which the authorised person has reason to believe controlled operations are being carried out.[15] Twenty-four hours notice of the intended entry must be given to the occupier before admission may be demanded as of right.[16] Once on the land, the authorised person may inspect any borehole, shaft, excavation, quarry or other works.[17] He may also employ any means for discovering the depth of any part of the works below the surface, and their location in respect to the controlled area.

Compensation

Where, as a result of the exercise of any of the entry powers under Schedule 6 to the Gas Act 1965 any land or chattels in which a person has an interest are damaged, or his enjoyment of them is disturbed, that person is entitled to compensation from the gas supplier for the damage or disturbance.[18]

Offences

(i) Disclosure. A person who discloses (otherwise than in the performance of his duty, or for legal proceedings, including arbitrations, or for a report of such proceedings) any information obtained by him in any premises entered under Schedule 6, will be guilty of an offence, punishable on summary conviction with a fine not exceeding level 3 on the standard scale, or up to three months imprisonment, or both.[19]

(ii) Obstruction. Wilful obstruction of a person exercising any of the powers

---

[11] *Ibid.*There are special provisions in respect of statutory undertakers, and water authorities.
[12] Para. 2(5).
[13] Para. 3(1).
[14] Para. 4. For the controlled operations, see Gas Act 1965, s.28(1). For the "protective area" see *ibid.*s.28(2).
[15] Para. 4(2).
[16] Para. 4(3).
[17] Para. 4(4)(a). Any apparatus or machinery used for works on the land may be used for this purpose.
[18] Para. 6.
[19] Para. 9.

under Schedule 6 is a summary offence, punishable with a fine not exceeding level 1 on the standard scale.[20]

C. Post Office

The Post Office has only one entry power, under section 57 of the Post Office Act **9.96** 1969, which enables it to survey land for exploratory purposes. A person duly authorised in writing by the Post Office may at any reasonable time enter and survey any land not covered by buildings or used as a garden or pleasure ground, for the purpose of ascertaining whether it would be suitable for the purposes of its business.[21] Sections 280(9) and 281(1) to (3) and (6) of the Town and Country Planning Act 1971 apply to this power,[22] except that there is no right to search and bore for the presence of minerals, and 28 days notice rather than 24 hours is required.[23] Compensation for damage to land or chattels, or disturbance of enjoyment of them, is payable,[24] with disputes being determined by the Lands Tribunal.[25]

D. Telecommunications and Broadcasting

Powers of entry in this area exist under the Wireless Telegraphy Act 1949, the **9.97** Telecommunications Act 1984 and the Cable and Broadcasting Act 1984.

(a) Wireless Telegraphy Act 1949

Section 15 of this Act, which still provides the general framework of controls over wireless telegraphy, contains two powers of entry. The more general power is in section 15(1). This enables a search warrant to be obtained from a justice of the peace who is satisfied by information on oath that there are reasonable grounds for suspecting that an offence under the Act has been or is being committed, and that evidence is to be found on any premises, vehicle, vessel or aircraft,[26] specified in the information. The warrant will empower named persons, authorised by the Secretary of State, to enter the specified premises, search them, and examine and test any apparatus found. This power is now backed up by the seizure provision under the Telecommunications Act 1984, s.79, described below.

The more specific entry power under the 1949 Act is contained in section 15(2). It supports the provision of sections 10 to 12 of the Act which are concerned with the use of apparatus which causes interference with wireless telegraphy. The section refers to a "written authorisation" rather than a warrant, for entry, but given the judicial view of the nature of a warrant there would seem to be little practical

---

[20] Para. 8.
[21] s.57(1).
[22] See above, para. 9.50.
[23] s.57(2).
[24] s.57(3).
[25] s.57(4).
[26] In the rest of the discussion of the powers under s.15, where the word "premises" is used, it includes "vehicle, vessel, or aircraft."

significance in this.[27] The authorisation may be obtained from a justice of the peace, on the basis of an application supported by sworn evidence. The justice must be satisfied that there are reasonable grounds for believing that there is on specified premises, apparatus to which section 10 applies, and which does not comply with regulations made under that section. He must also be satisfied that it is necessary to enter the premises to obtain information to enable a decision to be made whether to serve a notice under section 11 or 12, and that access to the premises has been demanded by a duly authorised person in the past 14 days, and has been refused. The justice must be shown either that seven days notice of this demand was served on the occupier and that the demand was made at a reasonable time, and was unreasonably refused, or that the Secretary of State has reasonable grounds for believing that the apparatus on the premises is likely to cause undue interference with wireless telegraphy used for safety of life service, or on which the safety of any person, vessel, vehicle, or aircraft may depend.

The authorisation will empower named persons, authorised by the Secretary of State, with or without any constables, to enter the premises. The premises may then be searched for apparatus; if any is found it may be examined and tested. Any person on the premises may be required to give reasonable assistance.[28]

Obstruction, or failing or refusing to give assistance, is an offence, as is disclosure, other than for the purposes of the Act, of information with regard to a manufacturing process or trade secret obtained in exercising the above powers. In each case the offence is punishable on summary conviction with a fine not exceeding level 5 on the standard scale.

(b) *Telecommunications Act 1984*

9.98 **(i) Seizure powers.** Section 79 gives two seizure powers. Both relate to apparatus which appears to the person exercising the power to have been used in connection with, or to be evidence of:

(a) an indictable offence under the 1949 Act;

(b) an offence under section 1(1) of the 1949 Act, other than one consisting of the installation or use, otherwise than under a wireless telegraphy licence, of apparatus not designed or adapted for emission (as opposed to reception); or

(c) an offence under section 7 of the Wireless Telegraphy Act 1967 (Restrictions on the manufacture or importation of apparatus).

The power to seize may arise either because it is included in a warrant issued under section 15 of the 1949 Act in relation to any of the above offences,[29] or simply, in any situation, where a person authorised by the Secretary of State has reasonable grounds to suspect that such an offence has been or is being committed.[30] Intentional

---

[27] See above, para. 1.20.
[28] s.15(3).
[29] s.79(2).
[30] s.79(3).

obstruction of the exercise of the power under section 79(3) is an offence under the 1949 Act.[31]

Any apparatus seized will be liable to forfeiture under the provisions of sections 80 and 81.

(ii) Survey. Under section 37 of the 1984 Act a person nominated by a public telecommunications operator, and duly authorised in writing by the Secretary of State, has an almost identical power of entry to survey for exploratory purposes as exists in relation to the Post Office under section 57 of the Post Office Act 1969.[32] The only difference is that the operator may make good any damage caused, instead of paying compensation.[33]

(c) *Cable and Broadcasting Act 1984*

The Cable Authority, which is established by this Act to exercise licensing and supervisory controls over cable programme services,[34] has a power of entry under section 32. The power is exercisable under a warrant obtainable from a justice of the peace who is satisfied that there is reasonable ground for suspecting that an offence connected with the provision of an unlicensed service is being or has been committed on specified premises. He must also be satisfied that evidence of the commissin of the offence is to be found on the premises. The warrant, which simply confers on persons authorised by the Authority and named in the warrant the power to enter and search the premises, must be executed within one month. **9.99**

Disclosure, other than in connection with legal proceedings, of any information obtained by such an entry or search, is an offence punishable on summary conviction with a fine not exceeding £1,000, or on indictment with a fine, or imprisonment for up to two years, or both.[35]

Intentional obstruction is an offence punishable on summary conviction with a fine not exceeding level 5 on the standard scale.[36]

E. *Water*

Entry powers of water authorities exist under a number of pieces of legislation. In addition, Schedule 3 to the Water Act 1945 constitutes the "modern waterworks code," which is incorporated as a "special Act" by various regulations.[37] **9.100**

1. General powers

The widest powers of entry are given by sections 111 and 112 of the Water

---

[31] s.79(4)—see above, para. 9.97, for the penalty.
[32] See above, para. 9.96.
[33] s.37(3).
[34] As defined in s.2.
[35] s.32(3).
[36] s.32(2).
[37] See, *e.g.* Water Authorities (Miscellaneous Provisions) Order 1974 (S.I. 1974 No. 607). For a full list of the situations in which the code is incorporated, see *Halsbury's Laws of England*, (4th ed.), Vol. 49, para. 570.

Resources Act 1963, which provide for entry with or without warrant. Very similar powers are given by section 82 of the special Act. The 1963 Act refers to "land"; the special Act to "premises."

(a) *Entry without warrant*

The purposes for which the power may be used are, in relation to the 1963 Act:

(i) performing any functions of the authority, in relation to the land entered or any other;
(ii) discovering whether, and if so how, any of the functions of the authority are to be performed, or whether any statutory provision is being or has been complied with.[38] In respect of this power the entrant may survey the land and inspect any articles thereon.[39]

Under section 82 of the special Act the powers may be used to:

(i)   inspect and examine water meters;
(ii) discover whether there is or has been any contravention of the special Act or the byelaws;
(iii) discover whether there are circumstances which would authorise the authority to take action or authorise works;
(iv) take such actions, or execute such works.

A person authorised in writing by a water authority may enter land for the above purposes at any reasonable time. He must produce evidence of his authority, if required.[40] He may take with him such other persons as may be necessary.[41] If entering under the 1963 Act he may also take with him necessary equipment.

The notice provisions under the special Act are simply that no admission may be demanded as of right unless 24 hours notice has been given to the occupier.[42] Under the 1963 Act no notice is required unless the land is used for residential purposes or heavy equipment is being taken on to it, in which case the occupier must be given seven days written notice.[43] This is not required, however, in an emergency. A person entering unoccupied premises under the 1963 Act must leave them as secure against trespassers as they were found.[44] Under the special Act this only applies to entries under warrant.[45]

(b) *Entry under warrant*

The power to obtain a warrant is identical under both Acts. A justice of the peace

---

[38] Note also the power to inspect local Acts, etc., under s.111(6).
[39] s.111(1). Similar powers are given to the Minister of Agriculture, and the Minister of Transport under s.111(2).
[40] 1963 Act, s.112(1); Special Act, s.82(1).
[41] 1963 Act, s.112(2); Special Act, s.82(3).
[42] s.82(1).
[43] s.112(3).
[44] s.112(5).
[45] s.82(5).

must be satisfied on sworn information in writing that there are reasonable grounds for entering for one of the purposes for which entry without warrant is allowed. He must also be satisfied of one of the following conditions[46]:

   (i) entry has been refused, or refusal is apprehended, and notice has been given to the occupier of the intention to apply for a warrant;
  (ii) the land or premises are unoccupied or the occupier is temporarily absent;
 (iii) the case is one of urgency;
 (iv) the giving of notice of intention to apply for a warrant would defeat the object of the entry.

The warrant will permit the use of force to enter, if necessary, and will remain valid until the purpose for which entry was required has been satisfied.[47]

(c) *Compensation*

This is only dealt with under the 1963 Act. Where any person's enjoyment of land or chattels in which he has an interest has been disturbed, or such land or chattels are damaged, he is entitled to compensation from the water authority,[48] disputes going to the Lands Tribunal.[49]

(d) *Offences*

(i) Disclosure. A person who discloses, other than in the course of duty, information with regard to a manufacturing process or trade secret, which he acquired as a result of entry under the above powers, commits a summary offence punishable with a fine not exceeding level 3 on the standard scale, or imprisonment for three months, or, under the 1963 Act, both.[50] Under the 1963 Act the offence extends to disclosure by a member or officer of a water authority to whom such information has been given by reason of his official position.

(ii) Obstruction. Wilful obstruction is a summary offence, punishable with a fine not exceeding level 1 on the standard scale.[51] Under the special Act there is in addition a daily fine of not exceeding £5 if the obstruction continues after conviction.

2. Byelaws

Where a water authority has made byelaws under section 17 or 18 of the 1945 Act, **9.101** section 19 gives a power of entry. The power is exercisable by an officer of the authority, on production, if required, of some duly authenticated document of his authority. It covers all premises in the area to which the byelaws apply, and may be exercised at all reasonable hours, for the purpose of ascertaining whether there has been a contravention of the byelaws, or exercising rights or powers under them.

---

[46] 1963 Act, s.111(3); Special Act, s.82(2).
[47] 1963 Act, s.111(4); Special Act, s.82(4).
[48] s.112(8).
[49] s.112(9).
[50] 1963 Act, s.112(7); Special Act, s.82(5).
[51] 1963 Act, s.112(6); Special Act, s.83.

3. Waste

(a) *Water Act 1945*

9.102   Section 14 of this Act is concerned with the waste, or excessive abstraction, of water from wells, boreholes or other works.

An officer of the water authority, authorised for the purpose, has a right, on production, if required, of documentary evidence of his authority, to enter any premises in the authority's area to ascertain whether there has been, on or in connection with the premises, any contravention of the provisions of section 14, or to execute an order of court, *e.g.* for the sealing of a well made under that section.[52]

All entry powers under the 1945 Act are subject to the provisions of section 48. Admission to any premises other than a factory, or a place where people are employed other than as domestic servants, shall not be demanded as of right unless 24 hours notice has been given to the occupier.[53] The authorised person may take with him such other persons as may be necessary, and must leave unoccupied premises entered under warrant as secure as they were found.[54] The power to obtain a warrant is given in the same terms as under the Water Resources Act 1963, s.111 (above, paragraph 9.100).[55] Disclosure, other than in the course of duty, of information which a person has discovered relating to a manufacturing process or trade secret, is an offence punishable on summary conviction with a fine not exceeding £1,000, or three months imprisonment, or both. On indictment the fine is unlimited, but the penalties are otherwise the same. Wilful obstruction is a summary offence punishable with a fine not exceeding level 1 on the standard scale.

(b) *Special Act*[56]

Section 62 of the special Act empowers an authorised officer of a water authority to enter any premises supplied with water by the authority, at any time between 7 a.m. and sunset, on production, if required, of evidence of his authority. The purpose of the entry is to discover whether there is any waste or misuse of water. Refusal of admission or other obstruction of the officer is a summary offence, punishable with a fine not exceeding level 1 on the standard scale.

4. Drought

(a) *Water Act 1945*

9.103   A water authority has power under section 16 of this Act to impose "hosepipe bans" in respect of watering gardens or washing cars. When a prohibition or restriction under this section is in force, an officer of the water authority has a right to enter any premises to which the prohibition or restriction applies to ascertain

---

[52] s.14(12).
[53] s.48(2).
[54] s.48(4).
[55] s.48(3).
[56] *i.e.* Water Act 1945, Sched. 3—see above, para. 9.100.

whether there has been a contravention of it. The power must be exercised at a reasonable hour, and the officer must produce his authority, if requested.

Section 48 of the 1945 Act applies to this power.[57]

(b) *Drought Act 1976*

An order made under the Drought Act 1976 may give a water authority power to enter land specified in the order to execute any works required for the discharge of their functions under the order.[58] If it does so, it must also require seven days notice of the intention to enter to be given to the occupier of the land, and others concerned with the land, as specified in the order.[59]

5. Pollution of water

Section 21 of the Water Act 1945 is concerned with the pollution of springs, wells, boreholes, or adits, used for human consumption or domestic purposes, or for manufacturing food and drink for human consumption. An officer authorised for the purpose by any local authority or water authority within whose area any spring, etc., is situated, has a right, on production if required of documentary evidence of his authority, to enter, at all reasonable hours, any premises, to ascertain whether there has been a contravention of this section.[60] Section 48 of the 1945 Act applies to this power.[61]

9.104

6. Survey

Where a water authority proposes to acquire land, a power of survey is given by section 8 of the Water Act 1948. An officer authorised for the purpose may enter the land to carry out the survey at any reasonable hour, on producing, if required, some duly authenticated document showing his authority. Experimental borings and other work may be carried out for the purpose of determining the nature of the subsoil, the presence of underground water, and its quality or quantity. Any person interested in the land may recover compensation for any damage caused.[62]

Section 48 of the 1945 Act applies to this section.[63]

9.105

7. Meters

Where, in relation to any premises, a water authority has fixed charges by reference to the volume of water supplied or effluent discharged, or both, or has given notice of its intention to do so, a power of entry is given under paragraph 2 of Schedule 2 to the Public Utility Transfer and Water Charges Act 1988. The power may be used for the purpose of installing, connecting, disconnecting, inspecting or

9.106

---

[57] See above, para. 9.102.
[58] s.3(4).
[59] s.3(5).
[60] s.21(2).
[61] See above, para. 9.102.
[62] For resolution of disputes as to compensation see section 91 of the special Act: 1948 Act, s.8(6).
[63] See above, para. 9.102.

examining meters, ascertaining the volume of water supplied or effluent discharged, or surveying the premises in connection with the powers under the Schedule. Seven days notice must be given before entry can be demanded as of right. Otherwise the power may be exercised at a reasonable hour by any officer authorised by the water authority, on production of some duly authenticated document of his authority.

In addition, a warrant may be obtained from a justice of the peace if there is reasonable ground for entry for one of the above purposes, and the justice is satisfied that admission has been refused or is reasonably apprehended, and that notice of the intention to apply for a warrant has been given to the occupier. Alternatively he must be satisfied that the premises are unoccupied, or that the occupier temporarily absent, or that the case is one of urgency, or that an application for admission would defeat the object of the entry. The warrant will authorise entry by force if necessary, and will apply until the purpose for which entry is necessary has been satisfied. This would appear to justify more than one entry under the same warrant.

An officer entering premises under these powers may take with him such other persons as may be necessary. Unoccupied premises must be left as secure against trespassers as they were found.

A person who discloses, other than in the course of duty or legal proceedings, information obtained on entered premises which relates to the water supplied, or effluent discharged, or to a manufacturing process or trade secret obtained in a factory or workplace, commits an offence punishable on indictment with a fine, and on summary conviction with a fine not exceeding the statutory maximum.

Intentional obstruction is an offence punishable on summary conviction with a fine not exceeding level 3 on the standard scale.

8. Reservoirs

9.107   The Reservoirs Act 1975 contains general powers for the supervision and control of reservoirs. Powers of entry, with or without warrant, are given by section 17. The person entering must produce evidence if required of his authority, and may take with him such other persons and equipment as may be necessary.[64]

(a) *Entry without warrant*

A person duly authorised in writing by an enforcement authority,[65] may enter any land on which a reservoir is situated. The purposes for which entry is allowed are:

(i)   to carry out a survey or other operations in relation to discovering whether the reservoir is a large raised reservoir, or whether it is in use as a reservoir at all;

(ii) to carry out a survey or other operations in relation to measures for safety under section 9, 10 or 14 of the Act;

(iii) to inspect the reservoir under section 15(1), or carry out a survey or other operations in that connection;

(iv) to carry out a recommendation under section 15(2);

[64] s.17(7).
[65] *i.e.*the local authority in whose area the reservoir is situated.

(v) to carry out a survey or other operations to determine what measures, if any, to take under section 16, or to carry out such measures. In relation to this purpose the power to enter extends to land neighbouring the reservoir.

Seven days written notice is required to be given to the occupier before entry may be demanded for purposes (i) to (iv).[66] The notice should specify the purpose of the entry, and, as far as possible, the nature of any powers to be exercised.

(b) *Entry under warrant*

A warrant may be obtained from a justice of the peace who is satisfied on sworn information in writing that there is reasonable ground for entry for the purpose specified, and that admission has been refused or is apprehended (notice of the intention to apply for a warrant having been given to the occupier), or that the occupier is temporarily absent.[67] The warrant will authorise entry by force if necessary. It will remain valid until the purpose for which entry is required has been satisfied.[68]

(c) *Compensation*

Where land (not occupied by the water suppliers) is damaged, or a person is disturbed in his enjoyment of the land, any person having an interest in the damaged land, or whose enjoyment has been disturbed, is entitled to compensation.[69] Disputes go to the Lands Tribunal.[70]

(d) *Obstruction*

Wilful obstruction is a summary offence, subject to a fine not exceeding level 3 on the standard scale.

9. Laying mains, etc.

Powers to lay mains (s.19), and telephone wires, etc. (s.5), are given by the special Act.[71] Entry depends on consent, but this must not be unreasonably withheld. **9.108**

10. Mining

In order to ascertain whether mining works have been, are being, or are about to be carried on so as to damage any of a water authority's works, an authorised officer may, after 24 hours notice, and on production, if requested, of documentary evidence of his authority, enter land in, on, or near which the authority's works are situated, and under which they know or suspect that mining is, has been, or is about **9.109**

---

[66] s.17(4).
[67] s.17(5).
[68] s.17(6).
[69] s.18(1).
[70] s.18(2).
[71] See above, para. 9.100.

to be, carried on. The officer may enter the mines, using any machinery or apparatus of the owner, lessee, or occupier, of the mine for this purpose. In particular the officer may use all necessary means to discover the distance of the mines from the authority's works.[72]

11. Land drainage

9.110   The Land Drainage Act 1976 provides for "internal drainage boards" within each water authority area, to exercise a general supervision over all matters relating to the drainage of land in their district.[73] Local authorities are also given powers relating to drainage in their area under Part V of the Act. In both cases a power of entry is given by section 39.

    The power is exercisable by any person authorised by an internal drainage board or a local authority. It does not apply to land belonging to Her Majesty in right of the Crown, or the Duchy of Lancaster, land belonging to the Duchy of Cornwall, or land belonging to a government department. Otherwise the power may be used:

(a) to enter land for the purpose of exercising any of the functions of the Board or local authority under the Act;

(b) to enter and survey any land (including the interior of a mill through which water passes or in connection with which water is impounded) and take levels of the land and inspect the condition of any drainage work on it. The entry must be at a reasonable time, and the authorised person must, if so required, produce documentary evidence of his authority.

Admission may only be demanded without notice in an emergency. Otherwise notice in writing must be given to the occupier. No particular amount of notice is required, unless the land is used for residential purposes, or heavy equipment is to be brought on to the land, when seven days notice should be given.

    An authorised entrant may take with him such other persons and such equipment as may be necessary.[74] If damage is caused by the exercise of powers under section 39 the injured party is entitled to full compensation by virtue of section 17(5), disputes being determined by the Lands Tribunal. In the absence of negligence, this is the only remedy available.[75] Unoccupied land should be left as effectively secured against trespassers as it was found.

    Intentional obstruction or impeding an entry is a summary offence, punishable with a fine not exceeding level 4 on the standard scale.

Ditches

9.111   Part III of the Act deals with the restoration and improvement of ditches. A person authorised or required by order of an Agricultural Land Tribunal to do work

---

[72] Water Act 1945, Sched. 3, s.17—see above, para. 9.101.
[73] s.6.
[74] N.B. *Not* what he considers necessary.
[75] *Marriage* v. *East Norfolk Rivers Catchment Board* [1950] 1 K.B. 284.

in relation to a ditch may enter any land specified in the order for this purpose.[76] If work which has been ordered has not been carried out within three months,[77] the Minister of Agriculture (or in Wales the Secretary of State) or any drainage body authorised by him may enter any land which it is necessary to enter to carry out the work.[78]

Certain general provisions as regards these powers are contained in section 44. They require seven days written notice of any entry to the occupier. The person entering may take with him such other persons and equipment as may be necessary,[79] and must leave unoccupied land as secure against trespassers as it was found.

Damage suffered as a result of the exercise of the powers of entry under Part III must be compensated for by the person exercising the power unless the entry was to do work which the injured party had been ordered to do. Disputes as to the amount of compensation are to be determined by the Lands Tribunal. In the absence of negligence, this is the only cause of action available to an injured party.[80]

There is no obstruction offence attached to these powers.

---

[76] ss.40, 41.
[77] A longer period may be specified in the order.
[78] s.43.
[79] Not what he *thinks* necessary.
[80] *Marriage* v. *East Norfolk Rivers Catchment Board* [1950] 1 K.B. 254 (C.A.).

HEALTH AND SAFETY REGULATIONS

(see paras. 8.30 and 9.34)

Agriculture (Tractor Cabs) (Amendment) Regulations 1984 (S.I. 1984 No. 605)
Anthrax Prevention Act 1919 (Repeals and Modifications) Regulations 1974 (No. 1775)
Anthrax Prevention Order 1971 (Exemptions) Regulations 1982 (S.I. 1982 No. 1418)
Asbestos (Licensing) Regulations 1983 (S.I. 1983 No. 1649) (as amended by S.I. 1985 No. 279; S.I. 1986 No. 392; S.I. 1987 No. 2115)
Asbestos (Prohibitions) Regulations 1985 (S.I. 1985 No. 910)
Celluloid and Cinematograph Film Act 1922 (Exemptions) Regulations 1980 (S.I. 1980 No. 1314)
Celluloid and Cinematograph Film Act 1922 (Repeals and Modifications) Regulations 1974 (S.I. 1974 No. 1841)
Classification and Labelling of Explosives Regulations 1983 (S.I. 1983 No. 1140) (as amended by S.I. 1988 No. 712)
Classification, Packaging and Labelling of Dangerous Substances Regulations 1984 (S.I. 1984 No. 1244) (as amended by S.I. 1986 No. 1922; S.I. 1986 No. 1951)
Clean Air Enactments (Repeals and Modifications) Regulations 1974 (S.I. 1974 No. 2170) (as amended by S.I. 1987 No. 180)
Coal and Other Mines (Electricity) (Third Amendment) Regulations 1977 (S.I. 1977 No. 1205)
Coal and Other Mines (Electric Lighting for Filming) Regulations 1979 (S.I. 1979 No. 1203) (as amended by S.I. 1983 No. 710)
Coal and Other Mines (Fire and Rescue) (Amendment) Regulations 1980 (S.I. 1980 No. 942)
Coal and Other Mines (Metrication) Regulations 1978 (S.I. 1978 No. 1648)
Coal and Other Mines (Safety Lamps and Lighting) (Amendment) Regulations 1983 (S.I. 1983 No. 710)
Coal Industry Nationalisation Act 1946 (Repeals) Regulations 1974 (S.I. 1974 No. 2011)
Coal Mines (Precautions against Inflammable Dust) Temporary Provisions Regulations 1976 (S.I. 1976 No. 861)
Coal Mines (Respirable Dust) Regulations 1975 (S.I. 1975 No. 1433) (as amended by S.I. 1978 No. 807)

Compressed Acetylene (Importation) Regulations 1978 (S.I. 1978 No. 1723) (as amended by S.I. 1987 No. 605)

Construction (Metrication) Regulations 1984 (S.I. 1984 No. 1593)

Control of Asbestos at Work Regulations 1987 (S.I. 1987 No. 2115)

Control of Industrial Air Pollution (Transfer of Powers of Enforcement) Regulations 1987 (S.I. 1987 No. 180)

Control of Industrial Major Accident Hazards Regulations 1984 (S.I. 1984 No. 1902) (as amended by S.I. 1985 No. 2023; S.I. 1988 No. 1462)

Control of Lead at Work Regulations 1980 (S.I. 1980 No. 1248)

Dangerous Substances (Conveyance by Road in Road Tankers and Tank Containers) Regulations 1981 (S.I. 1981 No. 1059) (as amended by S.I. 1984 No. 1244; S.I. 1985 No. 1333; S.I. 1986 No. 1951)

Diving Operations at Work Regulations 1981 (S.I. 1981 No. 399)

Dry Cleaning (Metrication) Regulations 1983 (S.I. 1983 No. 977)

Explosives Act 1875 etc. (Metrication and Miscellaneous Amendment) Regulations 1984 (S.I. 1984 No. 510)

Explosives Act 1875 (Exemptions) Regulations 1979 (S.I. 1979 No. 1378)

Explosives Act 1875 and 1923 etc. (Repeals and Modifications) Regulations 1974 (S.I. 1974 No. 1885)

Explosives (Licensing of Stores and Registration of Premises) Fees Regulations 1985 (S.I. 1985 No. 1108)

Factories Act 1961 etc. (Metrication) Regulations 1983 (S.I. 1983 No. 978)

Factories Act 1961 etc. (Repeals and Modifications) Regulations 1974 (S.I. 1974 No. 1941)

Factories Act 1961 (Repeals) Regulations 1975 (S.I. 1975 No. 1012)

Factories Act 1961 etc. (Repeals) Regulations 1976 (S.I. 1976 No. 2004)

Factories (Standards of Lighting) (Revocation) Regulations 1978 (S.I. 1978 No. 1126)

Fire Certificates (Special Premises) Regulations 1976 (S.I. 1976 No. 2003) (as amended by S.I. 1985 No. 1333; S.I. 1987 No. 37)

Freight Containers (Safety Convention) Regulations 1984 (S.I. 1984 No. 1890) (as amended by S.I. 1986 No. 392)

Gas Quality Regulations 1972 (S.I. 1972 No. 1804)

Gas Safety (Installation and Use) Regulations 1984 (S.I. 1984 No. 1358)

Gas Safety Regulations 1972 (S.I. 1972 No. 1178) (as amended by S.I. 1980 No. 1851; S.I. 1984 No. 1358)

Health and Safety (Agriculture) (Miscellaneous Repeals and Modifications) Regulations 1976 (S.I. 1976 No. 1247)

Health and Safety (Dangerous Pathogens) Regulations 1981 (S.I. 1981 No. 1011)

Health and Safety (Emissions into the Atmosphere) Regulations 1983 (S.I. 1983 No. 943)

Health and Safety (Enforcing Authority) Regulations 1977 (S.I. 1977 No. 746) (as amended by S.I. 1980 No. 1744; S.I. 1985 No. 1107; S.I. 1986 No. 294)

Health and Safety (Fees) Regulations 1988 (S.I. 1988 No. 712)

Health and Safety (First-Aid) Regulations 1981 (S.I. 1981 No. 917)

Health and Safety (Genetic Manipulation) Regulations 1978 (S.I. 1978 No. 752)

Health and Safety (Leasing Arrangements) Regulations 1980 (S.I. 1980 No. 907)

Hydrogen Cyanide (Fumigation) Act 1937 (Repeals and Modifications) Regulations 1974 (S.I. 1974 No. 1840)

Hydrogen Cyanide (Fumigation of Buildings) (Amendment) Regulations 1982 (S.I. 1982 No. 695)

Ionising Radiations Regulations 1985 (S.I. 1985 No. 1333)

Mines and Quarries Acts 1954-1971 (Repeals and Modifications) Regulations 1974 (S.I. 1974 No. 2013) (as amended by S.I. 1979 No. 318)

Mines and Quarries Acts 1954 to 1971 (Repeals and Modifications) Regulations 1975 (S.I. 1975 No. 1102)

Mines and Quarries Act 1954 (Modification) Regulations 1978 (S.I. 1978 No. 1951)

Mines and Quarries (Metrication) Regulations 1976 (S.I. 1976 No. 2063)

Mines (Miscellaneous Amendments) Regulations 1983 (S.I. 1983 No. 1130)

Mines (Precautions Against Inrushes) Regulations 1979 (S.I. 1979 No. 318)

Ministry of Fuel and Power Act 1945 (Repeal) Regulations 1974 (S.I. 1974 No. 2012)

Notification of Accidents and Dangerous Occurrences Regulations 1980 (S.I. 1980 No. 804) (as amended by S.I. 1981 No. 1059; S.I. 1984 No. 1114; S.I. 1985 No. 1333)

Notification of Installations Handling Hazardous Substances Regulations 1982 (S.I. 1982 No. 1357)

Notification of New Substances Regulations 1982 (S.I. 1982 No. 1496) (as amended by S.I. 1984 No. 1244; S.I. 1985 No. 1333)

Nuclear Installations Act 1965 etc. (Repeals and Modifications) 1974 (S.I. 1974 No. 2056)

Offices, Shops and Railway Premises Act 1963 (Repeals and Modifications) Regulations 1974 (S.I. 1974 No. 1943) (as amended by S.I. 1981 No. 917)

Offices, Shops and Railway Premises Act 1963 (Repeals) Regulations 1975 (S.I. 1975 No. 1011)

Offices, Shops and Railway Premises Act 1963 (Repeals) Regulations 1976 (S.I. 1976 No. 2005)

Operations at Unfenced Machinery (Amendment) Regulations 1976 (S.I. 1976 No. 955)

Petroleum (Consolidation) Act 1928 (Carriage of Dangerous Substances in Packages, etc.) Regulations 1986 (S.I. 1986 No. 1951)

Petroleum (Consolidation) Act 1928 (Enforcement) Regulations 1979 (S.I. 1979 No. 427) (as amended by S.I. 1982 No. 630; S.I. 1981 No. 1059; S.I. 1984 No. 1244)

Petroleum (Regulation) Acts 1928 and 1936 (Fees) Regulations 1983 (S.I. 1983 No. 1640)

Petroleum (Regulation) Acts 1928 and 1936 (Repeals and Modifications) Regulations 1974 (S.I. 1974 No. 1942) (as amended by S.I. 1986 No. 1951)

Petroleum-Spirit (Plastic Containers) Regulations 1982 (S.I. 1982 No. 630)

Pipe-lines Act 1962 (Repeals and Modifications) Regulations 1974 (S.I. 1974 No. 1986)

Poisonous Substances in Agriculture Regulations 1984 (S.I. 1984 No. 1114)

Protection of Eyes (Amendment) Regulations 1975 (S.I. 1975 No. 303)

Radioactive Substances Act 1948 (Modification) Regulations 1974 (S.I. 1974 No. 1821)

Reporting of Injuries, Diseases and Dangerous Occurrences Regulations 1985 (S.I. 1985 No. 2023)

Safety Representatives and Safety Committees Regulations 1977 (S.I. 1977 No. 500)

Safety Signs Regulations 1980 (S.I. 1980 No. 1471)

STANDARD SCALE FOR FINES

(see para. 1.32)

The current amounts for the "standard scale" for fines for criminal offences are given below. They may be varied by order made under the Magistrates' Courts Act 1980, s.143.

Level 1	£25
Level 2	£50
Level 3	£200
Level 4	£500
Level 5	£1000

INDEX